JOURNAL FOR THE STUDY OF THE OLD TESTAMENT
SUPPLEMENT SERIES

40

JSOT Press
Sheffield

DIRECTIONS in BIBLICAL HEBREW POETRY

edited by
Elaine R. Follis

Journal for the Study of the Old Testament
Supplement Series 40

Published by JSOT Press
JSOT Press is an imprint of
Sheffield Academic Press Ltd
The University of Sheffield
343 Fulwood Road
Sheffield S10 3BP
England

Typeset by Sheffield Academic Press
and
printed in Great Britain
by Billing & Sons Ltd
Worcester

British Library Cataloguing in Publication Data

Directions in biblical Hebrew poetry.—
(Journal for the study of the Old Testament
supplement series, ISSN 0309-0787; 40).
1. Hebrew poetry, Biblical—History and
criticism
I. Follis, Elaine R.
223′.07 BS1405.3

ISBN 1-85075-013-0
ISBN 1-85075-012-2 Pbk

CONTENTS

PREFACE

The essays included in this volume are, as its title suggests, indicative of some of the directions in which the study of biblical Hebrew poetry is presently being pursued. Additionally the essays reflect directions in which such study has been pursued in the past, and point the way for future explorations along this highly creative and exciting line of inquiry.

Those who have contributed are for the most part individuals who have participated in the meetings of the Biblical Hebrew Poetry Section of the Society of Biblical Literature during the past five years. One important feature of their work, and of the volume in general, is its interdisciplinary character. Biblical study which focuses on a literary form cannot help but touch upon the larger field of literary criticism with its methodologies. Authors have also drawn insights from the fields of music, drama, classics, philosophy and the social sciences in the preparation of their essays. One hopes that the result will prove of interest and use to persons engaged, not only in the field of biblical studies, but in disciplines which are seen more and more as relating to it.

In selecting essays for the collection, no effort has been made to create an exhaustive catalog of even the most important approaches to the subject, although many of them are represented here in one form or another. Rather, the editor has sought to include a variety of approaches—some traditional, some quite innovative and controversial—in order to suggest the richness of the study itself and to provide a sense of its expansiveness in the future.

ELAINE R. FOLLIS
Principia College
Elsah, Illinois

ABBREVIATIONS

AJSL	*American Journal of Semitic Languages and Literature*
ANET	J.B. Pritchard (ed.), *Ancient Near Eastern Texts*
BASOR	*Bulletin of the American Schools of Oriental Research*
BDB	F. Brown, S.R. Driver, and C.A. Briggs, *Hebrew and English Lexicon of the Old Testament*
BHS	*Biblia hebraica stuttgartensia*
Bib	*Biblica*
CBQ	*Catholic Biblical Quarterly*
CTA	A. Herdner, *Corpus des tablettes en cunéïformes alphabétiques*
Cur TM	*Currents in Theology and Mission*
ETL	*Ephemerides theologicae lovanienses*
FOTL	Fortress Old Testament Library (also OTL)
HALAT	W. Baumgartner *et al.*, *Hebräisches und aramäisches Lexicon zum Alten Testament*
HUCA	*Hebrew Union College Annual*
IDB	G.A. Buttrick (ed.), *Interpreter's Dictionary of the Bible*
JANES	*Journal of the Ancient Near East Society*
JBL	*Journal of Biblical Literature*
JNES	*Journal of Near Eastern Studies*
JQR	*Jewish Quarterly Review*
JR	*Journal of Religion*
MT	Masoretic Text
NEB	*The New English Bible*
OBO	*Orbis biblicus et orientalis*
OTL	Old Testament Library
RHPR	*Revue d'histoire et de philosophie religieuses*
UF	*Ugarit-Forschungen*
UT	C.H. Gordon, *Ugaritic Textbook*
VT	*Vetus Testamentum*

CONTRIBUTORS

David Noel Freedman is Arthur F. Thurnau Professor of Biblical Studies, University of Michigan, Ann Arbor, and Endowed Chair of Hebrew Biblical Studies, University of California, San Diego.

Duane L. Christensen is Professor of Old Testament Languages and Literature, American Baptist Seminary of the West, Berkeley, California.

John T. Willis is E.W. McMillan Distinguished Professor of Old Testament, Abilene Christian University, Abilene, Texas.

David J.A. Clines is Professor of Biblical Studies, University of Sheffield, Sheffield.

Jerome T. Walsh is Associate Professor of Biblical Studies, St. John's Provincial Seminary, Plymouth, Michigan.

Theodore Hiebert is Associate Professor of Hebrew Bible/Old Testament at the Divinity School, Harvard University, Cambridge, Massachusetts.

Adele Berlin is Professor of Hebrew, University of Maryland.

Harris Lenowitz is Associate Professor of Hebrew at the Middle East Centre, University of Utah.

Michael Patrick O'Connor, who lives in Ann Arbor, Michigan, is the author of *Hebrew Verse Structure* (1980).

Elaine R. Follis is Professor of Religion, Principia College, Elsah, Illinois.

Syliva Huberman Scholnick, who lives in Williamsburg, Virginia, is currently completing a book-length study of the book of Job.

Carole Fontaine is Associate Professor of Old Testament at Andover Newton Theological School, Newton Centre, Massachusetts.

William J. Urbrock is Professor of Religion and Associate Dean of Humanities, College of Letters and Science, University of Wisconsin Oshkosh.

Alan J. Hauser is Professor of Old Testament and department chair of the Department of Philosophy and Religion, Appalachian State University, Boone, North Carolina.

Bernhard W. Anderson is Professor Emeritus of Old Testament Theology, Princeton Theological Seminary, and currently Adjunct Professor of Old Testament, Boston University School of Theology.

Walter Brueggemann is Professor of Old Testament Language and Literature, Columbia Theological Seminary, Decatur, Georgia.

1

ANOTHER LOOK AT BIBLICAL HEBREW POETRY

David Noel Freedman

The purpose of this presentation is to establish two points or theses about biblical Hebrew poetry. Neither is exactly new, and both have been regarded as plausible if not probable. In recent years, however, a plethora of data, many of them statistical, has become available, and these data have provided both the evidence and the stimulus for reformulating and refining the points under present discussion.

Briefly these points may be stated as follows:

1. The long-standing recognition that certain particles are typical of and commonly used in Hebrew prose, but not (or not as frequently) in Hebrew poetry, can be converted into a criterion for separating passages of prose from those of poetry throughout the Hebrew Bible. The so-called prose particles are the definite article *h-*, the relative pronoun *'ᵃšer*, and the sign of the definite object *'et*. For a discussion see Andersen–Forbes 1983:165-168 and Freedman 1977:6-8.

2. The question of meter (or more properly, quantity) has been much debated and discussed, with opinions ranging from the conviction that there is no meter or measurable quantity in Hebrew poetry, to the equally strong conviction that Hebrew poetry can be quantified in a very precise manner, comparable to the poetry of Greece or Rome, or at least to that of France or England. Unfortunately, much of the work of scholars in recent decades has had a tendency to impose a meter or rhythm on a text by altering the text to suit the presumed rhythm, an ultimately self-defeating procedure. Now it can be affirmed that certain kinds of Hebrew poetry are quantifiable, and a demonstration can be made as to the

nature of the meter or measure so employed and how it produces closely similar if not identical results in a series of poems. For it is one thing to find some sort of rhythmic pattern in a poem, but a much more important matter to show that the results are duplicated or repeated in other pieces. In the process we will see that quantity in Hebrew poetry, where it has been observed, is quite unlike that in other languages and literature, since there are opposing processes at work: a centralizing or regularizing one which defines the average, mean, or total length of a line or half-line, and a random effect which incorporates lines of variable length, or pronounced deviations from a norm. But even these deviations can be plotted so that in the end we can say of a certain group of poems at least, that their pattern and totality are predictable (within limits) and meet appropriate aesthetic requirements.

The conclusion I wish to draw is that on the basis of these points, it should be possible to tackle the great bulk of biblical literature and on the one hand divide between poetry and prose, identifying the former and even isolating that intermediate group that lies between the two classes and, on the other hand, determine the real quantity or metrical character of Hebrew poetry, recognizing both its regularity, or normality, and its random aspects, or its freedom, at one and the same time. These two main points raise two basic questions about biblical poetry. First, how does one distinguish poetry from prose? That question may seem simplistic, but a simple mechanical test could do wonders in clearing the air, in view of all the complexities involved in formulating a definition or articulating a philosophy. Second, how does one decide whether there is anything like quantity in Hebrew poetry? This question involves matters of rhythm and meter, but is really an attempt to deal with another basic question, and to give it an answer.

Dealing with the first question begins with the so-called prose particles and what they can indicate if not determine; my comments are based on statistics cited in Andersen–Forbes 1983. The investigation raises implications as to the possible evolution of poetic canons. There is some evidence to show that the so-called prose particles are almost entirely absent from the earliest poetry, while they increase in number in late poetry. This observation has to be made carefully, because while there is a considerable amount of late poetry which has very low particle counts, the reverse is not true. No early poetry has a high count.

Using Andersen–Forbes's table 0 (Andersen–Forbes 1983:170), we note that the data are clearly decisive, even though we must always bear in mind the important qualification that their counts and percentages and the like are all based on the chapter as a unit. Thus, Psalm headings (obviously prose) are mixed in with the psalms themselves; and the same is true of other mixtures of poetry and prose, e.g. Exodus 15, which is listed at 5.6%, fairly high for old poetry, although very low for prose. In this case, the percentage shown in the table is relatively meaningless, because the chapter consists of a clearly marked poem embedded in surrounding prose. The poem itself, vv. 1-18 and 21, has no prose particles at all, and is an outstanding example of early Hebrew poetry, indeed of poetry in general, as everyone would agree. The surrounding material is clearly straightforward prose. The prose particle count can be calculated easily, since there are 18 such particles in that material, while the number of words in the prose section is the total for the chapter, 321, minus the number in the poem, 177, for a net of 144 words. The prose particle percentage is 12.5%, so the chapter figure of 5.6% conceals a really impressive contrast between the poem, which is 0.0%, and the rest of the chapter, which has a count of 18 for 12.5%. In spite of such roughness, the figures are nevertheless impressive and convincing, as the following summary and comparison will show.

On the basis of the data presented, we can say that practically everything with a reading of 5% or less will be poetry, whereas practically everything with a reading above 15% will be prose. If we consider only the books which are commonly regarded as poetic, in comparison with books regarded as prose (taking Andersen–Forbes's first column and comparing it with a combination of columns 3 and 4, Torah and History), then for 5% or under we have 186 chapters of poetry and seven chapters of prose. But four of the prose chapters are in fact poems, as we know; so there are only three chapters of prose writing which come in under 5%, and in every case an explanation can be given. After all, there is nothing intrinsic in prose that requires that there be these particles, and in some situations they would be scarce.

Contrariwise, in the case of readings of 15% and up, one counts 248 chapters of prose, against four of poetry. While in view of the data and the method we could hardly expect the compartments to be airtight, the shift from one end of the spectrum to the other corresponds precisely to the shift from prose to poetry and vice versa. There can be little question that the proposed criterion works; it not only reflects the traditional divisions between poetry and prose, but also can be used to identify poetry and prose respectively, by the counts and proportions.

We can sort out the intermediate range by drawing the line at 10% and suggest that under that figure we would be inclined to see poetry, while over it we would see prose. The figures generally support this conclusion, but the distinction is not so sharply drawn as the larger numbers show: we would have 216 chapters of poetry under 10% and only nine over that number; we would have fifty-two chapters of prose under 10% (of which some are demonstrably poems hiding out in prose books), with 389 over 10%. If we look at the nine poems over 10%, we find that they are all Psalms, and all belong to the last or fifth book of the Psalter. While these are generally considered late Pslams, we can hardly date them exactly. They include, however, Psalm 137, which cannot be earlier than the middle of the sixth century, hence almost by definition a late poem. The fact that all of the Psalms over 10% are to be found in the single book of the Psalter is an indication of an inner development in poetry, whereby the use of such prose particles gradually became possible or acceptable. More than half of the same collection of the Psalter remains well below 10%, so it is clear that it was possible and acceptable to compose poems in the old manner, with few if any prose particles. It is also possible that low counts indicate an earlier date for those poems, since there is no way to decide the date of each poem in the collection. For example, we have poetry of the sixth century with very low counts, such as II Isaiah generally (beginning with ch. 40 we have percentages of 5.0, 5.4, 4.2, 3.2, 1.5, 3.3, 3.3, 2.6, 3.9, 2.8, 6.9, 5.4, 4.2, 2.3, 9.7, 6.7, 6.2, 1.4, 2.5, 4.7, 2.4, 7.9, 2.9, 2.3), but for chs. 65–66 we have 11.1 and 12.4 (a point made by M. Pope many years ago), and for Lamentations we have 2.9, 2.6, 2.6, 4.2, and 1.4. And Ezekiel, normally written in dense prose, has a number of chapters in the poetic range, including especially ch. 19, regarded by all as a poem and having a prose particle percentage of 0.6.

What remains to be examined is the large group of books generally listed as Prophecy. Here the distribution falls roughly between the poetic and the prose books, with a relatively even apportionment among all the percentages from zero to over 20%. Once again we must bear in mind the nature of the analysis, which runs according to chapters—however heterogeneous the chapters may be in containing both prose and poetry. Thus, it would be important to sort the parts out more carefully in order to gain a truer picture of the prose-poetry ratios in the prophets. But even on the basis of the rather crude data we have, some judgments can be made. First of all, there is considerable straight poetry in the prophetic collection, including fifty-two chapters that have percentages under 5%. Most, if not all, of these would be classified as poetry. At the other end, we have fifty-six chapters over 15%: most of these would be reckoned as prose, especially the large sections of Jeremiah and Ezekiel that are obviously prose by any standard. Then there are roughly equivalent segments in the 5-10% bracket (seventy-two chapters) and another fifty-four chapters in the range from 10-15%. Discounting mixed chapters, of which there are clearly a number, we could divide roughly at 10% and say that 124 chapters of the prophets are below 10%, and hence more likely to be poetry than prose, and another 110 chapters are over 10%, and are more likely to be prose than poetry.

Nevertheless, and especially with regard to prophecy, there is another possibility to consider. One might establish a third category, which is neither prose nor poetry, but shares features with each and could tentatively be called *prophetic discourse*. As we know from other languages and literatures, there are few if any sharp lines between prose and poetry, and there are various stages between pure poetry and pure prose which can be categorized as prose-poetry, or poetic prose, or prosaic poetry. It is in the middle range that we should look for this phenomenon, which seems to be reflected in the prophetic category although we should not exclude it from the other groups of books. It is important to exclude accidental combinations of prose and poetry in the same and succeeding chapters, where the resulting average falls in between those for poetry and those for prose. Frank Andersen and I suggested as much in our analysis of the prosody of Hosea, but were still uncertain as to how to classify or categorize such material (Andersen–Freedman 1980). Similar phenomena have turned up in the book of Amos, so it seems likely that a third or middle category should be identified, with a range between 5% and 15% for the prose particle count. It will be noted that a majority of the chapters in the prophetic corpus falls between these limits (126, in contrast to 108 either lower or higher), and that almost half of all the chapters found in the 5% to 10% range come from the prophetic corpus (72 out of a total of 147). While it is too early to make a definite statement about this situation, the overall data and a preliminary analysis suggest that the biblical divisions (modified as indicated by Andersen–Forbes in their notes) have a strong correlation with prose-particle counts. It is possible to summarize the findings of this line of inquiry in the following fashion:

1. The so-called poetic books are predominantly poetic in fact, and the great bulk of the chapters have counts under 5%, with a substantial but smaller group in the next bracket (5%-10%), and only a handful above 10%.
2. The predominantly prose books (Torah and History categories) are predominantly prose, with the majority of chapters (248) above 15%, while a substantial minority (141) are between 10% and 15%. A much smaller group is in the 5%-10% range (45), and there are practically none below 5% (seven, but several of these are clearly poems embedded in the prose text).
3. The prophetic corpus has an entirely different profile, and overall is spread out fairly evenly over the whole range. We posit, however, that the chapters below 5% constitute poetry, and those over 15% are clearly prose. The remainder may to a substantial degree constitute a third category of elevated speech, which we call prophetic discourse. In any event, the question of a third category is worthy of further investigation.

The prose particle counts confirm the traditional division of the Hebrew Bible to a remarkable extent, and show that the Masoretic Text reflects and preserves those distinctions. The poetic books, with their distinctive arrangements and cantillation, are overwhelmingly poetic in terms of the prose particle counts, while the prose books are overwhelmingly prosaic. Exceptional are certain poems which are arranged as poems in the prose books, although there are several other poems which are written as prose, but the prose particle counts are a better indicator of what is prose and what is poetry.

The prose particle count, overall, is an excellent indicator and discriminator in separating prose from poetry, and also in indicating the possible middle category, especially for the prophetic corpus. Discounting mixed chapters of prose and poetry, we can suggest the following:

1. Anything with a count under 5% is almost certainly to be regarded as poetry.
2. Anything with a count over 15% is almost certainly to be regarded as prose.
3. Anything with a count between 5% and 10% is more likely to be poetry than prose, but I think that many of these units will turn out to be prophetic discourse or some form of poetic speech.
4. Anything between 10% and 15% is more likely to be prose than poetry, but may share some of the qualities of the adjacent category (between 5% and 10%), having some poetic elements in it.

The chief value of this method is that it is simply applied, is purely mechanical (with some slight interpretative requirements), and obviously works in the great majority of cases. It identifies as poetry what most scholars would agree was poetry, and as prose what most scholars would agree was prose. Hence it is likely that it will work in areas and passages where there is disagreement among scholars.

We can test the system in a provisional way against the book of Ezekiel, which, as is well known, poses severe problems of analysis and identification in terms of what is prose and what is poetry in the text. First, it is clear from every point of view that much of Ezekiel is straight prose. There are fourteen chapters over 15%, while another eighteen are in the range between 10% and 15%. The remaining sixteen chapters are under 10%; of these, twelve are in the range 5% and 10%, while four are below 5% (chs. 19, 21, 27, 28). These latter would be the obvious targets for identification as poetry, and the printed versions tend to reflect and confirm this identification. We will use Kittel's Biblia Hebraica (BHK) and the Stuttgart Biblia Hebraica (BHS) for comparison. Thus ch. 19 in both BHK and BHS is printed as poetry in full; the prose particle count is 0.641%, which would be decisive in any case. Chapter 21 has a count of 4.9% and is printed partly as poetry and partly as prose in both BHK (vv. 13-22 as poetry, the rest as prose) and BHS (same). In chs. 27 and 28, the prose particle count is 3.2% and 3.7% according to Andersen–Forbes, and again BHK and BHS render the material partly as poetry and partly as prose. It may be noted that BHS renders ch. 28 entirely as prose, but this seems to be an arbitrary decision in view of the prose particle count.

If we look at a pair of controversial or questionable chapters in BHK and BHS, we may find a comparison of the prose particle counts useful. Thus in BHK, ch. 7 is printed entirely as prose, while ch. 15 is printed as a poem. In BHS, ch. 7 is printed entirely as poetry, while ch. 15 is printed exclusively as prose. The prose particle count for ch. 7 is 11.95% while for ch. 15 it is 16.5%. On the basis of the prose particle counts we would judge that ch. 15 is certainly a piece of prose, and that the same is probably true of ch. 7, although the categorization is slightly less certain. Reexamination of both chapters reinforces the conclusion that both chapters are pieces of Ezekielian prose; so BHK and BHS are each half right.

We must turn now to the other major point to be made about Hebrew poetry, and that concerns the question of meter and rhythm, or as I prefer to speak of it, the question of quantity. Here we rely mainly on the study of the five chapters of Lamentations, which I published in *The Harvard Theological Review* in 1972 (Freedman 1972). I used syllable-counting in order to establish a basis of comparison between the poems in terms of length. As I have noted in this paper, an equivalent is to count words, since they show the same correlations, and it is possible to argue that ancient Israelites could have counted words rather easily since they generally wrote using word dividers. The main point I wish to make here is that there really is quantity in Hebrew poetry, and that we can prove it, and that it cannot therefore be ignored in any overall estimate of the nature, quality or character of Hebrew poetry. While the examples I have used in the article cited are all acrostic poems (or modelled on them), I have no doubt that the same principles apply to Hebrew poetry generally, and that there will be many other examples that can be classified and quantified in the same or similar ways. The advantage of acrostics is that they provide us with stanza and (occasionally) line limits, so that we can be relatively sure where such units begin and end.

The nature of quantification in Hebrew poetry has to be defined carefully, since it is different from what we regard as quantity or meter in other kinds of poetry. In Hebrew poetry, or at least in the sample examined in my paper, the regulation or control of quantity refers to the whole poem rather than to its discrete parts. We have an apparently anomalous situation in which the poems or chapters are almost identical in length (with a range of 1%) or proportionately so: i.e. ch. 4 of Lamentations is ⅔ as long as chs. 1–3, since it consists of

2-line stanzas instead of 3-line stanzas. The same principle applies to the 16-syllable acrostics including Lamentations 5 (special case) and the different Psalms listed in the paper. Strangely enough, the range in length between the whole poems is less or not more than it is between lines and stanzas of the same poems. While the average length of line in each of the first three chapters of Lamentations is thirteen syllables, the lines may vary from as few as nine or ten syllables to as many as sixteen or seventeen. The same is true proportionately of stanzas. But the overall length of the poems is the same, or only negligibly different, as the charts show.

We may contrast this phenomenon with an example drawn from English poetry. We are confident, for example, that English sonnets, especially of the Shakespearean variety, will have a total length of 140 syllables, plus or minus one or two. We can be sure of this, because the rule for such sonnets is that they consist of fourteen lines of iambic pentameter, and thus will come out as indicated. Some slight variations are allowed, but the reason for the regularity in the total is that each line is roughly the same length as the other lines. In other words, the regulating feature is the length of each line; adding them up, we get a predictable total. What is different about Hebrew poetry is that, while the sum-total is predictable within a very narrow range, the total is not based upon the repetition of lines of the same length, as in the case of the English sonnet. Unless we engage in wholesale emendation and improvement of the text, we must recognize it as a basic fact of Hebrew poetry that individual lines (and stanzas) vary considerably in length. Nevertheless—and this is all the more remarkable—the length of the whole poem is fixed. We have poems which vary widely in line and stanza length, but which come out with the same total length. That this is no accident, but the result of careful planning and deliberate decisions throughout the poem, is clear from the statistical tables and the theoretical considerations in determining the difference between deliberate and chance arrangements. While the distribution of lines and stanzas according to their lengths follows the pattern of the familiar bell-shaped curve (reflecting random distribution), there can be little question that these cases reflect conscious artistic choices and decisions.

When we look at Frank Cross's reconstruction of ch. 1 of Lamentations on the basis of a 4Q manuscript (Cross 1983), we note that there are many differences from MT, and that few if any of the lines are the same in the two versions. But amazingly enough, his total length for the poem (838 syllables, on the basis of his counts, verse by verse) is exactly the same as one of my counts for the same chapter. (I refer to it as type 'A' in ch. 1, although the basis for counting is quite different.) The point is that a set of controls is at work in these poems which constrains not only the original poet, but any scholarly reconstructor, whether that person is aware of it or not. There are different hypothetical ways in which the poet could control the overall length of the poem while allowing himself freedom in dealing with individual lines and stanzas. But the point is that the control is there, and that quantity cannot be disregarded as an element in the construction of poems. How to count it is almost immaterial, and I have opted for syllables because there are a lot of them, and hence a disagreement about a few of them will not make much difference. I steer a middle course between counting words, which will work but may be a little too crude, and counting morae, which may be more precise but seems overly fussy and produces more detailed information than is necessary or desirable. But so long as a system is applied consistently, it should work reasonably well and tell us what we want to know—namely, how long a line, a stanza, or a poem is.

What do we learn from this investigation of quantity? Chiefly, that the Israelite poets counted something, and made their poems come out according to a predetermined scheme. At the same time, they allowed themselves a freedom in composing individual lines and stanzas, which has been a source of confusion and misunderstanding about Hebrew poetry since Day One. Scholars have gone in two directions. One group began by assuming that Hebrew poetry was severely metrical; but when they discovered that lines and stanzas do not conform to any strictly metrical system, they either gave up, or went ahead to reconstruct the poem so as to conform to the meter they had already established for the poem. The other group decided that lines and stanzas are irregular, and hence that there is no meter in Hebrew poetry. Both sides are right in their way, and wrong in another. The specifically Hebrew phenomenon has not been recognized for what it is: it is quantitative, but with a degree of freedom rarely seen in metrical poetry. The result is that we should recognize the phenomenon for what it is, and we should also recognize our limitations in dealing with Hebrew poetry.

Perhaps it is best to start on the negative side, that is, what the quantitative factor will *not* do for us in dealing with Hebrew poetry. It won't allow or encourage us to emend the text. What that means is that the degree of freedom allowable in lines and stanzas will make it impossible to demonstrate any emendation on the basis of meter or rhythm. Adding or subtracting a word would not be permissible in this situation, unless there were some other indication of excessive line length (or the reverse). While the bulk of the lines hover around the 13-syllable mark in chs. 1–3, there are many, too many, which vary widely from the norm, to indicate that there is some ultimate limit below or above which we cannot go. The same is true of stanzas. We have in chs. 1 and 2 two stanzas (one each) with four lines instead of the standard three. I don't believe that there is any way to decide the question whether the fourth line is part of the original composition or an editorial or scribal addition which should be removed, on the basis of quantitative considerations. In fact, the presence of the extra line in those poems brings their totals in closer harmony with ch. 3, which has 22 3-line stanzas. But the difference is too slight to ensure that the longer count in chs. 1 and 2 is better than a shorter count.

I consider this sort of variation to be an instance of a larger phenomenon, namely, general deviation or variation from a norm to avoid monotony or to demonstrate versatility and virtuosity. The fact that lines and stanzas vary so considerably in the poems we have (and be it noted that except for making all the stanzas consist of three lines, and other sporadic efforts at conformity to a preconsidered plan, Cross's reconstruction has the same wide variation in individual line length and also in stanza length) suggests that the poet exercised sovereign freedom in all respects except for the total length of the poem. Whether the different chapters of Lamentations were written by one or several poets, the result is the same. The constraints are too sharply drawn and specific to be regarded as mere happenstance or accident. Although we may not be able to describe the mechanism by which Israelite poets achieved such precision in total length while at the same time exercising considerable freedom in the case of individual lines and stanzas, we must face the fact that they did this quite consciously, and it must enter into our judgment about the quantitative factor in Hebrew poetry.

On the basis of the data secured in the research into Lamentations and other acrostics, we can make additional inferences and suggest some ideas about the way in which Hebrew poets worked. We have noted that the standard acrostic poem in the Bible (i.e. Prov 31 and several Psalms, especially Ps 119) has lines that average 16 syllables in length, and that these lines are divided generally in the middle. They are bicola of sixteen syllables, generally with the pause in the middle, so that each colon has eight syllables. This is equivalent to the familiar 3:3 pattern of stress or accent-counting systems. The same rules apply: overall length, averages and means all come out strictly according to preplanned construction, but there is considerable range in individual length of lines and stanzas. Chapter 5 of Lamentations, which as we all know lacks the alphabetic element in the acrostic (although there may be a hidden system or cipher which has not yet been elucidated), nevertheless conforms admirably to the 16-syllable pattern, evenly divided. This stands in marked contrast to the other four chapters, in which the line length is three syllables shorter, and comes out in average and mean at thirteen syllables with the usual variations. The difference is certain, and certainly deliberate and marked. While there are 13-syllable lines in the 16-syllable poems, and 16-syllable lines in the 13-syllable poems, there is no question about the general pattern or the role of the shorter or longer lines in the different configurations. These poems are not accidentally different, but deliberately so.

Furthermore, the pattern in chs. 1–4 is clearly different in another respect as well. We can confirm the Budde hypothesis about Qina-meter or falling rhythm, on the basis of the data. Statistically, Budde is right about the 3:2 pattern (using the old stress system): the lines are divided unevenly for the most part, and especially in chs. 2–3 (but also 4) the falling rhythm is nearly universal. There are nevertheless variations, so that some lines balance out evenly, and others are in reverse order. But the great majority are in a 3:2 pattern, or if we use syllables, then the major group is in the 7:6, or 8:5 pattern, or somewhere in between, depending upon the total number of syllables in the line. So, not only do we have a different average line length in chs. 1–4, but also a distinctive pausal arrangement: that the first colon is regularly longer than the second, although not always so. There is too much freedom to justify emendation on the basis of so-called meter, but there is more than enough regularity to show that these acrostic poems (Lam 1–4) are quantitatively different from the other acrostics, while in and among themselves they are absolutely regular in terms of overall length, but nevertheless exhibit wide variation in individual lines and stanzas. The same is true of the 16-syllable group.

Perhaps this presentation will suffice to show that the phenomenon of quantity is clearly demonstrable in Hebrew poetry, at least of a certain kind, and that it must be taken into consideration in any discussion of Hebrew poetry or the way in which Israelite poets constructed their poems. At the same time, the facts in the case discourage manipulation or emendation of the text in order to produce a certain narrow conformity to a standard or pattern, which is itself only an average or a norm, and from which deviation was expected and taken for granted. I think that this is the best way to describe a curious phenomenon, with which we are generally not acquainted from experience with other poetry in the ancient world (or modern one): that is, quantity in terms of the large or overall constructions, and freedom at the level of smaller units. Another way of looking at the phenomenon is that the poet had a model or structure in mind which would cover the whole poem (e.g. my treatments of Ps 23 [Freedman 1976] and Ps 137 [Freedman 1971]), and then while following it generally and on the average, he deliberately varied or deviated from it at specific points. So we are justified in the first place in trying to determine the overall pattern, and then in the second of recognizing deviations and variations as part of the deliberate activity of the poet rather than the mistaken activity of editor or accidental alteration on the part of the scribe. I should add that in all this I do not want to appear to be a defender of the MT or any other text against all emendations. On the contrary, I believe that there is a very important place for textual reconstruction on the basis of other texts and versions, and that there is a place for conjectural emendation as well (as a last but very important resort nonetheless). What I object to is conjectural emendation on the basis of supposed meter or rhythm. Even this is possible in a general way, and it might be argued that we have a right to move in the direction of the norm or average: but it is very risky, often overdone, and therefore on the whole to be avoided.

Before drawing a few conclusions from this survey, I want to mention some of the implications and ramifications of these two main points. First there is the matter of the difference between prose and poetry related to the so-called prose particles. I want first of all to apologize for the use of the term 'prose' particles, since this seems to prejudge the case. The exercise is entirely inductive, and we have simply recorded the occurrence of certain particles, and then only on the basis of distribution and frequency have come to the conclusion that they are characteristic of prose and unusual in poetry, the two categories (prose and poetry) having been defined and the examples chosen on the basis of other criteria entirely. But the terms were called prose particles long before this exercise was undertaken, and it was simply a convenient way to label them. In view of the results, the label is appropriate, and so the technique can be used diagnostically in dealing with difficult passages. One obvious implication of their usage or non-usage is that poetry tends to be shorter and more elliptical, or more parsimonious in the use of particles and other terms. Thus ellipsis generally is a phenomenon more common in poetry than in prose. And to be more specific, there are other particles which are in shorter supply in poetry than in prose. We have used as the most striking and flagrant examples the three particles mentioned.

But the investigation could be extended, and should be, to include particles such as conjunctions and prepositions. I believe that the distribution of the basic conjunction is quite different in poetry from what it is in prose, but the statistics are not easy to come by, and we are working on a program that will sort out the conjunctions in poetry. What we are interested in is the use of conjunctions at the beginning of cola. And we would want to screen out simply coordinating conjunctions between nouns and other parts of speech. The impression I have is that for standard Hebrew poetry, the conjunction is not used at the beginning of the first colon, but is used before the second and third. The oldest poetry may have been still more sparing in their use, while later poetry may have used them even at the beginning of first cola. In any case, the usage is probably considerably below that of prose, although the difference may not be as striking as what we have seen in the case of the three particles selected so far.

Prepositions are another matter entirely, although the same pattern may obtain. In the case of prepositions, meaning is significantly involved, especially if the Hebrew poets made a habit of omitting prepositions where they should be understood. Once again, the overall statistics are not easy to arrive at, but we have the impression that fewer prepositions are used in poetry than in prose. What this means for understanding and interpreting Hebrew poetry is not altogether clear, but we can suggest a rationale. From time immemorial, at least in inflected languages, it has been possible to express various relations between verbs and nouns and nouns and nouns either by use of various case-endings or by the use of prepositions. There is no reason to suppose that these possibilities did not exist side by side. Once the inflections were lost, however, then inevitably, prepositions as well as other parts of speech were called upon to bear a larger share of the burden in sentence constructions. What we suggest is that originally Hebrew, like other Semitic languages, was inflected and that prepositions were used alongside of case-endings. When the case-endings were lost, then the use of prepositions was increased. That is what happened in prose in the normal development of the language. In poetry, however, the older pattern was preserved, with partial use of prepositions and partial use of inflections. When the inflections were lost (and most of the few surviving ones are in the poetry), then poetry persisted without them, but also without adding prepositions, or supplying them in smaller number. This left a number of cases in which the meaning would have been clear if the case-endings had been preserved, but without them, the absence of a preposition is or poses a difficulty in interpretation.

We do not wish to pursue this point further, but simply to point out that the shortage of prepositions is a characteristic feature of Hebrew poetry as compared with prose, and that it has implications for the interpretation of Hebrew poetry. In some cases, it may belong to the pattern of so-called double-duty particles, in which one preposition does duty for more than one noun or phrase. A striking example is to be found in Amos 6.5, where it would be appropriate to apply the preposition *'al* to both cola, and thus interpret the second colon as referring to the devising or composing of songs *on* instruments of music, rather than the anomalous (but persistent) interpretation that Amos is referring to the invention of new instruments. In another case, we can supply the preposition on the basis of a parallel passage. In this situation, the meaning is clear in one passage where the preposition is used, and less clear where it fails to put in an appearance. Thus, in Amos 2.7, the words are normally interpreted as a verb plus a construct chain and rendered: 'They turn aside the way of the afflicted'. The related passage is in Job 24.4, where the same or synonymous words are used, but we have the preposition *min* before the word for 'way' (*drk*). The meaning there is plain: 'They push the poor out of the road'. That that is what Amos intended, seems clear from the passage and its parallel in Amos 2.7, namely, that a violent physical action is presumed. That the preposition was omitted is the all-important element in the picture. We can suppose that the original reading was based upon usage at a time when case-endings were in vogue, and that the judicious use of these would have shown that no construct chain was intended, and hence, the phrase *derek ʿanāwim* was not meant as a construct chain. Had that been the situation, then the word *drk* would have been vocalized as an accusative: *darka*. With the sense derived from the Job passage, the reading would have been *darki*, the oblique case to be interpreted in context as spatial.

With regard to the question of quantity, there are implications for further study, namely, that we should look more closely at large structures, expecting to find rigid constraints and nearly equal counts of length for major parts and complete poems. We have been able to determine the existence of such gross structures for poems widely scattered in the Bible; so it stands to reason that the same is true of other poems in the Bible, although it may be more difficult to determine these because they lack the obvious markers which acrostic poems provide. With regard to lines and verses and small structures, the message seems to be both sharp and certain: there is too much freedom and variation to discern any but statistical patterns, and it is time to turn attention more to large configurations and units, including whole poems. It seems likely that a handful of such patterns will merge, and we will begin to gather clues and form opinions as to desirable length and the constraints that produced the variety of poems that we have in the Bible.

The following are some provisional conclusions about Hebrew poetry:

1. Out of the welter of debate and discussion I wish to draw attention to certain objective data, which should play a significant role in future research. The first is both basic and obvious: the determination of what is poetry and what is not. The new technique, which is simply the formulation and application of an old impression, has proved to be basically right. It consistently supports the older tradition about what was prose and what was poetry (although with refinements), and offers the possibility of clearing up disputed and debated compositions. It also points the way to clarifying and perhaps resolving a question that has surrounded the prophetic corpus since scholars first began to identify poetic materials in this

body of literature. It may be that in addition to prose and poetry in the corpus as we have elsewhere, there is also a *tertium quid*, which needs to be defined and described more accurately, but which lies between the extremes indicated by the other categories. Analysis of this category might also help to explain why, in the tradition, prophecy was not transmitted simply as poetry, as the books such as Proverbs, Psalms, and Job were, along with some poems in the Primary History.

2. I wish to make a second point, which has to do with the scansion of Hebrew poetry. I think it is clear now that both sides of the debate as to whether there is quantity, definable and countable, in Hebrew poetry were partly right and partly wrong. There is quantity, but there isn't meter in the usual sense of the word. Quantity can only be determined and calculated for large structures, whole poems, or large units; whereas there is considerable freedom and irregularity in small units, especially lines and cola. Both sets of facts seem indisputable, and therefore both elements must be considered when talking about poetry. There are other factors as well, but we must include quantity as a basic fact, along with freedom. The method of counting seems to be less important, although the case should be made for the most objective and mechanical system possible, so as to avoid argument and debate about injecting interpretive criteria and conclusions in the statistical analysis and actual counting. I have opted for syllables, but word counting would probably serve almost as well, and counting morae (if the rules were set down carefully so as to decide the question of which vowels are really long and which are artificially so in the Masoretic system) might be even better. But there is no doubt that syllable counting gives a very reliable picture of comparable length, which is the essential purpose of the analysis. That Israelite poets had a system for counting seems both clear and inescapable, as otherwise it is impossible to explain how they produced poems of exactly equal length. No doubt music played a role, but that is an investigation in and of itself.

Bibliography

Andersen, F.I. and Forbes, A.D.

1983 '"Prose Particle" Counts of the Hebrew Bible', *The Word of the Lord Shall Go Forth. Essays in Honor of David Noel Freedman in Celebration of His Sixtieth Birthday* (ed. Carol L. Meyers and M. O'Connor, Philadelphia: American Schools of Oriental Research), pp. 165-83.

Andersen, F.I. and Freedman, D.N.

1980 *Hosea* (Anchor Bible, 24; Garden City: Doubleday).

Cross, F.M.

1983 'Studies in the Structure of Hebrew Verse: The Prosody of Lamentations 1.1-22', *The Word of the Lord Shall Go Forth. Essays in Honor of David Noel Freedman in Celebration of His Sixtieth Birthday* (ed. Carol L. Meyers and M. O'Connor. Philadelphia; American Schools of Oriental Research), pp. 129-55.

Freedman, D.N.

1971 'The Structure of Psalm 137', *Near Eastern Studies in Honor of William Foxwell Albright* (ed. Hans Goedicke; Baltimore: The Johns Hopkins University Press). Reprinted as pp. 303-21 in Freedman 1980.

1972 'Acrostics and Metrics in Hebrew Poetry', *Harvard Theological Review* 65, pp. 367-92. Reprinted as pp. 51-76 in Freedman 1980.

1976 'The Twenty-Third Psalm', *Michigan Oriental Studies in Honor of George G. Cameron* (ed. Louis L. Orlin, *et al.*; Ann Arbor: Department of Near Eastern Studies, University of Michigan), pp. 139-66. Reprinted as pp. 275-302 in Freedman 1980.

1977 'Pottery, Poetry and Prophecy: An Essay on Biblical Poetry', *Journal of Biblical Literature* 96, pp. 5-26. Reprinted as pp. 1-22 in Freedman 1980.

1980 *Pottery, Poetry and Prophecy: Studies in Early Hebrew Poetry* (Winona Lake, Indiana: Eisenbrauns).

2

NARRATIVE POETICS AND THE INTERPRETATION OF THE BOOK OF JONAH*

Duane L. Christensen

The interpretation of any literary work is shaped in large measure by presuppositions determined by the literary genre to which the work belongs. Herein lies the crux for the book of Jonah, since there is no agreement as regards its literary genre. It has been described as historical narrative, legend, parable, allegory, short story, prophetic tale, midrash, parody, drama and satire—to name only the more frequent categories mentioned. This paper is not an attempt to add still one more category to the list of candidates, but rather it is an endeavor to explore a more fundamental distinction. Almost every critic of this remarkable literary composition recognizes in it a work of art. But, as a work of art, is it to be classified as prose or poetry? The distinction is a rather important one!

T. Georgiades has argued that the distinction between the terms prose, poetry, and music was unknown in ancient Greece. As he put it, 'For the ancient Greeks, music existed primarily as verse. The Greek verse line was a linguistic and, simultaneously, a musical reality. The element common to both language and music was rhythm.'[1] He went on to argue that the English word 'music' is a quite inadequate translation of the Greek term *musiké*. *Musiké* is a

*The substance of this paper was written while in residence at the École Biblique in Jerusalem and was presented to the seminar on 'The Bible as Literature' at the Institute for Advanced Studies for the Hebrew University under the direction of Professors Shemaryahu Talmon and Menahem Haran. I am grateful to members of that seminar for their criticism and suggestions, particularly to Jack Sasson and Nahum Sarna.

form of musically determined verse, from which our familiar concepts of 'music' and 'prose' (and ultimately 'poetry') are both derived. He claimed that 'The ancient Greek line was a singular formation for which there is no analogy in Western Christian civilization. It was, if you will, music and poetry in one, and precisely because of this it could not be separated into music and poetry in two tangibly distinct components.'[2] For Georgiades, poetry is to be defined as linguistically determined verse, as opposed to prose, which he described as rhythmic chaos. It is quite possible that a somewhat analogous situation existed in ancient Israel.

This paper explores the relationship between traditional poetry and prose in the Hebrew Bible through the text of the book of Jonah. This remarkable narrative consists of only 48 'verses'—a term which, though applied to the whole of the biblical text as arranged by medieval scholars, belongs more to the realm of poetry than prose. Moreover, the book contains a 'psalm' (2.3-10), uttered from the belly of the GREAT FISH,[3] which is clearly of a different literary genre than the rest of the book. The thesis explored here is that the entire book of Jonah belongs to the category of poetry as this term is normally used in the field of literature. In short, the book of Jonah is not only a composition in verse, in the Masoretic tradition; it is also a composition in metrical language. The difference in structure between the psalm of Jonah (2.3-10) and its so-called 'prose' narrative context is more a matter of degree in terms of 'heightened language', than it is a distinction between poetry and prose genres as such. The book moves between narrative and lyric poetry, within the context of a delightful literary masterpiece.

It should be noted at the outset that this particular study is not the first attempt to apply a theory of metrical analysis to 'prose' sections of the book of Jonah. In his monumental study, *Metrische Studien* (1901-1907), Eduard Sievers included Jonah 1–2 in his first volume, where he subjected both chapters to a meticulous metrical analysis.[4] Wilhelm Erbt (1907) went even further as he used Sievers's principles to divide the entire book of Jonah into two separate literary sources.[5] And more recently, D. Arvid Bruno (1957) has studied the whole of the book of Jonah according to his theory of metrical and strophic analysis.[6] Though I believe that the conclusions of both Erbt and Bruno must be rejected or modified substantially, their basic approach is worth a second look.

The traditional approach to Hebrew meter remains that of the Ley–Sievers method, which focuses on patterns of word-stress within given poetic lines.[7] Recently, Jerzy Kurylowicz has criticized this approach, suggesting an important modification which will be used in this study. By paying careful attention to the diacritical marks of the Masoretic accentual system, Kurylowicz has devised a system of 'Syntactic-Accentual Meter'.[8] In short, he counts syntactic units rather than individual words. Thus, some independent nouns and verbs lose their accent altogether when considered from a metrical point of view.

A second approach to the study of Hebrew meter in vogue at the present time focuses on the actual length of poetic lines in terms of counting syllables.[9] Though this particular approach does produce interesting, and often persuasive, insights into the prosodic structure of some texts, the method itself is in need of refinement. Since counting syllables is essentially a means of assessing the length of poetic lines rather than the rhythmical manner in which these same lines were spoken (or sung), there is no real reason to see the method of syllable-counting as inherently different from that of stress-counting. But because the Hebrew language makes a distinction between long and short vowels, there is a need to modify such an approach if one hopes to assign a meaningful number to the length of a particular line, especially if that number is to represent a measure of the actual length of time required to speak that line.

The most useful approach to measuring the length of lines in Hebrew poetry is that of counting morae, i.e. the length of time required to say the simplest syllable from a phonetic point of view. Though this particular approach to scanning Hebrew poetry has been around a long time, it has not been the subject of serious discussion in recent years. It was a dominant approach in German scholarship from the middle of the seventeenth to the early nineteenth century.[10] The most influential of the early advocates were J. Alting (1608-79) and J.A. Danz (1654-1727), and the so-called 'Alting–Danzian System' survived into the nineteenth century.[11] B. Spinoza (1677) was an advocate of this approach, as were such scholars as H.B. Starke (1705), J.W. Meiner (1748, 1757) and J.F. Hirt (1771).[12] Nineteenth- and twentieth-century 'Metriks' who counted morae include J. Bellermann (1813), J. Saalschütz (1825), H. Grimme (1896-1903), and E. Isaacs (1918).[13] The basic problem with virtually all of these earlier approaches to counting morae is that the systems were much too complex and overly refined. As with similar scanning devices in other languages where vowel length is significant, it is sufficient to ascribe individual vowels to one of two categories—

either phonetically short or long, assigning a count of one for the former and two for the latter.[14]

In the following analysis of the book of Jonah the first column of figures in the right hand margin is the mora-count for that particular line in the Hebrew text, which is simply the syllable count plus one additional unit for each long vowel. The second column of figures is an assessment of syntactic-accentual stress units based on a close reading of the Masoretic accentual system, following the work of Kurylowicz. The vertical slash marks in the text of the English translation indicate the presence of disjunctive accents, with the *ṣilluq* and *'atnaḥ* indicated by a double slash. The triple slash after 2.10, 2.11 and 4.3 indicates the *setuma* and *petucha* markings in the Masoretic division of the text into paragraphs.[15] Disjunctive accents indicate a pause in pronunciation which is roughly equivalent to rhythm or metrical beat as such. The numbers in the third column are simply the sum of the syntactic-accentual stress units in various groupings of lines which fall into discernible prosodic patterns. In short, the two approaches to Hebrew meter were found to complement each other. Together, they comprise a system which is the basis of a structural analysis of the entire book of Jonah. The end result is remarkable in its simplicity as well as in its beauty. A surprising result of the analysis as such is a glimpse into some of the theological concerns of the author of the book of Jonah as reflected in the architectural design of the narrative poem taken as a whole.

Rules for Counting Morae

1. Short vowels which are counted as one mora include the standard short vowels ***i e a o u*** and the reduced vowels; i.e. the vocal shewa and the composite shewas *ᵉ ă ĕ ŏ*.
2. Long vowels which are counted as two morae include the unchangeable long vowels ***î ê ô û*** and normally the changeable long vowels *ē ā ō* as well.
3. The *furtive pataḥ* is counted; i.e. *librōaḥ* (4 morae) in 1.3.
4. Postaccentual *qameṣ* in nonverbal situations is considered short and counted as one mora; i.e. *'ālêha* (5 morae) in 1.2.
5. The shewa under the labial consonants (b m p) following the conjunction is considered vocal and is counted as one mora; i.e. *ûbᵉhēmâ* (7 morae) in 4.11. Elsewhere such shewas are considered silent; i.e. *ûqrā'* (4 morae) in 1.2).

Rules for Counting Syntactic-Accentual Units

1. The boundaries of the syntactic-accentual stress units are normally marked by the appearance of one of the 18 disjunctive accents (*distinctivi vel domini*) as listed on the insert to *Biblia Stuttgartensia*.
2. The versification of the MT is sometimes in error. When the *'atnaḥ* or *ṣilluq* does not fall at the boundary of a grouping of syntactic-accentual units, it may be necessary to change the *tipḥā* which precedes that *'atnaḥ* or *ṣilluq* to a conjunctive accent; i.e. 1.3, 4, 16; and 3.5.
3. There is apparently some inconsistency in the use of the *y*ᵉ*tîb* in monosyllabic particles when followed by the *zāqēp qāṭôn*. In some cases it is to be taken as the conjunctive accent *mahpak* which shares the same sign, though in a different position; i.e. 1.12 and 2.5 (but compare 1.6).

THE BOOK OF JONAH: A METRICAL READING[16]

Part One (1.1-8): | 5:5 | 4:4:4 | 5:5 || 5:5 || 5:5 | 4:4:4 | 5:5 |

1.1	Now /	4	1	
	the word of Yhwh came / to Jonah ben-Amittai, /	14	2	5
1.2	(Saying): // 'Arise! /	6	2	
	Go to Nineveh /	8	1	
	THAT GREAT CITY /	10	1	
	And proclaim against it; //	9	1	5
	For their evil has come up / before Me.' //	18	2	
1.3	But Jonah arose / to flee to Tarshish, /	16	2	
	Away from Yhwh; //	7	1	4
	And he went down to Joppa. /	8	1	
	And he found a ship /	9	1	
	plying the Tarshish route; /	7	1	
	And he paid the passage money; /	9	1	4
	And he went down in it—/	6	1	
	To go with them /	8	1	
	to Tarshish /	4	1	4
	away from / Yhwh. //	7	2	

1.4	So Yhwh / hurled a GREAT WIND /	16	2	
	toward the sea; /	4	1	5
	And there was a GREAT TEMPEST / on the sea. //	12	2	
	And the ship / had a mind to break up; //	18	2	
1.5	And the sailors were afraid; /	12	1	5
	And they cried out, /	5	1	
	each one to his own god. /	8	1	
	And they hurled the cargo, /	13	1	
	Which was in the ship / into the sea—/	13	2	5
	to lighten / its load; //	11	2	
	But Jonah / went down, /	8	2	
	Into the farthest reaches of the vessel; /	11	1	5
	And he lay down / and he went deep in sleep. //	9	2	
1.6	So the captain of the sailors / came to him; /	13	2	
	And he said to him: / 'What is this, O sleeper? //	12	2	5
	Arise! /	2	1	
	Call out to your God! /	9	1	
	Perhaps / the God will give a thought / to us, /	18	3	5
	so that we do not perish.' //	7	1	
1.7	And they said / each one to his companions: /	15	2	4
	'Come! / Let us cast lots—/	15	2	
	That we may know / on whose account, /	11	2	4
	This evil / has come upon us.' //	13	2	
	So they cast / lots; /	11	2	4
	And the lot fell / on Jonah. //	14	2	
1.8	And they said to him: / 'Tell us, now! /	20	2	5
	On whose / account has this evil / come upon us? //	19	3	
	What is your profession? /	4	1	
	And where do you come from? /	10	1	5
	What is your country? /	4	1	
	And of what people / are you?' //	10	2	

Transition (1.9-10a): |5:5|

1.9	And he said to them: / 'I am a Hebrew! //	17	2	5
	And it is Yhwh / the God of heaven / I fear—	22	3	
	The one who made the sea / and the dry land.'//	18	2	
1.10	And the men feared / a GREAT FEAR; /	21	2	5
	And they said to him: /	10	1	

Part Two (1.10b-16): |6|4:4:3:5||4:4||5:3:4:4|6|

	What is this you have done?' //	9	1	
	For the men knew, /	14	1	6
	That it was from Yhwh / he was fleeing; /	15	2	
	Because he confessed / to them. //	8	2	
1.11	And they said to him: /	10	1	
	'What shall we do with you, /	6	1	4
	That the sea may calm down / for us?' //	15	2	
	For the sea / grew more and more tempestuous.//	14	2	4
1.12	And he said to them: 'Take me up! /	14	2	
	And hurl me into the sea! /	12	1	3
	And the sea will calm down / for you. //	13	2	
	For I know / that it is because of me /	15	2	5
	That this / GREAT TEMPEST / has come upon you.' //	14	3	
1.13	And the men rowed hard, /	12	1	
	To return / to the dry land; /	12	2	4
	And they were unable to do so; //	9	1	
	Because the sea /	5	1	
	grew more and more tempestuous / against them; //	13	2	4
1.14	And they called out to Yhwh. /	9	1	
	And they said: /	6	1	
	'O Yhwh / let us not perish /	15	2	5
	with the soul-life / of this man. /	9	2	
	And do not put to our account / innocent blood; //	17	2	3
	For You are Yhwh! /	8	1	
	What pleases You / is what You have done!' //	14	2	4
1.15	And they picked up / Jonah; /	10	2	
	And they hurled him / into the sea; //	12	2	4
	And the sea ceased / its raging. //	12	2	
1.16	And the men feared /	13	1	
	Yhwh with a GREAT FEAR; //	12	1	6
	And they offered a sacrifice / to Yhwh; /	11	2	
	And they vowed / vows. //	10	2	

Transition (2.1): |4:4|

2.1	And Yhwh appointed / a GREAT FISH //	12	2	4
	to swallow / Jonah; //	9	2	

	And Jonah was / in the belly of the fish /	13	2	
	three days /	9	1	4
	and three nights. //	10	1	

Part Three (2.2-10): |6:5|4:4||6:4:4:6||4:4|6:5|

2.2	And Jonah prayed / to Yhwh / his God //	18	3	
	From the belly / of the fish; //	9	2	6
2.3	And he said: /	4	1	
	'I cried out / in my distress / to Yhwh; /	17	3	
	And He answered me, //	7	1	5
	from the womb of Sheol. /	6	1	
	I cried for help—/ You heard my voice; //	12	2	
2.4	You cast me toward the depth /	13	1	4
	into the heart of the seas; /	6	1	
	And River / swirled about me. //	13	2	4
	All Your breakers and Your waves / passed over me. //	19	2	
2.5	And then I said: /	9	1	
	"I am driven away / from Your presence; //	11	2	6
	Yet I persist in looking / to Your holy / Temple. //	15	3	
2.6	Waters choked me / to death; /	12	2	4
	The Abyss / swirled about me. //	11	2	
	Weeds / tangled about my head; //	11	2	4
2.7	To the roots of the mountains / I went down. /	13	2	
	The Netherworld / with its bars closed upon me /	15	2	
	forever. //	5	1	6
	But You brought me up from the Pit / alive, /	8	2	
	O Yhwh, my God." //	8	1	
2.8	When my soul-life had expired / within me, /	11	2	4
	I remembered / Yhwh. //	10	2	
	And my prayer / came to You, /	15	2	4
	to your holy / Temple. //	6	2	
2.9	Those who cling / to empty nothings, //	10	2	
	Their covenant trust / they have abandoned. //	9	2	6
2.10	But I / with the voice of thanksgiving—/	11	2	

	Let me sacrifice to You! /	6	1	
	What I have vowed / let me pay! //	13	2	5
	Salvation belongs / to Yhwh!' ///	11	2	

Transition (2.11-3.2): \|4:3:3:4\| or \|7:7\|

2.11	So Yhwh spoke / to the fish; //	10	2	
	And it vomited out Jonah /	10	1	4
	upon the dry land. ///	7	1	
3.1	And the word of Yhwh / came to Jonah /	13	2	3
	a second time (saying): //	8	1	
3.2	'Arise! / Go to Nineveh, /	10	2	3
	THAT GREAT CITY; //	10	1	
	And proclaim to it / the proclamation, /	17	2	4
	That I / am about to tell you.' //	16	2	

Part Four (3.3–4.2): \|4:5:6:4\|4:4\|7:6\|\|5:5\|\|7:6\|4:4\|6:4:4:5\|

3.3	So Jonah arose / and he went / to Nineveh; /	18	3	4
	according to the word of Yhwh. //	5	1	
	And Nineveh /	6	1	
	was a GREAT CITY / to God, /	18	2	5
	a journey / of three days. //	11	2	
3.4	And Jonah began / by going into the city, /	16	2	
	a journey / of one day; //	8	2	6
	And he cried out / and he said: /	8	2	
	'There remain but / forty days, /	9	2	4
	And Nineveh / shall be "overturned"!' //	10	2	
3.5	And the people of Nineveh / believed / God; //	21	3	4
	And they proclaimed a fast. /	7	1	
	And they put on sackcloth, /	8	1	
	From the greatest of them to the least of them;//	12	1	
3.6	And the word reached /	8	1	4
	the king of Nineveh. /	8	1	
	And he arose / from his throne; /	8	2	
	And he threw off / his royal robe; //	15	2	7
	And he donned sackcloth; /	4	1	
	And he sat / in ashes. //	10	2	
3.7	And he cried out; /	4	1	
	And he said / in Nineveh, /	10	2	
	From a "judgment" of the king /	6	1	6
	and his grandees / (saying): //	10	2	

	'Human beings and beasts—/	13	1	
	Cattle and sheep, /	9	1	5
	Let them not taste / anything. /	10	2	
	Let them not graze (be evil). /	4	1	
	And water / let them not drink; //	8	2	
3.8	Let them don sackcloth, /	8	1	5
	Human beings and beasts. /	13	2	
	Let them call out to God / mightily; //	17	2	
	Let them turn / each one /	8	2	7
	From his evil way / and from the violence /	18	2	
	Which is in their hands. //	7	1	
3.9	Who knows, He may yet turn; /	11	1	
	The God / may repent. //	10	2	6
	He may turn / from His burning anger, /	11	2	
	So that we do not perish.' //	7	1	
3.10	And the God saw / their deeds, /	15	2	4
	That they turned / from their evil way. //	16	2	
	And the God repented / from the evil, /	19	2	
	Which He said He would do to them; /	11	1	4
	And He did not do it. //	7	1	

Part Five (4.1-11): |6:4:4:5|6:5:5:5||6:5:6||6:5:5:5|5:4:4:6|

4.1	But a GREAT EVIL / came upon Jonah; //	18	2	
	And he / became angry; //	5	2	6
4.2	And he prayed to Yhwh / and he said: /	13	2	
	'O Yhwh, / is this not what I said, /	15	2	4
	When I was still / in my own country? /	12	2	
	That is why I made haste / to flee to Tarshish.//	15	2	4
	For I knew / that You are—/	12	2	
	"A God who is gracious and merciful, /	9	1	
	full of patience, /	5	1	5
	And abounding in steadfast love; /	4	1	
	Who repents / from the evil." //	11	2	
4.3	So now Yhwh / take my life / from me; //	18	3	6
	For / I am better off dead / than alive.' ///	13	3	
4.4	And Yhwh said: / 'Do you do well / to be angry?//	18	3	5
4.5	And Jonah went out / from the city. /	14	2	

	And he sat down / east of the city; //	11	2	
	And he built for himself there / a Sukkah; /	10	2	5
	And he sat down beneath it—/	8	1	
	in its shade—/	3	1	
	Until / he should see / what would become /	11	3	5
	of the city. //	4	1	
4.6	And Yhwh-God appointed / a Qiqayon; /	16	2	
	And it grew up, /	3	1	6
	Over Jonah / to be a shade / over his head, /	18	3	
	To deliver him / from his evil. //	14	2	
	And Jonah rejoiced /	7	1	5
	over the Qiqayon / a GREAT JOY. //	16	2	
4.7	So the God appointed / a worm, /	14	2	
	As Dawn came up / the next morning; //	12	2	6
	And it smote the Qiqayon, /	10	1	
	so that it withered. //	5	1	
4.8	And then, /	4	1	
	as the sun arose, /	7	1	6
	God appointed / a 'burning' / east / wind; /	20	4	
	And the sun smote / upon Jonah's head; /	12	2	
	And he grew faint. //	5	1	5
	And he asked / that he might die. /	11	2	
	And he said: / 'I am better off dead / than alive!' //	15	3	5
4.9	And God said to / Jonah: /	14	2	
	'Do you do well to be angry /	10	1	
	because of the Qiqayon?' //	9	1	5
	And he said: / 'I do well to be angry /	14	2	
	unto death!' //	4	1	
4.10	And Yhwh said: /	7	1	
	'You have compassion / for the Qiqayon; /	13	2	5
	For which / you did not labor; /	10	2	
	Nor did you cause it to grow—//	7	1	
	Which came up in a night / and perished in a night. //	17	2	4
4.11	And I—/	4	1	
	Should I not have compassion / on Nineveh, /	12	2	4
	THAT GREAT CITY // in which there are /	15	2	
	More than 120,000 / persons /	16	2	
	who do not know /	7	1	6
	Their right hand from their left—/	12	1	
	and much / cattle?' //	10	2	

From a rhetorical point of view the structure of the book of Jonah clearly consists of four major sections which correspond, for the most part, to the chapter divisions. The two-fold use of the phrase '(THAT) GREAT CITY' (1.2; 3.2,3; and 4.11) frames the two major parts of this narrative poem, the first of which focuses on Jonah with respect to a fish which houses him, and the second on Jonah in relation to the city of Nineveh. In this regard it is interesting to note the observation made by E.A. Speiser some years ago, that the cuneiform texts sometimes use a pseudo-logographic form NINA for the term Nineveh. The sign NINA (AB + ḪA) combines two signs, those of an enclosure (AB) with a fish (ḪA) inside it.[17] With this fact in mind, it is easy to see the spatial chiasm which forms the over-all structural design of the composition:

1.1-16	A—Jonah Outside the House of the Fish
2.1-3.2	B—Jonah Inside the House of the Fish
3.3-10	B′—Jonah Inside another 'House of the Fish'
4.1-11	A′—Jonah Outside the 'House of the Fish'

The prophet moves from outside the 'House of the Fish' to inside, and then from inside another 'House of the Fish' (Nineveh) to outside, where the story ends.

The chiastic relationship between the four chapters may also be described theologically as follows:

ch. 1	A—What Yahweh requires is 'fear' (cf. Deut 10.12-20)
ch. 2	B—Jonah as an anti-Moses figure
ch. 3	B′—The King of Nineveh as a Mosaic prophet
ch. 4	A′—In place of anger, Yahweh desires compassion

Jonathan Magonet has shown the 'mirror image' parallelism between chs. 2 and 3 which he sees as conclusive evidence that the 'psalm' from the belly of the fish was from the very outset an integral part of the author's composition.[18]

From a metrical point of view a rather different structural pattern emerges which, though also concentric in nature, consists of five major divisions rather than four—with transitional elements between each of these divisions, except for the last two which share a metrical element. Each of these five metrical divisions has a similar structural design; and the repetition of key words ties the five parts together in a sort of two-dimensional manner, both vertically and horizontally. This metrical structure may be described as follows:

1.1-8	A—Jonah's flight as a descent (*yrd*, 'to go down')
1.10-16	B—The men try to return (*l^{e}hāšîb*) to dry land.
2.2-7a	C—Jonah's final descent (*yrd*, 'to go down')
2.7b-10	C′—Jonah's ascent (*'lh* 'to go up')
3.3–4.2	B′—The people of Nineveh turn (*šwb*) from evil.
4.1-11	A′—Jonah's plight portrayed as a possible ascent (*'lh*)

Each of the five major parts of this narrative poem is arranged concentrically from a metrical point of view; and in each case the key verbs (*yrd*, *šwb* and *'lh*) appear at the structural center of metrical configurations. Thus, in terms of accentual-stress units the first part (1.1-8) scans as follows:

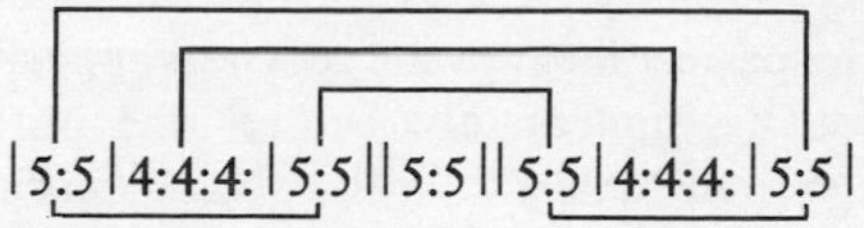

Here the second part of the |5:5| element at the center of this structure (1.5b) focuses on the root *yrd*.

> But Jonah / went down (*yārad*) /
> into the farthest reaches of the vessel /
> And he lay down /
> and he went deep in sleep (*wayyērādam*) //

This particular metrical unit is preceded by a |5:5|4:4:4|5:5| unit (1.1-5) which has its center the first of two concentric sentences (1.3 and 3.7b-8a) which also focuses on the root *yrd* in parallel lines:

> And he went down (*wayyēred*) to Joppa. /
> And he found a ship / plying the Tarshish route; /
> And he paid the passage money; /
> And he went down (*wayyēred*) in it—/

The next, and final, appearance of the root *yrd* in the book of Jonah is at the structural center of the third major section (2.2-10), which scans as follows:

Jonah's descent takes him away from the presence of Yahweh (2.4-5; cf. 1.3); and his final descent (2.6-7a) takes him to 'the roots of the mountains', i.e. to hell itself. It is precisely when Jonah reaches the farthest possible limits in his flight that Yahweh himself appears to raise him up (*watta'al*) 'from the Pit alive' (2.7).

The poet has used a most interesting technique to communicate the nature of Jonah's descent. On the one hand, he has carefully connected the journey down with Jonah's earlier descent at the outset of the larger narrative poem. In the only other use of the perfect form *yārad* (1.5b) Jonah 'went down' into the *yark^{e}tê hass^{e}pînâ* ('the farthest reaches of the vessel'). Here the poet has used a form of anticipatory paronomasia, as J. Ackerman has suggested, playing on the mythic *yark^{e}tê ṣāpôn* ('the farthest reaches of Zaphon/ the North').[19] The perfect form of the root *yrd* appears only twice in the book of Jonah—immediately before the phrase *'el-yark^{e}tê hass^{e}pînâ* (1.5) and immediately after the phrase *l^{e}qiṣbê hārîm* ('to the roots of the mountains', in 2.7). The mythic abode of the gods in the *yark^{e}tê ṣāpôn* is thus associated with the farthest point in Jonah's 'descent' from the presence of Yahweh in a theological reversal. It is in hell itself that Yahweh reappears to Jonah in a most unexpected theophany.

The poet uses still other literary techniques to underscore the nature of Jonah's descent from the presence of Yahweh. After descending into the innermost reaches of the vessel (1.5), Jonah lay down and went into a 'deep sleep' (*wayyērādam*). In this latter term the poet repeats all three consonants of the root *yrd*. Moreover, this unusual word has interesting overtones for the sensitive reader, for the same root is used to describe the sleep (*tardēmâ*) of Adam when Eve was created (Gen 2.21), and the sleep of Abraham when the covenant promises were revealed to him (Gen 15.12)—two rather familiar passages. The experience of Jonah may thus be understood as being preparatory to some new creation—a resurrection from death, with covenant implications for the people of God. This particular message took on striking new meaning in the New Testament context where this imagery was applied to Jesus' redemptive activity which is clearly associated with the experience of Jonah.[20]

A further literary technique has been explored by Magonet, who has shown that the allusions to the Psalter in Jonah's psalm form a concentric pattern.[21] Magonet found sixteen places where Jonah's psalm makes explicit allusion to the Psalter, with some thirty possible sources. But the interesting factor is the distribution of these allusions. Nine allusions are to be found in 2.3-6a and seven in 2.7b-10, but none in the lines between, which read as follows:

> The Abyss / swirled about me. //
> Weeds / tangled about my head; //
> To the roots of the mountains / I went down (*yāradtî*). /
> The Netherworld / with its bars closed upon me / forever. //

At the very point where Jonah makes his 'final descent' to hell itself, he leaves the familiar world of the Psalter. All contact, at least for the moment, with the familiar world of the psalms ceases until Yahweh himself re-enters the picture. It is a bit like a technique used by Shakespeare in *Othello* where he reproduced almost perfect Greek iambic pentameter until the point at which Othello goes insane. And at that precise moment the meter dissolves and the reader (or hearer) is left with an uneasy feeling that something is wrong, even if he or she knows nothing about the intricate world of Greek metrical structures.[22] Here in the narrative of Jonah the numerous allusions to various psalms at the beginning and end of Jonah's psalm can be understood as a literary technique on the part of an author who, perhaps at a subliminal level, is urging the reader to 'think Psalter' at this particular point in the narrative. As Jonah resumes his journey downward, to the very depths of hell itself, the language in turn soars to lyrical heights. But in the very center of the psalm, which is also the structural center of the book of Jonah as a whole from a metrical point of view, Jonah slips beyond the pale in his flight from Yahweh's presence. As Magonet put it, 'In parallel to the situation he describes, the sudden change from familiar to unfamiliar language takes one into the depths of a frightening new world, far from God, where only the sudden intervention of God Himself can restore the lost soul'.[23]

Like the root *yrd*, the verbal root *ʿlh*, 'to go up', also occurs only four times in the book of Jonah—once in the perfect form (*ʿāl*^{e}*tâ* in 1.2), twice in the converted imperfect (*wattaʿal* in 2.7 and *wayyaʿal* in 4.6), and in the infinitive construct form with a prepositional suffix (*baʿ*^{a}*lôt* in 4.7). Both of these occurrences of *ʿlh* in the fifth major section of the book of Jonah (4.1-11) appear in the structural center of another concentric metrical configuration which scans as follows:

| 6:4:4:5 | 6:5:5:5 || 6:5:6 || 6:5:5:5 | 5:4:4:6 |

The verbal roots *yrd* and *ʿlh* thus each appear four times in the book of Jonah and only in parts one, three and five of the five-part metrical structure. The narrative movement in these three sections is in a vertical direction and can be described in the form of the letter 'U'. Jonah's flight from the presence of Yahweh takes him downward until he literally reaches hell itself; but at the bottom of that journey Yahweh appears to bring him up out of the Pit alive (2.7). The shift in direction occurs precisely at the structural center of the book of Jonah from a metrical point of view.

Although the verbal root *ʿlh* appears only twice in part five (4.1-11), the two occurrences are part of a group of four terms which contain the same sounds (4.6-8): *wayyaʿal . . . tôlaʿat* / *ba*ʿ^{a}*lôt . . . wayyitʿallāp*. Thus even when Jonah faints (*wayyitʿallāp*), assonance provides a hint of an upward journey.

In a somewhat similar fashion there is a four-fold use of the verbal root *šwb* as one moves out of the center of another concentric metrical structure in part four (3.3–4.2) which scans as follows:

| 4:5:6:4 | 4:4 | 7:6 || 5:5 || 7:6 | 4:4 | 6:4:4:5 |

In 3.8-10 the root *šwb* appears four times, twice in the plural and twice in the singular, arranged chiastically: *w*^{e}*yāšūbû . . . yāšûb . . . w*^{e}*šāb . . . kî-šābû*. The people of Nineveh are the subject of the two plural forms, while God (*hāʾ*^{e}*lōhîm*) is the subject of the two singular forms in the center. The root *rʿʿ*, 'to be evil', appears six times in 3.8–4.2, lending further support to the close structural tie between parts four (3.3–4.2) and five (4.1-11) which share a metrical unit. A seventh use of the root *rʿʿ* occurs at the center of part four on the level of paronomasia in the phrase *ʾal yirʿû*, 'let them not graze (be evil)'.[24]

The only other use of the root *šwb* in the book of Jonah is at the center of still another concentric metrical structure in part two (1.10b-16), which scans as follows:

| 6 | 4:4:3:5 || 4:4 || 5:3:4:4 | 6 |

Here it is the 'sailors'[25] who are trying 'to return (*l*^{e}*hāšîb*) to the dry land'. Unable to do so, they pray to Yahweh (*wayyiqr^{e}'û 'el-Yhwh*) and thus demonstrate that they are the ones who truly 'fear God' rather than the prophet Jonah, in spite of the latter's great confession (1.9).[26]

The narrative movement in parts two and four of the book takes place on a horizontal plane, focusing on the 'turning/repentance' of the sailors on the one hand, and the people of Nineveh on the other. Part two (1.10-16) focuses much more on the sailors than on Jonah. In part four (3.3–4.2) the prophet is absent altogether, until one reaches the shared metrical element (4.1-2). The king of Nineveh has taken Jonah's place, even to the point of commanding the people (including Jonah?) to turn from their evil (3.7-8).

A poem may be defined as 'a composition designed to convey a vivid and imaginative sense of experience, characterized by the use of condensed language, chosen for its sound and suggestive power as well as its meaning, and by the use of such literary techniques as structured meter, natural cadences, rhyme, or metaphor'.[27] In light of the foregoing metrical reading of this delightful literary masterpiece, it is clear that the book of Jonah can be described as a narrative poem, written in metrical language in five parts which are integrally structured along two primary dimensions. The dominant dimension (parts one, three and five) is vertical, focusing on the flight of Jonah/ Israel from Yahweh's presence and Yahweh's grace in raising him/ them up from the Pit alive and restoring him/them to his/their prophetic task. The other dimension focuses on the outsiders, both friend and foe of Jonah/Israel (parts two and four), who are called to worship Yahweh by 'fearing him', thus turning from their evil ways.

The 'psalm of Jonah' (2.3-10) is thus an integral part of the structural design of the book of Jonah as a whole and not a secondary insertion, as is often claimed. At the very point in the narrative where Jonah makes his final descent to the depths of hell itself, the language soars to lyrical heights. And once the GREAT FISH 'turns Jonah around' en route to Nineveh, the language of the poet returns to the level of narrative poetry.

NOTES

1. T. Georgiades, *Music and Language* (Cambridge: Cambridge University Press, 1982), p. 4.

2. *Ibid.*, p. 6.

3. The capital letters are for emphasis to call attention to the twelve occurrences of the adjective *gādôl* or *gᵉdôlâ* in the book of Jonah (1.2, 4, 10, 12, 16; 2.1; 3.2, 3; 4.1, 6, 11) which appear to be arranged according to carefully determined rhetorical patterns.

4. E. Sievers, *Metrische Studien*, I (Leipzig, 1901), pp. 482-85.

5. W. Erbt, *Elia, Elisa, Jona: Ein Beitrag zur Geschichte des IX. und VIII. Jahrhunderts* (Leipzig, 1907).

6. D.A. Bruno, *Das Buch der Zwölf: Eine rhythmische und textkritische Untersuchung* (Stockholm: Almqvist & Wiksell, 1957), pp. 82-89, 213-14.

7. For a description of this approach see W.H. Cobb, *A Criticism of Systems of Hebrew Metre: An Elementary Treatise* (Oxford, 1905), pp. 83-107, pp. 169-84.

8. J. Kurylowicz, *Studies in Semitic Grammar and Metrics* (London: Curzon Press, 1973), p. 176. The term 'Syntactic-Accentual meter' is that of T. Longman, 'A Critique of Two Recent Metrical Systems', *Bib* 63 (1982), pp. 230-54.

9. See T. Longman, *ibid.*, pp. 232-38 for a convenient summary of this approach which has been associated primarily with F.M. Cross, D.N. Freedman and their students. The most common objection to this method of scansion remains that of the frequent emendation of the text practiced by most adherents. Though continuing to count syllables, Freedman has taken a stand against such emendation and has turned to statistical approaches to explore structural patterns with minimal alteration of the MT. See in particular his article in *The Bible World* (Festschrift C.H. Gordon; New York: Ktav, 1980), pp. 25-46, and my response in *Bib* 65 (1984), pp. 382-89.

10. For a brief discussion of this period see B. Pick, 'The Study of Hebrew Among Jews and Christians', *BibSac* 42 (1885), pp. 490-93. I am grateful to Walter Bodine for this reference and the one to the work of E. Isaacs in note 13 below.

11. The system was subsequently discredited by Vater and Gesenius.

12. See Pick's article (note 10 above) for specific references to works of these scholars.

13. J.J. Bellermann, *Versuch über die Metrik der Hebräer* (Berlin, 1813); J.L. Saalschütz, *Von der Form der hebräischen Poesie* (Konigsberg, 1825); H. Grimme, *ZDMG* 50 (1896), pp. 529-84; 51 (1897), pp. 683-712; *Vierteljahrsschrift für Bibelkunde* 1 (1903), pp. 1-14; and E. Isaacs, 'The Metrical Basis of Hebrew Poetry', *AJSL* 35 (1918), pp. 20-54.

14. J. Hoard, professor of linguistics at the University of Oregon, has

described such a system for scanning Japanese poetry (private communication). For a similar counting system based on *mātrās* ('instants') with the same long vs. short vowel distinction, see V.P. Vatuk, 'Poetics and Genre-typology in Indian Folklore', *Studies in Indian Folk Traditions* (New Delhi, 1979), pp. 38-47. I am grateful to Sue Clark, one of my students, for this reference. Elcanon Isaacs made a strong case for the same point in *AJSL* 35 (1918), pp. 25-26.

15. See I. Yeivin, *Introduction to the Tiberian Masorah* (MS, 5; Missoula: Scholars Press, 1980), pp. 40-41; and J.M. Oesch, *Petucha and Setuma* (OBO, 27; Göttingen, 1979).

16. For this study I have chosen to accept the MT as it stands without emendation, including the major disjunctive marks of the Masoretic accentual system. Omission of a disjunctive accent is indicated by a blank space in the English translation (1. 3, 4, 12, 16; 2.5 and 3.5). There is a problem as regards 2nd m.s. pronominal suffixes, since the use of the final *kaph* in the MT suggests that the Masoretes have normalized the longer *-kā* for what may have been a dialectal variant. E. Sievers rejected the longer form and read instead **-ak* after singular nouns and **-êk* after plural nouns (*Metrische Studien*, I, pp. 316-17). P. Kahle amassed an enormous amount of evidence to support a similar conclusion in *The Cairo Geniza* (London, 1947), pp. 95-102. F.M. Cross and D.N. Freedman presented still further arguments for the same conclusion in *Early Hebrew Orthography: A Study of the Epigraphic Evidence* (AOS, 36; New Haven, 1952), pp. 55, 65-66. For this study I have chosen to vocalize such forms *-êk(a)* when a *yodh* appears with the suffix, *-ek(a)* when the *yodh* is not present, and *lēk(a)* in the two occurrences of the term *lᵉkā* in the MT (1.6 and 4.9). In all cases the final syllable, indicated by the parentheses, is not counted in the mora-count.

17. 'Nineveh', *IDB*, III (1962), p. 552.

18. J. Magonet, *Form and Meaning: Studies in Literary Techniques in the Book of Jonah* (Sheffield: Almond Press, 1983), p. 62.

19. J. Ackerman, 'Satire and Symbolism in the Song of Jonah', in *Traditions in Transformation: Turning Points in Biblical Faith* (Winona Lake: Eisenbrauns, 1981), pp. 229-35.

20. See Matt. 12.38-41 and Luke 11.29-30.

21. Magonet, *Form and Meaning*, pp. 44-50.

22. I owe this observation to Professor H. Ridlon of Bridgewater State College in Bridgewater, Massachusetts.

23. Magonet, *Form and Meaning*, p. 49.

24. For a more detailed discussion of this passage see my article, 'Anticipatory Paronomasia in Jonah 3.7-8 and Genesis 37.2', *RB* 90 (1983), pp. 361-63.

25. It should be noted that once one reaches the center of this metrical structure the 'sailors' (*hammallāḥîm*) are referred to only as 'men' (*hāʾᵃnāšîm*).

26. Jonah's confession in 1.9 is at the center of another concentric structure which includes the whole of ch. 1. See R. Pesch, 'Zur konzentrischen Struktur von Jona 1', *Bib* 47 (1966), pp. 577-81.

27. *The American Heritage Dictionary of the English Language* (New York: Houghton Mifflin, 1976), p. 1011.

3

ALTERNATING (ABA'B') PARALLELISM IN THE OLD TESTAMENT PSALMS AND PROPHETIC LITERATURE

John T. Willis

Research into the characteristics of Hebrew (along with Ugaritic and Akkadian) parallelism has led to the discovery of various arrangements of lines within couplets as well as of longer and more complex pieces. Much attention has been given to synonymous,[1] 'pivot-pattern',[2] 'Janus',[3] ABCB,[4] and chiastic[5] parallelism in particular. In addition, in more general studies dealing with parallelism, some work has been done on antithetic, emblematic, 'stairlike' or 'staircase' and other types.[6] Occasionally 'alternating parallelism' is mentioned, sometimes with an example,[7] but as far as this writer knows, no special study has been devoted to this phenomenon. Over the past several years, my attention has been drawn to several examples in which the biblical text is arranged so that lines 1 and 3 correspond or balance each other, and also lines 2 and 4. The purpose of this paper is to enumerate several examples of this phenomenon in the Old Testament psalmic and prophetic literature (in the hope that it might stimulate others to seek and find additional examples), and to suggest ways in which this phenomenon is used to communicate the author's message. The texts presented contain more than an alternating arrangement of the same or similar verbs or nouns (as is the case with several of the passages cited in connection with the ABCB arrangement in the articles mentioned in n. 4 above); rather, they concern the whole thought of the passage under consideration. Matters of meter, syllable-count, word-count, and letter-count are left aside in this paper, and emphasis is placed on the flow of thought and clear breaks in the thought.

1. *Examples in the Psalms*

Ps 9.20-21

קומה יהוה אל־יעז אנוש	Arise, O Yahweh! Let not man prevail;
ישפטו גוים על־פניך	let the nations be judged before thee!
שיתה יהוה מורה להם	Put them in fear, O Yahweh!
ידעו גוים אנוש המה	Let the nations know that they are but men![8]

As printed in *Biblia Hebraica Stuttgartensia*, these are the last two lines under the letter *kaph* in the acrostic consisting of Pss 9–10. The first line contains a clear example of synonymous parallelism. These last two lines are composed of four separate sentences. The first and third are addressed directly to Yahweh (*yhwh* is the second word in both lines, and functions as a vocative). Both begin with an imperative with the emphatic ending *-â*. By way of contrast, the second and fourth lines consist of a prayer of execration against the 'nations' (*gôyim* without the fully written *ḥireq* is the second word in both lines). The verbs at the beginning of these lines are both jussives. Even though *'ĕnôš* appears in lines A and B′, it is used with a singular verb in A and with a plural pronoun in B′. Here the alternating pattern tends to stress the urgency of the situation and of the psalmist's plea.

Ps 10.3-4

כי הלל רשע על־תאות נפשו	For the wicked (one) boasts of the desire of his soul,
ובצע ברך נאץ יהוה	and the greedy (one) curses, he renounces Yahweh.
רשע כגבה אפו בל־ידרש	The wicked (one) in[9] the pride of his countenance does not seek (him);
אין אלהים כל־מזמותיו	'There is no God' are all his thoughts.

Lines A and A′ concern 'the wicked one' (*rāšā'* is the subject of both lines). They both condemn his pride or arrogance, and contain construct expressions which have similar meanings: 'the desire of his soul' in A, and 'the pride of his countenance' in A′. Then lines B and B′ state his attitude toward God: he curses or renounces him (B); he thinks (or would like to think, or behaves as if he thought) God does not exist (B′). The alternating pattern has the effect of defining the wicked in broad strokes as one who feels or acts as if he is of ultimate importance and, as a direct corollary to this, denies any need for

God. In other words, the fundamental feature which identifies the wicked is that he is self-sufficent or independent rather than dependent on God.

Ps 22.15

כמים נשפכתי	I am poured out like water,
והתפרדו כל־עצמותי	and all my bones are out of joint;
היה לבי כדונג	my heart is like wax,
נמס בתוך מעי	it is melted within my breast.

The use of running water and melting wax together in parallel similes seems to have been common in ancient times.[10] In this passage, the similes occur in lines A and A′, followed by metaphors in lines B and B′. Certainly B′ is not to be taken literally, and it is unlikely that B refers to an actual physical condition. Rather, the whole point of this verse is that the psalmist is wholly distraught. Everything is against him. He is soundly defeated and hopelessly torn within himself.

Ps 24.7-10

שאו שערים ראשיכם	Lift up your heads, O gates!
והנשאו פתחי עולם	and be lifted up, O ancient doors!
ויבוא מלך הכבוד	that the King of glory may come in.
מי זה מלך הכבוד	Who is the King of glory?
יהוה עזוז וגבור	Yahweh, strong and mighty,
יהוה גבור מלחמה	Yahweh, mighty in battle!
שאו שערים ראשיכם	Lift up your heads, O gates!
והנשאו פתחי עולם	and be lifted up, O ancient doors!
ויבא מלך הכבוד	that the King of glory may come in.
מי הוא זה מלך הכבוד	Who is this King of glory?
יהוה צבאות	Yahweh of hosts,
הוא מלך הכבוד	he is the King of glory!

The alternating character of these verses is obvious. Each verse has three lines or stichoi. Because of the style and thought of this text, A and A′ should probably be read as identical. This requires only one emendation in v. 9 to agree with v. 7, viz. from *ûś*^{e}*'û* to *w*^{e}*hinnāś*^{e}*'û*; *h* and *n* dropped out for some reason in transmission. B and B′ exhibit a gradual crescendo. In this way, the psalmist emphasizes the magnificence of this particular deity, Yahweh, who appears in the theophany, apparently in connection with the ark procession.[11]

Ps 27.1

יהוה אורי וישעי	Yahweh is my light and my salvation;
ממי אירא	whom shall I fear?
יהוה מעוז־חיי	Yahweh is the stronghold of my life;
ממי אפחד	of whom shall I be afraid?

Lines A and A′ declare Yahweh's relationship to and care for the psalmist; then B and B′ relate the psalmist's resolution in light of this. A and A′ begin with *Yhwh* and contain the first person pronominal suffix. B and B′ both begin with *mimmî* and conclude with the first person singular imperfect form of a verb for 'fear'. The psalmist's purpose is to relate his own experience in order to encourage his hearers to 'wait for Yahweh' (note v. 14).

Ps 27.3

אם־תחנה עלי מחוה	Though a host encamp against me,
לא־יירא לבי	my heart shall not fear;
אם־תקום עלי מלחמה	though war arise against me,
בזאת אני בוטח	yet I will be confident.

Lines A and A′ both consist of the apodosis of a conditional sentence introduced by the particle *'im* + the imperfect, *'ālay*, and a noun which sounds very much like the noun in the parallel line (*maḥăneh* in A and *milḥāmâ* in A′), and states hypothetically the worst type of crisis conceivable. Then B (negatively) and B′ (positively) proclaim the psalmist's resolution to trust in Yahweh irrespective of the circumstances.

Ps 30.6

כי רגע באפו	For only a moment is his anger,
חיים ברצונו	(but) a lifetime is his favor.
בערב ילין בכי	In the evening weeping may tarry,
ולבקר רנה	but in the morning, joy.

The last two lines depict a metaphorical analogy to the reality affirmed in the first two lines. Thus a manifestation of God's anger is illustrated by the heavy heart and disappointment which one often feels at the end of a hard and trying day, while God's never-ending favor is likened to the feeling of freshness and renewed vigor frequently experienced when one rises after a good night's sleep. The rather unusual word order (which the translation here seeks to convey), followed invariably in all four lines, suggests that the ABA′B′ arrangement in this case is intentional.

Ps 38.4

אין־מתם בבשרי	There is no soundness in my flesh
מפני זעמך	because of thy indignation;
אין־שלום בעצמי	there is no health in my bones
מפני חטאתי	because of my sin.

Lines A and A′ describe the psalmist's condition, and lines B and B′ state the reason for it. The OT frequently uses the word-pair 'flesh' (*bāśār*) and 'bones' (*'eṣem* is the lexical form) (Gen 2.23; 29.14; Exod 12.46; Judg 9.2; 2 Sam 5.1; 19.13-14; 1 Chr 11.1; Job 2.5; 4.14-15; 10.11; 19.20; 33.21; etc.). Furthermore, both 'reasons' are introduced by *mippᵉnê*. Clearly the arrangement is alternating by the author's design.

Ps 68.3

כהנדף עשן	As smoke is driven away
תנדף	so drive them away;
כהמס דונג מפני־אש	as wax melts before fire,
יאבדו רשעים מפני אלהים	so let the wicked (ones) perish before God!

The first two lines are much shorter than the last two lines in Hebrew. But this could be intentional to create a crescendo effect. Lines A and A′ contain a simile denoting quick and complete destruction, and lines B and B′ relate the attendant prayer of the psalmist that God's enemies suffer a like fate.

Ps 68.16

הר אלהים	O mighty mountain,
הר בשן	mountain of Bashan;
הר גבננים	O many-peaked mountain,
הר בשן	mountain of Bashan!

Lines B and B′ are identical. Lines A and A′ both contain construct expressions in which the *nomen rectum* ends in *-îm*. The parallelism supports the rendering of *'ᵉlōhîm* as a descriptive noun ('mighty') rather than a proper noun ('God'). The psalmist's purpose is to emphasize the awesome majesty of Mount Bashan in order to exalt

Mount Zion as even more imposing because it had been chosen by Yahweh as his dwelling place (see v. 17).

Ps 69.7

אל־יבשו בי קויך	Let not those who hope in thee be put to shame through me,
אדני יהוה צבאות	O Lord Yahweh of hosts;
אל־יכלמו בי מבקשיך	let not those who seek thee be brought to dishonor through me,
אלהי ישראל	O God of Israel.

It is obvious that B and B′ correspond. There is also a tightly-knit agreement in the semantic structure of A and A′ (as well as in the meaning): the negative *’al*—the imperfect with passive meaning—*bî*—the plural participle—the second person masculine singular suffix. The alternating pattern underlines the urgency of the psalmist's request.

Ps 78.63-64

בחוריו אכלה־אש	Their young men fire devoured,
ובתולתיו לא הוללו	and their maidens had no marriage song.
כהניו בחרב נפלו	Their priests by the sword fell.
ואלמנתיו לא תבכינה	and their widows made no lamentation.

This literal translation is intended to show that in each of the four lines the substantive stands in first position, even though in A it is the direct object rather than the subject. Lines A and A′ pertain to masculine groups, whereas B and B′ pertain to feminine.[12] 'Fire' (*’ēš*) and 'sword' (*ḥereb*; A and A′) are often paired in Hebrew poetry as means of destruction (see Deut 13.16-17; Josh 11.11; Judg 1.8; 18.27; 2 Chr 36.17, 19-20; Isa 66.16; etc.). The alternating pattern here aids in depicting the total distress under which the Israelites were suffering at Shiloh.

Ps 79.9

עזרנו אלהי ישענו	Help us, O God of our salvation,
על־דבר כבוד־שמך	for the glory of thy name;
והצילנו וכפר על־חטאתינו	deliver us and forgive our sins,
למען שמך	for thy name's sake!

Lines A and A′ contain the supplication of the psalmist and his fellows, then B and B′ give the reason. The concern of the poet is to preserve God's reputation ('name', *šēm*, in both B and B′), which those observing the defeat and oppression of God's people associate with their relative well-being. The alternating pattern stresses the urgency of the psalmist's supplication, and the importance which he attaches to Yahweh's reputation (see also v. 13).

Ps 94.18-19

אם־אמרתי מטה רגלי	When I thought, 'My foot slips',
חסדך יהוה יסעדני	thy steadfast love, O Yahweh, held me up.
ברב שרעפי בקרבי	When the cares of my heart are many,
תנחומיך ישעשעו נפשי	thy consolations cheer my soul.

It is not certain whether the verbs should be read as all past, or as all present, or the latter (v. 19) as a present conviction derived from a previous experience (v. 18). In any case, A and A′ contain the protasis stating the precarious situation of the psalmist, then B and B′ praise Yahweh for intervening in his behalf and delivering him. The function of the alternating parallelism is to stress the sharp contrast between the human predicament and the divine rescue.

Ps 95.1-2

לכו נרננה ליהוה	O come, let us sing to Yahweh;
נריעה לצור ישענו	let us make a joyful noise to the rock of our salvation!
נקדמה פניו בתודה	Let us come into his presence with thanksgiving;
בזמרות נריע לו	let us make a joyful noise to him with songs of praise!

This is a call to worship. It may be argued that the four lines are simply synonymous. However, the recurrence of 'let us make a joyful noise' (Hebrew *nārîʿâ* in B, and *nāriʿa* in B′, although the latter probably should be emended to agree with the former) in the second and fourth lines tends to justify an analysis as alternating parallelism. Such a pattern reflects excitement and suggests a crescendo.

Ps 99.1

יהוה מלך	Yahweh reigns;
ירגזו עמים	let the peoples tremble!
ישב כרובים	He sits enthroned upon the cherubim;
תנוט הארץ	let the earth quake!

In A and A′ the psalmist affirms that Yahweh is ruling over his world as king, then in B and B′ he states an obvious and natural response to this, namely, that the whole earth should be awed by his presence.

Ps 101.5

מלושני בסתר רעהו	Him who slanders his neighbor secretly
אותו אצמית	I will destroy.
גבה־עינים ורחב לבב	The man of haughty looks and arrogant heart
אתו לא אוכל	I will not endure.

The speaker is probably the king. His primary domestic responsibility is to maintain and preserve justice in the land.[13] B and B′ both begin with *'ôtô*, the direct object 'him', for the sake of emphasis. The king is resolving and promising before Yahweh that he will strive to overthrow the propagators of injustice in his kingdom.

Ps 104.28

תתן להם	When thou givest to them,
ילקטון	they gather it up;
תפתח ידך	when thou openest thy hand,
ישבעון טוב	they are filled with good things.

Ps 104.29

תסתיר פניך	When thou hidest thy face,
יבהלון	they are dismayed;
תסף רוחם	when thou takest away their breath,
יגועון ואל־עפרם ישובון	they die and return to their dust.

Both of these verses describe Yahweh's activity in A and A′, then the effect that has on his creatures in B and B′. In 28A′ and 29A, the psalmist uses a figurative expression (opening the hand, and hiding the face), and in the corresponding line a literal statement. The effect of the alternating pattern is to call attention to the consequence of God's action on his creatures.

Ps 105.1

הודו ליהוה קראו בשמו	O give thanks to Yahweh, call on his name,
הודיעו בעמים עלילותיו	make known his deeds among the peoples!
שירו־לו זמרו־לו	Sing to him, sing praise to him,
שיחו בכל־נפלאותיו	tell of all his wonderful works!

The psalmist calls on his fellows to praise Yahweh (A and A′) and to tell the nations what he has done (B and B′). The verbs are imperative plural throughout, but in A and A′ there are two verbs each, while in B and B′ there is one. The alternating parallelism suggests excitement and urgency.

Ps 106.24-25

וימאסו בארץ חמדה	And they despised the pleasant land,
לא האמינו לדברו	and they did not have faith in his promise,
וירגנו באהליהם	and they murmured in their tents,
לא שמעו בקול יהוה	and they did not obey the voice of Yahweh.

Lines A and A′ state the external sinful act of the Israelites in failing to try to take the land of Canaan in the days of Moses when the ten spies returned with an 'evil' report about the superior size and number of the inhabitants of the land (Num 13.31-33; 14.1-10). Then lines B and B′ declare the inward sinful attitude which motivated them to behave in this way. The effect of the alternating pattern is to demonstrate the direct connection between a sinful attitude and a sinful act.

Ps 109.17

ויאהב קללה	He loved to curse;
ותבואהו	let curses come on him!
ולא־חפץ בברכה	He did not like blessing;
ותרחק ממנו	may it be far from him!

The first two lines stand in antithesis to the last two lines. The latter state in the negative what the former state in the affirmative. A and A′ describe the wicked person's frame of mind, then B and B′ express the psalmist's wish or desire that he be punished in like kind (*jus talionis*).

Ps 114.3-6

הים ראה וינס הירדן יסב לאחור
ההרים רקדו כאילים גבעות כבני־צאן
מה־לך הים כי תנוס הירדן תסב לאחור
ההרים תרקדו כאילים גבעות כבני־צאן

The sea looked and fled, Jordan turned back.
  The mountains skipped like rams, the hills like lambs.
What ails you, O sea, that you flee? O Jordan, that you turn back?
  O mountains, that you skip like rams? O hills, like lambs?

A glance at the Hebrew text is compelling to understand these lines as alternating parallelism. Line A refers to Israel's crossing of the Reed Sea and later the Jordan. It does so by personifying the Reed Sea and Jordan as retreating or withdrawing from the channels in which they ordinarily flowed. Then A′ asks what caused such a catastrophic withdrawal, implying that is was only the power of Yahweh that could perform such a deed. Similarly, line B alludes to the earthquake which accompanied Yahweh's theophany on Mount Sinai to give Moses the law (cf. Exod 19.16-23). It does so by personifying the mountains and hills as playfully skipping about like young rams and lambs. Then B′ asks what caused these apparent towers of strength to behave in such a manner, suggesting that only Yahweh's might could bring about such a phenomenon. The effect of the alternating parallelism is to emphasize the magnitude of Yahweh's power over nature, and how he used this power to deliver his people.

Ps 118.19-21

פתחו־לי שערי־צדק	Open (pl.) to me the gates of righteousness,
אבא־בם	that I may enter through them
אודה יה	and give thanks to Yahweh.
זה־השער ליהוה	This is the gate of Yahweh;
צדיקים יבאו בו	the righteous (pl.) shall enter through it.
אודך כי עניתני ותהי־לי	I thank thee that thou hast answered me
לישועה	and hast become my salvation.

These verses represent a kind of 'expansion' of the alternating pattern: ABCA′B′C′. A, B, and C contain the psalmist's request of some group (perhaps the priests at the Jerusalem sanctuary—see vv. 26-27) to allow him entrance into the sanctuary so he might give Yahweh thanks. Then A′, B′, and C′ relate the favorable response to his request, and his promised thanksgiving to Yahweh for answering and delivering him. The function of the alternating parallelism is to demonstrate the realization of the request.

Ps 119.99-100

מכל־מלמדו השכלתי	I have more understanding than all my teachers,
כי עדותיך שיחה לי	for thy testimonies are my meditation.
מזקנים אתבונן	I understand more than the aged,
כי פקודיך נצרתי	for I keep thy precepts.

In A and A′, the psalmist describes the fortunate spiritual situation in which he finds himself, then in B and B′ states the reason for this, namely, that he had spent his time and energies learning God's word and applying it to his life. The alternating pattern stresses the intimate and inseparable connection between an individual's activities and the results that issue from them.

Ps 119.109-110

נפשי בכפי תמיד	I hold my life in my hand continually,
ותורתך לא שכחתי	but I do not forget thy law.
נתנו רשעים פח לי	The wicked have laid a snare for me,
ומפקודיך לא תעיתי	but I do not stray from thy precepts.

Lines A and A′ depict the danger facing the psalmist, but B and B′ record his fidelity to Yahweh's law in spite of this. Thus the alternating parallelism stresses the determination of the poet to remain faithful to God's word irrespective of the circumstances.

Ps 126.6

הלוך ילך ובכה	He that goes forth weeping,
נשא משך־הזרע	bearing the seed for sowing,
בא־יבוא ברנה	shall come home with shouts of joy,
נשא אלמתיו	bringing his sheaves with him.

Line A′ states the result of the activity portrayed in A, and B′ declares the result of that mentioned in B. The alternating pattern emphasizes the natural consequences of human activity in view of Yahweh's creative or providential intervention (see vv. 4-5).

Ps 138.4-5

יודוך יהוה כל־מלכי־ארץ	All the kings of the earth shall praise thee, O Yahweh,
כי שמעו אמרי־פיך	for they have heard the words of thy mouth;

וישירו בדרכי יהוה	and they shall sing of the ways of Yahweh,
כי גדול כבוד יהוה	for great is the glory of Yahweh.

Lines A and A′ proclaim what the kings of the earth will do, then B and B′ state the reason for doing this. They will praise Yahweh, because of certain impressive ways he has demonstrated his presence and power to them. The alternating parallelism brings out the connection between man's activities and the divine motivations prompting them.

Ps 139.21-22

הלוא־משנאיך יהוה אשנה	Do I not hate them that hate thee, O Yahweh?
ובתקוממיך אתקוטט	And do I not loathe them that rise up against thee?
תכלית שנאה שנאתים	I hate them with perfect hatred;
לאויבים היו לי	I count them my enemies.

The psalmist states the same ideas twice each: first, by a negative question expecting an affirmative answer (A and B); then, by a forthright declaration (A′ and B′). It seems obvious that he is anxious to express his strong distaste for God's enemies unequivocally. Thus he uses the alternating pattern to underscore his feelings.

2. *Examples from the Prophets*

Amos 3.8

אריה שאג	The lion has roared;
מי לא יירא	who will not fear?
אדני יהוה דבר	The Lord Yahweh has spoken;
מי לא ינבא	who can but prophesy?

The first and third lines contain an affirmation, while the second and fourth ask rhetorical questions. Thus A′ clarifies the sense of A: the roaring of the lion refers to Yahweh's speaking through the prophets. Naturally, then, B′ makes clear the meaning of B: the true prophets can no more evade proclaiming the message of doom which God has given them than one can keep from fearing a lion that roars.

Amos 5.11c-f

בתי גזית בניתם	Houses of hewn stone you have built,
ולא תשבו בם	but you shall not dwell in them;

כרמי־חמד נטעתם	pleasant vineyards you have planted,
ולא תשתו את־יינם	but you shall not drink their wine.

The Hebrew word order, which this translation attempts to reproduce as closely as possible, betrays the finely constructed alternating parallelism here. The prophet contrasts the human achievements of the aspiring Israelites (A and A′) with the divine reversals which they will experience (B and B′) because of their injustices toward the poor.

Amos 5.19

כאשר ינוס איש מפני הארי	As if a man fled from a lion,
ופגעו הדב	and a bear met him;
ובא הבית וסמך ידו על־ הקיר	or went into the house and leaned with his hand against the wall,
ונשכו הנחש	and a serpent bit him.

Lines B and B′ function as sudden, delayed-action, surprising turns of events. The author's purpose is to portray vividly the futility of human efforts to escape God's punishments. He describes an apparently successful evasion of calamity (A and A′), followed by an inescapable affliction (B and B′). The effect is traumatic.

Amos 5.22

כי אם־תעלו־לי עלות ומנחתיכם	Even though you offer me your burnt offerings and cereal offerings,
לא ארצה	I will not accept them,
ושלם מריאירם	and the peace offerings of your fatted beasts
לא אביט	I will not look upon.

Amos uses alternating parallelism to declare Yahweh's disapproval of Israel's external religious activities as a means of covering their sinful activities. Lines A and A′ refer to various sacrifices which the people are offering, while B and B′ state Yahweh's disapproval. The 'deep structure'[14] of this passage suggests one should understand A′ to mean, 'and (even though you offer me) the peace offerings of your fatted beasts, (I will not look upon them)'.

Hos 4.6b-e

כי־אתה הדעת מאסת	Because you have rejected knowledge,
ואמאסאך מכהן לי	I reject you from being a priest to me.

ותשכח תורת אלהיך And since you have forgotten the law of your God,
אשכח בניך גם־אני I also will forget your children.

The correspondence of the verbs in A and B on the one hand, and in A′ and B′ on the other, brings out sharply the direct connection between one's activities and the consequences which result from them. The punishment fits the crime perfectly. This is further underlined by the reversal of roles in the person addressed; he is the subject of the verb which shows his rejection of God's law in A and A′, but the object of Yahweh's punitive action in B and B′.

Hos 10.1c-f

כרב לפריו The more his fruit increased
הרבה למזבחות the more altars he built;
כטוב לארצו as his country improved
היטיבו מצבות he improved his pillars.

These lines depict the sinfulness of Israel by contrasting Yahweh's blessings on his people (A and A′) with the selfish way in which they used these blessings (B and B′). Instead of being grateful for increased fruit of the field crops and trees and for the improved conditions in the country, and showing that gratitude by serving Yahweh in appropriate ways both in worship and in daily life, the Israelites built many altars and pillars for the worship of Baal (cf. Hos 3.4; 11.2).

Isa 1.15a-d

ובפרשכם כפיכם When you spread forth your hands,
אעלים עיני מכם I will hide my eyes from you:
גם כי־תרבו תפלה even though you make many prayers,
אינני שמע I will not listen.

Line A and A′ describe the attempts of the Judeans to placate Yahweh's wrath and to obtain his approval. By way of contrast, lines B and B′ affirm God's disapproval and refusal to accept their empty prayers. Here the function of the alternating pattern is to denounce very pointedly man's vain attempts to please God by mere external acts of religion without a change of heart and life.

Isa 1.18b-e

אם־יהיו חטאיכם כשנים	Though your sins are like scarlet,
כשלג ילבינו	as white as snow they shall be;
אם־יאדימו כתולע	though they are red like crimson,
כצמר יהיו	like wool they shall become.

The prophet's purpose here is to emphasize the seriousness of his hearers' predicament (A and A′) in order to call attention to the magnitude of God's forgiveness (B and B′). He accomplishes this through color similes.[15]

Isa 2.7

ותמלא ארצו כסף וזהב	Their land is filled with silver and gold,
ואין קצה לאצרתיו	and there is no end to their treasures;
ותמלא ארצו סוסים	their land is filled with horses,
ואין קצה למרכבתיו	and there is no end to their chariots.

The repetition of the first two words in A and A′, and again in B and B′, in Hebrew reveals clearly the deliberate alternating character of this verse. The same thing occurs in v. 8a, but not in v. b, suggesting that perhaps a line has dropped out of the text immediately after 8a. The author's intention is to emphasize the great extent of Judah's sins. The choice of the terms 'filled' and 'no end' arranged in an alternating pattern communicate this thought admirably.

Isa 5.5c-f

הסר משוכתו	I will remove its hedge,
והיה לבער	and it shall be devoured;
פרץ גדרו	I will break down its wall,
והיה למרמס	and it shall be trampled down.

By alternating an infinitive absolute functioning as a finite verb in the first person singular (A and A′ as is shown by the antecedent in lines a and b) with the waw consecutive + *hāyâ* (B and B′), the prophet intensifies the announcement of divine punishment vividly.

Isa 5.7c-f

ויקו למשפט	He looked for justice,
והנה משפח	but behold, bloodshed;
לצדקה	(he looked) for righteousness,
והנה צעקה	but behold, a cry.

Here the prophet depicts Yahweh's great disappointment over the sins of his people. They dashed his expectations (A and A′) to the ground (B and B′). Notice that what is stated figuratively of grapes and wild grapes in two lines in vv. 2 and 4 is explained literally in this verse in four lines because of the alternating parallelism.

Isa 7.8a-b + 9a-b

כי ראש ארם דמשק	For the head of Syria is Damascus,
וראש דמשק רצין	and the head of Samaria is the son of Remaliah.
וראש אפרים שמרון	And the head of Ephraim is Samaria,
וראש שמרון בן־רמליהו	and the head of Samaria is the son of Remaliah.

The context suggests that Isaiah is showing the futility of human efforts against God's determined will. It is futile for Ahaz of Judah to fear Syria and Israel, because their 'heads' (rulers, kings) are human. Lines A and A′ use 'head' for the capital, then B and B′ use 'head' for the earthly king. The implication is that Yahweh is the 'head' of Judah (cf. 6.1, 3, 5), and thus there is no reason to doubt that the plans of Rezin and Pekah to conquer Jerusalem will fail.

Isa 14.27

כי־יהוה צבאות יעץ	For Yahweh of hosts has purposed,
ומי יפר	and who will annul it?
וידו הנטויה	His hand is stretched out,
ומי ישיבנה	and who will turn it back?

Lines A and A′ declare Yahweh's determination to punish the Assyrians (cf. v. 25). Then lines B and B′ ask rhetorically, Who can prevent him from carrying out his decision? Obviously, the answer is that no one can stop him. Consequently, the overthrow of Assyria is certain.

Isa 15.1

כי בליל שדד ער	Because Ar is laid waste in a night
מואב נדמה	Moab is undone;
כי בליל שדד קיר	Because Kir is laid waste in a night
מואב נדמה	Moab is undone.

Except for the different place names in A and A′, the alternating lines are precisely the same. This has the effect of emphasizing the impact of the sudden calamity on those who are smitten.

Isa 24.6

על־כן אלה אכלה ארץ	Therefore a curse devours the earth,
ויאשמו ישבי בה	and its inhabitants suffer for their guilt;
על־כן חרו ישבי ארץ	therefore the inhabitants of the earth are scorched,
ונשאר אנוש מזער	and few men are left.

The repetition of A in A′ and of B in B′ stresses the effect of the divine punishment on the inhabitants of the city. It is not necessary to repeat 'therefore' (Heb. *'al-kēn*) in lines A and A′ unless the author has in mind creating some sort of parallelism for the sake of emphasis. It connects the punishment announced in v. 6 with the sins condemned in v. 5.

Isa 25.6b-e

משתה שמנים	A feast of fat things,
משתה שמרים	a feast of wine on the lees;
שמנים ממחים	of fat things full of marrow,
שמרים מזקקים	of wine on the lees well refined.

It is questionable whether these lines are strictly 'poetic'. In any case, A′ picks up and extends A, and B′ picks up and extends B. The effect this has on the reader or hearer is to draw attention to the richness and vastness of God's blessings.

Isa 29.8a-d

והיה כאשר יחלם הרעב והנה אוכל	As when a hungry man dreams he is eating
והקיץ וריקה נפשו	and awakes with his hunger not satisfied,
וכאשר יחלם הצמא והנה שתה	or as when a thirsty man dreams he is drinking
והקיץ והנה עיף ונפשו שוקקה	and awakes faint, with his thirst not quenched,
	[so shall the multitude of all the nations be that fight against Mount Zion].

The prophet is describing the futility of the efforts of the nations to overthrow Jerusalem when Yahweh is in her midst. Lines A and A′ depict the confidence of the nations that their plots will be successful, then B and B′ portray the reality that their plans will fail. The figures of unsatisfied hunger and unfulfilled thirst graphically denote the thwarted anticipations of the nations as they attempt to execute the strategy they had designed.

Isa 30.16

	[But you said,]
לא־כי על־סוס ננוס	'No! We will speed upon horses',
על־כן תנוסון	therefore you shall speed away;
ועל־קל נרכב	and, 'We will ride upon swift steeds',
על־כן יקלו רדפיכם	therefore your pursuers shall be swift.

This is the response of the leaders of Judah to Yahweh's appeal to them to trust in him (v. 15), and an announcement of the consequences they must suffer because of this response. A and A′ picture the decision of the leaders to trust in military strength. B and B′ then state that if it is military strength they want, it is military strength they will get—that of their invading enemies!

Isa 34.6b-e

[חרב ליהוה]	[The Lord has a sword];
מלאה דם	it is sated with blood,
הדשנה מחלב	it is gorged with fat,
מדם כרים ועתודים	with the blood of lambs and goats,
מחלב כליות אילים	with the fat of the kidneys of rams.

In this passage, the prophet is announcing Yahweh's intervention to overthrow Israel's enemies. He compares this overthrow with a sacrifice (see lines f-g). Lines A′ and B′ in the alternating pattern clarify what is meant by the somewhat vague 'blood' and 'fat' of A and B respectively. Consequently, the structure of these lines has a crescendo effect.

Isa 44.5

זה יאמר ליהוה אני	This one will say, 'I am Yahweh's',
וזה יקרא בשם־יעקב	another will call himself by the name of Jacob,
וזה יכתב ידו ליהוה	and another will write on his hand, 'Yahweh's',
ובשם ישראל יכנה	and surname himself by the name of Israel.

These lines describe the return of penitent exiles to Yahweh. Lines A and A′ picture the converts as declaring their desire to be 'the Lord's', while B and B′ describe them as designating themselves 'by the name of' Jacob or Israel.

Isa 51.1c-2b

הביטו אל־צור חצבתם	Look to the rock from which you were hewn,
ואל־מקבת בור נקרתם	and to the quarry from which you were digged.
הביטו אל־אברהם אביכם	Look to Abraham your father,
ואל־שרה תחוללכם	and to Sarah who bore you.

These words apparently are addressed to the Babylonian exiles who are about to return to Jerusalem. The prophet is urging them to believe in Yahweh's power to restore them to Jerusalem and to build them up, since he had demonstrated his ability to multiply his people by what he had done through Abraham and Sarah. The alternating structure shows that the rock from which his hearers were hewn is Abraham (A and A′), and the quarry from which they were digged is Sarah (B and B′). Accordingly, A′ and B′ clarify the meaning of A and B respectively.

Isa 51.18

אין־מנהל לה	There is none to guide her
מכל־בנים ילדה	among all the sons she has borne;
ואין מחזיק בידה	there is none to take her by the hand
מכל־בנים גדלה	among all the sons she has brought up.

In order to emphasize the magnitude of Yahweh's deliverance of the ruined city of Jerusalem, the prophet describes her present hopeless condition. Lines A and A′ depict her solitude and loneliness, while B and B′ stress the totality of this destitute and helpless condition.

Isa 53.7

נגש והוא נענה	He was oppressed, and he was afflicted,
ולא יפתח פיו	yet he opened not his mouth;
כשה לטבח יובל וכרחל לפני גזזיה נאלמה	like a lamb that is led to the slaughter, and like a sheep that before its shearers is dumb,
ולא יפתח פיו	so he opened not his mouth.

The thrust of this verse is the patient resilience with which Yahweh's servant absorbs the suffering which is heaped upon him, which is emphasized in B and B′. Whether one counts the syllables or the letters in A′, this line seems excessively long, and as a matter of fact many think it should actually be divided into two lines. At the same time, these two similes appear to correspond to the two statements in A and thus to function as vivid examples to illustrate their force. If so, the content or subject matter may take precedence over metrical considerations in analyzing this passage.

Isa 55.10-11

כי כאשר ירד הגשם והשלג מן־השמים
ושמה לא ישוב כי אם־הרוה את־הארץ
והולידה והצמיחה
ונתן זרע לזרע ולחם לאכל
כן יהיה דברי אשר יצא מפי
לא־ישוב אלי ריקם
כי אם־עשה את־אשר חפצתי
והצליח אשר שלחתיו

For *as* the rain and the snow *come down from heaven*,
and *return not* thither *but* water the earth,
making it bring forth and sprout,
giving seed to the sower and bread to the eater,
so shall my word be that *goes forth from my mouth*;
it shall *not return* to me empty,
but it shall accomplish that which I purpose,
and prosper in the thing for which I sent it.

This well-known passage follows an alternating ABCDA′B′C′D′ pattern in a remarkable way, so that the four lines in the simile of v. 10 correspond as well as could be expected to the four lines of the straightforward affirmations of v. 11. Yahweh is declaring to the penitent exiles that his promise that they will return to Jerusalem and prosper is as certain as the productivity of the earth when adequate moisture falls upon it.

Isa 62.4

לא יאמר לך עוד עזובה	*You* shall no more be termed Forsaken,
ולארצך לא יאמר עוד שממה	and *your land* shall no more be termed Desolate;

כי לך יקרא חפצי־בה	but *you* shall be called My delight is in her,
ולארצך בעולה	and *your land* Married;
כי חפץ יהוה בך	for Yahweh delights in *you*,
וארצך תבעל	and *your land* shall be married.

The pattern is clearly ABA′B′A″B″. Lines A, A′, and A″ are addressed to Zion or Jerusalem (second person sing. 'you'), while B, B′, and B″ refer to 'your land'. Further, there is a contrast between the present undesirable situation in A and B, and the promised desirable circumstance in A′ and B′, followed by an explanation of the reason for this transformation in A″ and B″.

Isa 65.13b-14b

הנה עבדי יאכלו	Behold, my servants shall eat,
ואתם תרעבו	but you shall be hungry;
הנה עבדי ישתו	behold, my servants shall drink,
ואתם תצמאו	but you shall be thirsty;
הנה עבדי ישמחו	behold, my servants shall rejoice,
ואתם תבשו	but you shall be put to shame;
הנה עבדי ירנו מטוב לב	behold, my servants shall sing for gladness of heart,
ואתם תצעקו מכאב לב	but you shall cry out for pain of heart.

These lines contain four contrasts between God's people who have returned from exile and their adversaries ('you' in the B lines is pl., *'attem*). In each case, line A states the blessing to be enjoyed by Yahweh's servants, whereas B affirms that their enemies experience just the opposite.

Mic 1.4

ונמסו ההרים תחתיו	And the mountains shall melt under him
והעמקים יתבקעו	and the valley will be cleft,
כדונג מפני האש	like wax before the fire,
כמים מגרים במורד	like waters poured down a steep place.

The theophany in vv. 3-4 is designed to announce Yahweh's intention to punish his sinful people, Israel and Judah. The simile of wax in A′ corresponds to the melting of the mountains in A, and that of water rushing down a steep place in B′ with the cleaving of the valleys in B. A recognition of this alternating structure renders unnecessary the proposal to rearrange the lines.[16]

Jer 2.18

ועתה מה־לך לדרך מצרים	And now what do you gain by going to Egypt,
לשתות מי שחור	to drink the water of the Nile?
ומה־לך לדרך אשור	Or what do you gain by going to Assyria,
לשתות מי נהר	to drink the waters of the Euphrates?

Here the prophet's purpose is to dissuade the leaders of Judah from making foreign alliances to secure their defenses against a powerful foe, and to encourage them rather to trust in God. The strength to be gained from drinking the waters of the Nile or of the Euphrates is nothing compared with that available from 'the fountain of living waters' (v. 13). Lines A and A′ denounce the effort involved in attempting a treaty with foreign nations, then B and B′ deny the value of the goal of that effort.

Jer 25.35-36b

ואבד מנוס מן־הרעים	No refuge will remain for the shepherds,
ופליטה מאדירי הצאן	nor escape for the lords of the flock.
קול צעקת הרעים	Hark, the cry of the shepherds,
ויללת אדירי הצאן	and the wail of the lords of the flock!

Here the prophet is describing the thoroughness of Yahweh's punishment, and the attendant futility of human attempts to escape. In lines A and B, he portrays the desperate situation by depicting the hopeless plight of one group in society—the shepherds. Then in A′ and B′, he pictures the grief-stricken response of this group to its plight. He does this dramatically by alternating the terminology between 'shepherds' in A and A′, and 'lords of the flock' in B and B′.

Jer 49.9

אם־בצרים באו לך	If grape-gatherers came to you,
לא ישארו עוללות	would they not leave gleanings?
אם־גנבים בלילה	If thieves came by night,
השחיתו דים	would they not destroy only enough for themselves?

The prophet addresses Edom in behalf of Yahweh of hosts. He uses two metaphors to depict the thoroughness of Yahweh's destruction of her land. The two negative questions in B and B′ require a positive reply. Grape-gatherers (A) would leave gleanings, and thieves (A′) would leave much potential spoil. But by way of contrast, Yahweh has left nothing in Edom.

Ezek 7.15

החרב בחוץ	The sword is without,
והדבר והרעב מבית	pestilence and famine are within,
אשר בשדה בחרב ימות	he that is in the field dies by the sword,
ואשר בעיר רעב ודבר יאכלנו	and him that is in the city famine and pestilence devour.

This verse depicts the widespread effect of the divine punishment. Outside the walls of Jerusalem, God's people are slain by the sword of the invaders (A and A′). Within the city, famine and pestilence take their toll of lives (B and B′). The definition of the danger in A and B prepares the hearers or readers for the effect on the people in A′ and B′.

Ezek 16.45a-d

בת־אמך את	The daughter of your mother are you,
געלת אישה ובניה	who loathed her husband and her children,
ואחות אחותך את	and the sister of your sisters are you,
אשר געלו אנשיהן ובניהן	who loathed their husbands and their children.

Here the prophet's purpose is to portray the extent of Judah's sins. Thus he compares Judah with the daughter of an unfaithful wife and mother who imitates her mother, and with the sister of two unfaithful sisters and mothers who are just like her sisters. Lines A and A′ state the relationship, then B and B′ state the sinful character of the relatives.

3. *Summary and Conclusions*

The present writer has found 199 instances of alternating parallelism in the OT psalmic and prophetic material: 64 in the Psalms, and 135 in the prophetic literature. All these examples appear in the summary classifications below, but only certain selected texts are cited in the discussion above. Due to the nature, purpose, and content of psalmic and prophetic literature, each has its own reasons and intentions for using alternating parallelism, but still sometimes they use this type of parallelism for the same purpose. Accordingly, an analysis of the function of this alternating pattern may be divided into three parts: (1) common usages in the psalms and prophets; (2) unique usages in the psalms; (3) unique usages in the prophetic literature.

1. *Common Usages in the Psalms and Prophets*

Alternating parallelism is used frequently to portray the totality, completeness, or thoroughness of the distress or affliction which has come or is about to come on an individual or the people (Pss 22.15; 38.4; 55.13; 69.3, 5; 77.4; 78.63-64; Isa 5.5c-f; 14.6, 12, 26; 15.5d-g; 17.12; 18.6b-e; 19.8; 29.4; 51.6a-d; Mic 1.4; 5.9-13; Jer 49.9; 50.2e-h; Joel 1.4; Zech 11.2, 3; 12.12-14). Several passages in the psalms and prophets emphasize Yahweh's magnificence by this means (Pss 24.7-10; 68.16; 78.38; 103.17-18; Isa 54.5). Both psalmists and prophets use it to register God's disapproval of man's wicked activities (Pss 26.4-5; 101.5; Amos 5.22; Hos 8.4; Isa 1.15a-d; Jer 23.21, 30-31), although the psalmists do this by expressing their own disapproval of sin (obviously intended as empathizing with God's view), whereas the prophets do it by speaking in God's behalf.

The alternating pattern may be used very effectively in both psalmic and prophetic texts to depict vividly the supplication of the worshipper (Ps 40.17; Jer 14.8c-9b; Hab 1.2), especially imprecations on enemies (Pss 28.4; 35.26; 40.15; 68.3; 70.3; 79.6; 109.17; Jer 17.18a-d). Quite often it functions to bring out the striking contrast between the human predicament and the divine deliverance (Pss 22.10-11; 94.18-19; 118.8-9, 10-12; Isa 1.18; 9.1; 25.9; 49.21c-f; 58.9a-d; 60.14a-d; 61.7; 62.4; Ezek 36.13-14; Jon 2.2). Finally, several speakers and writers use it to stress the direct connection between one's attitudes and the deeds which they produce, or between one's actions and the results which follow from them (Pss 106.24-25, 32-33; 119.99-100, 124-25, 145-46, 169-70; 126.6; Hos 4.6b-e; 12.12; Isa 1.19; 58.13a-d; 65.13-14b; Jer 18.7-10; 51.35).

2. *Unique Usages in the Psalms*

Perhaps because of the nature and function of psalms, alternating parallelism occurs in them to communicate certain ideas and feelings in connection with which it is not found in the prophetic literature. By far the largest category here is instances in which the alternating pattern appears to emphasize the effects of Yahweh's activities on man. These include bolstering the psalmist's faith (27.2; 118.6-7), causing the nations to tremble (99.1), giving or withholding life or food (104.28, 29), demonstrating Yahweh's power (114.3-6), providing reasons to trust in Yahweh (115.9-11), eliciting the psalmist's thanksgiving (118.28), enabling some human activity to succeed (127.1), and evoking praise of Yahweh by the nations (138.4-5).

In addition, some psalmists use the alternating pattern to express urgency (9.2-21; 69.7; 70.6; 142.7; 143.7, 8). It may aid in sharpening a definition (10.3-4). Some psalmists employ it to declare their resolution to trust in Yahweh (27.3) or to delight in his word (119.15-16, 69-70, 109-10) or to praise him (145.1-2). It helps the psalmist bring the hearer or reader in contact with reality by using an experience with which the hearer or reader is intimately acquainted (30.6). It naturally lends itself to contributing to the excitement which exists at the time of worship (95.1-2; 100.4; 105.1; 118.1-4; 119.1-2; 136.2-3). It may help explain how the psalmist's request is granted (118.19-21). It effectively illuminates the author's feelings (139.21-22). And it aids in delineating the sharp contrast between Yahweh's blessings of his people and his overthrow of their enemies (44.3).

3. *Unique Usages in the Prophetic Literature*

In keeping with the function of the prophets and the nature of their proclamation, alternating parallelism is used primarily in the prophetic literature in connection with the themes of sin and punishment, and of God's blessings on his faithful, penitent people. It is often used to emphasize the extent of the sin of Israel or of some other nation (Isa 2.7; 5.11, 20; 56.10a-d; 58.3e-4b; Mic 1.5c-f; Jer 4.22a-d; 6.10c-f, 13; 8.10; 9.7;. 22.18b-e; 23.17; Ezek 16.28; 45a-d; Obad 12-14; Mal 1.6c-f, 8a-d). It helps bring out the obvious ingratitude manifested in the sins of God's people (Isa 10.1c-f; Jer 5.3b-e; 7.27). It is employed in showing the futility of trusting in idols or in human strength rather than in God (Isa 30.2b-3, 16; Jer 2.18; 10.5a-d). It appears in Yahweh's words to Jeremiah when he rebukes him for his lack of faith (Jer 12.5), and when he calls him to repentance (Jer 15.19b-e).

The alternating pattern functions well in oracles which announce the imminence of the divine punishment and accordingly urge the hearers to repent (Amos 3.4; Hos 7.9; Zeph 2.2c-f; Ezek 21.14c-15b; Joel 4.13a-d). Closely connected with this, it appears in many prophetic texts which declare the futility of all human efforts to escape or avoid God's punishment (Amos 5.19; 9.2-4b; Hos 2.9a-d; Isa 7.8a + 9a-d; 9.9, 19; 14.24, 27; 24.18; 29.16c-f; 47.1a-d, 11a-d; Jer 14.12a-d; 25.35-36b; 48.44a-d). Correspondingly, it is used to help emphasize the horrible effect of calamity on its victims (Isa 5.1; 24.6; 51.18, 19; 57.1a-d; Jer 4.23-26b; 14.18a-d; 50.35-38b; Ezek 7.15; Zech 11.17). Isa 5.7 uses it in describing Yahweh's disappointment because of his dashed expectations of his people. And it occurs in a few passages which seek to show how divine punishment is able to thwart the apparent prevalence of human achievements (Amos 5.11c-f; Zeph 1.13c-f; Ezek 27.33 [cf. v. 34]; 28.9).

As far as Yahweh's blessings upon the faithful and penitent is concerned, alternating parallelism functions to underscore the richness and vastness of these blessings, as well as their effect on those who observe them (Isa 25.6b-e; 35.2c-f; 55.10-11; Ezek 44.28; Obad 20). It may aid in portraying assurances to God's people (Isa 56.3, 5; 61.4; 65.16a-d, 21-22b; 66.7, 10, 11; Jer 50.20b-e). Jer 32.7-8b use it to help show the fulfilment of God's promise. Isa 53.7 employs it effectively in depicting the extent of the suffering of Yahweh's servant. It appears in three passages in Isa 40–55 to describe the return of penitent exiles to Yahweh or to summon them to return (Isa 44.5; 50.11a-d; 55.7c-f). Isa 58.6b-e uses it in describing the godly treatment of one's fellowman. And several times in the book of Isaiah its function is to help bring out the futility of the efforts of the nations to overthrow the people of Yahweh (Isa 29.8a-d, 11c-f; 33.1; 41.11; 50.8b-e).

The prophets also use the alternating pattern to show the variety of God's activities (Amos 4.7c-f; Isa 54.7-8b), and to clarify the meaning of figures in their respective contexts (Amos 3.8; Hos 9.10; Isa 28.27; 34.6b-e; 37.22b-e; 51.1c-2b; 62.5; 63.13b-14b; Jer 46.7-8b; Ezek 37.16).

This survey of occurrences of alternating parallelism in the OT Psalms and Prophetic Literature suggests that it is a prevalent phenomenon in Hebrew poetry. Consequently, it deserves fair treatment in studies of ancient Semitic poetry. A recognition of its presence, and the various usages to which it may be put in the composition of oral or written communication genres, may become an important aid in appreciating the literary skills of ancient Semitic authors and in interpreting their works. The pervasiveness of the alternating patterns in the Psalms and Prophetic Books suggests that this manner of composition was natural because it belonged to the thought patterns of the people. And this is probably due to the contacts which the Israelites had with other nations throughout her history. This phenomenon is attested, for example, in Ugaritic literature (see e.g. *UT* 68.25 'nt.II.32-34; *UT* 51.I.26-29). But this would be the task of another study.

NOTES

1. See e.g. R.G. Boling, '"Synonymous" Parallelism in the Psalms', *JSS* 5 (1960), pp. 221-55; N.K. Gottwald, 'Poetry, Hebrew', *IDB* 3 (1962), pp. 831-32; W.G.E. Watson, 'Gender-Matched Synonymous Parallelism in the OT', *JBL* 99 (1980), pp. 321-41; 'Gender-Matched Synonymous Parallelism in Ugaritic Poetry', *UF* 13 (1981), pp. 181-87.

2. M. Dahood, 'A New Metrical Pattern in Biblical Poetry', *CBQ* 29 (1967), pp. 574-82; W.G.E. Watson, 'The Pivot Pattern in Hebrew, Ugaritic and Akkadian Poetry', *ZAW* 88 (1976), pp. 239-53.

3. G. Rendsburg, '"Janus Parallelism" in Genesis 49.26', *JBL* 99 (1980), pp. 291-93; E. Zurro, 'Disemia de brḥ y paralelismo bifronte en Job 9,25', *Bib* 62 (1981), pp. 546-47; C.H. Gordon, 'Asymmetric Janus Parallelism', *EI* 16 (1982), pp. 80*-81*.

4. B. Porten and U. Rapaport, 'Poetic Structure in Genesis IX 7', *VT* 21 (1971), pp. 363-69; J.S. Kselman, 'The ABCB Pattern: Further Examples', *VT* 32 (1982), pp. 224-29.

5. N.W. Lund, 'Chiasmus in the Psalms', *AJSL* 49 (1932/33), pp. 281-312; A.R. Ceresko, O.S.F.S., 'The Function of Chiasmus in Hebrew Poetry', *CBQ* 40 (1978), pp. 1-10.

6. G.B. Gray, *The Forms of Hebrew Poetry*, with a Prolegomenon by D.N. Freedman (The Library of Biblical Studies; New York: KTAV, 1972; first published in 1915); T.J. Meek, 'The Structure of Hebrew Poetry', *JR* 9 (1929), pp. 523-50; T.H. Robinson, 'Hebrew Poetic Form: The English Tradition', *SVT* 1 (1953), pp. 128-49; Gottwald, 'Poetry, Hebrew', pp. 829-38.

7. See e.g. S.A. Geller, *Parallelism in Early Biblical Poetry* (Harvard Semitic Monographs, 20; Missoula: Scholars Press, 1979), p. 15, with reference to Exod 15.9b-c; E.L. Greenstein, 'How Does Parallelism Mean?', *A Sense of Text: The Art of Language in the Study of Biblical Literature* (JQR Supplement; Winona Lake, Ind.: Eisenbrauns, 1983), p. 62 n. 54, with reference to Deut 32.21.

8. There are serious textual problems here. Several scholars seek to solve certain issues by transposing v. 21 after v. 18. See e.g. E.J. Kissane, *The Books of Psalms: Vol. I* (Dublin: Browne and Nolan, 1953), pp. 39, 42; R. Gordis, 'Psalm 9–10—A Textual and Exegetical Study', *JQR* 48 (1957),

pp. 104-105. But in defense of the arrangement in the MT, see M. Dahood, *Psalms I: 1–50* (AB, 16; Garden City, N.Y.: Doubleday, 1966), pp. 54, 58-59. Other than the few exceptions which are noted, the biblical passages which are quoted follow the RSV. The numbering of the chapters and verses correspond to the MT.

9. The text is admittedly difficult, and several emendations and suggestions for improving it have been made. The present rendering is one attempt to stay as close to the MT as possible.

10. See Mic 1.4; and cf. Pss 68.3; 97.5.

11. See H.-J. Kraus, *Psalmen*. 1. Teilband (BKAT, XV/1; 3rd edn; Neukirchen-Vluyn: Neukirchener Verlag, 1966), pp. 194-95; Dahood, *Psalms I*, p. 151; F.M.Th. de Liagre Böhl, *De Psalmen* (Nijkerk: G.F. Callenbach, 1968), p. 149. However, A. Weiser, *The Psalms* (OTL; trans. H. Hartwell; Philadelphia: Westminster, 1962), pp. 234-35, argues that vv. 7-10 are based on an ancient creation myth in which Yahweh defeated the powers of chaos, and does not involve the ark.

12. On this, see Watson, 'Gender-Matched Synonymous Parallelism in the OT'.

13. See further Pss 45.7-8; 72.1-4, 7, 12-14; Jer 23.5-6.

14. On this, see Greenstein, 'How Does Parallelism Mean?', p. 54.

15. On the different interpretations of this verse, see J.T. Willis, 'On the Interpretation of Isaiah 1.18', *JSOT* 25 (1983), pp. 35-54.

16. This rearrangement has been advocated by W. Nowack, *Die kleinen Propheten übersetzt und erklärt* (3rd edn; GHKAT III/4; Göttingen: Vandenhoeck & Ruprecht, 1922), p. 201; A. van Hoonacker, *Les douze petits prophètes* (Paris: Gabalda, 1908), p. 355; B. Duhm, 'Anmerkungen zu den Zwölf Propheten: III. Buch Micha', *ZAW* 31 (1911), p. 82. J.T. Beck, *Erklärung der Propheten Micha und Joël* (Gütersloh: C. Bertelsmann, 1898), p. 79, who defends the alternating order of the MT, refers to it as a 'Tetrakolon'.

4

THE PARALLELISM OF GREATER PRECISION
Notes from Isaiah 40 for a Theory of Hebrew Poetry

D.J.A. Clines

The purpose of this paper[1] is to draw attention to a hitherto generally unobserved feature[2] of the parallelistic couplet in Hebrew poetry, a feature which may offer a *point de départ* for a revised perception of the nature of the parallelistic couplet as such.

The feature in question is that the second half of a parallelistic couplet (line B) is often more precise or specific than the first half (line A). In the first section of this paper (I) I will present some examples from Isaiah 40, which will enable me to construct a tentative theoretical statement about it (section II). I will then examine some further couplets from Isaiah 40, with a view to judging the usefulness of the concept, 'the parallelism of greater precision', for exegetical work (section III). In section IV some similar features of the parallelistic couplet, previously recognized and named, will be examined by way of contrast and comparison. The final section (V) will raise the question whether any new insights into the nature of Hebrew poetry may be developed from the identification of the parallelism of greater precision.

1. *Examples from Isaiah 40*

a. *Isa. 40.16*

ולבנון אין די בער	And Lebanon is not enough to burn
וחיתו אין די עולה	and its animals not enough for a burnt offering.

Line A taken by itself raises the question, Why should anyone want to burn Lebanon? Lebanon is not elsewhere in the Hebrew Bible usually connected with burning[3] and while it is natural enough—even while we are still in line A—to suppose that it is the *trees* of Lebanon that are for burning, even though they are typically used for *building*, it is impossible to discern from line A what purpose is in view in burning Lebanon's trees, and thus why Lebanon's trees are insufficient for burning. Not to know that is to be ignorant of the whole point of the affirmation. Only with line B, and with its last word, is it made clear that the image of the whole couplet is of sacrifice; the burning of line A must be of wood upon the sacrificial altar. We are confirmed in our impression that line A is not perspicuous by the fact that a modern version like NIV finds it necessary to offer an expanded rendering: 'Lebanon is not sufficient for *altar* fires' (my italics).

We may say, then, that line A is less precise, less specific than line B. Line A is not swallowed up in line B, however; it is not the case that once we have line B we can dispense with line A. Rather, line B provides the clue or the context within which the uncertainty of line A is resolved. Line B drives us back to read line A again in the light of what line B has added to line A.

b. *Isa 40.22*

הנוטה כדק שמים	who stretches out the heavens like a thin thing,
וימתחם כאהל לשבת	and spreads them out like a tent to dwell in.

In reading line A we may well ask, What, precisely, are the heavens like that God stretches out? The problem is not primarily that דק is a hapax legomenon, for there can be little uncertainty that it means 'something thin' (from דקק 'crush'). Even if we knew from a multiplicity of attestations that the thinness in question was specifically a thin curtain or veil or gauze,[4] we would still not know what precisely the image was, for a curtain could be vertical or horizontal, it could be used to divide or screen or cover, it could serve the one who spreads it out, or someone else for whom it is spread out. Line B, however, disambiguates line A. From line B we learn that the 'thin thing' is a 'tent for dwelling in', i.e. a tent from the viewpoint of its occupants, a curtain that is both horizontal and vertical, and spread out not to hide the one who spreads it but to serve as a covering for those under it. The blurred and indefinite image of line A is brought into focus in line B. The 'parallelism' of דק and אהל is a parallelism of increasing precision.

c. *Isa 40.3*

במדבר פנו דרך יהוה	In the wilderness prepare the way of Yahweh,
ישרו בערבה מסלה לאלהינו	make straight in the desert a highway for our God.

The imprecision of line A, as compared with line B, lies in the meaning of דרך, 'way', in the genetival relation דרך יהוה, 'the way of Yahweh', and in the connection between 'prepare' (פנו) and 'make straight' (ישרו). דרך, of course, may mean not only 'way, road, path' in a literal sense, but also 'way, manner, habit; way of life, moral behaviour'. In genetival relation with a personal name it can be taken for granted that דרך has a metaphorical meaning, e.g. 'the way of Jeroboam' (1 Kgs 15.34; 16.2), 'the way of David' (2 Kgs 22.2).[5] When דרך is linked with יהוה, as it is frequently, the usages can be analysed, with BDB, as meaning (i) his creative activity (Job 26.14), (ii) his moral administration (Exod 33.13; Deut 32.4); (iii) his commandments (Gen 18.19, 'to keep the way of the Lord'; and often). Even if this analysis is open to question at some points, it cannot be doubted that some such metaphorical sense is the most natural one (within the same writing as our text, Yahweh's 'ways' are clearly his 'way of life' or 'moral administration' at Isa 55.8, 9). Natural or not, however, such an understanding of the present text would be wrong; for the parallel term מסלה, 'highway', is certainly used in a literal sense. Indeed it is used, in 26 of its 27 occurrences, literally; in the other case, 'The highway of the upright is to depart from evil' (Prov 16.17), we have the impression that the metaphor is freshly minted for the occasion, and there can be little question that מסלה is typically a literal road.

What line B also makes precise is the relation of the 'road' to God. The construct chain in line A is open to many interpretations, but the phrase 'a highway *for* our God' in line B is unambiguous: it must mean a road for Yahweh to walk along—just as a 'highway for the remnant of his people' (מסלה לשאר עמו) in Isa 11.16, and a 'way for the redeemed to pass over' (דרך לעבר גאולים) in 51.10 are paths for Israel to walk on. Here, the 'way of Yahweh' (line A) has meaning in the sense of 'a highway for our God' (line B); line B then specifies line A.

Furthermore, we may perhaps see in 'make smooth, straight' (ישרו) a greater precision than in 'prepare' (פנו). פנו in line A is properly 'clear away', i.e. 'remove any obstacles', which could apply to an already existing road—which might be what is meant by '*the* way of Yahweh'. Line B, however, in specifying that the 'clearing' is a matter of 'making smooth, or straight' *a* highway *for* God, more evidently envisages the building of a *new* road. פנו 'clear' is to be understood *in the sense of* ישרו 'make smooth, straight'. The obstacles to be cleared away are not just boulders or other debris lying on the road (which פנו דרך could refer to) but are the natural features (v. 4 will mention them as mountains and valleys) that are to be overcome and eliminated in the construction of an entirely new road.

d. *Isa 40.6*

כל־הבשר חציר	All flesh is grass
וכל־חסדו כציץ השדה	and all its loyalty is like the flower of the field.

The metaphor in line A is open to various understandings. Grass is indeed a symbol of what is short-lived, and is sometimes used of mankind's transitoriness. So we find, for example, that men are like grass renewed in the morning but withered by the time of evening (Ps 90.5); their days are like grass which is gone when the wind (רוח, as here) passes over it (103.15-16); the 'son of man who is made like grass' (בן־אדם חציר ינתן) is parallel to 'man who dies' (Isa 51.12). It is in a rather different sense that it is said of the wicked that they will soon fade like the grass (Ps 37.2), for there it is not an inbuilt weakness of the human constitution that accounts for the imminent death of the wicked but a fate peculiar to wrongdoers. In other passages, however, the symbolism of grass is completely different: in Isa 44.4, though the text is open to doubt,[6] the redeemed are to spring up like grass; in Isa 66.14 restored Israel will find its bones flourish like grass (דשא), in Job 5.25 Eliphaz promises Job that his descendants will be many and his offspring like (i.e. as plentiful as) the grass (עשב) of the earth.

The image of grass is therefore ambivalent, and nothing in the lines preceding our present text has conditioned its readers to interpret the image of line A in the way that line B requires. Indeed, the previous reference to 'all flesh' in v. 5 as being about to see the glory of Yahweh could have created an expectation that the image in v. 6 will be positive rather than negative. At best, any reading of line A is bound to be provisional; the precise sense of the 'grass' image—that it is grass in its aspect of impermanence (absence of חסר)—awaits a reading of line B.

e. *Isa 40.17*

כל הגוים כאין נגדו	All nations are as nothing beside him;
מאפס ותהו נחשבו־לו	less than nothing and emptiness they are reckoned by him.

What line A leaves open and what is further specified by line B is the question: in whose estimation are the nations as nothing beside him? Without line B, we might reasonably conclude that this evaluation is the poet's judgment, just as we would suppose for the preceding verses, 15-16 (though the presence of נחשבו in v. 15 may give us second thoughts). What line B specifies is that the reckoning is God's: the לו indicates 'the efficient cause (or personal agent)' with the passive (GKC, §121f). Line B makes clear that the perspective upon the nations and their significance in comparison with God (נגדו, line A) is God's own.

There may be a further precision in line B's phrase מאפס ותהו by comparison with line A's כאין. Being literal-minded about it, we might say that כאין means only '*about* nothing', '*roughly* nothing', whereas מאפס means 'to be precise, *less than* nothing'. But it is not at all certain that the מן signifies 'less than'[7] rather than 'consisting of, made from',[8] and there is also the possibility that the text should read כאפס (so 1QIs^{a}).[9]

No doubt ותהו 'and emptiness' adds a further precision or perhaps elaboration to the אין of line A; that is to say, to the idea of ignorable non-existence is added that of chaotic absence of form. But the most significant precision in line B is that which I have mentioned first: the specification of the standard or judge which gives value and significance to the comparison (כ) contained within line A.

f. *Isa 40.21*

הלוא תדעו הלוא תשמעו	Have you not known? Have you not heard?

הלוא הגד מראש לכם	Has it not been told to you 'from beginning'?
הלוא הבינתם מיסדת הארץ	Have you not understood from the foundations of the earth?

This tricolon displays a double specificity. Line B adds precision to line A, and line C to line B. What is not specified in line A is *when* Israel's coming to know and hearing is supposed to have taken place. In line B it is more specifically said to be 'from the beginning' (מראש), but that also raises a question: the beginning of what? Line C explicates B by its phrase 'from the foundation of the earth' (מיסודת הארץ, emended text);[10] the 'beginning' in question is the beginning of the earth. There is certainly a difficulty in understanding how Israel can be expected to have known anything from primeval times,[11] when it did not exist, but there is no doubt that we have here a parallelism of increasing precision.

2. *A Theorem*

In the parallelism of greater precision, line B specifies line A or some element of line A. There are different functions which precision or specification may serve:

1. B may disambiguate A (as in examples *a*, *b*, *c*, and *d* above). In these cases A is to a greater or lesser extent unclear, ambiguous. It is not incomplete, but it is vague or question-provoking, especially when compared with B or with the total effect of A plus B.

2. B may explicate A (as in examples *e* and *f* above). In these cases there is no ambiguity or uncertainty about A, but it is patient of further elaboration, in directions that it does not perhaps explicitly state, but which can be seen—especially on reflection after reading B—to be latent in it.

Further Comments

1. The movement toward greater precision is characteristically from A to B. This does not mean that A cannot contain *more* than B, but that when there is a relation of greater *precision* between A and B, it is B that typically exhibits that greater precision. Some examples of where A contains *more* than B but is not more precise may be noted.

a. *Isa 40.27*

למה תאמר יעקב	Why do you say, Jacob,
ותתבר ישראל	and speak, Israel?

A contains למה, 'Why', a surplus to B. But just because B follows A, למה is implied in B, and B is therefore no less precise than A.

b. *Isa 40.18*

ואל־מי תדמיון אל	And to whom will you liken God,
ומה־דמות תערכו לו	and what image/likeness will you compare to him?

Let us suppose for the sake of the discussion that 'liken God' and 'compare a likeness to him' are strictly synonymous, or else strictly separate (i.e. that line A refers to a deity and line B to his image). Let us suppose, that is to say, that B is not more *precise* than A. Then, we may ask, is A more precise than B? It contains 'God' (אל) whereas B contains only '(to) him' (לו). A *is* indeed more precise, but only in a trivial sense, for לו in B does present us with the same referent as אל in A. If, on the other hand, the lines changed places, so that we read:

ומה־דמות תערכו לו	And what image/likeness will you compare to him,
ואל־מי תדמיון אל	and to whom will you liken God?

or even if just the noun and pronoun changed places:

ואל־מי תדמיון אתו	And to whom will you liken him,
ומה־דמות תערכו לאל	and to what image/likeness will you compare God?

B *would be* more precise than A, for in A we should not know who was being spoken of ('him') but in B we should find it stated ('God').

2. Not all parallelistic couplets, of course, exhibit the parallelism of greater precision. And because the comparison is between sense-units and not just words, there is often enough room for debate over whether a particular B-line is more precise than its A-line. But I would argue that in Isaiah 40 slightly more than half the parallelistic couplets exhibit it. In Psalm 21, almost every verse is an example of this parallelism. It is a common enough feature of Hebrew poetry to

make it worth asking of every parallelistic couplet whether any gain in understanding may result from applying the present concept to it.

3. *Exegetical Applications*

Under this heading I am examining some texts in Isaiah 40 for which the possibility of an analysis as the parallelism of greater precision may have some exegetical value.

a. *Isa 40.26*

המוציא במספר צבאם	who brings out by number their host,
לכלם בשם יקרא	to all of them by name he calls.

This is a textbook example of a parallelistic couplet, with a mirror chiasmus.[12] מוציא is parallel to יקרא, and צבאם to לכלם. Those parallelisms are syntactic rather than morphological, whereas with במספר // בשם 'by number' // 'by name' we have a strict morphological parallelism as well (preposition plus noun).[13]

Such an analysis is accurate as far as it goes, but when we consider the sense of the lines it is quite misleading.[14] For 'by number' is not a method of summoning the stars that is parallel to 'by name'. Each star has a name, but each does not have a number. במספר in fact does not mean '*by* number' at all but 'in full number' (cf. 1 Chr 9.25). As far as the sense goes, we would be better to say that line B specifies the way in which God brings the army of the stars out in full number: it is by summoning each one of them by name. Line A acquires its specific meaning in the light of line B. It is not so rewarding to ask which terms of A correspond to which terms of B, as to ask whether and in what way line B specifies line A.

b. *Isa 40.31*

קוי יהוה יחליפו כח	Those who wait for Yahweh will gain new strength;
יעלו אבר כנשרים	they will put forth (?) plumage like eagles.

Here the parallelism of greater precision may help to solve a long-standing exegetical problem. Is יעלו qal or hiphil? Do they 'rise up (on) wings like eagles'[15] or 'put forth,[16] or grow, wings (*or*, plumage) like eagles'?[17] In favour of the former is the use of עלה qal with נשרים

in Jer 49.22, and 'soaring' is undoubtedly an obvious thing for eagles to do. But in favour of the latter is the awkwardness of the absence of a preposition before אבר, the LXX rendering πτεροφυήσουσιν, 'they will grow wings', and the Targum's *wytḥdtwn l'wlymwthwn kṣymwḥ dslyq 'l gdpy nšryn* 'and they will be renewed in their youth like the sprouting (of plumage) that rises up upon the wings of eagles'.

If line B may be more specific than line A, we can ask, In what way can the somewhat vague language of A, יחליפו כח, 'they will change, substitute, renew (their) strength', be specified further by B? *Going up* on wings in no way specifies 'changing strength', but *putting forth* new wings or new plumage is indeed a sign of new strength, whether or not there is an allusion to a belief that in old age eagles grow new wings.[18] The exiles would then substitute new strength for old strength, and 'change' their strength *in the sense that* old eagles 'change' theirs.

c. *Isa 40.27*

נסתרה דרכי מיהוה	My way is hidden from Yahweh,
ומאלהי משפטי יעבור	and from my God my right is disregarded.

A further example of the parallelism of greater precision may be found here, though commentators do not generally see the connection of thought between the two lines. The A-line taken by itself is open to more than one interpretation. For Israel's way to be hidden מן Yahweh could mean that God cannot see Israel's way, or will not see Israel's way, or has caused Israel not to be able to see its own way. 'Way' itself can mean here 'course of life' (BDB, *s.v.*, §5), perhaps with the sense of 'destiny', 'fate'[19] (NEB 'plight') or its 'direction' in some metaphorical sense.

The B-line however makes everything plain, not without some help from the A-line. משפט is itself not very precise (RV 'judgement'; RSV 'right'; NEB 'cause'). But for a משפט to עבר can only mean that a 'right' (which perhaps already became a legal 'cause' or 'case') has 'vanished', sc. from the notice of the one to whom it ought to be a matter of concern. In such a light, the A-line most probably means that Israel's 'course of life' or 'state' (or 'plight', since it is a *bad* state) is deliberately ignored by God ('hidden from Yahweh'). Israel's state is hidden from God (A) *in the sense that* its claim to restitution has failed to attract his attention (B). And Israel only knows that its 'way is hidden from Yahweh' (A) *in that* its cause is ignored, it does not receive its rights (B). The resulting interpretation of the couplet is no spectacular advance on the appropriate sense many readers attain very quickly; but our investigation has built a surer foundation for the validity of the interpretation.

We should also note that the principle of the parallelism of greater precision concerns primarily the relation between the two *lines* of a couplet; it does not focus on the relationship between the *members* of the two lines, either grammatically or semantically. In the present case, for example, we have an example of a complete or 'mirror' chiasmus (as in 40.26, discussed above), but that is of no significance for the relation of the lines. It is likewise unimportant whether דרך is a good parallel to משפט or not both because the relation of the *lines* does not depend upon the relation between the *terms* that are 'in parallel' (as we say), and because the notion that an ideal parallelism is a truly synonymous parallelism has been exploded by the principle of the parallelism of greater precision. Duhm found the parallelism here 'rather feeble' (*etwas ärmliche*)—which is indeed the case if the ideal is synonymity, but not at all the case if other relationships between the lines of a couplet can exist.

The foregoing examples yield evidence of the value of having the model of the parallelism of greater precision in mind when approaching the exegesis of an individual text. I conclude this section with an exegetical example of where the parallelism of greater precision is a 'false friend' and potentially misleading.

d. *Isa 40.28*

אלהי עולם יהוה	God of eternity / the world is Yahweh,
בורא קצות הארץ	Creator of the ends of the earth.

To anyone approaching this verse with a background in rabbinic or medieval Hebrew, the A-line is quite ambiguous: is עולם 'eternity' or 'the world, universe'? The parallelism of greater precision would seem to set the matter beyond doubt: 'the ends of the earth' must surely function as specification of the ambiguous עולם. It is generally argued, however, that the meaning 'world' of עולם is a post-Biblical development,[20] and a mere possibility in the relationship of parallelistic lines ('greater precision') cannot be set against a linguistic certainty.

The couplet exhibits the parallelism of greater precision, nevertheless—in another respect. For if we ask, In what respect is the 'eternity' of Yahweh significant in the present context, it is *in the* sense of line B, that he was in distant times (עולם) creator of the earth; and it is his creative power that lies behind the subsequent lines (vv. 28c-31).

4. *Some Similar Aspects of the Parallelistic Couplet*

It is perhaps unlikely that at this stage in the history of research into Hebrew poetry any completely new observations can be made. There are indeed several points at which the parallelism of greater precision corresponds to features that have previously been noted. But no one, I think, has focused upon the matter of 'greater precision' as an important definition of the relation of the lines of the parallelistic couplet.

To take the last point first, it is true that several scholars have observed that 'specification' is a function of the B-line of a couplet. James Kugel, for example, has recently remarked that

> there are quite a few lines in which B is clearly a continuation of A, or a going-beyond A in force or specificity.[21]

But his principal concern is to affirm that the relationship of A to B is only in a minority of cases an exact repetition, or a saying of the same thing in different words. Kugel's emphasis is on the *additive* or *emphatic* aspect of the B-line: 'A is so, and *what's more*, B is so'. He portrays the B-line as a continuing, seconding, emphatic carrying further, echoing, reiterative statement. All of that may be true of various couplets of Hebrew poetry, but it is quite other than what is being urged in this paper.

To similar effect J. Muilenburg remarked that

> parallelism is in reality very seldom precisely synonymous. The parallel line does not simply repeat what has been said, but enriches it, deepens it, transforms it by adding fresh nuances and bringing in new elements, renders it more concrete and vivid and telling.[22]

More 'concrete', yes; but he said nothing about 'more specific, more precise'.

Other aspects of parallelism fall now to be compared to and contrasted with the parallelism of greater precision.

a. *Staircase parallelism*

This feature of the parallelistic couplet, otherwise known as 'climactic' or 'repetitive' parallelism, or the 'expanded colon', has long been recognized.[23] W.G.E. Watson notes some forty examples,[24] including Jer 31.21:

שובי בתולת ישראל	Return, O Virgin Israel,
שאבי אל עריך אלה	Return to these your cities.

From a formal perspective, the description 'staircase' is apt, but from a more semantic perspective it is easily seen that such a form is an instance of the parallelism of greater precision. In the example quoted, the first line leaves unstated the place to which Israel is to return; the B-line specifies the full significance of 'return' in A. It is true of course that it is not only that the B-line is more specific than the A-line but also that the A is more specific than the B. Such cases do not negate the parallelism of greater precision; they are a subset of the examples of our feature.

b. *Number parallelism*

Examples of number parallelism can be divided into two categories: those with itemization and those without.

i. *Itemized number parallelism*. The best known example is Prov 30.18-20:

שלשה המה נפלאו ממני	There are three things too wonderful for me,
וארבע לא ידעתים	four I do not understand:
דרך נשר בשמים	(1) the way of a vulture in the sky;
דרך נחש עלי צור	(2) the way of a serpent on a rock;
דרך אניה בלב ים	(3) the way of a ship in the middle of the sea;
ודרך גבר בעלמה	(4) and the way of a man with a maiden.

The itemization makes it plain that it is precisely *four* things that the speaker does not understand. Line A contains the approximate number ('three'), line B the precise number. In all cases of itemization the precise number is the second one mentioned.[25] It is true that 'three' is in itself just as precise as 'four', but *in the context* 'three' is imprecise. M. Haran has listed twelve such instances, six from the OT,[26] five from Ben Sira, and one from the Babylonian Talmud citing Ben Sira. All of these, we may now say, exhibit parallelism of greater precision.

The recurring couplet in Amos, though it is not usually followed by an itemization, fits here best:

על שלשה פשעי . . .	For three transgressions of X,
ועל ארבעה לא אשיבנו	And for four, I will not revoke it.
	(Amos 1.3, 6, 9, 11, 13; 2.1, 4, 6)

In these cases (except perhaps in 2.6-8) it is only the fourth trangression that is specified, almost certainly because the fourth is so climactic that the others may be left out of consideration.[27] It is because of the fact that they total to *four*, and so include the fourth, climactic one, that Yahweh's punishment falls. So again the B-line of the couplet is the more precise or specific.

ii. *Unitemized number parallelism*. Most such instances display ordinary 'synonymous' parallelism, though of course no number is ever strictly synonymous with another.[28] For example, Mic 5.4:

והקמנו עליו שבעה רעים	Then we will raise against him seven shepherds,
ושמנה נסיכי אדם	eight chiefs of men.

We cannot say that 'eight' is more precise, in the context, than 'seven' (nor vice versa). Haran has suggested however that in a few cases 'the intended number is the first of the two';[29] but in Job 33.14 and Ps 62.12, which he cites, it can be maintained much more convincingly that it is the *second* number that is 'intended' or the more precise. This category of graded numerical sayings thus yields two more examples of the parallelism of greater precision, but on the whole it does not display the feature under consideration here.

c. *Automatism*

The phenomenon of 'automatism' as set forth by Haran[30] involves the use of one element of a word-pair solely for balance between the lines, and not at all for its semantic significance. An example that is adduced is Prov 24.30:

על־שדה איש עצל עברתי	I passed by the field of a sluggard,
ועל־כרם אדם חסר־לב	and by the vineyard of a man without sense.

The argument is that שדה and כרם form a fixed pair, corresponding to other pairs like bread and wine, threshing-floor (גרן) and wine-vat (יקב), corn (דגן) and new wine (תירוש), farmers (אכרים) and vintners (כרמים). But in the context *only* the vineyard is really meant, for the following verse refers to 'it' as having a stone fence—which points to a single parcel of ground, and that a vineyard, not a field. 'Field' is not 'intended' at all.

If such is the case, the line that contains the 'intended' word is inevitably more precise than the one with the 'automatic' variant. So for those cases where the 'automatic' variant occurs in line A,[31] we would have the parallelism of greater precision.[32] However, the existence of such automatism is, in my opinion, open to question.

In the example above, it is entirely probable that שדה, 'field', is a more general term that includes 'vineyard'—as is amply attested by Judg 9.27, 'they went out into the field (שדה) and harvested their vineyards (כרם)'. So it is not true that the place the wisdom poet saw 'can be either a field *or* a vineyard, but not both'.[33] The relationship between A and B is not one of 'automatic' word-pairing but of what is here being referred to as greater precision: the שדה in question is a כרם.

As for cases where it is claimed that the A line contains the more specific term, here also the existence of 'automatism' may be doubted. Haran cites Prov 4.3 as an example:

כי בך הייתי לאבי	For I was a son to my father,
רך ליתיד לפני אמי	tender and alone before my mother.

He comments, 'Only the father is actually kept in the poet's mind, while the mother is mentioned because of a mere automatic adherence to the verbal pattern'.[34] Indeed, the succeeding lines do refer exclusively to the father: 'and *he* taught me, and *he* said to me, "Let your heart hold fast *my* words . . ."' So it is quite true that it is the father that is principally in focus; but that does not necessarily mean that 'mother' is only there by accident. For if we suppose, quite reasonably, that the sense of the couplet is *distributed* across the two lines,[35] we have a perfectly satisfactory meaning, viz. 'When I was a young only child with my parents . . .'[36] This is certainly not an example of the parallelism of greater precision, but neither is it an example of automatic writing.

My conclusion is, though I have not reviewed here all the examples adduced for the phenomenon of 'automatism', that the phenomenon does not exist in the Hebrew Bible,[37] and that some supposed examples of it really exhibit the parallelism of greater precision, while other examples contain other types of parallelistic relationships.

d. *Ballast variants*

A ballast variant is defined by W.G.E. Watson as 'simply a *filler*, its function being to fill out a line of poetry that would otherwise be too short'.[38] As an example he cites Judg 5.28:

מדוע בשש רכבו לבוא	Why is his chariot so slow in coming?
מדוע אחרו פעמי מרכבותיו	Why does the clatter of his war-wagons tarry so?

On this he comments: 'Since *lābō* (or its equivalent in meaning) does not reappear in the second colon, the longer expression *pa'^a^mê mark^e^bôtâyw* is ued instead of simply one word (e.g. *mark^e^bôtâyw* // *rikbô*)'. No doubt a major question is begged here, viz. which comes first, the overshortness of the line or its filling? Being unanswerable, it suggests that the terms of the discussion are wrong. And the premise of the whole concept of 'ballast' or 'filling' depends on the 'isocolic principle' that the two lines of a parallelistic couplet should balance—which is open to question.[39]

The language of 'compensation' long ago introduced by G.B. Gray, falls under the same criticism,[40] and so too perhaps the use of 'expletive' by R. Austerlitz.[41] But there can be no doubt that some such terminology is needed for this feature of the parallelistic line.

Another conceptualization of the same phenomenon uses the language of 'gapping', which refers to the absence in the B-line of the verb or some other term of the A-line. This conceptualization, no different intrinsically from that of 'filling', has been used with discretion in the systemic analysis of M. O'Connor.[42] His primary example is Num 23.7:

מן־ארם ינחני בלק	Balak brought me from Aram,
מלך־מואב מהררי־קדם	the king of Moab from the Eastern Hills.

'Gapping' refers to the absence of anything equivalent to ינחי in line B. It is not clear what corresponding term O'Connor would use to describe the relationship of 'Aram' to 'the Eastern Hills' *and* of 'Balak' to 'the king of Moab'. He does indeed regard the latter case as a splitting of the name 'Balak, king of Moab' across two lines[43] (he calls it 'binomination'), but that cannot be said of the former case.

Our present description of the parallelism of greater precision of course prescinds from questions of causes or poetic psychology and even from issues of grammatical relationship and cuts across distinctions that have previously been made. That is to say, in some cases, perhaps many, of ballasting, filling, expletives, or gapping, the parallelism of greater precision can be seen; but in other cases, other parallelistic relationships occur.

A consideration of Num 23.7, just quoted, which certainly contains parallelism of greater precision, leads to a closer definition of 'greater precision'. It could well be argued that both 'Balak' and 'Aram' in line A are more specific or precise than their counterparts in line B, 'the king of Moab' and 'the Eastern Hills', because they use proper names for identification. Yet, on the other hand, it could just as well be argued that many people may be called Balak, and 'king of Moab' specifies which one is meant. In reality, such a debate misses the point of the parallelism: the question is not whether, taken in isolation, B is more precise than A, but whether 'king of Moab' in B adds any precisions to what we already have in A. Unquestionably it does; however, we must admit that in the case of 'Aram' // 'the Eastern Hills' we cannot say that B adds precision to A (unless perhaps the poet knows something that we do not).

In brief, so-called 'ballast variants' are *prima facie* candidates for the parallelism of greater precision, but a roughly synonymous parallelistic relationship is also quite possible.

e. *Word-pairs*

This very frequently discussed feature of Hebrew poetry needs to be mentioned here primarily in order to *distinguish* it from the subject of this paper. At its most conventional, the use of word pairs is a substitute for creative poetic activity, whereas the parallelism of greater precision is a subtle relationship between or among the lines of poetry that can only be designed in by a relatively sophisticated artist.

In a recent analysis building upon psycholinguistic studies, A. Berlin has argued persuasively that pairing of words is a manifestation of a common linguistic phenomenon of word association.[44] Two principal types of word associates can be denominated paradigmatic (e.g. good—bad, father—mother, descend—ascend) and syntagmatic (Zion—Jerusalem, mercy—truth, heavens—earth [as a merismus]). The phenomenon of *fixed* word-pairs, which has been a primary focus of attention in Hebrew poetry especially since the discovery of Ugaritic poetry, is only a subset of the broader category of word-pairing. It may indeed be possible to regard the present subject of study as yet another type of word-pairing—except of course that the 'greater precision' may be a function of the whole line in relation to the previous line, and not just of one word in relation to another word.

My principal concern here, however, is to observe that the phenomenon of the *fixed* word-pair is a contra-indication of the parallelism of greater precision—at least as far as those words are concerned. It is indeed true that in word-pairs the B-word is often less frequently attested, more poetic, more esoteric than the A-word.[45] But it is not typically more *specific* than the A-word; indeed, whether the pair is classified as paradigmatic or syntagmatic,[46] or as 'synonymous', 'antonymous' or 'correlative',[47] there is usually a parallelistic relationship of *balance*, in which there is no question of *progress* from word A to word B.

Things may be different, however, if we adopt a more flexible definition of 'word-pair', as is advocated by several recent authors. A. Berlin, for example, affirms that 'there is no qualitative difference between the so-called "fixed" pairs and pairs that have not so been labelled. The only difference is that fixed pairs are attested more often than non-fixed pairs.'[48] M. O'Connor writes that 'any single word in a language can be paired with another', a process he terms 'dyading'.[49] And W.M. Watters uses throughout his study, *Formula Criticism and the Poetry of the Old Testament*, a concept of word-pairs that can incorporate almost any kind of associative relatonship.[50] In such cases the 'word-pair' may exhibit a parallelism of greater precision—or any of the other kinds of parallelistic relationship.

It may finally be noted that the presence of a 'synonymous' word-pair within a parallelistic couplet may not necessarily form an obstacle to the parallelism of greater specificity. For example, Ps 7.17:

ישוב עמלו בראשו	May his sin redound upon his head,
ועל קדקדו חמסו ירד	and upon his pate may his violence descend.

Here 'head' (ראש) and 'pate' (קדקד) are the pair, and are perhaps completely synonymous (though the latter could reasonably be thought more specific or 'concrete' than the former). But there is nevertheless a greater precision in line B, since חמסו 'his violence' specifies the kind of 'sin' or 'trouble' (עמלו) that the A-line speaks of.

5. *Towards a (Somewhat) New Theory of Hebrew Poetry*

The new feature that has emerged from this study of the parallelistic couplet is not so much the identification of a particular relationship of the lines of the couplet (greater precision) as a movement towards a statement of relationships within the poetic couplet. Within the couplets that we have examined here, we can affirm, *the relationship of the two lines is unpredictable*. What is predictable about Hebrew poetry generally is its structure as couplets (or triplets, i.e. extended couplets). What is unpredictable is how the lines of that couplet (or, triplet) will turn out to relate to one another. Will they be synonymously parallel, will they exhibit the parallelism of greater precision, or staircase parallelism or synonymous-sequential parallelism,[51] or some other parallelistic relation—or no parallelism at all?[52]

This unpredictability is encountered by the reader at the beginning, middle, and end of the poetic couplet. At the beginning, before we start to read a couplet, we are aware that it is a couplet (whether through modern conventions of typography, or through our familiarity with the poetic convention itself); we can see that it will end after a snatch of words of between four and about ten, and we can expect that the couplet will constitute a complete sense-unit. But we do not know how that self-contained unity will present itself to us. We have some patterns of expectation available to us, indeed, but we are at the mercy of the poet for which of those patterns may lie ahead of us. At the end of the first line (colon) when we pause momentarily for processing the sense so far, we make a provisional judgment on the completeness or otherwise, the self-sufficiency or open-endedness, of the sense-unit thus far read or heard. But here also we cannot predict how the couplet will proceed; not only do we not yet know the grammatical or syntactic pattern of the next line, or its lexical contents, but, more importantly, we do not know *what kind of a relationship* what we have read will bear to what we have yet to read. (Many popular expositions of parallelism, formulaic poetry, word-pairs and the like implicitly encourage us to believe that we do.) The unpredictability remains even when we have read to the end of the couplet. For even when we have processed both lines of the couplet, our understanding will not be complete until we have gone back over the lines from the viewpoint of their relationship. And what that relationship will be is not securely indicated by any surface clues (like grammatical morphology or the presence of a fixed word-pair).

It is often not difficult to determine that relationship, but the point about it is that it is *not given but must be figured out by every reader*.[53]

James Kugel was entirely right in asserting, as against a crude popularization of Lowthian parallelism, that 'Biblical parallelism is of one sort . . . or a hundred sorts; but it is not three'.[54] But I believe he is wrong to describe the 'one sort' as a matter of 'A, and what's more, B', since that restricts the relationship of the lines to those of emphasis, repetition, seconding, and so on. The relationships of A and B are so diverse that only some statement such as 'A is related to B' will serve as a valid statement about *all* parallelistic couplets. And such a statement is equally valid for non-parallelistic lines. Biblical poetry in general is overwhelmingly composed of couplets (or triplets, extended couplets), and of such couplets we could state that they are of one sort (A is related to B) or of a hundred, but not of three or four or five.

Our study of the parallelism of greater precision has alerted us to something that is true of Hebrew poetry generally. The meaning of the couplet does not reside in A nor in B; nor is it in A + B (if they are regarded as capable of being added like 2 + 2 or 3 + 2). It is in the whole couplet of A and B in which A is affected by its juxtaposition with B, and B by its juxtaposition with A. The whole is different from the sum of its parts because the parts influence or contaminate each other.[55] A has its meaning within the couplet only in the light, or sense, of B, and B in the light, or sense, of A. In the case of Isa 40.3, for instance, the couplet does not mean B, even if B is more precise than A. It means (i) prepare Yahweh's way *in the sense of* making straight a highway, and it means (ii) make straight the highway *as an act of* preparing a way for Yahweh, and it means both of these things concurrently.

Because the relationship of the two lines within the couplet is not predetermined, the reader is more fully engaged in the process of interpretation, a more active participant in the construction of meaning, than when a text presents itself in more straightforward linear fashion. E.L. Greenstein has reminded us of Marshall McLuhan's distinction between 'hot' and 'cool' media, 'hot' media presenting a complete pattern of stimuli, 'cool' presenting an incomplete pattern and therefore requiring greater processing and hence a higher level of engagement on the reader's part.[56] Such engagement, I would suggest, is systematically demanded by the nature of the Hebrew poetic couplet. The reader is constantly involved in the delicate and tantalizing[57] question of the relation of the parts and the product of their interrelationship. That relation, as we have seen in the study of the parallelism of greater precision, is a dynamic one which cannot be mechanically delineated, but which often yields itself only to patient exegetical probing, each couplet in its own right. Any future theoretical study of such phenomena as that discussed in the present paper will have the converging resources of philosophical hermeneutics, current literary theory (especially reader-response criticism and reception theory), and psycholinguistics to draw upon.

NOTES

1. A draft of the present paper was read to the Hebrew Poetry Section of the Society for Biblical Literature at its Annual Meeting in Chicago, on December 11, 1984. I am grateful to colleagues at that session for several helpful comments.

2. This paper was in proof when there came into my hands the article of A. Berlin, 'Shared Rhetorical Features in Biblical and Sumerian Literature', *JANES* 10 (1978), pp. 35-42. The unspecific title of her paper disguises the fact, which I gladly acknowledge, that my initial observation was anticipated by Dr Berlin in her discussion (pp. 35-39) of the 'particularizing' parallelism, as she calls it. She cites a number of Sumerian examples, such as this triplet from *Dumuzi's Dream*, lines 1-3:

> His heart was filled with tears, he went out to the plain;
> The lad—his heart was filled with tears, he went out to the plain;
> Dumuzi—his heart was filled with tears, he went out to the plain.

From the Hebrew Bible, she notes Ps 29.5; 89.4; Deut 32.9 and others. It should be pointed out, however, that she is concerned only with cases of particularizing *words* and almost exclusively with cases where 'the first member of the pair is a general term and the second is a proper, or geographical name' (p. 37). It will be observed that the present paper extends the area of consideration in several new directions.

3. Zech 11.1 seems to be the only other place: 'Open your doors, O Lebanon, that the fire may devour your cedars'.

4. BDB renders 'veil', and the *Hebräisches und aramäisches Lexikon zum Alten Testament* gives *Flor* (gauze).

5. Isa 62.10 (דרך העם, 'the way of the people') is an evident exception, especially as the immediate context makes clear that it is a physical road that is envisaged, which is to be 'built up' (סלו) and 'cleared of stones' (סקלו מאבן). The phrase פנו דרך העם may indeed be modelled upon the text at present

under discussion. R.N. Whybray, in denying that it is a highway and affirming that it is the '"way" of life of devotion to Yahweh which the inhabitants of Jerusalem must lead' fails to distinguish between the concrete image and its metaphorical function (*Isaiah 40–66* [NCB; Oliphants: London, 1975], p. 251.

6. בְּבֵין חציר is indeed very improbable, but the usual emendation to כבין, 'as if among', though somewhat awkward, is satisfactory (כבין is supported by 1QIs[a], LXX and Targum). The emendation recommended by *BHS* to כְּבִין חָצוֹר, 'like a poplar of Hazor' is weak. It is doubtful moreover whether we should identify here a חָצִיר 'reed', separate from חָצִיר 'grass' (so *HALAT*, *s.v.*).

7. So RSV; it must be admitted that 'in point of language this *comparative* sense of the Hebrew preposition . . . is quite admissible' (O.C. Whitehouse, *Isaiah XL–LXVI* [CB; Edinburgh: T.C. & E.C. Jack, 1908], p. 57).

8. So e.g. B. Duhm, *Das Buch Jesaja* (HAT, 3/1; Göttingen: Vandenhoeck und Ruprecht, [3]1914), p. 269 ('"aus dem Nichts", ohne Kern und Wesenheit'); K. Marti, *Das Buch Jesaja* (KHAT, 10; Tübingen: J.C.B. Mohr [Paul Siebeck], 1900), p. 274 (partitive מן).

9. Thus e.g. K. Elliger, *Deuterojesaja* (BKAT, 11/1; Neukirchen: Neukirchener Verlag, 1978), p. 42.

10. So BHS and many moderns; MT מוֹסְדוֹת 'foundations' can hardly be the object of הבינתם.

11. The phrase probably means simply 'from ancient times', says Whybray (*Isaiah 40–66*, p. 55). It is perhaps better to see the temporal expressions as relating to the 'telling' rather to the 'hearing', 'knowing' or 'understanding'. Duhm (*Jesaja*, pp. 271f.) argued that the ראש was the beginning of Israel's history, and that the 'foundation of the earth' does not refer to the *time* of the earth's creation but to the *fact* of its creation; Israel should have discerned the existence of a creator God from the existence of the world of nature. But it seems much more probable that a temporal reference is made in both lines.

12. M. O'Connor finds no example of this mirror chiasm in his selected texts (*Hebrew Verse Structure* [Winona Lake: Eisenbrauns, 1980], p. 394). W.G.E. Watson, *Classical Hebrew Poetry. A Guide to its Techniques* (JSOTS, 25; Sheffield: JSOT, 1984), pp. 202f. reserves the term 'mirror chiasmus' for cases of exact repetition of terms, calling cases such as the present 'complete chiasmus' (abc // c′b′a′).

13. For the terminology, cf. A. Berlin, 'Grammatical Aspects of Biblical Parallelism', *HUCA* 50 (1979), pp. 17-43.

14. It should be noted that Berlin is of course quite aware that grammatical analysis does not permit semantic conclusions ('Grammatical Aspects', pp. 42-43).

15. So RSV.

16. So Elliger, *Deuterojesaja*, p. 101; Whybray, *Isaiah 40–66*, pp. 55f.

17. 'Put forth' or 'grow' are acceptable senses of עלה hi. (*HALAT*, p. 785b), *contra* Duhm, *Jesaja*, p. 274; Marti, *Jesaja*, p. 277; R. Levy, *Deutero-Isaiah* London: OUP, 1925), p. 128, who suppose a different verb עלה 'to grow' (cf. עָלֶה 'leaf'). Similar uses are found in Jer 30.17; 33.6; Ezek 37.6.

18. Some commentators find such an allusion 'doubtful' (Whybray, *Isaiah 40–66*, p. 60) or even 'fanciful' (North, *The Second Isaiah*, p. 89).

19. So North, *The Second Isaiah*, p. 89.

20. *HALAT*, p. 755b; E. Jenni, *THWAT*, cols. 242-43.

21. J.L. Kugel, *The Idea of Biblical Poetry* (New Haven: Yale University Press, 1981), p. 8.

22. J. Muilenburg, 'A Study in Hebrew Rhetoric: Repetition and Style', *VTS* 1 (1953), pp. 97-111 (98).

23. S.E. Loewenstamm, 'The Expanded Colon in Ugaritic and Biblical Verse', *JSS* 14 (1969), pp. 176-96; *id.*, 'The Expanded Colon Reconsidered', *UF* 7 (1975), pp. 261-64; Watson, *Classical Hebrew Poetry*, pp. 150-56.

24. Watson, *Classical Hebrew Poetry*, p. 151 n. 106, and pp. 152-55.

25. Cf. M. Haran, 'The Graded Numerical Sequence and the Phenomenon of "Automatism" in Biblical Poetry', *VTS* 22 (1971), pp. 238-67 (256).

26. Prov. 6.16; 30.15b, 18, 21, 29; Job 5.19.

27. Cf. Haran, 'Graded Numerical Parallelism', p. 266; Y. Zakovitch, '*For Three . . . and for Four*' (Jerusalem; Makor, 1979), ch. 3 [Hebrew]. I am not convinced by the argument of M. Weiss, 'The Pattern of Numerical Sequence in Amos 1–2', *JBL* 86 (1967), pp. 416-23, that there are *seven* transgressions (he argues that 'three' and 'four' are the break-up of a stereotyped phrase).

28. For a possible exception, see Watson, *Classical Hebrew Poetry*, p. 144 n. 84.

29. Haran, 'Graded Numerical Parallelism', p. 253. He is followed by Watson, *Classical Hebrew Poetry*, p. 148.

30. Haran, 'Graded Numerical Parallelism', pp. 243-53.

31. Haran adduces Prov 24.30; Amos 6.1; Ps 81.4 (pp. 243-47).

32. It is true that Haran also finds four examples where the automatism is in line B (Prov 4.3; 1.8 [similarly 6.20]; 23.22).

33. Haran, p. 244.

34. Haran, p. 247.

35. The language, as Kugel reminds us, goes back to Theodore of Mopsuestia (using the term διαίρεσις, 'dividing in two'; the corresponding term in Latin rhetoric was *distributio* (*Idea of Biblical Poetry*, pp. 40-42, 156f.).

36. Some would speak of this as the break-up of the stereotyped phrase 'father-mother'. On the principle, see E.Z. Melamed, 'Break-up of Stereotype Phrases as an Artistic Device in Biblical Poetry', *Scripta Hierosolymitana* 8 (1961), pp. 115-53; G. Braulik, 'Aufbrechen von geprägten Wortverbindungen

und Zusammenfassen von stereotypen Ausdrücken in der alttestamentlichen Kunstprosa', *Semitics* 1 (1970), pp. 7-11; Watson, *Classical Hebrew Poetry*, pp. 328-32. C.F. Whitley has, however, urged some important objections against both the concept and the detailed exemplifications of the break-up of stereotype phrases ('Some Aspects of Hebrew Poetic Diction', *UF* 7 [1975], pp. 493-502 [493-99]). It would indeed be better if we could avoid thinking of an 'ideal' or 'original' or 'simple' thought being 'broken-up' or 'distributed' into separate lines. Yet lines A and B are not separate and independent, but yield their meaning up only as a differentiated unity.

37. A much less clear-cut example (more difficult because of the rarity of its words) adduced by Haran may be discussed by way of illustrating that Haran's theory is less than persuasive. Judg 5.25 has

מים שאל חלב נתנה	Water he asked, and she gave milk;
בספל אדירים הקריבה חמאה	in a lordly bowl she presented curds.

Curds, says Haran (p. 250), are only mentioned for the sake of the parallelism (as in Gen 18.8 and Deut 32.14; but, unlike here, in both places חמאה 'curds' is the A-word). *Milk* is what she gave him, as the prose narrative says (4.19), and that in a 'bowl' (ספל), elsewhere a vessel for *liquids* (6.38). חמאה, by contrast, is something one eats (2 Sam. 17.29; Isa 7.15, 22); it is not a *drink*. Against these arguments we can assert: nothing is said in the poem (which is all that counts for this purpose) of *drinking*; a vessel which, in the one other place where the term is used, could be filled with the water wrung from a fleece (6.38) does not thereby become reserved exclusively for liquids. Prov 30.33 makes clear that חמאה is a milk-*product*, which is to say that it is a specific kind of milk. Is this not more probably a case of the parallelism of greater precision?

38. Watson, *Classical Hebrew Poetry*, p. 344.

39. M. O'Connor is perhaps extreme in asserting that the principle that all lines tend to be the same length is 'so far from being true that it is useless' (*Hebrew Verse Structure* [Winona Lake, Eisenbrauns, 1980], p. 136). Cf. also Kugel, *Idea of Biblical Poetry*, pp. 45-48, who however is ready to speak of a general balance of poetic lines (p. 71).

40. G.B. Gray, *The Forms of Hebrew Poetry* (London: Hodder and Stoughton, 1915), pp. 76-83, 94; his term was 'incomplete parallelism with compensation'.

41. R. Austerlitz, *Ob-Ugric Metrics* (Folklore Fellows Communications, 174/8; Helsinki, 1958), pp. 64f., 101. This work is known to me only from Watson, *Classical Hebrew Poetry*, pp. 344, 348.

42. O'Connor, *Hebrew Verse Structure*, pp. 123-29.

43. O'Connor, *Hebrew Verse Structure*, p. 113.

44. A. Berlin, 'Parallel Word-Pairs: A Linguistic Explanation', *Ugarit-Forschungen* 15 (1983), pp. 7-16.

45. Cf. e.g. R.G. Boling, '"Synonymous" Parallelism in the Psalms', *JSS* 5

(1960), pp. 221-55 (223f.); Watson, *Classical Hebrew Poetry*, p. 129.

46. Cf. Berlin (see note 42 above). The conceptualization she employs is not free from difficulties; see, briefly, S.A. Geller, *Parallelism in Early Biblical Poetry* (HSM, 20; Missoula: Scholars Press, 1979), pp. 32ff.

47. So Watson, *Classical Hebrew Poetry*, pp. 131f.

48. Berlin, 'Parallel Word-Pairs', p. 8.

49. O'Connor, *Hebrew Verse Structure*, pp. 96f.

50. W.M. Watters, *Formula Criticism and the Poetry of the Old Testament* (BZAW, 138; Berlin: de Gruyter, 1976); see, for example, pp. 102f.

51. See P.D. Miller, 'Synonymous-Sequential Parallelism in the Psalms', *Bib* 61 (1980), pp. 256-60.

52. The frequently encountered statement that parallelism is 'characteristic' of Hebrew poetry (e.g. Watson, *Classical Hebrew Poetry*, p. 114) must be taken to mean that it is not universally found (cf. Watson, p. 12).

53. The remarks of P.A. Boodberg on parallelistic couplets in Chinese poetry may be aptly cited: the function of the second line of a couplet is, he argues, 'to give us the clue for the construction of the first'; 'parallelism is not merely a stylistic device of formularistic syntactical duplication; it is intended to achieve a result reminiscent of binocular vision, the superimposition of two syntactical images in order to endow them with solidity and depth, the repetition of the pattern having the effect of binding together syntagms that appear at first rather loosely aligned' ('On crypto-parallelism in Chinese poetry' and 'Syntactical metaplasia in stereoscopic parallelism', *Cedules from a Berkeley Workshop in Asiatic Philology*, nos. 001-540701 and 017-541210 [Berkeley, 1954-55] [cited by R. Jakobson, 'Grammatical Parallelism and its Russian Facet', *Language* 42 (1966), pp. 399-429 (402)]).

54. Kugel, *The Idea of Biblical Poetry*, p. 58.

55. Cf. the sentence of Menahem b. Saruch (AD 960), 'One half of the line teaches about the other' (cited by Watters, *Formula Criticism*, p. 92).

56. E.L. Greenstein, 'How Does Parallelism Mean?', in S.A. Geller, E.L. Greenstein and A. Berlin, *A Sense of Text. The Art of Language in the Study of Biblical Literature* (A Jewish Quarterly Review Supplement; Winona Lake: Eisenbrauns, 1982), pp. 41-70 (54).

57. I am reminded of D.S. Brewer's remark à propos of the opening of Chaucer's *Parlement of Foulys* that the rhetorical devices are so deployed that the reader's mind is 'led forward by a combination of information and mild mystification, which arouses both expectation itself and pleasure in its ingenuity' (*The Parlement of Foulys*, ed. D.S. Brewer [Manchester: Manchester University Press, 1972], p. 49).

5

THE CASE FOR THE PROSECUTION
Isaiah 41.21–42.17

Jerome T. Walsh

Introduction

For the first half of this century, critical study of Isa 40–55 subscribed, almost without exception, to the view that the prophecy of Second Isaiah comprised a large number of short, independent literary units. Before 1950, very few contested this opinion.[1] Since 1950, on the other hand, a growing number of scholars have sought to identify larger literary units composed of materials thought by earlier commentators to be independent. Y. Kaufmann, J. Muilenburg, and M. Haran are among the first contemporary scholars to propose such readings. Haran, in turn, was the first to identify 41.21–42.17 as a single literary unit, using as his criterion a series of 'components' (defined as ideas and images, themes and motifs) that constitute the basic pattern followed by Second Isaiah in chs. 40–48. The same unit is identified by P. Bonnard on the basis of continuity of ideas and verbal correspondences. Most recently, J. Goldingay has added a contextual argument by showing the formal parallels between 41.1-20 and 41.21–42.17.[2]

The purpose of this essay is to investigate the stylistic and logical structure of this putative literary unity. A translation of the text will be followed by a close reading. Each of the unit's three sections shows a tight, careful symmetry, as does the passage as a whole. The logical coherence of the entire unit is revealed when it is read as the case for the prosecution in a trial scene. Yahweh challenges the claim of other gods to divinity; sets forth a clear, step-by-step procedure by which such claims can be demonstrated; and follows the procedure to prove his own claim to divinity.

1. *Text*

1. *Transliteration*

I A

21. *qārĕbû rîbĕkem*
yō'mar yhwh
haggîšû 'ăṣūmôtêkem
yō'mar melek ya'ăqōb

22. *yaggîšû wĕyaggîdû lānû*
'ēt 'ăšer tiqrênâ
hārī'šōnôt mâ hēnnâ haggîdû
wĕnāśîmâ libbēnû
wĕnēdĕ'â 'aḥărîtān
'ô habbā'ôt hašmî'ūnû
23. *haggîdû hā'ōtîyôt lĕ'āḥôr*
wĕnēdĕ'â kî 'ĕlōhîm 'attem
'ap-têṭîbû wĕtārē'û
wĕništā'â wĕnir'e yaḥdāw
24. *hēn-'attem mē'ayin*
ûpo'olkem <mē'epes>[3]
tô'ēbâ yibḥar bākem

I B

25. *ha'îrôtî miṣṣāpôn wayya't*
mimmizraḥ-šemeš <yiqqārē'> bišmî
wĕyābō' sĕgānîm kĕmô-ḥōmer
ûkĕmô yôṣēr yirmos-ṭîṭ

26. *mî higgîd mērō'š wĕnēdā'â*
ûmillĕpānîm wĕnō'mar ṣaddîq
'ap 'ên maggîd 'ap 'ên mašmîa'
'ap 'ên-šōmēa' 'imrêkem
27. *rī'šôn lĕṣîyôn <.. >*
wĕlîrûšālaim mĕbaśśēr 'ettēn
28. *wĕ'ēre' we'ên 'îš*
ûmē'ēlleh wĕ'ên yô'ēṣ
wĕ'eš'ālēm wĕyāšîbû dābār

29. *hēn kullām <'ayin>*
'epes ma'ăśêhem
rûaḥ wātōhû niskêhem

II A

1. *hēn ʿabdî ʾetmok-bô*
bĕḥîrî rāṣĕtâ napšî
nātattî rûḥî ʿālāyw

mišpāṭ laggôyim yôṣîʾ
2. *lōʾ yiṣʿaq wĕlōʾ yiśśāʾ*
wĕlōʾ-yašmîaʿ baḥûṣ qôlô
3. *qāneh rāṣûṣ lōʾ yišbôr*
ûpištâ kēhâ lōʾ yĕkabbennâ
leʾĕmet yôṣîʾ mišpāṭ
4. *lōʾ yikheh wĕlōʾ <yērôṣ>*

ʿad-yāśîm bāʾāreṣ mišpāṭ
ûlĕtôrātô ʾîyîm yĕyaḥēlû

5. *kōh-ʾāmar hāʾēl yhwh*
bôrēʾ haššāmayim wĕnôṭêhem
rōqaʿ hāʾāreṣ wĕṣeʾĕṣāʾêhā
nōtēn nĕšāmâ lāʿām ʿālêhā
wĕrûaḥ lahōlĕkîm bāh

II B

6. *ʾănî yhwh*
qĕrāʾtîkā bĕṣedeq
wĕʾaḥzēq bĕyādekā
wĕʾeṣṣorkā wĕʾettenkā
librît ʿām lĕʾôr gôyim
7. *lipqōaḥ ʿênayim ʿiwrôt*
lĕhôṣîʾ mimmasgēr ʾassîr
mibbêt kele ʾ yōšbê ḥōšek
8. *ʾănî yhwh hûʾ šĕmî*
ûkĕbôdî lĕʾaḥēr lōʾ-ʾettēn
ûtĕhillātî lappĕsîlîm

III A

9. *hāriʾšōnôt hinnēh-bāʾû*
waḥădāšôt ʾănî maggîd
bĕṭerem tiṣmaḥnâ ʾašmîaʿ ʾetkem

10. *šîrû layhwh šîr ḥādāš*
tĕhillātô miqṣēh hāʾāreṣ

yôrĕdê hayyām ûmĕlō'ô
'îyîm wĕyōšĕbêhem
11. *yiś'û midbār wĕ'ārāyw*
ḥăṣērîm tēšēb qēdār
yārōnnû yōšĕbê sela'
mērō'š hārîm yiṣwāḥû
12. *yāśîmû layhwh kābôd*
ûtĕhillātô bā'îyîm yaggîdû

III B

13. *yhwh kaggibbôr yēṣē'*
kĕ'îš milḥāmôt yā'îr qin'â
yārîa' 'ap-yaṣrîaḥ
'al-'ōyĕbāyw yitgabbār

14. *heḥĕšêtî mē'ôlām*
'aḥărîš 'et'appāq
kayyôlēdâ 'ep'eh
'eššōm wĕ'eš'ap yāḥad
15. *'aḥărîb hārîm ûgĕbā'ôt*
wĕkol-'eśbām 'ôbîš
wĕśamtî nĕhārôt lā'îyîm
wa'ăgammîm 'ôbîš
16. *wĕhôlaktî 'iwrîm bĕderek lō' yādā'û*
bintîbôt lō'-yādĕ'û 'adrîkēm
'āśîm maḥšāk lipnêhem lā'ôr
ûma'ăqaššîm lĕmîšôr

'ēlleh haddĕbārîm
'ăśîtīm wĕlō' 'ăzabtîm

17. *nāsōgû 'āḥôr*
yēbōšû bōšet
habbōṭĕḥîm bappāsel
hā'ōmĕrîm lĕmassēkâ
'attem 'ĕlōhênû

2. *Translation*

I A

21. Bring near your lawsuit
Says Yahweh.

Bring close your arguments
Says the king of Jacob.

22. Let them bring (it) close and tell us
Whatever will occur.
The first things—tell us what they were
That we might consider them
And that we might know their aftermath.
Or the coming things, make us hear them.
23. Tell us the things arriving later
That we might know that you are gods.
In fact, do anything—good or bad!
That we might see (it) and revere (you).

24. Look! You are less than nothing
And your doing is <less than zero>!
An abomination is he who chooses you!

I B

25. I aroused (one) from the north, and he arrived.
From the orient he is called in my name
That he might come to rulers as to mortar
And as a potter trampling his clay.

26. Who told it from the first that we might know
And from beforehand that we might say, 'He was right!'?
In fact, none told it; in fact, none made it heard,
In fact, none heard you say anything.
27. First of all, to Zion <I declared it>,
And to Jerusalem I am giving a herald.
28. But I look, and there is none;
Among them, there is no counsellor
That I may ask them and they might respond something.

29. Look! They are all <nothing>!
Their work is zero!
Breath and brouhaha are their statues.

II A

1. Look! My servant: I support him;
My chosen one: my heart delights.
I have placed my breath upon him—

He shall bring about justice to the nations.
2. He shall not cry out, he shall not lift up,
He shall not make heard in the street his voice.
3. A weakened reed he shall not break,
A fading lamp he shall not blow out.
Justice to rely on he shall bring about;
4. He'll not weaken nor fade—

While justice he establishes on the earth
And the sea-lands await his guidance.

5. Thus spoke God Yahweh
Who created the heavens and deployed them
Who spread out the earth and its growth
Who gave air to the people upon it
And breath to those who go about it:

II B

6. I am Yahweh
I have called you rightly
That I may grasp your hand
And form you and give you
To (be) a covenant of people,
To (be) a light of nations,
7. To open eyes that are blind,
To bring out from jail the prisoner,
From the dungeon those who dwell in the dark.
8. I am Yahweh: that is my name.
My glory I will not give another,
Nor my praise to images.

III A

9. The first things—see!—have come.
Now new things I foretell.
Before they develop, I make you hear (them).

10. Sing Yahweh a new song,
His praise from the ends of the earth—
Those who go down to the sea and fill it,
Sea-lands and their dwellers;
11. Let the desert and its towns lift up (their voice),
The villages where you dwell, O Qedar;

Let the dwellers of Sela exult,
From the mountaintops let them shout—
12. Let them establish glory for Yahweh
And in the sea-lands let them tell his praise!

III B

13. Yahweh goes forth like a warrior
Like a man of war he arouses passion
He yells, in fact, he roars;
Against his enemies he 'warriors'.

14. I've been unresponsive for a long time;
I've kept myself silent and in check.
Like a woman in childbirth I've been groaning;
I've been appalled and eager at the same time.
15. I will lay waste mountains and hills
And all their green I will dry up.
I will make the rivers into sea-lands
And pools I will dry up.
16. I will lead the blind by a route they do not know
And by paths they do not know I will route them.
I will make the darkness before them into light
And the twists into a straightaway.

These things are my evidence,
I have done them and I have not abandoned them.

17. They have turned away!
They blush with shame!—
Those who trust in images
And say to statuary,
'You are our gods'.

3. *Notes on the translation*

41.23 (1) Read *têṭîbû wĕtārē'û* as second person jussives. The phrase is a merism. (2) Read *wnr'* with the Ketib. The Qumran variant (*wnšm'h* for *wnšt'h*) is an attractive alternative to the MT.

41.24 Emend *m'p'* to *m'ps*, with most commentators. The initial *mem* in the words *m'yn* and *m'p'* can be understood as comparative, and need not be deleted as dittography.

41.25 (1) Read niphal *yiqqārē'* (the LXX also reads a passive form here). Might the Q variant (*wyqr'*) point to an indirect jussive with final force: 'that he might call upon my name'? (2) Read *wĕyābō'* as a jussive with final force. The couplet may be a reference to Cyrus's march of conquest across northern Mesopotamia and Asia Minor through Media, Lydia, and the vassal kingdoms that he cemented into his growing empire.

*41.26b*β Literally, 'none heard your sayings'.

41.27 A conjectural emendation *ad sensum* for the unintelligible *hnh hnm.*[4]

41.28 Read *wĕ'ēre'* as conjunctive *waw* with the imperfect.

41.29 Emend *'wn* to *'yn*, with Q and most commentators.

42.3 The phrase *le'ĕmet* appears only here in the OT. It is not simply a synonym for *be'ĕmet*, 'reliably, faithfully', describing the servant's manner of establishing justice. The preposition conveys a purposive nuance: the servant's mission of establishing justice is done with a view toward reliability.

42.4 Read niphal *yērôṣ* for *yārûṣ*.

42.6 Read the verbs as a series of cohortatives with final force.

42.14 Read the imperfect verbs as expressing the durative past. The last two verbs have been variously understood. Formally they are an alliterative pair, joined by conjunctive *waw*. Most commonly *'eššōm* is derived from a verb *nšm*, 'to pant' (cf. *nĕšāmâ*, 'breath'); such a verb would be a *hapax* here. The line is then understood to refer to the labored gasping and panting of a woman in childbirth. Schoors,[5] following Joüon, rejects this reading and has proposed to read *'eššōm* as a unique transitive qal use of the verb *šmm*, 'to be desolate', and *'eš'ap* as 'to swallow up, to devour'; he translates the line 'I will destroy and also devour'. Both readings must postulate an otherwise unattested Hebrew usage. Attention to the emotional overtones of the terms offers a better possibility: *šmm* can refer to being distressed or appalled (cf. Isa 52.14); *š'p* can connote eager desire (cf. Ps 119.131; Job 5.5). The image is thus an accurate depiction of the mixed feelings of one in excruciating pain (typified in biblical imagery by the 'woman in childbirth') whose relief can be gained only through further endurance.

42.16c 'These things are my evidence'; literally, 'These are the things'.

2. *41.21-29*

The passage falls into two parallel parts, vv. 21-24, 25-29. The last verses of each section describe the worthlessness of the gods, of their deeds, and of their worshippers (v. 24c) or their idols (v. 29c); the two verses are marked by verbal parallels as well.

v. 24	*v. 29*
Look!	Look!
You are less than nothing	They are all nothing!

And your doing is less than zero!	Their work is zero!
An abomination is he who chooses them.	Breath and brouhaha are their statues.

1. *Vv. 21-24.* The first verse shows Yahweh calling for a trial and daring his opponents to present their case. Two legal terms establish the courtroom as the frame of reference and the scene as a trial: *rîb*, a legal case; and *qrb* (piel), to present a case in court (cf. Job 31.35-37).[6]

Verses 22-23 are a challenge to the defendants to do or say something noteworthy in their own defense. Like a clever lawyer, Yahweh uses first person plural forms to imply an identification of his own point of view with that of the court. The challenge follows an ABB′A′ pattern. The outer elements are shorter (distichs) and more general; the central elements are tristichs and more specific. Each central element opens with an imperative ('tell us', v. 22bα; 'make us hear', v. 22cβ) and ends with 'that we might know'.

A. Tell us anything that happens (v. 22a)
  B. Explain the past (v. 22bcα)
  B′. Or explain the future (v. 22cβ-23a)
A′. In fact, do anything at all (v. 23b)

In the concluding verse Yahweh declares to the defendants that they are useless. By addressing the gods in the second person, he makes the insult part of the challenge.

2. *Vv. 25-29.* The second part opens with Yahweh recalling his past action in calling forth Cyrus to begin his march of conquest (v. 25). This deed is evidence upon which Yahweh will build his own case.

Verses 26-28 are also arranged in an ABB′A′ pattern:

A. Question: Who foretold the affair of Cyrus? (v. 26a)
  B. No one (of the gods) foretold it (v. 26b)
  B′. I, Yahweh, foretold it (v. 27)
A′. Comment: None of them answers the question! (v. 28)

The outer elements concern the question Yahweh hurls at the defendants; v. 26 poses the question, v. 28 comments on the gods' silence in face of it. The central elements comprise Yahweh's argument that the question points to him as revealer of history, not to the gods.

In v. 26a, Yahweh continues to address the other gods, using first person plurals as in vv. 22-23 to identify himself with the court. The repeated key word 'that we might know' (*wĕnēdĕʿâ*, vv. 22, 23; *wĕnēdāʿâ*, v. 26, in pause), also alludes to the opening challenge. In vv. 26b-27 Yahweh contrasts the gods' past silence about the coming of Cyrus with his own announcement of it. Foreknowledge of an event implies control, and any being claiming divinity must possess demonstrable foreknowledge. In v. 28, Yahweh turns to address the court (first person singular forms, references to the defendants in the third person) to call attention to the gods' continuing silence. They not only were unable to foretell Cyrus's coming; they remain unable even now to answer a simple, obvious question posed to them by Yahweh.

In the concluding verse Yahweh again declares to the court that the defendants are useless. By speaking of the gods in the third person he suggests a verdict based on his foregoing argument.

3. *Symmetry*. The symmetry of the two parts is evident.

41.21 He calls the gods to trial	I Yahweh's initiative	*41.25* He called Cyrus to conquest
41.22-23 Challenge to the gods	II Yahweh's speech (ABB′A′ pattern)	*41.26-28* Evidence against the gods
41.24 Insulting challenge	III Conclusion: the gods are worthless	*41.29* Suggested verdict

Each part begins at Yahweh's bidding. In v. 21 he summons his opponents to trial; in v. 25 he recounts how he initiated Cyrus's march of conquest. The central speeches are both chiastic in structure, and build on the opening summons. Verses 22-23 challenge the gods to reveal either the past or the future in order to substantiate their claim to divinity; vv. 26-28 give evidence that, whereas the other gods were unable to foretell Cyrus's coming, Yahweh himself had done so. The conclusions of each part are parallel in wording and content, but different in force. Verse 24 is an insult addressed to the gods; v. 29 is a judgment proposed to the court.

3. *42.1-8*

Numerous connective techniques link 41.21-29 to 42.1-8. The words *hēn* and *rûaḥ* appear at structurally significant junctures: the end of 41.21-24 (*hēn*); the end of 41.25-29 (*hēn* and *rûaḥ*); the beginning of 42.1-4 (*hēn* and *rûaḥ*); and the beginning of 42.5-9 (*rûaḥ*). The verb *ntn* is a 'linked keyword'[7] (41.27; 42.1, 5, 6, 8). Finally, the sevenfold negation *'yn* in 41.24-29 is balanced by the sevenfold *lō'* in 42.2-4.

The passage comprises two divine speeches (vv. 1-4, 6-8) separated by the prophet's words in v. 5.

1. *Vv. 1-4.* The first verse of the first divine speech is usually treated as a quatrain. For example, the RSV reads:

42.1 Behold my servant, whom I uphold,
  my chosen, in whom my soul delights;
I have put my Spirit upon him,
  he will bring forth justice to the nations.

In such a reading the last two lines are held to be a sort of 'synthetic parallelism': the divine spirit given to the servant is related to his mission to bring forth justice. But this overlooks the discontinuity between v. 1abα (numerous first person morphemes) and vv. 1bβ-4 (all third person morphemes). The first element of the speech is to be read as a tercet (v. 1abα) recounting Yahweh's choice of the servant. The 'parallelism', if such is to be sought, is between the delight of Yahweh's *npš* and the gift of his *rûaḥ*.

The second element is a description of the servant's mission. It is usually held to extend through v. 3, leaving v. 4a as a concluding description of the servant's personal endurance in his mission. For example, the RSV reads for vv. 3-4:

42.3 a bruised reed he will not break,
  and a dimly burning wick he will not quench;
  he will faithfully bring forth justice.
42.4 He will not fail or be discouraged
  till he has established justice in the earth;
  and the coastlands wait for his law.

Such a reading ignores two rhetorical devices that connect the last line of v. 3 and the first of v. 4 closely with what precedes them: (i) a sevenfold repetition of *lō'* and (ii) two interlocked verbal chiasms:

mišpāṭ . . .yôṣî' (v. 1bβ) // *yôṣî' mišpāṭ* (v. 3b)

and

rāṣûṣ . . .*kēhâ* (v. 3a) // *yikheh* . . .*yārûṣ* (v. 4aα).

The effect of these chiasms is to make vv. 3b-4aα a kind of summary couplet for the whole of vv. 1bβ-4aα: the servant is to bring forth 'justice to rely on'; he will be indomitable in accomplishing his mission.

The third element is the final couplet (v. 4aβb). It contains two clauses in chiastic parallelism (ABCC′B′A′), governed by *'ad*. The clauses are usually read as dependent upon v. 4aα and indicative of the extent of the servant's personal endurance (see the RSV quoted above).

The break between v. 4aα and 4aβ allows another possibility. The description of the servant's mission (vv. 1bβ-4aα) is rhetorically unified by the interlocked verbal chiasms already mentioned. This unit may be read as suspending a syntactic connection between the opening tercet (v. labα) and the final couplet. Since the particle *'ad* can convey a nuance of purpose,[8] the final couplet thus expresses Yahweh's goal in choosing the servant and endowing him with the divine *rûaḥ*: 'I have placed my breath upon him . . . while he is establishing justice . . . '

2. *Vv. 6-8*. The second speech is composed of four tercets, the first and last of which begin with the phrase 'I am Yahweh'. This inclusion establishes the boundaries of the unit.

The first tercet (v. 6a) consists of short lines, and describes Yahweh's choice of his servant. The second and third tercets (vv. 6b-7) describe the servant's mission. The second, like the first, has short lines and is connected to it by a series of cohortatives (*wĕ'aḥzēq*, *wĕ'eṣṣorkā*, *wĕ'ettenkā*). It is connected to the longer lines of the third tercet by a series of purposive clauses beginning with *lĕ*—nominal phrases in v. 6b and infinitival phrases in v. 7. The three tercets form a single syntactic unit. The fourth tercet is a divine self-description. Its tone is polemic and expresses Yahweh's hostility to other gods.

3. *Symmetry*. On the 'surface' of the text, v. 5 acts as an introduction to the second divine speech. But on a deeper level of symmetry, it can be seen as the final element in the first of two parallel units:

*42.1ab*α About the servant	I Yahweh proclaims that he has chosen his servant	*42.6* To the servant
*42.1b*β-4 *mišpāṭ*	II The servant's mission	*42.6b-7* Rescue
42.5 Praise of his majesty as creator	III Description of Yahweh	*42.8* His claim to exclusive glory and praise

Both units begin with an announcement of Yahweh's choice of a servant and continue with a description of the servant's mission. While vv. 6-7 are clearly addressed to the servant himself, vv. 1-4 are a presentation of the servant to an unspecified third party. Context suggests that the addressee is the court, to whom Yahweh was speaking in the preceding verses (41.28-29).

The final element in each unit focuses on Yahweh. Verse 5 is a description of the Creator by an unnamed speaker; the verse is most easily read as an intervention by the prophet in his own right. The verse marks, perhaps intentionally, the approximate midpoint of the unit 41.21–42.17. Verse 8, on the other hand, is a self-description by Yahweh that reveals his underlying motivation in calling for the trial in the first place: he refuses to share his divine glory with rival claimants. Each description of Yahweh introduces a new emotional element that will be developed more extensively in 42.9-17. The participial phrases of v. 5 are elements of the genre of the hymn of praise; the hostile tone of v. 8 portends a declaration of war.

4. *42.9-17*

The third section has only one verbal link to the second: the parallel pair 'glory'/'praise' (42.8) recurs in 42.12. A more substantive link is seen in the expansion of the two elements introduced in vv. 5, 8 into major units, the hymn of praise (vv. 10-12) and the declaration of a war of rescue (vv. 14-17).

The inner structure of this section is less clear than those of the preceding ones. The first step is to identify the individual units by means of stylistic and rhetorical indicators. The section begins with a short statement, presumably by Yahweh (v. 9). This is followed by the hymn of praise—or, more precisely, the first element of such a hymn, the invitation to the singers. The invitation is issued, presumably, by the prophet and is marked by an inclusion with the word 'his praise' (vv. 10-12). There follows a description, presumably still by the prophet, of Yahweh the warrior (v. 13); it is marked by an inclusion with the root *gbr* and an internal paronomasia (*yā'îr* / *yārîa'*). The next unit is Yahweh's declaration of war in three quatrains (vv. 14-16b). These four units are arranged in parallel sequences: two brief announcements about Yahweh's future deeds (vv. 9, 13), each followed by a longer speech (vv. 10-12, 14-16b). Verses 16c-17 form a conclusion to the whole passage.

1. *42.9-12*. The first part begins with Yahweh's announcement that, just as he has foretold his past actions, so now he is about to reveal his future deeds (v. 9). The verse thus acts as an introduction to what follows; as we shall see below, it also has a pivotal function in the whole passage we are considering.

The response to Yahweh's announcement is a summons on the part of the prophet to universal praise of Yahweh. The summons begins with a general invitation to 'the ends of the earth'; the three central couplets specify those invited as inhabitants of the sea, the desert, and the mountains.

2. *42.13-16b*. This part begins with an announcement by the prophet that Yahweh's future deed will be done in the persona of a warrior (v. 13).

The response to the prophet's announcement is a divine speech. In three quatrains Yahweh reveals that his past inaction was due to heroic self-restraint rather than to disinterest (v. 14), that he is about to destroy his enemies (v. 15), and that he will rescue prisoners (v. 16ab).

3. *Symmetry*. The whole section consists of two parallel parts, with Yahweh and the prophet exchanging speaking roles in each.

42.9	I	*42.13*
Yahweh announces that he is about to foretell and accomplish 'new things'	Prophetic announcement	The prophet announces that Yahweh is about to act as a triumphant warrior

42.10-12	II	*42.14-16*
The prophet invites the whole earth to praise Yahweh (sea-lands, desert, mountains)	Response to the announcement	Yahweh declares war on sea-lands and mountains, and rescue for prisoners

5. *Unity of the whole passage*

1. *Stylistic unity*

The three sections of the passage are alike in that each comprises two parallel parts. Beneath this symmetry lies a further regular alternation of long speech and short description, a pattern that establishes an overarching rhythm for the whole passage:

41.21-23	Yahweh's speech of challenge to the gods
41.24	Description: the gods, their deeds and worshippers
41.25-28	Yahweh's speech about the summoning of Cyrus
41.29	Description: the gods, their deeds and idols
42.1-4	Yahweh's speech about his servant
42.5	Description: Yahweh the creator
42.6-7	Yahweh's speech to his servant
42.8	Yahweh's self-description
42.10-12	Prophet's speech: invitation to praise
42.13	Description: Yahweh the warrior
42.14-16	Yahweh's declaration of war
42.17	Description: the worshippers and idols of the gods.

2. *Logical unity*

The logical unity of the passage springs from the opening verse. It is a court scene: 41.21 is the summons; 41.22-24 present the opening challenge; 41.25–42.17 constitute Yahweh's case for the prosecution, with two laudatory interventions by the prophet (42.5; 42.10-13).

1. *The summons (41.21)*. We have already seen that the vocabulary establishes the courtroom as the scene of the divine speech.

2. *The opening challenge (41.22-24)*. The careful rhetorical structure of the case for the prosecution is foreshadowed in the central elements of the opening challenge. In 41.22-23 Yahweh challenges the gods to

(1) explain the past:
(i) 'the first things (*hārīʾšōnôt*)—tell us what they were'
(ii) 'that we might consider them'

(iii) 'and that we might know their aftermath'

(2) foretell the future:

(i) 'or the coming things, make us hear them (*hašmîʿūnû*)'

(ii) 'tell us the things arriving later (*ʾāḥôr*)'

(iii) 'that we might know that you are gods (*ʾĕlōhîm ʾattem*)'.

After issuing the challenge, Yahweh proceeds to demonstrate that he himself can fulfill both requirements. He can explain the past (41.25–42.8); and he can foretell the future (42.9-16b).

3. *The past (41.25–42.8).* In three speeches Yahweh explains the past: he summoned Cyrus and indeed foretold that he would (41.25-29); he chose his servant (42.1-4); he commissioned his servant (42.6-8). Each of the three speeches, as it were, brings the figure closer to the court. At first Yahweh merely speaks about the summoning; in 42.1-4 he introduces Cyrus to the court as his servant and details his mission; and in 42.6-8 he commissions him in the presence of the court.[9] There is even a correspondence between these three moments and the three lines of the challenge:

(i) 'The first things—tell us what they were'
—Yahweh summoned his servant, and he arrived

(ii) 'That we [Yahweh and the court] might consider them'
—The servant is presented to the court

(iii) 'And . . . know their aftermath'
—The servant's mission of rescue is spelled out.

4. *The future (42.9-16b).* 42.9 is a turning point in the entire argument, and its wording recalls both parts of the opening challenge. Having presented the evidence of his control over the past ('the first things', *hārīʾšōnôt*, 42.9a; cf. 41.22b), Yahweh turns to announce (*ʾašmîaʿ*, 42.9b; cf. *hašmîʿūnû*, 41.22cβ) the future.

The prophet's speech (vv. 10-13) at this point has multiple effect. Verses 10-12 act as an interlude between Yahweh's explanation of the past and his foretelling of the future. Verse 13 turns attention to that future by a series of imperfect verbs (*yṣʾ . . . yʿyr . . . yryʿ . . . ytgbr*). And it links the future to the past by repeating a key verb from Yahweh's first speech about the past ('arouse', *yāʿîr*, 42.13; cf. *haʿîrôtî*, 41.25).

The three quatrains of Yahweh's final speech (vv. 14–16b) fulfill the second part of his challenge to the gods by spelling out his future deeds.

5. *The conclusion*. The conclusion is in two parts. Verse 16c is Yahweh's summation of the whole case he has presented. *haddĕbārîm* is a general term referring not solely to the future actions listed in vv. 14-16b, but to all the deeds, past and future, that Yahweh has entered as evidence in the trial. The verbs *'ăśîtīm* and *'ăzabtîm* likewise reflect the past/future organization of his case: his evidence shows (1) that he has done what he claims and (2) that he has not left off doing such things.

Verse 17 is best understood, not as a further element in Yahweh's argument, but as an observation of the effect of his case on the opposition. Its tone of insult to other gods recalls 41.24, 29. It does not speak of the gods or their deeds directly, but shows their worthlessness reflected in the disillusionment of the worshippers (cf. 41.24c) of idols (cf. 41.29c). Whereas in those verses the gods' worthlessness was part of Yahweh's challenge and claim, that worthlessness has now been demonstrated, to the embarrassment of their partisans. The worshippers' reactions to Yahweh's case for the prosecution are tantamount to conceding the trial. Verbal correspondences link this concluding verse with the second part of the opening challenge: *'āḥôr* (41.23aα; 42.17aα) and *'ĕlōhîm 'attem* (41.23aβ) . . . *'attem 'ĕlōhênû* (42.17bβ).

Conclusion

Isa 41.21–42.17 is coherent as a single trial scene, carefully crafted, wherein Yahweh challenges the claim of the gods to divinity and, by proving his own claim according to the terms of the same challenge, demonstrates the gods' worthlessness. The verbal, stylistic, and rhetorical organization of the passage does not indicate that preexistent elements have not been utilized. The freedom with which 'Deutero-Isaiah' shaped materials and *Gattungen* available to him has long been recognized. But it does indicate that the reworking of any such elements was very thorough. From a large number of disparate materials and forms, the poet created a product of great symmetry, precision and force.

NOTES

1. T. Mettinger, *A Farewell to the Servant Songs* (Lund: Gleerup, 1983) documents the history of the question.

2. Y. Kaufmann, *History of the Religion of Israel*, IV (New York: Ktav, 1977 [Hebr. original, Tel Aviv: Bialik Institute-Dvir, 1956]); J. Muilenburg, 'The Book of Isaiah, Chapters 40–66', *IB*, V (1956), pp. 381-773; M. Haran, 'The Literary Structure and Chronological Framework of the Prophecies in Is. XL–XLVIII', *VTSup* 9 (Leiden: Brill, 1963), pp. 127-55; P.-E. Bonnard, *Le Second Isaïe, son disciple et leurs éditeurs* (ÉBib; Paris: Gabalda, 1972); J. Goldingay, 'The Arrangement of Isaiah xli–xlv', *VT* 29 (1979), pp. 289-99.

3. Angled brackets indicate emendations of the consonantal text. Such emendations are discussed in the notes following the translation.

4. See the discussions in A. Schoors, 'Les choses antérieures et les choses nouvelles dans les oracles deutéro-isaïens', *ETL* 40 (1964), pp. 28-29, and Schoors, *I Am God Your Saviour* (VTSup, 24; Leiden: Brill, 1973), pp. 220-21.

5. Schoors, *I Am God Your Saviour*, p. 91.

6. Elsewhere the hiphil of *qrb* is used in the same sense (Num 27.5; Deut 1.17).

7. For the terminology, see H. Parunak, 'Transitional Techniques in the Bible', *JBL* 102 (1983), pp. 525-48.

8. P. Joüon, *Grammaire de l'hébreu biblique* (Rome: Biblical Institute Press, 1947), §113k.

9. This unitary reading of the passage argues strongly for identifying the servant of 42.1-4 and the addressee of 42.6-8 as Cyrus, despite the contextual arguments raised by Goldingay ('The Arrangement of Isaiah xli–xlv') and, following him, Mettinger (*A Farewell to the Servant Songs*).

6

THE USE OF INCLUSION IN HABAKKUK 3

Theodore Hiebert

Attempts to find a coherent literary structure in Habakkuk 3 have varied widely, from Albert Condamin's proposal in the last century that this poem was composed like a Greek chorale with strophes and antistrophes, to M. O'Connor's recent suggestion that this poem is composed of three staves which may be subdivided into batches.[1] In addition to specific literary studies such as these, most commentaries on Habakkuk have made explicit or implicit judgments on the structure of ch. 3. Yet in all of these treatments, no literary analysis of Habakkuk 3 has taken sufficient account of the use of inclusion as a structuring device. The intention of this investigation is to illustrate the fundamental manner in which inclusion functions to mark the discrete sections of Habakkuk 3 and to give shape to the poem as a whole.

Inclusion is a well-known stylistic technique in biblical poetry. Its presence has been noted, for example, in the Psalms, Isaiah, Jeremiah, the Song of Songs, Judges 5, and the Psalm of Jonah.[2] Also called cyclic, envelope, and ring composition, inclusion is a poetic device through which the poet effects closure by linking the beginning and end of a poem or of a section or subsection within the poem. It operates at many levels. In Habakkuk 3 inclusion is apparent in the repetition of themes and motifs, of key words and phrases, of syntactic patterns, of parallelistic verse structure, and of phonetic elements.

The text of Habakkuk 3 is set out here in the four stanzas which are indicated by the presence of inclusive features in the poem. The term stanza is used, not to designate divisions of the poem which are regular in length and structure, but simply as a convenient term for the distinct literary units within the poem. No satisfactory designation has yet been found for subsections within biblical poems.

Text and Translation

I

2	יהוה שמעתי שמעך	Yahweh, I heard the account of you,	
	יראתי יהוה פעלך	I am in awe, Yahweh, of your work.	
	בקרב שנים חיית[3]	Through the years you sustained life,	
	בקרב שנים תודע[4]	Through the years you made yourself known,	
	ברגז רחם תזכור	In turmoil you remembered to have compassion.	

II

3	אלוה מתימן יבוא	'Eloah from Teman came,	A
	קדוש[5] מהר פארן	The Holy One from Mount Paran.	
	כסה שמים הודו	His majesty covered heaven,	B
	תהלתו מלאה ארץ[6]	His praise filled earth,	
4	נגה[7] כאור הוה[8]	He shone like a destroying fire.	
	קרנים . . . [9]	Horns . . .	C
	ישמח ביום[10] עזה	He rejoiced in the day of his strength.	
5	לפניו ילך דבר	Before him marched Deber,	D
	יצא רשף לרגליו	Resheph advanced at his feet.	
6	עמד וינדד[11] ארץ	He stood and shook earth,	C′
	ראה ויתר גוים	He looked and startled nations.	
	יתפצצו הררי עד	Ancient mountains were shattered,	B′
	שחו גבעות עולם	Eternal hills collapsed,	
7	הליכות עולם לתחתאן[12]	Eternal orbits were destroyed.	
	אהלי כושן ירגזון	The tents of Kushan shook,	A′
	יריעות ארץ מדין[13]	The tent curtains of the land of Midian.	

III

8	הבנהרם[14] חרה יהוה	Against River did it burn, Yahweh,	
	הבנהרם[15] אפך	Against River, your anger,	
	אם בים עברתך	Against Sea, your rage;	

	כי תרכב על סוסיך מרכבת ישועתך[16]	When you mounted your horses, Your chariot of victory?
9	ערה תער[17] קשתך שבעת[18] מטי[19] אשפתך[20]	You laid bare your bow, You sated the shafts of your quiver.
10	נהרות תבקע ארץ ראוך יחילו הרים	Earth was split open with rivers, Mountains saw you and heaved.
	זרמו מים עבות[21] נתן תהום קולו	Clouds poured down water, Deep uttered its voice.
11	רום ידיהו נשא שמש ירח עמד זבלה[22]	Sun lifted its hands high, Moon stood in its princely station.
	לאור חציך יהלכו לנגה ברק חניתך	Brightly, your arrows darted, Brilliantly, your lightning spear.
12	בזעם תצעד ארץ באף תדוש גוים	In indignation you marched on earth, In anger you trampled nations.
13	יצאת לישע עמך לישע עם[23] משיחך	You advanced for the victory of your militia, For the victory of the militia of your anointed one.
	מחצת במת[24] רשע ערית[25] יסוד עד צואר	You struck the back of the wicked one, You laid him bare, tail-end to neck.
14	נקבת במטיך[26] ראש . . .[27]	You pierced with your shafts his head,
15	דרכת בים סוסיך בחמר[28] מים רבים	You trod on Sea with your horses, On the surge of Many Waters.

IV

16	שמעתי ותרגז בטני לקול צללו שפתי	I heard, and my stomach churned, At the account, my lips quivered.
	יבוא רקב בעצמי תחתי תרגז[29] אשרי[30]	Rottenness entered my bones, Beneath me my steps trembled.
	אאנח[31] ביום[32] צרה לעלות[33] עם[34] יגודן[35]	I groaned in the day of distress, When the militia which attacked went up.
17	תאנה[36] לא תפרח אין יבול בגפנים	The fig tree did not bud, No produce was on the vines.

	כחש[37] מעשה זית	The yield of the olive tree recoiled,	
	שדמות[38] לא עשה אכל	Terraces did not provide food.	
	גזר[39] ממכלא[40] צאן	The flock was cut off from the fold,	
	אין בקר ברפתים	No cattle were in the stalls.	
18	ואני ביהוה אעלוזה	As for me, in Yahweh let me rejoice,	
	אגילה באלהי ישעי	Let me be joyful in the God of my victory.	
19	יהוה ארני חילי	Yahweh, my lord, is my might,	
	ישם רגלי כאילות	He made my feet like the does',	
	על במותי[41] ידרכני	On backs he made me tread.	

The use of inclusion in Habakkuk 3 indicates the presence of four stanzas: introductory and concluding units (Stanza I, v. 2; Stanza IV, vv. 16-19) which provide a literary framework for the theophany in vv. 3-15, which is itself composed of two distinct units (Stanza II, vv. 3-7; Stanza III, vv. 8-15). Before the inclusive structures which link the introductory and concluding stanzas to provide a literary framework for the poem as a whole are examined, the two stanzas which make up the body of the poem, the theophany, will be analyzed. Although the theophany is a continuous narrative, each of its two stanzas possesses its own literary integrity.

Stanza II (vv. 3-7)

The central literary feature of Stanza II is its inclusive structure. Inclusion here operates, not only to link the extremities of the stanza with one another, but also to link the material just within these opening and closing boundaries, so that a series of inclusive circles is constructed within the stanza. For this use of inclusion within multiple levels I have employed the term *concentric structure*. This structure has been illustrated in the text above by the use of capital letters to identify corresponding verse units. The three opening verse units (ABC) describe the appearance of God, while the three closing verse units (C′B′A′) describe the response to God's appearance. The description of the response is carefully matched through concentric structure to the description of the appearance. In order to illustrate the care with which this overall structure has been achieved, corresponding verse units will be discussed together rather than in the order in which they appear in the stanza.

3	אלוה מתימן יבוא	'Eloah from Teman came,	A
	קדוש מהר פארן	The Holy One from Mount Paran.	

7	אהלי כושן ירגזון	The tents of Kushan shook,	A′
	יריעות ארץ מדין	The tent curtains of the land of Midian.	

The opening and closing bicola[42] of Stanza II (A, A′) correspond to one another at almost every possible level. On the levels of grammar and parallelistic verse structure they are nearly identical. The first colon of each bicolon opens with the subject which is followed by a geopolitical term and the verb (prefix form: preterite) which serves both lines of the bicolon. The second colon opens with a repetition of the subject expressed by a parallel term which is followed by a ballast variant of the geopolitical term in the first colon. The only significant difference is the appearance of the geopolitical terms of bicolon A in prepositional phrases and those of bicolon A′ in construct chains.

In addition to these similarities should be noted the phonetic parallels between these bicola, particularly prominent between the geopolitical terms *têmān*//*har pā'rān* and *kûšān*//*'ereṣ midyān*. The repetition of *-ān* is particularly apparent. And when the probable historical pronounciation of these terms—*tayman*//*harr pa'ran*, *kūšan*//*'arṣ madyan*—is taken into account, two other types of phonetic correspondence become clear: the identical stress pattern and syllable length of these terms, and the assonance produced by the repetition of 'a' in all but two syllables. Also to be noted is the phonetic similarity between the opening terms in each bicolon, *'ĕlôah* and *'ohŏlê*.

Finally, the content of these two bicola is carefully matched to the appearance/response contrast upon which Stanza II is constructed. The location of the theophany, expressed nowhere else in the poem, is the focus of both of these bicola. In bicolon A, God leaves his sanctuary, Teman/Mount Paran. In bicolon A′, the inhabitants of this area, Kushan/Midian, tremble in awe at his appearance.[43]

3	כסה שמים הודו	His majesty covered heaven,	B
	תהלתו מלאה ארץ	His praise filled earth,	
4	נגה כאור הוה	He shone like a destroying fire.	

6	יתפצצו הררי עד	Ancient mountains were shattered,	B′
	שחו גבעות עולם	Eternal hills collapsed,	
7	הליכות עולם לתחתאן	Eternal orbits were destroyed.	

Verse units B and B′ which form a concentric circle within the opening and closing bicola (A, A′) show many similarities as well. They are both tricola in which chiasm is employed as a structuring device. In tricolon B *hwdw* and *thltw* are arranged chiastically, as are *ksh šmym* and *ml'h 'rṣ*. A chiastic patterning is apparent also in the final long *a* (represented by *h*) of *ksh*/*ml'h*/*hwh*. In tricolon B′ the final colon is related chiastically to the straight order parallelism of the first two cola: *ytpṣṣw*/*šḥw* and *tḥt'n* are arranged chiastically, as are *hrry ʿd*/*gbʿwt ʿwlm* and *hlykwt ʿwlm*. In both tricola the final line represents the 'unique' colon. And in both tricola the subject of the verbs (with one exception, *ngh*, a reconstruction) is not God, but a common noun. These tricola also reflect the appearance/response contrast of Stanza II. Whereas tricolon B describes God's majestic and splendorous appearance in heaven and on earth, tricolon B′ describes the tumultuous response on earth and in heaven, in concentric structure.

4	קרנים . . .	Horns . . .	C
	ישמח ביום עזה	He rejoiced in the day of his strength.	
6	עמד וינדד ארץ	He stood and shook earth,	C′
	ראה ויתר גוים	He looked and startled nations.	

Bicola C and C′ may not be compared as extensively, due to the problematic text of v. 4, but some observations may be made on the basis of the partial reconstruction which has been proposed. Three of the four cola in these verse units begin with verbs of which God is the subject. These bicola also reflect the appearance/response contrast. Bicolon C describes the strength of God (*qrnym*, *ʿzh*), and bicolon C′ describes the result of his strength: earth and nations are shaken by God's appearance.

5	לפניו ילך דבר	Before him marched Deber,	D
	יצא רשף לרגליו	Resheph advanced at his feet.	

At the heart of the concentric construction of Stanza II lies bicolon D, a description of God's entourage marching out before and behind. It is fashioned with chiasm, *lpnyw* and *lrglyw* being positioned chiastically together with *ylk dbr* and *yṣ' ršp*. Though it represents a unique image within the stanza, this bicolon has links to preceding and succeeding sections of Stanza II. The verbs *ylk* and *yṣ'* and the position of *dbr* and *ršp* in relation to *'lwh* recall the opening bicolon of Stanza II describing God's march from his sanctuary. And the prepositional phrases *lpnyw* and *lrglyw* appear to be related in chiastic order to the initial verbs in the two cola which immediately follow (*ʿmd*//*r'h*).

In addition to the unifying concentric construction which marks off Stanza II as a distinct unit within the poem, several other literary features indicate the distinctive character of this stanza. First, the perspective is not the first person perspective of the poet in Stanza I, which reappears again in Stanza IV. First person verbs and suffixes are absent,[44] and the focus is entirely on God's activity and the general response to it. Second, God is not addressed in the second person as he is in Stanzas I and III but is referred to entirely in the third person. Third, the title of God is *'lwh/qdš*, whereas *yhwh* is used in the other stanzas.

Stanza III (vv. 8-15)

Stanza III continues the narrative of God's theophany, but the appearance of a new inclusive structure distinguishes this section of the theophany from that which precedes it. In order to bring out the use of inclusion to structure this stanza, the opening and closing sections of Stanza III (vv. 8-9a, 13b-15) will be dealt with first; then the inner section (vv. 9b-13a) will be examined.

Stanza III opens with a description of the preparation of the divine warrior for battle. He turns his anger against his foe (v. 8a), mounts his chariot (v. 8b), and makes ready his weapons (v. 9a). This description is unified stylistically by the vocative *yhwh*, which concludes the first colon, and by the 2ms suffixes which conclude the six following cola. This phonetic pattern is enhanced by additional alliteration in the final terms of these cola: the repetition of gutturals and labials in *'pk//'brtk* and of *š*, *t*, and gutturals in *yš'tk/qštk// 'šptk*.

Whereas Stanza III opens with a description of the preparation of the divine warrior for battle, it concludes with a description of the battle itself. The divine warrior attacks his foe (vv. 13b-14) and treads on it in triumph (v. 15). The description of the battle is unified stylistically by the series of 2ms perfect verbs which begin each colon but the last, a colon intended as the climax for the description of the battle.

These opening and concluding sections of Stanza III contain many prominent correspondences which serve to produce an inclusion unifying the stanza as a whole. The relationship of the content of these sections—the preparation for battle and the battle itself—has already been noted. This thematic association is supported by numerous literary connections. These can be most clearly seen by an examination of the corresponding verse units within these sections of

Stanza III which exhibit the same kind of concentric structure present in Stanza II.

8	הבנהרם חרה יהוה	Against River did it burn, Yahweh,
	הבנהרם אפך	Against River, your anger,
	אם בים עברתך	Against Sea, your rage;
	כי תרכב על סוסיך	When you mounted your horses,
	מרכבת ישועתך	Your chariot of victory?
15	דרכת בים סוסיך	You trod on Sea with your horses,
	בחמר מים רבים	On the surge of Many Waters.

Foremost among the literary connections between these verses is the identification of the enemy in the opening cola (v. 8a) and in the concluding cola (v. 15) of Stanza III. The alternate titles of the enemy are arranged in a concentric pattern: *nhr-m//ym* (v. 8a), *ym// mym rbym* (v. 15). The terms *nhr-m* and *mym rbym* are in inclusive position, making up the first and last words of the stanza as a whole.

Other literary connections linking the opening and concluding sections of Stanza III occur in the description of the divine warrior. Yahweh begins the battle by mounting his horse-drawn chariot (*swsyk//mrkbt yšʿtk*, v. 8b) and ends the battle by trampling Sea with his horses (*swsyk*, v. 15). The phonetic and semantic similarities between the verbs mount (*trkb*, v. 8b) and trample (*drkt*, v. 15) and the semantic similarity between the prepositions *ʿl* and *b* related to these verbs further link these two acts with one another. Finally, the mention of Yahweh's victory at the beginning of the stanza (v. 8b) clearly anticipates the final victory scene which concludes Stanza III (v. 15).

9	ערה תער קשתך	You laid bare your bow,
	שבעת מטי אשפתך	You sated the shafts of your quiver.
13	מחצת במת רשע	You struck the back of the wicked one,
	ערית יסוד עד צואר	You laid him bare, tail-end to neck.
14	נקבת במטיך ראש	You pierced with your shafts his head,
	...	...

Further connections can be seen between the final verse of the opening section (v. 9a) and the initial verse units of the concluding section (vv. 13b-14) of Stanza III. The reference to Yahweh's baring his bow (*ʿrh tʿr*, v. 9a) is recalled when Yahweh lays his enemy bare (*'ryt*, v. 13b) in the actual battle. And the reference to Yahweh's shafts (*mṭy-*, v. 9a) is recalled when Yahweh pierces his enemy's head with these shafts (*mṭy-*, v. 14a). These correspondences between v. 9a and vv. 13b-14, together with those between vv. 8 and 15, reveal a concentric construction including various levels of inclusion which functions to set off Stanza III as a distinct unit within the poem.

The medial section of Stanza III (vv. 9b-13a) reflects and develops themes and motifs from the opening and closing sections of the stanza. The first verses of this medial section (vv. 9b-11a) picture the response to the divine warrior's preparation for battle described in the opening of Stanza III.

9	נהרות תבקע ארץ	Earth was split open with rivers,
10	ראוך יחילו הרים	Mountains saw you and heaved.
	זרמו מים עבות	Clouds poured down water,
	נתן תהום קולו	Deep uttered its voice.
11	רום ידיהו נשא שמש	Sun lifted its hands high,
	ירח עמד זבלה	Moon stood in its princely station.

Earth and mountains crack and heave (vv. 9b-10a), waters above and below burst out (v. 10a-b), and sun and moon stand in the heavens (vv. 10b-11a). Particularly prominent in these verses is the 'water' motif, which is found in three of the six cola and which reflects the titles of God's enemy in the opening and closing sections of Stanza III. The term *nhrwt* (v. 9b) recalls *nhr-m* (v. 8a); *mym* (v. 10a) anticipates *mym rbym* (v. 15); and *thwm* (v. 10b) may echo *ym* in vv. 8a and 15. The agitation of the cosmic waters here is a response to the preparation of the divine warrior for battle at the beginning of Stanza III as well as a foreshadowing of the actual battle with the water monster at the conclusion of Stanza III.

The final verses of the medial section of Stanza III (vv. 11b-13a) picture the charge of the divine warrior into battle, the battle described in the concluding section of Stanza III.

11	לאור חציך יהלכו	Brightly, your arrows darted,
	לנגה ברק חניתך	Brilliantly, your lightning spear.
12	בזעם תצעד ארץ	In indignation you marched on earth,
	באף תדוש גוים	In anger you trampled nations.
13	יצאת לישע עמך	You advanced for the victory of your militia,
	לישע עם משיחך	For the victory of the militia of your anointed one.

His weapons fly (v. 11b) as he advances, trampling earth and nations (v. 12), to gain the victory for his people (v. 13a). In all three bicola, prepositions are repeated in parallel cola: *l* in the first and third, *b* in the second. The mention of Yahweh's anger in these verses (*zʿm*//*ʾp*, v. 12) recalls the reference to it in the opening section of Stanza III (*ʾpk*//*ʿbrtk*, v. 8a). The mention of victory (*yšʿ*, v. 13a) recalls its earlier use as well (v. 8b). The reference to Yahweh's weapons here (v. 11b) recalls the mention of them at the beginning of Stanza III (v. 9a) and anticipates mention of them again at the conclusion of the stanza (v. 14a). Finally, the description of Yahweh's charge with the use of the verbs *tṣʿd*//*tdwš* (v. 12) anticipates Yahweh's trampling on his enemy (*drkt*, v. 15) at the conclusion of the stanza.

Stanza III, like Stanza II, is thus marked off by the use of inclusion, a technique which in this case links the first and last sections of the stanza and shapes the character of the medial section. In addition to this structural pattern, several other literary features mark off Stanza III as a distinct unit. The title for God is *yhwh*, rather than *ʾlwh*/*qdš* as in Stanza II. Yahweh is addressed directly in the second person, rather than indirectly in the third person as in Stanzas II and IV. A number of motifs which are dominant in Stanza III—divine anger and weaponry, the cosmic waters—are absent elsewhere in the poem.

Stanzas I (v. 2) and IV (vv. 16-19)

Stanzas I and IV are linked to one another by the use of inclusion to provide a literary framework for the theophany in Stanzas II and III and to effect closure in the poem as a whole. The use of inclusion in the opening and closing stanzas of Habakkuk 3 can best be illustrated by comparing Stanza I with individual sections of Stanza IV. Each of these subsections of Stanza IV was designed to develop specific themes introduced succinctly in Stanza I.

I

2	יהוה שמעתי שמעך	Yahweh, I heard the account of you,
	יראתי יהוה פעלך	I am in awe, Yahweh, of your work.
	בקרב שנים חיית	Through the years you sustained life,
	בקרב שנים תודע	Through the years you made yourself known,
	ברגז רחם תזכור	In turmoil you remembered to have compassion.

IV

16	שמעתי ותרגז בטני	I heard, and my stomach churned,
	לקול צללו שפתי	At the account, my lips quivered.
	יבוא רקב בעצמי	Rottenness entered my bones,
	תחתי תרגז אשרי	Beneath me my steps trembled.
	אאנח ביום צרה	I groaned in the day of distress,
	לעלות עם יגודן	When the militia which attacked went up.
17	תאנה לא תפרח	The fig tree did not bud,
	אין יבול בגפנים	No produce was on the vines.
	כחש מעשה זית	The yield of the olive tree recoiled,
	שדמות לא עשה אכל	Terraces did not provide food.
	גזר ממכלא צאן	The flock was cut off from the fold,
	אין בקר ברפתים	No cattle were in the stalls.

The motif of hearing opens both Stanzas I and IV. The verb *šm‘ty* which opens Stanza I also, and in the same form, opens Stanza IV. The object of the hearing, the account about Yahweh, is referred to in Stanza I by the cognate accusative of *šm‘ty*, *šm‘*, and in Stanza IV by the term parallel to *šm‘ty*, *qwl*. Both *šm‘* and *qwl* should be translated ‘account’.

The motif of hearing is followed immediately in both stanzas by the motif of fear. In the opening bicolon of Stanza I, the verb *yr’ty* is in parallel relationship to *šm‘ty*. The response of the poet to hearing the account is fear. The term *rgz* in the concluding colon of Stanza I picks up this motif by referring to the general agitation and trembling which accompany God’s appearance (*twd‘*, v. 2a).

In Stanza IV, the motif of fear introduced in Stanza I is developed at length. The first three bicola of Stanza IV (v. 16) describe in vivid detail the terror of the poet at hearing the account and thus represent an extended amplification of the verb *yr’ty* from Stanza I. In these initial bicola the root *rgz*, introduced at the conclusion of Stanza I, is used again twice. The next three bicola of Stanza IV (v. 17) describe in detail the terror in the world around the poet: plant and animal life are devastated together with the poet. This description of turmoil among all living things represents an amplification of the general use of the term *rgz* in Stanza I. All of nature is shaken by the theophany of the divine warrior.

I

2	יהוה שמעתי שמעך	Yahweh, I heard the account of you,
	יראתי יהוה פעלך	I am in awe, Yahweh, of your work.
	בקרב שנים חיית	Through the years you sustained life.
	בקרב שנים תודע	Through the years you made yourself known,
	ברגז רחם תזכור	In turmoil you remembered to have compassion.

IV

18	ואני ביהוה אעלוזה	As for me, in Yahweh let me rejoice,
	אגילה באלהי ישעי	Let me be joyful in the God of my victory.
19	יהוה ארני חילי	Yahweh, my lord, is my might,
	ישם רגלי כאילות	He made my feet like the does',
	על במותי ידרכני	On backs he made me tread.

The third motif prominent in Stanzas I and IV is fascination. The term is taken from Rudolf Otto, who has used it to describe the attraction felt by one who experiences the immediacy of the divine presence because of a sense of its essentially merciful character.[45] The poet, terrified by the power of divine presence, also recognizes its gracious intent. This recognition is expressed in Stanza I by the verb *ḥyyt* (v. 2a) and the verbal phrase *rḥm tzkwr* (v. 2b; note the repetition of *ḥ* and *t* in these terms and their inclusive position in the tricolon in which they occur). The poet recalls that when God appeared (*twd*ʿ) he sustained life and remembered to show compassion.

As was the case with the motif of fear, the motif of fascination succinctly introduced in Stanza I, is developed at greater length in Stanza IV. This development is accomplished in the bicolon and tricolon which conclude Stanza IV (vv. 18-19), thus providing the poem as a whole, as the theophany within it, with a triumphant climax. The sustenance of life mentioned in Stanza I is here identified with victory in battle. The poet applauds *yhwh*, the source of his military might (*ḥyly*), for giving him sure footing in battle and causing him to tread in triumph on the backs of his foes. On account of this compassionate act, the poet rejoices in the God of his victory.

Several literary features other than inclusion which link Stanzas I and IV deserve mention. One is the first person perspective in which both are composed. First person verbal forms, pronouns, and pronominal suffixes predominate. The focus is on the poet and his situation. This contrasts with the theophany in vv. 3-15 where first person forms are absent and where second and third person verbal forms and pronominal suffixes predominate. In this section of the poem the focus is on God and his acts.

Another literary feature linking Stanzas I and IV is the introduction of the poem with a bicolon and a tricolon in Stanza I and the conclusion of the poem with this same sequence at the end of Stanza IV. A third feature is the use of the divine name. It is employed twice at the beginning of Stanza I and twice again at the conclusion of Stanza IV. It is the initial word of the first verse of the poem and of the last verse. Elsewhere the name only occurs in the opening cola of Stanzas III and II (with the alternate forms *'lwh/qdš*).

Although Stanza IV is constructed as a development of Stanza I and achieves its coherence in this process, it does at the same time contain its own inclusive structure which must not be overlooked. Stanza IV opens with an expression of terror and an image of trembling steps (v. 16). It concludes with an expression of joy and an image of steady steps (vv. 18-19). An inclusive pattern is thus produced, uniting Stanza IV and providing a literary link between the contrasting aspects of theophany, its awe-fulness and graciousness, also linked within the concluding colon of Stanza I: *brgz rḥm tzkwr*.

The coherent literary structure of Habakkuk 3, as has been shown in the preceding analysis, derives fundamentally from the use of inclusion. Very often inclusion operates, not only as a single circle uniting the beginning and end of a literary unit, but as a series of concentric circles carefully fashioned to produce a concentric structure in which many layers of inclusion may be found. This inclusive structure operates at all levels of the poem. It links Stanzas I and IV to provide a literary framework for the poem as a whole. It also links beginnings and endings of stanzas, in particular Stanzas II and III, to mark them off as distinct units within the poem as a whole.

Implications for Interpretation

Though the major intent of this analysis is to provide literary grounds for the four stanza structure of Habakkuk 3 which has been described above, a word may be in order about some of the more important implications this literary structure has for the interpretation of the poem. The design of the theophany at the heart of the poem, as well as its literary framework in Stanzas I and IV, provide exegetical clues to the text.

The most striking characteristic of the theophany (vv. 3-15) is its two-part structure. In the first stanza (II, vv. 3-7) the divine warrior leaves his mountain sanctuary and marches to battle, in response to which nature convulses. In the second stanza (III, vv. 8-15) the divine warrior attacks and subdues his foe. This two-part structure conforms closely to one segment of an archaic mythic pattern which has been recognized by Frank Cross in Ugaritic and Hebrew poetry.[46]

This ancient pattern is made up of two segments or genres within which the theophany of the storm god is described in formulaic fashion. In the genre which comprises the first segment of this pattern, the storm god marches out from his mountain to do battle with Sea, in response to which nature is devastated. In the genre which comprises the second segment of this pattern, the storm god returns victoriously from the battle to take up kingship on his mountain, in response to which nature is renewed.

Of these two genres within the old mythic pattern, the theophany of Habakkuk 3 clearly fits the first. The divine warrior marches out (Stanza II) to battle Sea (Stanza III). In response to the march and the attack itself the cosmos collapses. The correspondence between the two stanza theophany of Habakkuk 3 and the initial segment within the ancient mythic pattern suggests that the Israelite poet based the structure of this theophany on the traditional mythic pattern used to describe the conquest of Sea by the god of the storm. The selection of a literary pattern associated with cosmic conflict indicates that the intention of the theophany is not narrowly historical. The poet seeks rather to place the earthly exploits of Yahweh into the context of the primordial conquest of chaos. The victory of the storm god celebrated in Habakkuk 3 is not only the victory of Israel's divine warrior over Israel's historical enemies but also, and fundamentally, the victory of Yahweh over Sea, the ancient dragon of chaos.

The fact that the theophany in Habakkuk 3 reflects only one of the two parts of the larger mythic pattern does not in any way negate the validity of the connection between the two. Brief biblical theophanies tend to fall into types representing either the initial or final segments of the entire mythic pattern. Theophanies, like Habakkuk 3, which describe the divine warrior's march into battle are found in Israel's oldest hymns: Exod 15.1-18; Judg 5.4-5, 19-21; the framework of Deuteronomy 33 (vv. 2-5, 26-29); and Pss 18.8-16; 68.8-9 (= Judg 5.4-5); 77.16-20; and 114.1-8. Examples of theophanies reflecting the second element of the larger pattern, the enthronement of the victorious divine warrior, are Psalms 29, 89.6-19, and a number of the enthronement psalms (e.g. 97, 98).[47]

As the literary structure of the theophany is instructive for the interpretation of Habakkuk 3, so is the literary structure of Stanzas I and IV which provide a framework for the theophany. As has been noted, the motifs of hearing, fear, and salvation are prominent in these stanzas and serve to link them together to provide an inclusion for the poem as a whole and a setting within which the theophany is to be understood.

The first of these motifs, that of hearing, indicates that the theophany (vv. 3-15) has been received by the poet through the medium of the spoken word. The theophany is an account (*šm'*, *qwl*) which the poet has heard (*šm'ty*). The source of the account is human rather than divine, as is indicated by the fact that the divine subject of the account does not address the poet in the first person but is addressed by the narrator in the second and third persons. The poet thus locates himself within the milieu of recital. Habakkuk 3 represents the preservation and passing down of sacred traditions. Having heard the account of God's deeds, the poet takes his place among those preserving these traditions by his re-citation of these events. The poem is thus not the result of a private, prophetic audition or vision in the heavenly council, as it is commonly understood, but a recitation of the *magnalia dei* from Israel's shared experience.

The other two motifs which link Stanzas I and IV, fear and fascination, are to be taken together as representing the response to the recitation of the theophany. They are woven closely together in Stanza I, as is illustrated by the sequence 'I am in awe / you sustained life / In turmoil you remembered to have compassion', and they are developed independently in greater detail in Stanza IV. The way in which these emotions are combined with one another suggests that they are to be understood as aspects of a single experience, the confrontation with God through the account of his theophany.

The contrasting emotions of terror at God's appearance and rapture at God's salvation are conventional elements in the human response to theophany. Fear before the awful power of God and exultation for the redemptive effect of his appearance are combined in Israel's oldest theophanies, in those associated with the royal cult, in the epic traditions which record the Sinai theophany, and in the eschatological divine warrior hymns of the postexilic era.[48] Terror is the natural reaction to the immediate presence of God, a presence so overwhelming that it could be fatal to those experiencing it.[49] And exultation is the expected response to the saving effects of this awful power.

Rudolf Otto has called attention to these contrasting emotions as typical elements in the encounter with the holy. The experience of the *mysterium tremendum* is characterized by what appear to be contradictory feelings: a deep dread at the tremendous mystery and power of the holy, and a rapture at the gracious intent of the deity. 'The qualitative *content* of the numinous experience, to which "the mysterious" stands as *form*', writes Otto, 'is in one of its aspects the element of daunting "awefulness" and "majesty" . . . but it is clear that it has at the same time another aspect, in which it shows itself as something uniquely attractive and *fascinating*. These two qualities, the daunting and the fascinating, now combine in a strange harmony of contrasts, and the resultant dual character of the numinous consciousness . . . is at once the strangest and most noteworthy phenomenon in the whole history of religion.'[50]

My own judgment about Habakkuk 3, which has been defended elsewhere in more detail than is possible here, is that the poem was composed in the premonarchic era as a recitation of the victory of the divine warrior over cosmic and earthly enemies.[51] The original text (as nearly as it can be reconstructed), the archaic linguistic features, prosodic style, historical allusions, and the use of mythological motifs all point in this direction. After being preserved for some time in a collection of psalms (the origin of the musical notations), the old hymn was eventually reinterpreted as a prophecy of God's eschatological victory and was added to the Habakkuk corpus by postexilic editors who were caught up in the apocalyptic fervor of this era. Once included in the corpus of Habakkuk, the hymn was understood as a prophetic vision described within the prophet's prayer for God's salvation.

The aim here has been to illustrate that in its original form Habakkuk 3 was composed as a theophany in two stanzas (II, III) enclosed within a literary framework (Stanzas I, IV), and that the primary stylistic device by which this structure was achieved was inclusion. Inclusion was employed to link the introduction and conclusion of the poem (Stanzas I, IV) as well as the beginnings and endings of the stanzas (II, III) within this framework. It was often employed in multiple levels to produce concentric structures, and it involved every aspect of literary structure: phonemes, syntax, verse structure, key words and phrases, themes and motifs. Inclusion is so pervasive and fundamental in Habakkuk 3 that any attempt to follow the movement of the poet's thought within this composition must take it into serious consideration.

NOTES

1. I am grateful to M. O'Connor for the extensive catalogue of the types of lines and variety of tropes employed in Hebrew verse structure (*Hebrew Verse Structure* [Winona Lake, Indiana: Eisenbrauns, 1980]). My analysis of Habakkuk 3 differs from his primarily because I have given more weight in my examination of gross structure to literary devices which transcend verse types. These are devices such as inclusion, repetition of key words, change in perspective indicated by shifts in verb forms and suffixes, and such patterning devices as series of similar verb forms or identical suffixes. I have also taken into greater consideration the content. I agree with O'Connor that literary variation creates the boundaries of larger units within Hebrew poems, but I am not yet convinced that the variation which marks larger units is primarily of the tropological and typological kind that O'Connor proposes. The attempt to find Greek literary forms in Hebrew poetry such as that of A. Condamin ('La forme chorale du ch. III d'Habacuc', *RB* 8 [1899], pp. 133-40) is no longer in fashion and properly so. Some of the variety among literary judgments about Habakkuk 3 can be seen in the analyses of B. Duhm (*Das Buch Habakuk* [Tübingen: J.C.B. Mohr, 1906], pp. 71-101), who divides the poem into twelve strophes with a liturgical conclusion, F.T. Kelley ('The Strophic Structure of Habakkuk', *AJSL* 18 [1901-2], pp. 113-19), who sees within the poem eight strophes with a liturgical addition, and D.H. Bévenot ('Le Cantique d'Habacuc', *RB* 42 [1933], pp. 521-25), who divides the poem into three main strophes with an introduction to the whole and three refrains falling outside the strophes themselves. A recent trend has been to divide the poem into four parts, which coincide in most cases with the four stanzas described in this literary analysis, but primarily on the basis of content with no serious literary defense (e.g. W.F. Albright, 'The Psalm of Habakkuk', in *Studies in Old Testament Prophecy* [ed. H.H. Rowley; Edinburgh: T. & T. Clark, 1950], pp. 8-18; J.H. Eaton, *Obadiah, Nahum, Habakkuk and Zephaniah* [London: SCM, 1961], pp. 108-18; W. Rudolph,

Micha, Nahum, Habakuk, Zephanja [KAT, XIII/3; Gütersloh: Gerd Mohn, 1975], pp. 241-48.

2. M. Dahood (*Psalms* [3 vols.; Garden City, N.Y.: Doubleday, 1966-1970]) and L.J. Liebreich ('Psalms 34 and 145 in Light of Their Key Words', *HUCA* 27 [1956], pp. 181-92) have discussed the use of inclusion in the Psalms; L.J. Liebreich ('The Compilation of the Book of Isaiah', *JQR* 46 [1956], pp. 259-77; 47 [1956], pp. 114-38) in Isaiah; J.R. Lundbom (*Jeremiah: A Study of Ancient Hebrew Rhetoric* [Missoula: Scholars, 1975]) in Jeremiah; F. Landsberger ('Poetic Units Within the Song of Songs', *JBL* 73 [1954], pp. 203-16, esp. pp. 213-14) in the Song of Songs; M. Coogan ('A Structural and Literary Analysis of the Song of Deborah', *CBQ* 40 [1978], pp. 151-58) in Judges 5; and F.M. Cross ('Studies in the Structure of Hebrew Verse: The Prosody of the Psalm of Jonah', in *The Quest for the Kingdom of God* [ed. H.B. Huffmon, F.A. Spina, and A.R.W. Green; Winona Lake, Indiana: Eisenbrauns, 1983], pp. 159-67) in the Psalm of Jonah. Compare the comments on inclusion of R.G. Moulton (*The Literary Criticism of the Bible* [Boston: Heath, 1899]) in the last century.

3. Read *ḥiyyîtā*, the Piel perfect 2ms form of *ḥyh*. The MT is problematic because the pronominal suffix lacks an antecedent. The G *Vorlage*, *ḥywt*, likely reflects a corruption of this original, arising from the common graphic confusion of *waw* and *yod*. The readings proposed here are defended in more detail in *God of My Victory: The Ancient Hymn in Habakkuk 3* (Atlanta: Scholars, 1986).

4. Read with the G the Niphal with reflexive meaning. This verb and the other verbs in the prefix conjugation in the remainder of the poem are to be understood as old preterite forms rather than imperfect forms, and they should be translated in the simple past tense. The best explanation for the alternation of suffix and prefix conjugations of the verb in Habakkuk 3 is the archaic practice of using these forms interchangeably to express past narrative. See D.A. Robertson, *Linguistic Evidence for Dating Early Hebrew Poetry* (Missoula: Society of Biblical Literature, 1972), pp. 7-55, esp. pp. 33-34.

5. Conjunctions which introduce cola have been omitted as prosaic accretions (except in v. 18). The secondary status of conjunctions in the MT is often indicated by their absence in the versions (vv. 4a, 6a, 16a, 19a) and by the lack of any consecutive function (here and v. 19a).

6. Articles, like conjunctions, are suspect in poetry as prosaic additions. In a number of instances (vv. 8, 18) the Masoretes have introduced them into Habakkuk 3, as their vowel points indicate, where the versions lack them. In this case, the article appears to be an unnecessary and secondary addition since the term parallel to *'rṣ*, *šmym*, lacks one and since elsewhere (vv. 6, 12) *'rṣ* is used without the article.

7. Read with W.R. Arnold ('The Interpretation of קרנים מידו לו, Hab 3.4', *AJSL* 21 [1905], p. 168) and W.A. Irwin ('The Psalm of Habakkuk', *JNES* 1

[1942], p. 20) the qal perfect 3ms of *ngh*.

8. Read *hawwâ*, 'destruction', as the *nomen rectum* of *'ôr*, 'fire'; thus, 'like a destroying fire' (as suggested to me by F.M. Cross). Compare Ps 91.3: *dbr hwh*, 'the destroying Deber/Pestilence'.

9. Attempts to reconstruct and interpret this colon have been unsuccessful, including those which construe *qrnym* as 'rays of light'. Because of its parallel relationship with *'zh*, *qrnym* must mean 'horns', a symbol of divine power (cf. Ps 18.3; *CTA* 10.2.21; 18.4.10; *Ugaritica* 5.1.1.20).

10. Read with W.F. Albright, *yśmḥ bywm* ('The Psalm of Habakkuk', pp. 11, 14), from which the MT developed through several simple errors: the misdivision of the first two words and the common graphic confusions of *waw* and *yod*, and *mem* and *nun* (written similarly in the seventh century BCE).

11. Read the polel of *nwd* on the basis of the LXX *esaleuthē*, a better parallel than *ymdd* for *ytr* in the following colon. The MT represents another example of the graphic confusion of *mem* and *nun*.

12. Problems with sense, grammar, and poetic style together with disagreement among the versions indicate the corrupt character of vv. 6b and 7a. The best reconstruction is that of W.F. Albright ('The Psalm of Habakkuk', pp. 11, 14-15) who reads the qal passive 3fp of *ḫt'* (**tuḫta'na*), 'crush, ruin, vanquish', preceded by the emphatic *lamed*. Though not attested elsewhere in biblical Hebrew, *ḫt'* is a common Semitic verb occurring in Ugaritic literature (e.g. *CTA* 6.2.23) and the Amarna correspondence (102.11-13), with cognates in Akkadian (*ḫatû*) and Arabic (*ḫata'a*).

The following term, *r'yty*, should be deleted. The first person form is anomalous here. Furthermore, once *tḥt'n* is recognized as the conclusion of the previous tricolon and the following bicolon is divided as suggested below, *r'yty* becomes extraneous. It is likely a gloss which arose on the basis of the theophanic character of the poem, the first person verbs in the framework of the poem (vv. 2, 16-19), and the development of the reading *taḥat 'āwen* (cf. Hab 1.3, *tar'ēnî 'āwen*).

13. This redivision of the lines in the MT, proposed by B. Duhm (*Das Buch Habakuk*, pp. 81-82), solves the major grammatical problem in the MT (masculine verb with feminine subject) and produces two poetic lines metrically similar to those in the rest of the poem. The original character of the resulting bicolon is further confirmed by its striking similarities to the opening bicolon of this stanza (v. 3a).

14. Read *mem* as enclitic rather than as masculine plural. Compare v. 9 where the ordinary feminine plural is employed.

15. Read *he* interrogative twice for stylistic reasons.

16. Read the construct singular, *mrkbt*, with the LXX; and locate the 2ms suffix on the *nomen rectum yšw'h* in accordance with the conventions of Hebrew grammar and the reading of the Peshitta.

17. The consonants *t'r* are to be understood as the old short preterite form

of the final weak verb *'rh*. When the preterite use of the prefix conjugation became confined in Hebrew to cases following the *waw* consecutive, this form could only have been understood as being derived from the middle weak verb *twr* and spelled accordingly. The old preterite *t'r* is preceded by the infinitive absolute which functions to strengthen the verbal idea.

18. Read the piel perfect 2ms of *śb'* with the Barberini Greek text, hereafter abbreviated Barb, the non-LXX G translation of Habakkuk 3 found in five medieval MSS (Holmes and Parsons nos. 23, 62, 86, 147, 407).

19. On the basis of the masculine plural in v. 14a and in Ugaritic literature, where *mṭm* occurs together with *qšt* as weapons of 'Anat (*CTA* 3.2.15-16), the masculine plural construct *mṭy-* should be read here.

20. The MT and LXX are puzzling. Their text *'mr* (*yhwh*) has all the hallmarks of a gloss and may have arisen together with the interpretation of *śb't* as related to the verb *šb'*, 'swear'. The *Vorlage* of Barb, *'šptw*, is superior, except for its 3ms suffix, which could not have been original in this context.

21. Read the poel perfect 3mp of *zrm* together with *'bwt* on the basis of Ps 77.18 and the text of Hab 3.10 in the Hebrew MS from the Wadi Murabba'at.

22. The form is the noun *zbl* with the 3ms suffix represented by *-h* as in preexilic spelling (cf. *'zh* in v. 4b).

23. Restore *'am*, 'people, militia', with F. Horst and W.F. Albright ('The Psalm of Habakkuk', pp. 16-17). Either *'m* was lost by haplography, its two letters being identical with the preceding and following ones, or *'m* was understood as the preposition *'im* and replaced with its alternate *'ēt*. The sign of the direct object is a prosaic particle uncommon in old poetry.

24. Read the 3fs construct form of *bāmâ*, with the meaning 'back' (cf. Ugaritic *bamtu*) rather than the usual rendering 'height', as the original lying behind the MT *mbyt*, the LXX *mwt*, and the Barb *mty*. If this proposal is correct, the preceding term *r'š* must represent the intrusive member of an ancient conflate text in which two parts of the enemy's body have been combined. It should be deleted.

25. Read with all of the versions against the MT the piel perfect 2ms form of *'rh*.

26. On the basis of the sense of the context and the reading of Barb, the suffix on *bmṭy-* should be understood as originally 2ms.

27. The conclusion of v. 14 is corrupt as indicated by problems with sense and poetic form in the MT and significant variants in the versions. It remains obscure and is perhaps best left untranslated.

28. The form *ḥmr* should be interpreted as a noun form of *ḥāmar*, 'ferment, boil, foam up' (see Ps 46.4); thus, the 'surge/swell of Many Waters'. The preposition *b* is present in the Vg and Tg, provides a parallel to *bym* in the previous line, and reflects the repetition of prepositions common in this poem (cf. vv. 2, 11, 12, 13).

29. The third person form of the LXX, OL, and Vg fits the context better than the first person form of the MT. The form *trgz* represents the old 3cdu rather than the 3fs form. For use of the *t-* form with duals, see W.F. Albright, 'The Psalm of Habakkuk', p. 17; F.M. Cross and D.N. Freedman, *Studies in Ancient Yahwistic Poetry* (Missoula: Scholars, 1975), p. 27; and C.H. Gordon, *UT* no. 9.15.

30. As most recent commentators have recognized, the original reading must have been the dual form of *'šr*, 'step', with the 1cs suffix. The relative pronoun in the MT is prosaic and damages the poetic lines.

31. B. Duhm (*Das Buch Habakuk*, p. 97) has suggested this reading, the niphal 1cs form of *'nḥ*. The verb *nwḥ* from which the form in the MT is derived hardly suits the context of agitated emotions.

32. Read with the LXX, Barb, and the Vg the preposition *b* in place of the preposition *l* of the MT.

33. For *l* with the infinitive to express time, W.F. Albright ('The Psalm of Habakkuk', p. 17) calls attention to Gen 24.63, Judg 19.26, and 2 Sam 18.29.

34. Delete the preposition. It results in an awkward construction and may have arisen as a dittography of the *'ayin/lamed* sequence a few letters before.

35. This is the energic form of the verb *gwd*. The suffix varies to such an extent among the versions that it may be considered an interpretive addition.

36. Omit *ky* with Barb. It serves no real consecutive, causal, conditional, or temporal function. It may have been added when the following lines came to be understood as agricultural adversity through which the poet retained faith ('When/even though . . . still, let me rejoice') rather than as part of the response to the theophany in which the poet participated.

37. For this translation, compare Deut 33.29 and Ps 18.45.

38. For the translation 'terraces', see L.E. Stager, 'The Archeology of the East Slope of Jerusalem and the Terraces of the Kidron', *JNES* 41 (1982), pp. 111-21.

39. Read with M. Dahood (*Ugaritic-Hebrew Philology* [Rome: Pontifical Biblical Institute, 1965], pp. 21-22) the internal qal passive.

40. The MT *mklh* is an orthographic error for *mkl'*.

41. In the three occurrences of this stock expression in Hebrew poetry (Ps 18.34 = 2 Sam 22.34; Hab 3.19), *bmwty* appears in exactly this form before the hiphil of *drk/'md*. This could be an archaic stereotyped phrase in which the old genitive case ending has been preserved and is represented by the final *yod* (**bamāti* > *bāmôtī*, spelled *bmwty*). Here, as in v. 13b, the old meaning of *bāmâ*, 'back', should be read. The image here is that of the conqueror astride the backs of his foes: 'on the backs (of my foes) he made me tread'. This in fact was the understanding of Barb: *kai epi tous trachēlous tōn echthrōn mou epibiba me*, 'and on the necks of my enemies he puts me'.

42. I use the term bicolon to refer to a verse unit composed of two related cola or lines of verse. Thus Hab 3.3 contains two bicola, one in v. 3a, another in v. 3b. Tricolon refers to a verse unit (e.g. v. 8a) with three related cola or lines of verse.

43. I take Kushan and Midian here to be Yahwists living near the mountain of God in the southeast, Teman/Mount Paran, and who react in awe to God's appearance together with the poet. For early links between Israel and Kushan/Midian, see Exod 2, 3, 18; and Num 12.1.

44. The only first person verb in this section, *r'yty* (v. 7), is in an area where the text is corrupt. I consider it a gloss (see note 12 above).

45. R. Otto, *The Idea of the Holy* (London: Oxford University Press, 1973), pp. 31-40.

46. F.M. Cross, *Canaanite Myth and Hebrew Epic* (Cambridge: Harvard University Press, 1973, pp. 147-63. The same pattern can also be discerned in *Enūma eliš*, the Babylonian version of the conflict between the storm god and the sea.

47. Cross, *Canaanite Myth and Hebrew Epic*, pp. 156-63.

48. See, for example, Exod 15 (vv. 1-2, 6, 11, 14, 16), Judg 5 (vv. 3-5), Ps 18 (vv. 1-15), Ps 97 (vv. 1-5), Exod 19 (vv. 16, 21) and 24 (v. 3), Deut 4 (vv. 32-40) and 5 (vv. 22-33), Isa 59 (vv 15b-20), and Zech 9.

49. Deut 4.33; 5.24; Exod 33.20; Judg 13.22; etc.

50. Otto, *The Idea of The Holy*, p. 31.

51. Hiebert, *God of My Victory: The Ancient Hymn in Habakkuk 3.*

7

ON THE INTERPRETATION OF PSALM 133

Adele Berlin

Psalm 133 is a short but perplexing poem. I became interested in it when I noticed that it contains a particular cohesive device that I was investigating. The device—one of several linguistic strategies whereby one line of a poem is linked to the next so as to form a unified poem—is a 'word chain'. This is the occurrence of word A in verses 1 and 2, word B in verses 2 and 3, word C in verses 3 and 4, and so forth. Word chains are not exclusively biblical; they have been noted by textlinguists in English and elsewhere. But, as far as I know, they have not been identified in the biblical text before.[1]

In most cases word chains, like other cohesive devices, serve to aid the perception of the relationship between the parts of the discourse in which they are located. In Ps 133, however, the presence of the word chain may be responsible for the modern misperception of the structure of the psalm, and hence its misinterpretation.

The word chain in Ps. 133 is

v. 1	טוב
v. 2	הטוב
v. 2	ירד על
	שירד על
v. 3	שירד על

It is the occurrence of *ṭwb* in the first two verses, I think, that has led to linking them together as parts of a simile: 'dwelling together' is like 'good oil'. But despite the many ingenious explanations found in the commentaries, I fail to see the sense of such a comparison, and I am not convinced that this simile exists at all. I offer here a radically different reading of the entire psalm.

Verse 1

שבת אחים גם יחד, 'the dwelling of brothers in unity'. This is the psalm's main topic, announced at the beginning, yet it has been largely misinterpreted. Most recent commentators take it to signify family unity and harmony. Typical is A. Weiser's comment that 'we are dealing here with a "Wisdom saying" which . . . has taken a feature from family life and has made it the subject of its teaching on the practical conduct of life . . .'[2] But praise of family life, in itself not a common theme in Psalms, is more likely to speak of wife and children (cf. Pss 127, 128) than of brothers. Nor is שבת אחים גם יחד a common phrase with a transparent meaning. *yšb yḥd* is a technical expression meaning 'living together on undivided land holdings'—a kind of joint tenancy. 'Living together with someone' in a non-technical sense is *yšb ʿm* (cf. Josh 20.4; Gen 27.44; Ps 26.4).

yšb yḥd occurs in the following verses:

ולא נשא אתם הארץ לשבת יחדו
כי היה רכושם רב
ולא יכלו לשבת יחדו

> And the land could not support their living in joint tenancy, for their possessions were too many, and they were not able to live in joint tenancy (Gen 13.6).

כי היה רכושם רב משבת יחדו

> For their possessions were too many for joint tenancy (Gen 36.7).

These two similar verses recount the separation of Lot and Abraham, and Esau and Jacob into separate households on different tracts of land.

כי ישבו אחים יחדו . . .

> If brothers live on undivided land holdings . . . (Deut 25.5)

Thus begins the levirate law; and it is apparently only in such a situation that the levirate would be necessary if its purpose were to preserve inherited allotments.[3]

It seems likely that Ps 133.1 is using the phrase שבת אחים גם יחד in the same sense as Gen 13.6, 36.7, and Deut 25.5. The image is not one of a quarrel-free family snuggling around the hearth, but of undivided land holdings. This is a metaphor for an undivided kingdom. The psalm expresses a hope for the reunification of the north and south with Jerusalem as the capital of a united kingdom.

Ironically, Weiser, whose view of this psalm was quoted earlier, cites the three verses containing *yšb yḥd* but completely missed this point. There are, however, a few earlier commentators who either hinted at or stated explicitly an interpretation similar to mine, although they do not bring supporting evidence from the verses in Genesis and Deuteronomy.

The most explicit is that of the eighteenth-century Jewish exegete, David Altschuler, in his commentary, *Meṣudat David*:

> How very good and how very pleasant is the thing when the whole house of Israel will dwell on its land; they are called 'brothers' for the great affection that is among them . . . And they will be together in one kingship and will not be divided into two kingdoms any more.[4]

J.J. Stewart Perowne (commentary first published 1873) does not see this as the primary meaning but notes that 'Hermon in the north, and Zion in the south, may also further suggest the union of the northern and southern tribes'.[5] At about the same time, G. Heinrich A.V. Ewald suggested that

> Although the praise holds good of every house: yet the poet certainly proceeded from a higher point of view. The fresh settlement of several tribes in Canaan, the image of those united in love to Jahve and Sion, and through such concord blessed, is plainly present to his mind, as also the recollection of the sorrows which finally arose through disunion . . . the song then proceeds . . . from the domestic relation, but conducts the thought immediately into the related but much higher sphere of the national.[6]

Verse 2

כשמן הטוב, 'like good oil'. The immediate significations of oil are fragrance (as a cosmetic), anointing (king and priest), and, by extension, a sign of joy.[7] Most interpretations choose fragrance,[8] but again I think Perowne has a better understanding of the image in our psalm.

> The point of comparison does not lie in the *preciousness* of the oil, or in its *all-pervading fragrance*; but in this, that being poured on the head, it did not rest there, but flowed to the beard, and descended even to the garments, and thus, as it were, consecrated the whole body in all its parts.[9]

The image of flowing oil is described more concretely by Othmar Keel (although not in connection with our psalm): '. . . perfumed fat . . . was set on the heads of the guests at festive banquets. During the course of the meal, it melted on the head and gave forth a beguiling scent.'[10]

It is, of course, not necessary or even desirable to limit the sense of a poetic image. It is quite likely that the initial impression of 'good oil' is fragrance; that the 'flowing' aspect is added by the words ירד על הזקן and by the following verse, 'like the dew of Hermon that flows down . . .'; and that, furthermore, the mention of Aaron's beard calls to mind the use of oil for the consecration of priests. In other words, the reader's interpretation of the image changes as he reads on.

The real question, however, is *whether this is a simile comparing dwelling together with good oil*, as has almost universally been assumed. In what sense do any of the associations with 'oil' relate to v. 1? Various scholars have exercised their ingenuity in making a connection, but it is unnecessary, if not harmful, to a correct understanding of the poem.

The structure of the psalm has generally been taken to be: 'dwelling in unity' is like 'good oil' and like 'dew of Hermon'. But as E. Beaucamp has recognized, the two comparative particles (*k*) do not introduce two similes which relate back to 'dwelling in unity'. Rather the 'similes' in vv. 2 and 3 relate to each other.[11] Oil is compared to dew and dew to oil; that is, oil and dew are equated. (The significance of this will be discussed shortly.) This construction is documented by P. Joüon[12] in, for example, Josh 14.11 and 1 Sam 30.24. For a poetic usage see Ps 139.12, כחשיכה כאורה, 'darkness and light are the same'. Rashi also analyzes our psalm in this way, citing Isa. 24.2.[13]

זקן אהרן, 'Aaron's beard'. The reference to Aaron is quite specific. It serves to restrict the more diffuse associations with oil and focuses attention on one particular use of it: for the consecration of Aaron to the priesthood (see Exod 29 and Lev 8).[14]

שירד על פי מדותיו, 'that flows down over the collar of his robe'. The *crux interpretum* has always been whether it is the oil or Aaron's beard that flows over the collar of his robe.[15] The text is ambiguous, perhaps intentionally so, for, whichever option is chosen, the effect is to enhance and reinforce the image of 'flowing'. This is the dominant image in the poem and is also present in the next verse.

Verse 3

כטל חרמון, 'like the dew of Hermon'. As in the case of 'oil', there are manifold associations with 'Hermon': height, moisture in all seasons, a northern land-mark which becomes representative of the north (cf. the comment by Perowne quoted earlier), and perhaps even a sound-play with 'Aaron'.

A strong connection between vv. 2 and 3 is achieved by the double use of *k*-, the repetition of the syntactic structure, the words 'that flows down', and the use of the lexical association 'oil' and 'dew' which both have connotations of flowing and of abundance, prosperity.[16] All of these are known cohesive devices and they suggest that the relationship between vv. 2 and 3 is stronger than between vv. 1 and 2 or 1 and 3.

Having presented the main points on which I base my understanding of this psalm, I now offer a translation and interpretation of the poem as a whole.

> A *ma'alot* song of David.
>
> Oh, how good and pleasant
> Is the dwelling of brothers (re)united.
>
> Like the fragrant oil on the head,
> Flowing down on the beard, Aaron's beard,
> That flows down over the collar of his robe;
>
> So is the dew of Hermon
> That flows down on the mountains of Zion.
> For there has the Lord ordained the blessing,
> Life everlasting.

The main theme is the unification of the country. This is achieved through the central image of flowing together.[17] The picture is one of continuous flow: from head to beard, from beard to collar, from Hermon to Zion. The higher to lower movement in v. 3 is an echo of the top to bottom movement in v. 2.[18] The combination of vv. 2 and 3 not only plays on the association of oil and dew, and the idea of flowing, but may also suggest a connection between hair and mountains reminiscent of Song 4.1 and 6.5. In fact, one might say that Ps 133 reverses the type of description found in Song of Songs: the Song compares the human body to geographical or topographical features (Song 4.4; 7.5-6); Ps 133 describes the land in terms of human features. The image in v. 3 is, then, an explanation for v. 2. The entire country is pictured as a priestly visage: from Hermon to Zion—from head to body. And to return to the equation of vv. 2 and 3, the land is anointed with dew as Aaron is anointed with the consecrating oil. The country is thus not only united, it is also holy; and not only is it holy, it is also blessed. The very things that symbolize its consecration—oil/dew—also symbolize its prosperity.

The focal point of holiness and blessing is Zion, 'for there has the Lord ordained the blessing'.

The movement ceases here. The point of climax, geographically and poetically, has been attained.

According to this reading, Ps 133 is not a wisdom psalm at all. Like Pss 132 and 134 which are adjacent to it, Ps 133 is an ode to Zion with a religious and nationalistic message.[19]

NOTES

A draft of this paper was read at the Ninth World Congress of Jewish Studies, Jerusalem, August 12, 1985. Various members of the audience made suggestions that enrich the interpretation of the psalm. Among them, Baruch Margalit pointed out aspects of mountain imagery found in Ugaritic mythology. One might see here overtones of a supreme deity once associated with a northern mountain moving his domain to Mt Zion. However, I am not convinced that we have here—at least consciously—a form of the Israelization of Canaanite mythology, although mythic associations may lie deeply buried in the imagery.

1. Word chains also occur in Pss 111 and 147. The term 'word chain' is my own but the phenomenon of repeating a lexical item is a recognized cohesive device. Cf. M.A.K. Halliday and R. Hasan, *Cohesion in English* (London: Longman, 1976), pp. 288-92.

2. *The Psalms* (Philadelphia: Westminster, 1962), p. 783.

3. Thus the allotments of all brothers who are potentially heads of households are preserved. The law excludes the preservation of a deceased *unmarried* (presumably a minor?) brother's allotment. If a man died after the apportioning of allotments, he would have already received his share, and hence no levirate would be necessary. If he died childless, his share would pass to the next of kin.

4. *Meṣudat David* is found in Rabbinic Bibles (*Miqra'ot Gedolot*). The translation is mine.

5. *The Book of Psalms* (Grand Rapids: Zondervan, third printing, 1978), II, p. 420. Cf. also A.B. Ehrlich, *Die Psalmen* (Berlin: Poppelauer, 1905), p. 348.

6. *Commentary on the Psalms* (London: Williams and Norgate, 1881), II, p. 167.

7. Cf. *IDB*, III, pp. 593-95.

8. See, for example, G.B. Caird, *The Language and Imagery of the Bible*

(Philadelphia: Westminster, 1980), pp. 145, 153. Caird calls this a low degree of correspondence between vehicle and tenor.

9. *The Book of Psalms*, II, p. 419.

10. *The Symbolism of the Biblical World. Ancient Near Eastern Iconography and the Book of Psalms* (New York: Seabury, 1978), p. 335.

11. *Le Psautier* (Paris: Gabalda, 1979), II, p. 239.

12. *Grammaire de l'hébreu biblique* (Rome: Pontifical Biblical Institute, 1923), §174i. Compare the English idiom 'like father, like son'.

13. There is a superficial resemblance between the syntax of Ps 133 and Num 24.5-6 but I do not think that the relationship between the verses is the same. Num 24.5-6 may contain an 'effective simile' which occurs in 'prayers and in prophetic oracles . . . in contexts where the writer expects or desires some objective effect on his world' (D.R. Hillers, 'The Effective Simile in Biblical Literature', *JAOS* 103 [1983], p. 184). That is, Balaam is declaring, in a peformative manner, a blessing of beneficence on Israel, and invoking a series of similes to effect, through the quasi-magical power of the words, his blessing. Ps 133 is quite different.

14. Oil and fragrant incense occur together in Exod 30.22ff. (Jacob Milgrom). This further reinforces the connection between 'fragrance' and 'consecration'.

15. See W.G.E. Watson, 'The Hidden Simile in Psalm 133', *Bib* 60 (1979), pp. 108-109 and D.T. Tsumura, 'Sorites in Psalm 133,2-3a', *Bib* 61 (1980), pp. 416-17.

16. Cf. M. Dahood, 'Ugaritic-Hebrew Parallel Pairs', *Ras Shamra Parallels*, I (ed. L.R. Fisher; Rome: Pontifical Biblical Institute, 1972), pp. 189-91 #206, #207, #208; cf. also M. Dahood, *The Psalms, III* (Garden City: Doubleday, 1970), p. 251. For an idiosyncratic connection between Aaron and the dew of Hermon see J.-M. Rosenstiehl, 'Un commentaire du Psaume 133 à l'époque intertestamentaire', *RHPR* 59 (1979), pp. 559-65.

17. Compare the image of flowing in Isa 2.2 = Mic 4.1.

18. Moshe Greenberg cautioned me against viewing this as a north-to-south picture since to an Israelite 'north' did not equal 'top'—the main geographical orientation being 'east'. Rather the picture moves from higher to lower; Mt. Hermon is higher than Mt. Zion. This reflects geographic reality as opposed to the eschatological reversal when Mt. Zion will become the tallest of mountains (Isa 2.2; Mic 4.1).

19. On this theme see M. Weinfeld, 'Zion and Jerusalem as Religious and Political Capital: Ideology and Utopia', *The Poet and the Historian. Essays in Literary and Historical Biblical Criticism* (ed. R.E. Friedman; Chico: Scholars, 1983), pp. 75-115.

8

THE MOCK-*śimḥâ* OF PSALM 137

Harris Lenowitz

More than a suspicion, but something less than a demonstrated case, has existed for some time concerning the likelihood that the noun *śimḥâ* occasionally defines a particular sort of song: a song of joy.[1] The particularization of the noun in Hebrew in other ways, in comparison with the root's development in some other languages, has been dealt with.[2] This paper demonstrates that a particular concretion of the noun *śimḥâ*[3] does define a song of joy and that a *mock*-song of joy lies at the centre of Ps 137.[4]

Psalm 137[5]

1 We sat there and cried along Babylon rivers remembering
Zion.

2 We hung up our harps in Babylon trees
3 when our captors asked for songs,
when they mocked us, calling for a happy tune:

'Sing us one of those Zion songs!'

4 How could we sing a Zion-song in an alien's land?
5 If I forgot you, Jerusalem,
my right hand would wither,
6 my tongue would stick to the roof of my mouth
if I didn't remember you,
if I couldn't start up a tune with:
'Jerusalem . . '

7 YHWH, You remember Jerusalem's day for the
Edomites, when they said:
'Strip her down! Strip her bare!'

8 Now, you plundered Babylons, (your song for you):

'Happy He'll be to pay you
the reward you've rewarded us!
9 Happy He'll be to snatch your babies
and smash them against a rock!'

In order to counterpose the expression of an emotion and the emotion itself, the simple count versus non-count (mass) noun tests can be used.[6] Thus, *śimḥâ* in the plural (*ś^{e}māḥôt*), or *śimḥâ* with the definite article (involved in affixes or as *ha-*), or both plural and defined, is non-abstract and cleaves away from the singular, undefined noun. The plural occurs only twice in biblical texts, Pss 16.11 and 45.16. Both occurrences are problematic. The confusion of the abstract suffix *-ût* with that of the marker for (feminine) plural, *-ôt*, the occurrence of feminine absolute singulars in *-ôt*, other considerations, and particularly the defective spelling in the one case, all obscure the reading.[7] The clearest early plural occurrence of the noun in Hebrew comes with the euphemistic title of the Talmudic tractate concerning mourning practices, *Ś^{e}maḥot*, i.e. 'occasions of mourning'.

The defined singular of the noun is not at all infrequent in biblical Hebrew on the other hand, though the two cases of *haśśimḥâ* are more problematic than the cases where the noun occurs defined by a possessive pronoun suffix or a definite *nomen rectum*. The most instructive cases from the latter category are these two: Isa 66.6,

> Your fellow-countrymen who hate you, who spurn you because you bear my name, have said, 'Let Yhwh show his glory, then we shall see you[r] *śimḥâ*'; but they shall be ashamed;[8]

and Ezek 35.14f.,

> These are the words of Yhwh the god: 'I will make you [Edom/ Seir] so desolate that the whole world will gloat (*kiśmōaḥ*) over you. I will do to you as you did to Israel my own possession when you gloated (*k^{e}simḥāt^{e}kā*) over its desolation.'

In both of these cases the noun is defined, and is an objective noun-phrase in a predicate where the verb is active, transitive, and predicts a change which the senses will perceive. The second case is, of course, of particular significance to the examination of Psalm 137 and the *śimḥâ* there, because of its reference to Edom.

The expression of an emotion may be found in contexts that will show the circumstances of its typical expression: the time, place and personnel of its performance. If its performance is important to either the cultus or the nation, we will expect to find it *ordained*. As it is performed, we will expect to learn further particulars of its performance. Num 10.10 contains the ordinance of a *śimḥâ*:

> On the days of your *śimḥâ*, your appointed season and your first day of the month you shall sound the trumpets over your whole-offerings and your shared-offerings, and the trumpets shall be a reminder on your behalf before Yhwh . . .

Though *śimḥâ* may be a general term qualifying the celebration of the *mō'ēd*, etc., the commentary of ibn Ezra here is instructive:

> 'and on the day of your *śimḥâ* and your appointed seasons,' When you have returned from the land of the enemy or conquered the enemy who has attacked you, you shall establish a *śimḥâ*-day such as, for example, the days of Purim or the seven days of Hezekiah [elsewhere, Ḥanukkah] [is the proper understanding of this term as] against commentators who explain that the *śimḥâ*-day is a reference to the Sabbath.[9]

In addition to finding here the ordinance requiring a *śimḥâ*, we learn some particulars. A *śimḥâ* would seem to be celebrated in connection with victory in war, either immediate or eventual. Particular calls on the trumpet are required, precisely as they are for the other two occasions mentioned. We can derive some further information from the association of the *śimḥâ* with the rites in its surrounding pericope: it is a ritual which is not specifically cultic and whose celebration is not limited to priests, nor by age or gender of worshippers. Yet, unlike the *mō'ēd* or the first day of a month which recurs regularly, the occurrence of a *śimḥâ* is fixed relative to a specific occasion which engenders joy and expresses itself in a *śimḥâ*.

More particulars of the *śimḥâ*-performance can be drawn from the account of one in the reign of Hezekiah, the one to which ibn Ezra refers, in 2 Chronicles 30:

> And the Israelites who were present in Jerusalem kept the feast of Unleavened Bread for seven days *with great rejoicing*, and the Levites and the priests praised the Lord every day *with unrestrained fervour*. Hezekiah spoke encouragingly to all the Levites who had shown true understanding in the service of the Lord. So they spent the seven days of the festival sacrificing shared-offerings and making confession to the Lord the God of their fathers.

> Then the whole assembly agreed to keep the feast for another seven days; so they kept it for another seven days *with general rejoicing*. For Hezekiah king of Judah set aside for the assembly a thousand bulls and seven thousand sheep, and his officers set aside for the assembly a thousand bulls and ten thousand sheep; and priests hallowed themselved in great numbers. So the whole assembly of Judah, including the priests and the Levites, *rejoiced*, together with all the assembly which came out of Israel, and the resident aliens from Israel and those who lived in Judah. There was *great rejoicing* in Jerusalem, the like of which had not been known there since the days of Solomon son of David king of Israel. Then the priests and the Levites stood to bless the people: the Lord listened to their cry, and their prayer came to God's holy dwelling-place in heaven.

We may learn from this episode that the celebration of a *śimḥâ* is held at the behest of king, priests and people with no particular differentiation. We may further learn that music, in addition to a noteworthy amount of drinking and eating, is an essential component of the celebration. Here, this component has advanced considerably from the simple trumpet or shofar sounding of its ordinance, in Numbers, an elaboration we might expect in Chronicles.

Against the commonly accepted notion that v. 21's *biklê ʿōz* has to be understood as *b*^{e}*kol-ʿōz* (without a variant reading to support the claim), it is clear by now that instruments of public proclamation that can be heard over a fair distance are intended. Then, we may learn something of the particular forms of music, in addition to the trumpet soundings, which may be typical of the *śimḥâ*. Four of the verbs in this passage define specific musical, liturgical forms, though we cannot know very much about their individual characteristics. A *b*^{e}*rākâ* lies beneath the verb of v. 27; a *tôdâ*, beneath that of v. 22, *mitvadim*; a *maśkîl*, beneath *hammaśkîlîm* in the same verse; and a *hallēl* has generated *m*^{e}*hall*^{e}*lîm* of v. 21. This will lead us directly into Psalm 137 but it will be worthwhile to see it, or its fellow, ordained into the ritual in 2 Chron 23.18:

> Then Jehoiada committed the supervision of the house of Yhwh to the charge of the priests and the Levites whom David had allocated to the house of Yhwh, to offer whole-offerings to Yhwh as prescribed in the law of Moses, with the *singing and rejoicing* as handed down from David.

The verse is now clearer. The 'rejoicing' is the *śimḥâ* ordained in

Num 10.10; the 'singing as handed down from David' has been added as an essential element, essential especially for the Chronicler.

Thus, we have established that a *śimḥâ* is a celebration of success over the enemy which is carried out when there exist no other celebrations proper to the success, or as an addition to prescribed celebrations when agreeable. The primary component of the *śimḥâ* is a trumpet call; music including lyrics is expected, in one of the joyous genres. In addition, the most proper setting for a *śimḥâ* has to do with Jerusalem, David's city, the home of the people of Israel for which they struggle, to which they return, and which they rebuild (cf. the *śᵉmāḥôt* of Ezr 3.10 and Neh 12.27).[10]

II

The NEB translation of our term in Ezek 35.14ff. was 'gloat'. Though no explanation for this choice of term was given, it seems apposite. The word here suggests a well-formed (memorable) taunt. Otto Eissfeldt has discussed the related forms of the taunt—the boast and the mocking song and saying—at length,[11] and in summary in *The Old Testament: An Introduction*.[12] Recently Kugel[13] has added to our understanding of 'sharpness' as a pervasive feature in the literary art of Israel, particularly in connection with the term *māšāl*. A taunt, before some contest, and a boast, after the contest, can be seen together in 1 Samuel 14, and we can learn something of the power of the forms. They both belong to the level of magically potent speech. Jonathan tells his armor-bearer that a sure sign of their power over the enemy will be the enemy's taunt, 'Come up to us; we have something to show you', which comes in v. 12. After the foretold victory, a historical note includes this simile in describing Jonathan's success (v. 14): 'In that first attack Jonathan and his armor-bearer killed about twenty of them, like men cutting a furrow across a half-acre field'. The simile from agriculture is a boast, a mockery of the bravery and now-silenced speech of the Philistines. Such mockeries are not limited to occasions of strife in war; Isa 23.15f. shows both the features of well-formedness and memorability common to the mockery: '[the plight of Tyre shall be that of the harlot in the song:] "Take your harp, go round the city, poor forgotten harlot; / touch the strings sweetly, sing all your songs, / make them remember you again"'. But war is the most common occasion for the genre by far, as victory commonly leads to the recollection of the enemy's taunt and to a mockery of it. Something of this sort motivates the generalized 'Where is your god now?', addressed to the righteous or to Israel with such frequency.

The Song of Deborah (Judges 5) is replete with quotations from those who excused themselves from the battle, stated as mockeries (vv. 15-17 are a section devoted to the mockery). Those who lost are mocked as well, especially the court lady who advises Sisera's mother that everything is fine (v. 30). In ch. 4, even one of the victors (v. 9) undergoes formal ridicule. A bragging taunt turned into a mockery is highlighted in Exod 15.9. This taunt or its mockery is shown to be well-formed in its context, by the much longer verse parts which surround it in opposition to its single-word, single-stress parts, as well as by its alliterations. The latter aspect arises from the imperfect, first-person marker, sharply contrasted with the second-person which follows in a verse of greater length.

The suspicion that *śimḥâ* might define a particular form of song, celebrating immediate or long-withheld victory, is supported by the precise and lengthy account of the dedication of the wall (presumably this is the *ḥ^{a}nûkâ* which the other versions of ibn Ezra's comment refer to, as cited above,) in Nehemiah 12. Verse 43 reads, 'A great sacrifice was celebrated that day, and they all rejoiced because God had given them great cause for rejoicing; the women and the children rejoiced with them. And the *śimḥâ* of Jerusalem was heard a long way off.' It is to be noted that the *śimḥâ* is audible and that, although all—including women, children—join in its performance, the *śimḥâ* is led by the 'singers', the psalm-guild.

In Judges 16 an 'Israelite narrator [pictures] the Philistine festival celebrating the triumph over Samson, no doubt according to the pattern of celebrations known to him from among his own people'.[14] The victory song the Philistines sing is first introduced as a *śimḥâ*: 'The lords of the Philistines assembled together to offer a great sacrifice to their god Dagon and as a *śimḥâ* they said, "Our god has delivered our enemy into our hands, / the scourge of our land who piled it with dead"'. It is again to be noted here that the victory song is turned to mockery by the events which follow it immediately.

As is the case for the *qînâ*, where the very best example of the genre is the lengthy mock-*qînâ* of Isa 14.4-21, features other than circumstance and performers may be best illuminated for the *śimḥâ*-song in a mock-*śimḥâ*. The text from Judges (above) is one sort of mock-*śimḥâ*. Verses 8b-9 of Psalm 137 are another.

III

D.N. Freedman analysed Psalm 137[15] and found it to be a sixth-century example of 'a major revival of Hebrew poetry in Babylon'. The only feature of the poem that militates against the whole being composed even later, after the return, is the use of imperfects in the concluding couplet. It might be easier to understand that part of the psalm as being contemporary with the events described in the psalm itself. The narrative frame would then have been composed later, after the foe's defeat. This idea has several advantages, not least of which is support for the form *šᵉdûdâ* in v. 8 as an appropriate address to Babylon's defeat after that has occurred, against Freedman's proposal to 'interpret the reference as a proleptic statement of the irreversible fate already determined and soon to be accomplished'.

Otherwise there is no reason to dissent from Freedman's reading of the poem, up to the point of the identification of the song requested by the Babylonians, or particularly their Edomite mercenaries. It is his finding that the *'et* of v. 4a indicates that a specific composition is being demanded. The demand is for a joyous song, as is made clear by the aggravated sadness and despair of the exiles, perhaps particularly one of the Songs of Ascents. The 'demand leads in turn to the agonizing protest of vs. 4, and an entirely different kind of song about Jerusalem: the terrible oath of remembrance and return, as well as the prayer for divine vindication against the enemies of his people'. Whereas Freedman sees the same demand as we do for the same sort of song, he must compose a separate explanation for v. 6cd, the crux, *'al ro'š śimḥātî*. But the song the captors request is a *śimḥâ*'.

The psalmist makes it abundantly clear that as he understands his function (see Eissfeldt, *Introduction*, pp. 92f., for a fine explanation of the function of the mocking-word in politics) in the national cult, he would betray that in singing a Jerusalem victory song in defeat, a song of Jerusalem outside Jerusalem. In this moment his realities are sharply defined: death (perhaps) or submission to the annihilation of his self-image. In this moment of anguish he seeks an answer, 'How *can* we sing a Zion-song in an alien land?' Though irony is at work here, the question is a real one and the poem, especially the conclusion, is the answer. Having averred that his whole art depends on verifiable accuracy, and that his instruments would fail in their misappropriation, he recalls the *śimḥâ*-song of the victors (v. 7cd). Their boast is represented by the heavy sound play in v. 7—three *'ayins* in a row, the three matrices CaCuno in a row, the hard stressed imperatives—and cf. Exod 15.9. The psalmist responds with what the victors have requested: the *śimḥâ*-song of vv. 8b-9, introduced to the now-defeated Babylonians/Edomites.

The fact that Babylonians/Edomites do not speak Hebrew allows the psalmist to fill a recognizable form with an unexpected content. Although the form, as has been seen, is largely the form of the circumstance, several recognizable literary types have been mentioned in connection with the musical aspect of the *śimḥâ* celebration. In Ezra 3 the *hallēl* which is recited is Psalm 136. In Hezekiah's *śimḥâ*, several other forms were mentioned. It would not follow, then, that the *śimḥâ* song could be limited to a single form nor, likewise, that every *hallēl* constituted a *śimḥâ* or that on every occasion of the performance of Psalm 136 a *śimḥâ* was being celebrated. The form of vv. 8c-9 is undeniably that of an *'ašrê*, a sub-type of song of ascent or victory hymn particularly attached to Jerusalem and its wisdom or liturgical enterprises. Our verse-parts here are a little longer than the ones typical (cf. Ps 144.15; 84.5; among many others) of other verses so begun. But the *selâ'* at the end of our verses seems apposite to a formal theme (cf. the *selâ* of Ps 84.5) as well as to our personae from Petra, particularly after we recall the passage from Ezekiel. In fact, it now seems impossible not to recognize the long indictment of Edom there as being connected with the three Edomite boasts of vv. 10, 12 and 36.2. To each of these the god Yhwh responds with his own words—first in general terms describing the efficacy of his word, then in more particular terms matching both the manner and subject of the Edomite boast. *Zkhr* is at stake. The high ground shall not be Edom's; effective speech is Yhwh's. The courtroom-style debate is ended as Yhwh responds again for all nature to attend to the scorn Edom and others express against the Yahwists and the impotence of that scorn. The words of Yhwh are the more potent.

The *śimḥâ* of the psalmists too was more potent, at first for the guild at that moment, in the face of the Edomite taunters; then later, it proved to be so for the whole of Israel returned from exile, their enemy defeated. In the narrative frame composed then, a single word carries us back to the original event and to the psalmist's emotion: *tôlālênû*. Against the possibility that the word is an Aramaized form of Hebrew *šôlālênû*, Freedman's suggestion is one of several to be preferred. He suggests that our word rests on the root *hll*, 'to boast'. Whether that is so, or whether a causative pattern has generated the noun from *hll*, 'to praise' (thus 'those who would force us to sing praise'), or from *yll*, 'to those who howled at us (in joy)' or 'those who sought to make us howl (in despair)', cannot be settled. But given what we know from Ezekiel of the occasion, as well as from the sharpening of the parallelistic relationship between vv. 3a and 3b, something like boasting seems right. The general term *dibrê-šîr* sharpens to a particular expression of song, *a śimḥâ*. This expands and achieves its point in *šîr-ṣîyôn*, which is the sticking-point. As the psalmist refuses the call, while further defining the song-type as a *šîr* of Jerusalem-and-Yhwh, so the *šōbîm* display their cruelty, ascending from the general, 'captors', to the particular—whichever of the above explanations seems best for *tôlālênû* (other than from *š/tll*).

The theme from Ezekiel of the impotence of the foe's argument before the advocate of Israel is expressed in Ps 137 in the arena where songs oppose each other for eternal victory. Resembling that of the Egyptian, the Edomite boast in v. 7 loses to the Israelite *śimḥâ* in vv. 8b-9. The Edomite attempt to win by forcing the Israelite psalmist to ridicule the power of his own song by an inappropriate performance on demand fails, as the psalmist sings his *tolal*, a song of doom which the Edomite can understand as little as he understands the history of Yhwh's people.

NOTES

1. In addition to sporadic renderings of the noun as 'song of joy' in the *New English Bible* and other translations, see M. Dahood's notes in the Anchor Bible, *Psalms II*, pp. 6f. and *Psalms III*, pp. 268-74 and especially p. 271.

2. Jonas C. Greenfield, 'Lexicographical notes II; the root *śmḥ*', *HUCA* 30 (1959), pp. 141-51.

3. This paper will not examine the question of the root *śmḥ* in verbs. It is noteworthy that in spite of the qal participle/adjective occurring in a stative /e/ pattern, the perfect 3 m.s. does not so appear. The laryngeal-pharyngeal in the third consonant slot is perhaps the cause; but perhaps only the adjective conveys 'emotion of joy' and all other verb forms have come to do with the celebrating of a *śimḥâ*-emotion. That would appear to be case with verbs in the piel and hiphil.

4. In addition to the publications mentioned in note 5, I have also approached this subject in the SBL section on biblical poetry (see *SBL Abstracts* [1978], p. 44).

5. Translation, Harris Lenowitz (cf. *Panjandrum* IV (1975); *A Big Jewish Book* (1978); *Technicians of the Sacred* (2nd edn; 1985).

6. Leonard Bloomfield, *Language* (1933), pp. 205f.

7. Dahood, *Psalms III*, p. 379; etc.

8. The translations throughout, with some slight changes, are those of the *New English Bible*.

9. R. Abraham ibn Ezra, *Commentary*, *ad loc*.

10. These cases have been helpful in reaching conclusions concerning the nature of the *śimḥâ*. The list is limited to occurrences of the noun.

a. Judg 16.23.

b. 1 Sam 18.6.

c. 2 Sam 6.12.

d. 1 Kgs 1.30.

e. Isa 9.2.

f. Isa 24.11, in spite of the apparent synonymous parallelism here with *m*[e]*śôś* and an effort to refrain from dependence on occurrences of *śimḥâ* in parallel with any of the 'joy' words, e.g. *gîl*, *śasôn*, *rînâ*, etc., and in spite of its symbolic use, the *śimḥâ* here is trapped with festivity and potables. Other 'joy' terms may occasionally denote 'sounds of celebrations of joy' in analogy to *śimḥâ*.

g. Isa 30.29, another case where *śimḥâ* parallels *šîr* in music heard in Jerusalem.

h. Jer 31.7.

i. Zeph 31.7.

j. Ps 16.11, an interesting parallelism, preceding that of mishnaic Hebrew, between *śimḥâ* and a term that is well-known in its use for 'tune': *n*[e]*'imâ*.

k. Ps 30.12, a parade example. The theme of the psalm has something to do with the utility of psalmistry; the concluding couplet balances a technicality of the funeral with one of the triumph; then following the caesura, another funeral component and another of the triumph, perhaps fancy clothes but given David's actions in 2 Sam 6, more likely a bare and flapping loin cloth. The last verse picks up this singing, dancing image to make the envoi.

l. Ps 43.4, the acceptable offering is the psalmist's song with instrumental accompaniment.

m. Ps 68.4, a triumph and a taunt.

n. Ps 97.12, a verb, but paired with 'give thanks', *hôdû*.

o. Ps 100.2, as a definition of the time or manner of proper worship.

p. Ps 106.5, with *hll* and with the notion of the *naḥ*[a]*lâ*.

q. Prov 14.10, the exclusivity of the *śimḥâ*; excluded are all enemies, the wicked, foreigners.

r. Neh 8.12.

s. 1 Chron 15.16, David gives instruction on the instrumentation and performers for the *śimḥâ*-music.

t. 1 Chron 29.9, a Grand *Śimḥâ*, David himself performing in happiness at a welcome donation.

u. 2 Chron 20.27, after the conquest of Ammon, with instruments, returning to Jerusalem with Jehoshaphat leading.

v. 2 Chron 29.30, the music (according to David), performers, etc., for the offering of an *'ôlâ*; when completed, the music and poetry (according to David and Asaph), the dancing of a *śimḥâ* added to the *'ôlâ*!

11. O. Eissfeldt, 'Der Maschal im AT', *BZAW* 24 (1913).

12. O. Eissfeldt, *The Old Testament. An Introduction* (1965), pp. 64-101.

13. J. Kugel, *The Idea of Biblical Poetry*, pp. 11f.

14. Eissfeldt, *Intrduction*, p. 100.

15. D.N. Freedman, 'The Structure of Psalm 137', in *Near Eastern Studies in Honor of W.F. Albright* (1971).

9

THE PSEUDOSORITES: A TYPE OF PARADOX IN HEBREW VERSE

M. O'Connor

1. *Paradox*

In this century several varieties of paradox have commanded the attention of students of human communication.[1] The formalizations of logic introduced in the late nineteenth century led philosophers to clarify the workings of strict antinomies and their verbal analogues, the classical paradoxes such as that of the lying Cretan. Epimenides' Cretan makes his claim, 'I am lying', in an odd way, since his statement, if it is to beguile students of truth-value and meaninglessness, must be taken as self-referential, i.e. 'I am hereby lying'. But in ordinary discourse the statement 'I am lying' is taken to refer to some element of the speaker's discourse other than the statement itself. Philosophical consideration of the Cretan's paradox attributes to his statement a peculiar pragmatic force, i.e., it makes it 'mean' something it would not ordinarily 'mean', and leaches from it its ordinary sense.

There are paradoxes which, unlike the strict antinomies, have a powerful pragmatic effect, an effect of controlling and in some cases strangling any response. These are paradoxes of large-scale or long-term human interaction, associated with familial and other forms of intimate ties and with therapy and counseling ties which ape them, and they are generally paradoxes of a set of communicative gestures. Speech alone is not often sufficient to effect so powerful a communicative block as accompanies these paradoxes. Close and important relationships are crucial for these paradoxes to work. They may work to the good, as in stable families, when a child is told to be independent, or in therapeutic interaction, in which the patient is told to be spontaneous. Or they may have adverse effect, as in schizophrenogenic families, in which one member is told to love and not-love the others.[2]

Thus we have, on the one hand, logical paradoxes of little pragmatic force, and, on the other, the pragmatic paradoxes associated with major communicative stress. Between the abstract notions of the formal logician and the situational studies of the clinician, we may locate the large class of linguistic paradoxes. Among these is the category of philosopher's paradoxes, a category defined on the basis of philosophers' interest in its members.

It should be possible to examine the class of linguistic (*sprachlich*) paradoxes on a linguistic (*sprachwissenschaftlich*) basis. It may be that all such paradoxes will fall into linguistically describable and delimitable groups, and that all such groups will be mappable into formal logic and into pragmatics; that is, the 'space' of paradox may be tripartite and homologous. It is not this task, but the necessary preliminary of describing a particular group of linguistic paradoxes, that interests me, not only as a preliminary adventure in paradox theory, but also because paradoxes occur, not only in philosopher talk and intimate interaction, but in all variety of discourse. Paradoxes are common in ordinary conversation and in literary texts in a variety of languages; they are crucial to jokes, insults, and curses, and to those forms of language that look for what isn't there where it used to be.[3]

2. *Sorites and pseudosorites*

The class of paradoxes I am concerned with here is the pseudosorites.[4] A sorites is a predicate chain: 'If A, then its consequent B. If B, then its consequent C', etc. Let us observe that a sorites can be replete with negatives and still function well.

> I don't like crooks, and even if I did, I wouldn't like crooks that are stool-pigeons, and if I liked crooks that are stool-pigeons, I still wouldn't like you (Dashiell Hammett).

The first sentence is negative. The second sentence begins with a subordinate concessive clause and has a negative in the main clause, and the third sentence has the same structure.[5] The patterning of negatives and concessive clauses is such that the sentence is logical.

Let us also observe that the sorites uses repetition or anaphora among its parts. In the example cited repetition dominates; only the anaphoric process of verb-phrase deletion has operated, yielding *even if I did* from *even if I did like crooks*. If verb-phrase deletion were to operate again, along with one instance of noun-phrase anaphor formation, the example would read:

> I don't like crooks, and even if I *did*, I wouldn't like *those* that are stool-pigeons, and if I did, I still wouldn't like you.

The instances of *like* could also be replaced by sentential pronominalization; but the point about repetition and anaphora should still be clear.

The same features appear in sorites in Hebrew; I present two examples in which the negation is virtual rather than explicit. Consider the destruction catalog in Joel 1.4.[6]

Joel 1.4a	*yeter-haggāzām 'ākal hā'arbeh*
Joel 1.4b	*wĕyeter-hā'arbeh 'ākal hayyāleq*
Joel 1.4c	*wĕyeter-hayyeleq 'ākal heḥāsîl*

Joel 1.4a	Locust eats what cutter left.
Joel 1.4b	Grub eats what locust left.
Joel 1.4c	Hopper eats what grub left.

Alongside this verse example, consider the similar prose catalog in 1 Kgs 19.17-18.

> *wĕhāyâ hannimlāṭ mēḥereb ḥăzā'ēl yāmît yēhû' wĕhannimlāṭ mēḥereb yēhû' yāmît 'ĕlîšā' wĕhiš'artî bĕyiśrā'ēl šib'at 'ălāpîm.*

> Him who escapes Hazael's sword Jehu shall kill, and him who escapes Jehu's sword Elisha shall kill, and I'll leave in Israel seven thousand.

In both cases the repetition is dense and the virtual negatives powerful.[7]

The sorites is a chain of two or more propositions (linguistically, sentences, for the most part) tied by repetition or anaphora and rehearsing a logical relation. The pseudosorites is a type of paradox which has some elements of the form of the sorites, but in which the negatives pattern illogically. The first sorites quoted above is an insult, but the form occurs in a variety of uses. The pseudosorites, like other types of paradox, is well suited to insults, as in this example, from a more genteel speaker than the woman who didn't like crooks.

> I dare say you expect me to shake hands with you, but even if I would, I can't with this bicycle (Denis Johnston).

The connector *even if* appears here as in the earlier example, but this time the concessive works quite differently. The sentence *I dare say you expect me to shake hands with you* would, in itself, serve as a rebuff to the expectation, and *even if I would* confirms the rebuff. The fact that the speaker is holding a bicycle does not serve as an excuse; indeed it is all but explicitly excluded from that role. It is the ghost of an excuse.

If we consider another English example we shall see that the pseudosorites can be savage as well as genteel. Malvina Reynolds, in a series of 'Non-ads', resorts to a pseudosorites in the conclusion of this verse:

> Try our insecticides—
> We know they're sure to please.
> They kill the little bees
> That pollinate the trees.
> Buy our insecticides
> On easy payment terms.
> You won't have any apples
> But they won't have any worms (Malvina Reynolds).

The apples which do not exist in one sentence are the subject of the next; the anaphor *they* and the repetition of *won't have any* link the two sentences. Thus, parody is another function of the pseudosorites.

3. *The Pseudosorites in Hebrew Verse*

Parody and insult might suggest that in studying the pseudosorites we are on the ground of the prophets, though the sarcasm in the two English examples is not nearly as mordant as the classical prophets often are. So it should come as no surprise that the pseudosorites is a strategy to be found in their writings. I want to mention some examples of pseudosorites from the prophets. Not all are plainly sarcastic, though all the examples bring into play the kinds of claims to power proper to sarcasm.

Let us begin by looking at some examples of two-step pseudosorites.[8] In Hos 8.7de the subject is cereal cultivation.[9]

Hos 8.7d	*bĕlî-ya'ăśeh qemaḥ*
Hos 8.7e	*'ûlay-ya'ăśeh zārîm yiblā'uhû*

Hos 8.7d	He [Israel] makes no flour.
Hos 8.7e	Even if he makes (it), strangers eat it.

In the first sentence, which is also the first line, it is asserted that a not-explicitly identified subject can make no flour, and in the second that even if he makes it (or it is made), he will not be able to feed himself—the point of the flour-making—since strangers will consume the meal. The lines show, in addition to the logical relations characteristic of pseudosorites, the grammatical patterns, both repetition (*hr y'śh*) and anaphoric relation (*qmḥ* and *(ybl')hw*). One anaphoric relation is not morphologically realized: *y'śh* in 7e bears no object suffix, as verbs often do not in Hebrew verse. (The usual descriptions of this situation, invoking the notion that the object is 'understood' or the principle of the double-duty suffix, both reflect incomplete analyses.) The logic of irreal consequence is combined with a complex of grammatical ties between the two parts of the chain.

A later stage in agricultural economy is apparently treated in Mic 6.14cd. This pseudosorites is surrounded by a group of other curses, of simpler logical form. There are two one-line curses.

Mic 6.14a	*'attâ tō'kal wĕlo'-tiśbā'*
	You eat and are not satisfied.
Mic 6.15a	*'attâ tizra' wĕlō'-tiqṣôr*
	You sow and don't reap.

There is a three-line double curse.

Mic 6.15b	*'attâ tidrōk zayit*
Mic 6.15c	*wĕlō'-tāsûk šemen*
Mic 6.15d	*wĕtîrôš wĕlō'-tišteh yāyin*

Mic 6.15b	You tread olives
Mic 6.15c	And don't anoint with oil.
Mic 6.15d	[You tread] grape-pulp and don't drink wine.

These are logically straightforward lines, but Mic 6.14cd are not.[10]

Mic 6.14c	*wĕtassēg wĕlō'-taplîṭ*
Mic 6.14d	*wa'ăšer tĕpallēṭ laḥereb 'ettēn*

Mic 6.14c	You bear off (stores) but secure nothing.
Mic 6.14d	What you secure I give to the sword.

The philological problems here are numerous, as are those of Mic 6.14b, which I leave out of consideration. The traditional understanding (cf. AV), which I follow, is supported by the general sense of Mic 6.14-15, which moves from eating (14a) to provisioning (14cd) to the getting of cereal (15a), oil (15bc), and wine (15d). The hiphil of *s/śwg* 'to move (oneself) away' (viz. 'to backslide') means 'to move (something)', almost always a boundary marker (*hr gĕbûl*). Here the absolute sense is taken to refer to moving food (or perhaps valuables). The first form of *plṭ* 'to escape' is easier; the sense of the hiphil is 'to bring into security' (so BDB), the only other occurrence of the stem referring to prey (Isa 5.29). The omission of an object after a negative finite form of a transitive verb is standard. The piel, the form in 6.14d, is usually used in the same sense as the hiphil, but of personal objects. If we may take *taplîṭ* and *tĕpallēṭ* as having the same sense, the passage is a pseudosorites: that which is not *taplîṭ* in 6.14c is the object, *'ăšer tĕpallēṭ*, which Yahweh destroys in 6.14d. It may be worth noting that this reading would also carry on a elliptical understanding of *tassēg* as referring to a boundary stone: 'You move the boundary marker but make no one (*or* nothing) secure./ Those who (*or* That which) you make secure I give to the sword.'[11]

The pseudosorites in Mic 6.14cd is of a piece with the other material in vv. 14-15. Other examples of the pseudosorites may similarly be part of the texture of the passages in which they occur; this poetic strategy may interact with other strategies, engaging the same metaphoric realms or metadiegetic structures. Hos 8 evidences such complexity: the pseudosorites in v. 7 links itself to the set of allusion to foreign alliances in the rest of the chapter and exhibits the byplay of singular and plural references that crisscrosses the chapter. Hos. 2, 5, and 9 also show similar complexity. I will turn to the last of these and look at aspects of its logical structure.

The second half of Hosea 9 is a recital of Israel's spiritual history that focuses on the advent of the central relation—'I found Israel in the wilderness' (9.10 in part)—and studies it under the aspect of generation. Over and over the passage recurs to the processes of reproduction as indeterminable clues to the character of Yahweh's tie to Israel, both primordial and present. It is the emphasis on present time that leads to the description of those processes as failed and failing.

One of the descriptions occurs in the second last verse of the chapter. There the prophet begins by declaring Ephraim sterile.

Hos 9.16a	*hukkâ 'eprayim*
Hos 9.16b	*šoršām yābēš*
Hos 9.16c	*pĕrî bal(y)-ya'ăśûn*

Hos 9.16a	Ephraim is stricken.
Hos 9.16b	Their root is dry.
Hos 9.16c	They produce no fruit.

The language of *šrš* and *pry* is euphemistic, but the context of the chapter makes it clear that the male organ and the outcome of its implanting is meant. As elsewhere in Hos 9.10-17, the possibility of engendering, here specifically on the male side, is denied. The verse continues with a verbal paraphrase of 9.16c rather than an anaphor or a repeated item.

Hos 9.16d	*gam-kî-yēlēdûn wěhēmattî maḥămaddê biṭnām*
	Even if they engender, I'll kill their bellies' darlings.

That is, if the insuperable obstacle of sterility is surmounted, Yahweh will kill the results of the engenderings.

There is a comparable 'take' on reproduction earlier in the chapter, in vv. 11 and 12:

Hos 9.11b	*millēdâ ûmibbeṭen ûmēhērāyôn*
Hos 9.12a	*kî- 'im-yěgaddělû 'et-běnêhem*
Hos 9.12b	*wěšikkaltîm mē'ādām*

Hos 9.11b	No birth, no gestation, no conception.
Hos 9.12a	Even if they raise their children,
Hos 9.12b	I'll bereave them before maturity (*or* of men, NJPS).

The first line constitutes a sorites, presented in the reverse of the expected or 'natural' order; it is both short grammatically (three phrases) and complex logically (three steps). This feat of condensation reflects the character of the processes that lead from impregnation to giving birth; the middle term *bṭn*, 'belly', is marked in the sense of gestation by the two flanking terms. In 9.11b, then, the female side of the engendering process is presented as failed, and, as in 9.16, there is a grim follow-up in the form of a pseudosorites: even if they (the masculine verb has a generic sense) raise children, the children will be destroyed before maturity (or as mature individuals) and the parents bereaved.

Hos 9.11b-12 and 9.16 are similar in structure: there will be no functioning of one gender or the other in reproduction, but even if there is functioning, the children begotten and reared will be destroyed. It is occasionally suggested that two such similar verses would be happy side by side (see, e.g., the NJPS note), but aspects of the overall structure of 9.10-17 speak against that view. The first such aspect is the symmetrical position of the two pseudosorites, and the second is the location of a third pseudosorites between them. In 9.14 there is a passage spoken in a voice quite different from that of the rest of the chapter.

Hos 9.14a	*tēn lāhem yhwh*
Hos 9.14b	*mâ tittēn*
Hos 9.14c	*tēn lāhem reḥem-maškil*
Hos 9.14d	*wĕšadayim-ṣomĕqîm*

Hos 9.14a	Give them, Yahweh—
Hos 9.14b	What shall you give?
Hos 9.14c	Give them a miscarrying womb
Hos 9.14d	And a pair of breasts that is dried up.

The prophet prays that the women of Ephraim be given wombs that miscarry, wombs that do not come to term. But should the miscarrying wombs come to term anyway, he prays that Yahweh give those women breasts incapable of providing nurture.[12]

Over a third of the verse in 9.10-17 is concerned with reproduction and involved in more or less explicit pseudosorites. Are we to read the three passages together, as constituting one complex pseudosorites? The evidence of other, equally complex passages, e.g., Job 3.3-10, suggests that we should.

4. *Concluding Remarks*

We have examined a few examples of the pseudosorites, a form of paradox involving two or three clauses tied by repetition, anaphora, or their equivalents. The form begins by excluding an event or outcome and continues by denying what would follow from that event or outcome; it is logically irreal and grammatically counterfactual. The examples treated here and the few others I have examined do not favor a particular logical connector. Here, *kî*-compounds occur twice (*gam-kî* in Hos 9.16d and *kî-'im* in Hos 9.12a); there is no marked connector in two cases (Mic 6.14d and Hos 9.14d); the use of *'ûlay* in Hos 8.7e is eccentric. Other syntactic features await further study. The suffix *(bny)hm* with its phantom antecedent is particularly interesting.

The examples we have considered for the most part refer to natural processes, cultivation and reproduction. Such processes may be said to have an inherent 'logic', that is, a predictable set of relations of various elements to the whole, which lends itself to tricks of 'logic', in the stricter sense of a set of relations made explicit and subject to scrutiny. The natural scheme, that is, proposes that impregnation leads to childbirth, but that scheme, which seems so inevitable, is still only a possible scheme. Other schemes may emerge or be imposed. In the examples at hand it is immaterial whether the alternative orders emerge or are imposed; what is crucial is the agent to whom they are attributed. If natural processes are basic to the form, then the pseudosorites is a theological prototype of possible-worlds logics.[13]

The question of where the form comes from is comparable to that of why it appears in verse, and I have no firmer answer for the latter question than for the former. The condensation that is a hallmark of all verse in part explains the pairing of the pseudosorites and Hebrew verse. Even more basic may be the role of repetition and complex forms of anaphora in Hebrew poetry; these resources are rarely used as extensively in poetry as they are in Hebrew. But further consideration of this topic must await study of the other linguistic paradoxes of the Hebrew Bible.

NOTES

1. I mean by paradox, paradoxical utterance rather than, for example, the antinomies of Lutheran, Kierkegaardian, and Hegelian theology (law and grace, freedom and necessity). I also exclude here the pattern of the implicit exception, e.g., reference to a text as 'unpublished' in a scholarly work that publishes the text (where 'unpublished' should be 'previously unpublished); cf. Mark 1.44. The role of utterance as determinative of linguistic meaning is discussed in its philosophical context by Arthur Gibson in his illuminating essay, *Biblical Semantic Logic* (New York: St. Martin's Press, 1981). For a general review of the work on paradox summarized here, see P. Watzlawick, J.H. Beavin, and D.D. Jackson, *Pragmatics of Human Communication* (New York: Norton, 1967); cf. P. Watzlawick, *How Real Is Real?* (New York: Random House, 1976), and J.L. Mackie, *Truth, Probability and Paradox* (Oxford: Clarendon, 1973). On Epimenides' Cretan, see Mackie, p. 296.

Comments on earlier papers in this series from S.H. Elgin, L.K. Obler, B. Bicknell, and P. Schmitz are gratefully acknowledged. This paper was read to the Biblical Hebrew Poetry Section of the Society of Biblical Literature at its 1984 meeting in Chicago, and I wish to thank its members for their comments.

2. These paradoxes have not been discussed with regard to biblical theology, but is not Elijah's rebuke, 'How long halt ye between two

opinions?' (1 Kgs 18.21, AV) a description of schizophrenogenesis in action? Compare the torture of Japanese Christians in the early seventeenth century discussed by Watzlawick and his colleagues (*Pragmatics*, pp. 203-207): the Japanese Christians were required to affirm their loyalty to the 'great family' of Japan with its gods by adjuring themselves by the Christian god, an adjuration which logically required them to express disloyalty to Japan. The 'problem' of Ezekiel's 'psychic abnormality' (so W.F. Albright), *pace* the useful strictures of the Jesuit psychiatrist Ned Cassem ('Ezekiel's Psychotic Personality; Reservations on the Use of the Couch for Biblical Personalities', *The Word in the World: Essays in Honor of Frederick L. Moriarty, S.J.*, ed. R.J. Clifford and G.W. MacRae [Cambridge, Mass.: Weston College Press, 1973], pp. 59-70), should be seen as a reflection or perhaps a byproduct of the schizophrenogenic situation in which the prophet worked.

3. This definition of poetry (as opposed to verse) is Helen Vendler's. See Vendler, *Part of Nature, Part of Us* (Cambridge: Harvard University Press, 1980).

4. The phenomenon in Hebrew is treated by F.I. Andersen in *Job* (Tyndale Old Testament Commentaries; Downers Grove, Ill.: Inter-Varsity Press, 1976), and F.I. Andersen and D.N. Freedman, *Hosea* (AB, 24; Garden City: Doubleday, 1980); O'Connor, 'The Pseudosorites in Hebrew Verse', in *A Ready Scribe: Essays in Honor of F.I. Andersen*, ed. Ted Newing and Ed Conrad (Winona Lake: Eisenbrauns, 1987), and in English by O'Connor, 'Irish bull and pseudosorites: Two types of paradox in English'. To the catalogue of examples in 'The Pseudosorites in Hebrew Verse', Job 40.30 should be added. I rely heavily on the work of my teachers Andersen and Freedman in what follows, and recognition of the pseudosorites is due to Professor Andersen. For an important discussion of the sorites, especially in the Mishnah, the Talmud, and Christian Scripture, see H.A. Fischel, 'The Use of Sorites (Climax, Gradatio) in the Tannaitic Period', *HUCA* 44 (1973), pp. 119-51. Fischel provides full bibliography for the classical background of the sorites and an abundance of examples from the period he studies (for the Mishnah, note simply Pirke Aboth 1.1; for the New Testament, Rom 10.14f., 8.29). From the Hebrew Bible he cites as examples Joel 1.3, Hos 2.23, and Joel 1.4 (pp. 128, 131); cf. Wisdom of Solomon 6.17ff. Miriam Lichtheim's recent survey of the Demotic instructions deals with paradoxes in Egyptian and Hebrew wisdom literature; see *Late Egyptian Wisdom Literature in the International Contex: A Study of the Demotic Instructions* (Orbis Biblicus et Orientalis, 52: Freiburg: Universitätsverlag Freiburg, 1983), pp. 138-50; on the sorites, pp. 13-18.

5. The increasing specificity here is similar to the chain *bnk, yḥdk, 'šr 'hbt, yṣḥq* in Gen 22.2.

6. I borrow the translation of the entomological terms from NJPS.

7. I also owe these examples to Professor Andersen (in Andersen and Freedman, *Hosea*, pp. 497-83); Dr Loraine Obler forced me to figure out

how they are to be distinguished from the pseudosorites. Andersen also cites 2 Baruch (= the Syriac Apocalypse of Baruch) 70.8-10. W.H. Shea suggests as examples of the sorites Amos 5.3 (+ 6.9) and 5.19, noting the eighth-century date of both Amos and Hosea as a possible point for further consideration in the history of Israelite dialectic.

8. In the handling of Hebrew verse I follow O'Connor, *Hebrew Verse Structure*. On the recent study of anaphora, see the references in O'Connor, 'The Pseudosorites in Hebrew Verse'; the study of Konrad Ehlich, 'Anaphora and Deixis: Same, Similar, or Different?', in *Speech, Place, and Action*, ed. R.J. Jarvella and W. Klein (Chichester: John Wiley, 1982), is concerned in part with Hebrew. J. Hankamer and I. Sag, 'Deep and surface anaphora', in *Linguistic Inquiry* 7 (1976), pp. 391-428, are useful on anaphora in general; see pp. 425-26 on anaphora and discourse as a whole.

9. The rest of the passage is treated in O'Connor, 'The Pseudosorites in Hebrew Verse'.

10. In his scheme of biblical and other ancient Near Eastern curses, D.R. Hillers recognizes curses by gods, simile curses, simple maledictions, and a small category of futility curses. See *Treaty-Curses and the Old Testament Prophets* (Biblica et Orientalia, 16; Rome: Pontifical Biblical Institute, 1964), pp. 28-29. All pseudosorites curses are members of this last group. Hillers deals with the Mic 6 curses in particular.

11. The ellipsis of a common object after a verb requires schematic study; *ńs'* would provide a good starting point.

12. Hos 9, along with several other passages dealing with birth, notably the curses of Jer 20 and Job 3, are treated in the context of the full range of birth vocabulary by P. Trible, *God and the Rhetoric of Sexuality* (Philadelphia: Fortress, 1978), pp. 31-71; Jer 20 and Job 3, pp. 36-37, 55; Hos 9, pp. 61-62; cf. O'Connor, 'The Pseudosorites in Hebrew Verse'.

The dry-breast curse is paralleled in the Sefire treaty and in a treaty described in Ashurbanipal's annals. Hillers (*Treaty-Curses*, pp. 61-62) treats this topos.

I have looked for pseudosorites in other ancient Near Eastern texts but without success. This passage from the Ashurnirari V-Mati'ilu Treaty may be a candidate:

> rev iv 17 šumma ^{m}mati'ilu mārēšu rabūtišu ša ina adī 18 ša ^{m}aššurnirāri šar ^{mat} aššur iḫaṭūni 19 LU$_{2}$.ENGAR-šu ina ṣēri aj ilsā alala 20 urqīt ṣēri lu la [= aj] uṣṣā ^{d}šamaš lu la immar (IGI). (Cf. E. Weidner, 'Der Staatvertrag Aššurnirâris VI. von Assyrien mit Mati'ilu von Bît-Agûsi', *Archiv für Orientforschung* 8 [1932], pp. 17-34).
>
> If it is the case that it is Mati'ilu, his sons, or his nobles who err against this treaty of Ashurnirari, king of Assyria—may his farmer not sing the alala-song in the open country, may no vegetation come out in the open country and see the sunlight (cf. E. Reiner in *ANET*, p. 533).

The difficulty is with the exact force of the alala-cry; Reiner translates it 'harvest song', but the dictionary entries are less firm. (See also T. Jacobsen, *The Harab Myth* [Sources from the Ancient Near East, 2 no. 3], pp. 102-103, 113.) Similarly, the complex curse in the Tabnit inscription comes close, as P. Schmitz observes, but does not quite fit; cf. F. Mazza, 'Le formule di maledizione nelle iscrizioni funerarie e votive fenicie e puniche', *Rivista di studi fenici* 3 (1975), pp. 19-30.

13. The best introduction to possible-worlds logic is still provided by the Alice books, Lewis Carroll's *Alice in Wonderland* and *Through the Looking-Glass*; for another look, see Rudolf Carnap's table-talk in *An Introduction to the Philosophy of Science*, ed. M. Gardner (New York: Basic Books, 1974).

The three English quotations are from Dashiell Hammett, *The Thin Man* (New York: Vintage, 1972; originally 1933), p. 79; Denis Johnston's play *The Moon in the Yellow River* (1932), published in E.M. Brown's *Three Irish Plays* (Baltimore: Penguin, 1959), p. 27; and Malvina Reynolds's songbook, *Cheerful Tunes for Lutes and Spoons* (Berkeley: Schroeder Music Company, 1970), p. 39.

10

THE HOLY CITY AS DAUGHTER

Elaine R. Follis

This paper deals with the expression, 'daughter of Zion'—or more properly, 'the daughter, Zion'—which occurs twenty-six times in the Old Testament, all of them in poetic contexts. Why is the holy city of Yahweh described as a woman, and more specifically, as a daughter? A comparison between this image and descriptions of Athena, the patroness of Athens and the daughter of Zeus, suggests one answer to the question. This paper investigates the parallel, thereby presenting the well-known Hebrew expression *bat-ṣiyyôn* in a somewhat different light than has been customary, as seen against the backdrop of Greek tradition.

At least for the present, uncertainty and speculation surround the comparatively little hellenosemitic research which has to date been done. Its claims, therefore, must remain modest. Nothing in this essay is intended to ignore or negate the parallels which exist, on this topic and on other topics, between the culture of Israel and those of Canaan and Mesopotamia. Such parallels are unquestionably the most important ones to consider. And yet they may not be the only ones with significance for an understanding of the backgrounds of biblical tradition. The hellenosemitic line of inquiry developed here would be a footnote, at best, in a more traditionally focused study. But its subject matter merits closer attention than that. By design, this paper looks at biblical texts in an unusual—but not impossible—context in an effort to see what more subtle elements of meaning may thereby emerge from the text.

Specifically, this paper will suggest the following: first, that the idea of a holy city as a divine daughter is hellenosemitic in scope;

second, that the poetry of both Hebrews and Greeks was a channel within which this idea was certainly expressed, and quite possibly, transmitted; third, that the feminine quality of the holy city pertains particularly to an intimate, virtually inseparable relationship between place and people, between the land and its inhabitants, and to the whole notion of civilization as over against barbarity; and finally, that the holy city as daughter in Hebrew literature may represent a 'broken myth'—the Hebrews' radically modified version of the great goddess, who appears here (as in certain elements of Greek tradition) not as the consort but as the daughter of the high god.

Tangential to but corroborative of the thesis of this essay is the parallel, far more widely acknowledged and intensively studied, between the goddess of wisdom (in this case, Athena) and its feminine voice heard in chapters 3 and 7 of the book of Proverbs. Here surely is a trace of the goddess figure in Old Testament tradition, classical parallels to which seem both ancient and very apparent.

Certain statistical observations constitute a reasonable beginning for this study. As was noted earlier, the phrase *bat-ṣiyyôn* appears twenty-six times in the Old Testament,[1] without exception in poetic literature. Each occurrence appears to draw on figurative language and imagery. From the standpoints of context and meaning, it is therefore appropriate to describe the expression as characteristically poetic. The plural, *bĕnôt-ṣiyyôn*, occurs four times,[2] also in poetic contexts and always referring to female inhabitants of the city of Jerusalem, a literal signification which does not seem ever to fit the singular form of the phrase.

As is well known, the word Zion refers to the fortified hill of the pre-Davidic city of Jerusalem, but appears frequently, especially in poetry, as a synonym for the city itself. Barrois explains the latter usage as significant of Jerusalem, first of all, as a religious capital; then as an object of divine favor or punishment; then as a collective term, designating Jerusalem as community.[3] Each usage pertains to the fuller expression *bat-ṣiyyôn* as well. Of approximately 106 references to Zion in the Old Testament, 30 have the word 'daughter' attached, as we have seen. There are in addition three references to the sons of Zion, or 'children of Zion'; all of them occur in poetry, and all designate the collective population of the city of Jerusalem.[4]

The expression, 'daughter of...' connected with a city or nation occurs sixteen times in the Old Testament, all in poetry: twice in

Psalms, three times each in proto-Isaiah and deutero-Isaiah, five times in Jeremiah, twice in Lamentations, and once in Zechariah.[5] The referents include Tyre and Sidon twice, Babylon seven times, Tarshish once, Edom twice, Egypt three times, and Gallim once. The plural, 'daughters of...' connected with a place name, also occurs from time to time, not always in poetic contexts. Sometimes the referent, as in the case of *bĕnôt-ṣiyyôn*, is female inhabitants of a territory; sometimes the expression, when connected with the name of a nation or territory, may refer to cities and villages therein (as, for example, 'daughters of the Philistines' in Ezek 16.27). The expressions, 'daughter of Judah' and 'daughter of Jerusalem'—in the singular each time—occur only in conjunction with *bat-ṣiyyôn*, the former three times and the latter seven times.[6] Of these ten instances, half are in direct parallelism with *bat-ṣiyyôn*.

With specific reference to the twenty-six occurrences of *bat-ṣiyyôn* itself, the preponderance—fourteen passages—appear in pre-exile literature, from the late eighth to early sixth centuries BC. The balance are probably exilic or post-exilic; eight appear in the book of Lamentations. It is clear from these observations that the expression *bat-ṣiyyôn* was closely connected with the nationalistic traditions of Judah, epitomized and symbolized by a capital, the city of Jerusalem. While statistics do not suggest the expression enjoyed wide popularity, it was nevertheless significant to Hebrew poets as a word-image with meanings at several levels.

A study of the grammatical characteristics of the twenty-six instances of the phrase *bat-ṣiyyôn* indicates the following. In fifteen verses, it stands at the end of a full line of poetry, or directly before a major caesura. In twelve verses, it stands in the vocative case. In nine verses, it is in a construct chain with another noun. In four verses, it is part of a prepositional phrase. And in three verses, it immediately follows the verb. The first two observations here are probably the most significant. The placement of a term immediately before a major break in word flow generally suggests a sense of emphasis and climax. The ancient poets accorded to *bat-ṣiyyôn* an important place as an expression with considerable emotional and conceptual impact. It is also not surprising that a phrase used metaphorically to represent a group of people as a community should be the recipient of direct address.

The correct translation of *bat-ṣiyyôn* has received recent attention, probably most significantly in the article, 'No Daughter of Zion' by

W.F. Stinespring.[7] His contention is that the expression, a personification, represents an occurrence of the appositional genitive, and should properly be translated, 'the daughter, Zion'.[8] Stinespring goes on to advocate greater flexibility in the translation of the word *bat* (which, like the Arabic *bint*, as he points out, can mean 'daughter', but also 'girl', or 'maiden'). In his survey of modern English translations, he laments that in the King James Version, the Revised Standard Version, and others, 'By and large "the daughter of Zion" seems to be a favorite character',[9] whereas in the work of James Moffatt, Stinespring discovers consistently correct translations, with 'maiden Sion' appearing fifteen times and 'Sion the maiden' twice.[10]

Explanations of the signification of *bat-ṣiyyôn* vary somewhat, but the consensus seems to be that the expression is a collective noun, suggesting the inhabitants of Jerusalem, both male and female,[11] or, one might say, 'the people of Zion as a unit', following the comments in the Koehler-Baumgartner lexicon.[12] As Stinespring observes, one of the definitions in the Brown-Driver-Briggs lexicon plays up the element of figurative language in its approach to the noun *bat*, noting: 'with name of city, land, or people, poetical personification of that city or (its) inhabitants'.[13]

The expression, while clearly connotative of people, is so in a very specific way, with direct reference to a place where that people dwells. The phrase *bat-ṣiyyôn* cannot possibly be understood simply in terms of a collection of human beings somewhere in space; these people have a home, a place from which they derive identity. And that place is Zion, the city of the Lord. The holy city thereby becomes both a meeting point for God and people, and a center—a point of stability—around which the human community revolves. And that holy city is a daughter. Why?

One may seek the explanation of this phenomenon, at the deeper levels of thought, in the language of symbol and myth. It is common to speak of the sky and earth as male and female elements, respectively. It is thus that they appear in the mythology of the ancient Near East, within which cultural milieu Israel grew to nationhood; and they appear thus in Greek mythology as well. With specific reference to children, males are commonly regarded by cultures both ancient and modern as people who go abroad seeking their fortunes and conquest. Indeed, sons commonly are thought to represent the adventuresome spirit of a society, constantly pressing beyond established boundaries, at the outmost part, the circumference, of the community. Daughters, on the other hand, have been associated with stability, with the building up of society, with nurturing the community at its very heart and center. The stereotypical male spirit lies in conquest, while the stereotypical female spirit lies in culture.

Thus the expression *bat-ṣiyyôn* does not refer to the Hebrew people in their wilderness wanderings, nor even in their territorial conquests during the period of the tribal confederacy. Rather, the expression refers to the Hebrews as a settled people, a centered and stable people whose life and culture revolved around the divine-human encounter focused on the holy city, Jerusalem. The usage of the term in pre-exilic literature from the monarchic period, and in later literature whose theme was the recollection of the glory of that era, appears to be entirely appropriate.

The hellenosemitic frame of reference within which this study has proceeded contributes greatly to understanding the propriety of the femininity of Jerusalem, not merely in terms of the city as being the mother of its inhabitants (a concept traditionally held and widely stated), but also and perhaps rather, in terms of the city as divine daughter. As such, the city becomes the quintessence of civilization and culture, of a stable lifestyle, of permanent relationships. It also becomes in particular the recipient of divine favor, and also, conversely, of wrath and punishment. That these statements also hold true for Athena, patroness of the city of Athens, will be demonstrated.

The mood which prevails in the twenty-six settings in which *bat-ṣiyyôn* occurs is worthy of consideration in this regard. In thirteen, or precisely half of them, the phrase occurs so as to represent dignity, joy, favor, and exaltation. Nine verses pertain to the restoration of Zion after an experience of sadness and humiliation. The other thirteen references cite the city as the object of wrath, mortification, and destruction—a pitiful image indeed, made poignant by the fact that the expression itself probably originated to depict the city and her people in victorious, secure prosperity. Here, then, is found ironic reversal, the downfall of what has been cherished, refined, and cultured. In one instance, such refinement and culture are associated with *hybris*, as Jeremiah declares, 'The settled and spoiled Daughter of Zion I shall destroy' (6.2). Elsewhere, in Mic 4.10 and Lam 1.6, culture is set in contrast with images suggesting the relative barbarity of the countryside, the open field with its wildlife.

ḥûlî wāgōḥî bat-ṣiyyôn kayyôlēḏâ
kî-ʿattâ tēṣʾî miqqiryâ wĕšākant baśśādeh

Writhe and burst forth, Daughter Zion, like her bringing forth
child;
for you will go forth from the city and inhabit the open field.

wayyēṣēʾ min-bat-ṣiyyôn kol-hădārâ
hāyû śāreyhā kĕʾayyālîm lōʾ-māṣʾû mirʿeh

From Daughter Zion has gone forth all her honor;
Her princes are as rams who have not found pasture.

In summary, then, the expression *bat-ṣiyyôn*, the maiden Zion (following the lead of Stinespring), is more than simply the personification of a group of people. Rather, it is an image of the unity between place and people within which divine favor and civilization create a setting of stability, of home, of fixedness. To see the beauty of that setting defaced is, to the ancient poet, comparable to seeing a beloved and cherished maiden ravished; thus appears deep pathos, inherent in the juxtaposition of 'Maiden Zion' and descriptions of destruction.

With these notions in focus, attention may appropriately be turned to the thought of the Greeks, concentrating specifically on Athena, virgin daughter of Zeus. Athena was an ancient, pre-Hellenic deity,[14] originally perhaps a tutelary goddess of Minoan and Mycenean princes. As such, she may have had significant Asiatic connections, since both sites have been demonstrated by T.B.L. Webster as trading with Mari, Ugarit and Alalakh in the sixteenth century BC.[15]

Athena is notable as a goddess of civilization, warfare, and most significantly, as the patroness of the city of Athens. The Greek poet Pindar preserves what is probably the most ancient version of her birth (which appears in substantially the same form in Hesiod's Homeric Hymn 28):

ἀνίχ Ἁφαίστου τέχναισιν
χαλκελάτῳ πελέκει πατέρος Ἀθαναία κορυφὰν κατ' ἄκραν
ανορούσαισ' ἀλάλαξεν ὑπερμάκει βοᾷ·
Οὐρανὸς δ' ἔφριξέ νιν καὶ Γαῖα μάτηρ.

By the cunning skill of Hephaestos
with copper axe, broke forth Athena from her father's crown,
and shouted with a great cry;
both heaven and mother earth trembled before her
(*Olympian Ode* 7.35-38).

In the *Theogony* (886-900), Hesiod explains that Zeus, sky god and chief of the Olympian pantheon, had married Metis—whose name means intelligence—only to learn that Metis was fated to bear a son who would reign as lord of heaven. Zeus, in an act of cannibalism, devoured Metis; but in due time, Athena was born, springing full-grown and fully armed from the head of her father.

Hesiod describes her specifically as 'the maiden (*kourēn*), . . . having strength equal to her father, and wise counsel (*epiphrona boulēn*)' (*Theogony* 895-96). Homer in the Iliad frequently joins her name with those of Zeus and her brother Apollo in an invocation to a sort of supreme trinity of gods (see e.g. 4.288; 7.132; 16.97). According to H.J. Rose, Athena was Zeus' favorite daughter, his 'dear Grey-Eyes',[16] and an incident from Book 5 of the Iliad tends to corroborate this perspective. Aphrodite and Athena have both approached Zeus on behalf of their favorites in the great war—in the former case, the Trojans, and of course in Athena's case, the Greeks. Athena heaps scorn upon Aphrodite,[17] and this is how Homer describes Zeus' response:

> Ὣς φάτο, μείδησεν δὲ πατὴρ ἀνδρῶν τε θεῶν τε,
> καί ῥα καλεσσάμενος προσέφη χρυσῆν Ἀφροδίτην·
> 'οὔ τοι, τέκνον ἐμον, δέδοται πολεμήϊα ἔργα,
> αλλὰ σύ γ' ἱμερόεντα μετέρχεο ἔργα γάμοιο,
> ταῦτα δ' Ἄρηϊ θοῷ καὶ Ἀθήνῃ πάντα μελήσει.'
>
> Thus she spake, and the father of both men and gods smiled,
> and then, having summoned golden Aphrodite, said:
> 'Not to you, my child, is given martial deeds,
> but you see to the enchanting matters of wedlock,
> and all these affairs shall pertain to swift Ares and Athena'
> (ll. 426-30).

With these words, Zeus effectively dismisses the appeal of Aphrodite, though gently, and reinforces the character of Athena as a wager of war, privy to his own counsels. Indeed, Professor Van L. Johnson has suggested that Athena's common epithet 'Pallas' means 'Shaker', or 'Brandisher', particularly of the aegis, symbol of Zeus' authority.[18] This aegis was represented either as a short, tasseled goatskin cloak or a shield worn on the left arm, decorated with snakes, representations of the qualities of fear, fight, force, and pursuit, and having in the center a gorgon's head.[19] Wielding the aegis caused stormclouds to gather, and its use served either to terrorize or to protect soldiers in battle.

A favorite epithet of Homer, applied to Athena, was *glaukōpis*, variously translated as grey-eyed, owl-eyed, or bright-eyed. It is Glaukopis Athena who constantly operates as an unseen force on the field of battle, deflecting arrows (4.541; 11.438), guiding Greek spears to their mark (5.290), sending confusion on Trojan troops (18.311), and beguiling the Trojan prince Hector to his doom (22.299).

How does all of this display of might on the part of one whom Hesiod describes as 'the terrible (*deinēn*), strife-stirring (*egrekudoimon*), host-marshaling (*agestraton*), unflagging lady (*atrutōnēn potnian*), who joys in din of battle and war and combat' (*Theogony* 924-26), square with the Hebrew vision of the daughter Zion in Lamentations?

> *ṣā'aq libbām 'el-'ădōnāy ḥômat bat-ṣiyyôn*
> *hôrîdî ḵannaḥal dim'â yômām wālayĕlâ*
> *'al-titnî pûgat lāk 'al-tidōm bat-'ēnēk*
>
> Cry to the Lord, Daughter Zion,
> cause your tears to flow down like a wadi, day and night;
> do not give solace to yourself nor rest to your eyes (2.18).

It clearly does not. The warrior maiden Athena was never disposed to lament with tears nor to bewail her fate. She was, however, like Daughter Zion, under the condemnation of her father on at least one occasion for disobeying his orders.

The Hebrew poet sings, 'How the Lord in his wrath has placed Daughter Zion under a cloud' (Lam 2.1). Homer, in Book 8 of the Iliad, describes Zeus' threat to his rebellious daughter, delivered by the divine messenger, Iris.

> ὧδε γὰρ ἠπείλησε Κρόνου πάϊς, ᾗ τελέει περ,
> γυιώσειν μὲν σφῶϊν ὑφ' ἅρμασιν ὠκέας ἵππους,
> αὐτὰς δ'εκ δίφρου βαλέειν κατά θ' ἅρματα ἄξειν·
> οὐδέ κεν ἐς δεκάτους περιτελλομένους ἐνιαυτοὺς
> ἕλκε' ἀπαλθήσεσθον, ἅ κεν μάρπτῃσι κεραυνός·
> ὄφρα ἰδῇς, γλαυκῶπι, ὅτ' ἂν σῷ πατρὶ μάχηαι.
>
> For thus the son of Kronos threatens, who will accomplish it:
> to cripple the swift horses beneath your chariot,
> and hurl you from the chariot-board, and shatter the chariot.
> Nor ever in ten circling years
> will you recover thoroughly from the wounds which the thunderbolt will inflict;
> that you, O Grey-Eyes, may learn better than to defy your father! (415-20).

Here is threatened destruction much in keeping with the mood of Daughter Zion imagery in the Old Testament, made all the more striking by contrast with Zeus' especially tender expression of affection for Athena, a sentiment repeated only shortly before the incident involving threat.[20] Like Daughter Zion, Athena was her father's favorite, beloved child. But like Daughter Zion, and Yahweh's chosen people, Israel, the goddess was not exempt from punishment, should she defy her father! And, of course, her punishment by Zeus would affect directly the fate of her 'chosen people', the Greeks centered in her city, Athens. While strictly speaking Athena does not personify her city, she is intimately bound up with its identity and fortunes.

Of Athena's militarism, an important observation must be made, in light of previous remarks about the qualities of the daughter in connection with civilization and not conquest. Nowhere does Pallas or Glaukopis Athena appear as an instrument of imperialism. While she certainly does not quail before carnage, to her, war serves but one purpose: the protection of her land, her people, her city.

A third significant epithet of Athena is Polis, 'She of the city'. Her contest with Poseidon for divine sovereignty over the city of Athens is recorded by Herodotus (8.55), Apollodorus (3.177-179) and Ovid (*Metamorphoses* 6.75). Poseidon either produced a salt spring from the rock of the Acropolis with a blow of his trident, or created the first horse. Athena created an olive tree, a feat judged the more impressive, and thereby became the patroness of all Attica. In Hesiod's *Homeric Hymns* 11 and 28 she is hailed as Erusiptolin, Guardian and Savior of the City. Pausanias's description of Greece (26.6) includes mention of an image of Athena which supposedly fell from heaven and was subsequently enshrined in a temple which antedated the Parthenon on the Acropolis and was probably completed about 520 BC.

Athena's tie to the land itself, mentioned earlier as a characteristic of daughter imagery among Hebrews as well as Greeks, comes with the myth of Erechthonios, a child born from the seed of Hephaestos which spilled on the ground and fertilized it as he struggled unsuccessfully to subdue Athena. He is sometimes associated with Erechtheus, legendary king of Athens. H.J. Rose writes, '... it is not surprising that Athens, like other places, had tales of kings who had actually and literally sprung not from the womb of any mortal mother, but from the land which they ruled'.[21]

As the patroness of the great city of Athens, Athena represented the epitome of civilization. Accordingly, she was associated with spinning, weaving, and embroidery, with horse-taming, and with music—in particular, music of the salpinx or trumpet—as well as with sailing, pottery, and medicine.[22] C.J. Herington argues that two views of the goddess existed side by side in the Athenian cult, the first earth-rooted and warlike, the second evanescent and intellectual.[23] It is in the latter respect that Athena exemplifies the idea of 'Daughter Civilization' as parallel with the 'settled, spoiled' character of the Hebrew Daughter Zion. Clearly, Athens and Jerusalem were both cities regarded as divinely favored, the centers of their respective civilizations, close to the heart of the God of Heaven. And both were regarded in figurative language as the daughter of that high god.

A final point of comparison may be made as regards the original aspects of Greek and Hebrew divine daughters. Only four of the twenty-six references to *bat-ṣiyyôn* include the word *bĕtulâ*, and in Mic 4.10 and Jer 4.31, *bat-ṣiyyôn* is spoken of as a woman in travail, certainly not virginal. Athena, on the other hand, is always Parthenos, the eternal virgin. She is not, however, without maternal attributes, being described as Mater at her cultic center at Elis.[24] Kalinka has suggested Athena's maternal rather than virginal character.[25] Interesting in this regard is Homer's image in Book 4 of the Iliad, where Athena deflects an arrow from Menalaus 'even as a mother brushed aside a fly from her child as he lies in sweet sleep' (130-31).

The wider implications of this study now remain for discussion. The holy city as daughter is a theme that occurs in Greek as well as Hebrew tradition, and is tied in with the idea of a divinely chosen people centered and settled in their own land. It appears in the writings of the Greek poets Homer and Hesiod, both from the eighth century BC, and in Hebrew literature from the period of the divided monarchy into post-exilic times. We know that, although Athens was fortified in the thirteenth century and functioned as a center of Mycenean trade as early as 1050, it did not come into a position of prominence until the reformist tyrants of the sixth century and the Persian wars of 490 and 489-479 BC. The 'golden age' of Pericles coincided, in the middle of the fifth century, with the restoration efforts of Nehemiah in the city of Jerusalem. It seems inconceivable, given the mediating influence of the Persian empire, that information about the great holy city Jerusalem should not have come to the attention of the builders of Athens, including tyrants like Peisistratus, and possibly Pericles himself. Conversely, as the studies of the classicists Burton-Brown and Webster have shown, Greek civilization richly and consistently inflenced Eastern thought from the second millennium BC.[26] Cyrus Gordon's theories about the truly Mediterranean cultural substratum for the Hebrew people are well known.[27] It is therefore certainly not surprising to find both Hebrew and Greek poets describing their holy cities as divine daughters. It is impossible, and largely pointless, to guess which culture first used the image. It is also unreasonable to suggest that the descriptions had to be generated in a vacuum or in isolation from one another.

As Gordon has maintained, poetry is a flexible medium of intercultural communication, particularly at a period characterized by emphasis on oral tradition. Both Greek and Hebrew literatures had beginnings in oral tradition, and as such, were heirs to a cosmopolitan set of images, styles, and symbols. The holy city as daughter appears to be one such symbol. It is likely that there are others, which may reveal themselves to those who study each canon, in particular its poetic sections, with an open mind.

NOTES

1. 2 Kgs 19.21 par. Isa 37.22; Isa 1.8; 10.32; 16.1; 52.2; 62.11; Mic 1.13; 4.8, 10, 13; Zeph 3.14; Jer 4.31; 6.2, 23; Lam 1.6; 2.1, 4, 8, 10, 13, 18; 4.22; Zech 2.10 (MT 14); 9.9; Ps 9.14 (MT 15).
2. Isa 3.16, 17; 4.4; Cant 3.11.
3. In *The Interpreter's Dictionary of the Bible*, IV (Nashville: Abingdon Press, 1962), p. 959.
4. Ps 149.2; Lam 4.2; Joel 2.23.
5. Ps 45.12; 137.8; Isa 10.30; 23.10, 12; 47.1, 5; Jer 46.11, 19, 24; 50.42; 51.33; Zech 2.7; Lam 4.21, 22. Also worthy of note is Jeremiah's repeated use of the expression, 'daughter of my people', in 8.11, 19, 21, 22, 23; 9.7; 14.17.
6. Daughter of Judah, Lam 1.15; 2.2, 5. Daughter of Jerusalem, 2 Kgs 19.21, par. Isa 37.22; Lam 2:13, Mic 4.8; Zeph 3.14; Zech 9.9.
7. W.F. Stinespring, 'No Daughter of Zion', *Encounter* 26 (1965), pp. 133-41.
8. Stinespring, 'No Daughter', p. 135.
9. Stinespring, 'No Daughter', p. 137.
10. Stinespring, 'No Daughter', p. 138.
11. After Cruden (first edition, 1737).
12. Ludwig H. Koehler and Walter Baumgartner, *Lexicon in Veteris Testamenti Libros* (Leiden: E.J. Brill, 1953).

13. Francis Brown, S.R. Driver, and Charles A. Briggs, *A Hebrew and English Lexicon of the Old Testament* (Oxford, 1952).

14. H.J. Rose, *A Handbook of Greek Mythology* (New York: Dutton, 1959), p. 107.

15. T.B.L. Webster, *From Mycenae to Homer* (2nd edn; New York: Norton, 1964), p. 11.

16. Rose, p. 109. See also *Iliad* 22.183, where the term *philon tekos* appears.

17. In *Iliad* 21.423-33, Athena knocks down and terrorizes Aphrodite.

18. Professor Van L. Johnson, Department of Classics, Tufts University, developed this explanation in 1964.

19. See entry in N.G.L. Hammond and H.H. Scullard (eds.), *Oxford Classical Dictionary*, (2nd edn; Oxford, 1970).

20. Lines 38-40.

21. Rose, p. 110.

22. Rose, p. 111, and entry in *Oxford Classical Dictionary*.

23. C.J. Herington, *Athena Partheos and Athena Polias* (Manchester, 1955).

24. Rose, p. 110.

25. E. Kalinka, *In Epitumbion Heinrich Swoboda dargebracht* (Reichenberg, 1927), p. 116.

26. T. Burton-Brown, *The Coming of Iron to Greece* (Wincle, Cheshire: Top House, 1954); T. Burton-Brown, *Early Mediterranean Migrations* (Manchester, 1959); and T.B.L. Webster, *Mycenae*.

27. See, e.g., *Before the Bible* (London: Collins, 1962).

11

POETRY IN THE COURTROOM: JOB 38–41

Sylvia Huberman Scholnick

Anguished by the devastating loss of his children, health and wealth, the righteous hero of the book of Job calls God to account for his abusive action. When the Almighty makes his dramatic entrance from the whirlwind in chs. 38–41, he dazzles the man from Uz with a vision of the cosmos from the divine perspective. He reveals intimate details about the nature and structure of the universe he created and rules. But God never directly mentions the profound suffering of the hero which occasioned the call for his appearance. In fact, he seems to dismiss Job's powerful speeches with one brief question:

> *mî zeh maḥšîk ʿēṣâ*
> *b^{e}millîn b^{e}lî-dāʿat*
>
> Who is this that darkens my plan
> By words without knowledge? (38.2).

Instead of explaining this condemnation, the Almighty proceeds to enlighten Job with an elaborate description of his *ʿēṣâ*, his plan or design for the universe,[1] previously beyond human comprehension.

The answer God gives to Job raises a difficult critical problem in the book. What is the underlying artistic structure which unifies God's words with Job's? In what way is the creation poetry in Job 38–41 an adequate response to the hero's complaints about the unjust treatment he, an innocent man, is receiving from his divine opponent? The problem of the artistic integrity of the book of Job has most recently been raised by Robert Alter in 'The Voice from the Whirlwind'. He makes progress toward its solution by analysing the 'essential role *poetry* plays in the imaginative realization of revelation' and by exploring 'how its language and imagery flow directly out of the poetic argument that has preceded'.[2] While Alter sees a continuity in language and imagery between the speeches of Job and his friends and that of God, he identifies what appears to be a troublesome discontinuity in the poetic drama:

> God chooses for His response to Job the arena of creation, not the court of justice, the latter being the most insistent recurrent metaphor in Job's argument after Chapter 3. And it is, moreover, a creation that barely reflects the presence of man, a creation where human concepts of justice have no purchase.[3]

For Alter, then, there is a discontinuity between the issues of human justice which Job raises in the courtroom and the response that God provides in what appears to be the far-removed arena of creation.[4]

As many scholars have recognized, the poet chooses the court of justice as the setting for the dialogue between Job and his friends.[5] He dramatizes the hero's search for an acceptable definition of the meaning of divine justice by structuring the work around a lawsuit which the man from Uz initiates against God.[6] The case is comprised of several interwoven complaints. But when God speaks from the whirlwind, the setting of the drama appears to shift to what Alter calls the 'arena of creation'. Apparently ignoring the accusations made by his human legal opponent, God describes his creation and administration of the universe. The creation poetry in chs. 38–41 evokes the rich ancient Near Eastern tradition of the divine warrior who has sufficient power to bring the forces of chaos under control and to order the cosmos. As is typical of poetry with a creation motif, God's speeches are concerned with the affirmation of his credentials as King.[7]

There is, however, no discontinuity of setting in the drama. The entire poetic Dialogue is staged in the human court of justice where God addresses the juridical issues raised by the man from Uz. The traditional conventions of creation poetry have been adapted so that the Almighty's speeches can function as testimony in the suit initiated against him by his human opponent. Paradoxically, by entering the court of law, God has the opportunity to lead Job beyond the narrow confines of this legal order to a plane which allows the hero to see justice from the divine perspective. By accepting accountablity in man's forensic forum for what Job charges is injustice in his role as Judge of mankind, God enlightens the hero about his design for the cosmos where human juridical categories cease to be central and where man must assume accountability for his proper role in the Lord's kingdom. Creation poetry, then, has a unifying artistic function within the drama: as testimony it continues the lawsuit, while at the same time as revelation it facilitates its resolution.

There can be no doubt that chs. 38–41 were intended by the poet to be understood as the testimony of the divine defendant in the lawsuit brought by the plaintiff from Uz. This is confirmed in 38.3 and 40.7 by his use of the metaphor of belt-wrestling to express the Almighty's challenge to continue juridical proceedings in his presence:

> *'ᵉzor-nā kᵉgeber ḥălāṣêkā wᵉ'eš'ālkā wᵉhôdî'ēnî*
>
> Gird your loins like a hero;
> I will ask and you inform me (38.3; 40.7).[8]

Still another indication that God acknowledges his active participation in a *rîb*, a lawsuit, is found in 40.2 when he asks his human co-litigant:

> *hărōb 'im-šadday yissôr*
> *môkîaḥ 'ĕlôah ya'ănennâ.*
>
> May one who reproves contend against Shaddai?
> May one arraigning testify against him? (40.2).

Although the Hebrew of this verse is difficult, as the NJPS notes, there is no question that the poet continues to use the root *rîb* in God's answer, as he has in the speeches of Job (10.2, 13.6, 19; 23.6 and 31.35) and Elihu (33.13), to refer to the hero's lawsuit against his divine opponent.[9] Here the infinitive of *rîb* is used, as Tur-Sinai points out, as a substitute for the finite verb.[10] The language and imagery of jurisprudence, used in the previous section of the book, is carried over into the vocabulary of the Lord, as evidenced in 38.3, 40.2 and 7, and demonstrate God's eagerness to accept the challenge of his human opponent to engage in litigation.

There are several accusations comprising Job's case against God which the divine litigant will need to answer in his testimony. He gives the most serious consideration perhaps to Job's charge that he has committed what in human terms would be considered a justiciable offense. In 19.7 the plaintiff charges that God has committed *ḥāmās*, 'offense', which is a juridical term in the Hebrew Bible for the broad category of unlawful conduct.[11] Job complains in

9.12 that God has robbed him (*yaḥtōp*), but the specific wrongdoing on which he is basing his case is to be found in 10.3a: *hăṭôb*?[12] *lᵉkā kî-ta'ăšōq*, 'Is it defensible for you to commit a wrongful taking?' It is not possible to identify in Anglo-American law an exact equivalent to the ancient Hebrew and Aramaic offense *'šq*, the closest being 'conversion', which *Black's Law Dictionary* defines as: 'an unauthorized assumption and exercise of the right of ownership over goods or personal property belonging to another, to the alteration of their condition or the exclusion of the owner's rights. Any unauthorized act which deprives an owner of his property permanently or for an indefinite time. Unauthorized and wrongful exercise of dominion and control over another's personal property, to the exclusion of or inconsistent with rights of ownership'.[13] 'Wrongful deprivation' is its general intent or meaning, as can be documented from Hebrew and Aramaic law.[14] The Prologue of the book, important within the whole artistic work for introducing the facts of the case,[15] clearly states that God has taken from the hero his health (2.7), family (1.19) and wealth (1.10, 14-15) 'without cause (*ḥinnām*)' (2.3), not as punishment for wrongdoing, but simply as a test of his loyalty (1.8-11; 2.3-6). In the poetic Dialogue Job's case is one of wrongful seizure against God for the losses he has sustained: he was once a vigorous and prosperous man (29.2-17) who was highly regarded in his community (29.7-9, 21-25); now his property is gone (as in 3.24); and he holds God responsible for the abusive treatment, a point to which he gives special emphasis (as in 6.4; 9.12; 10.8, 16, 17; 12.9; 16.9-14; 19.8-12, 21; 30.18-23). Central to his case is his claim to innocence of wrongdoing that would justify the Lord's action, a claim which he reiterates throughout his speeches, from ch. 9 through ch. 27 (9.15, 20, 21; 10.7; 16.17; 23.7, 10-12; 27.5-6). For example, in 23.10-12, he attests to his righteousness:

kî-yāda' derek 'immādî
bᵉḥānannî kazzāhāb 'ēṣē'.
ba'ăšurô 'āḥazâ raglî
darkô šāmartî wᵉlō'-'āṭ.
miṣwat śᵉpātāyw wᵉlō' 'āmîš
mēḥuqqî ṣāpantî 'imrê-pîw.

But he knows the way I take;
Would he assay me, I should emerge pure as gold.
I have followed in his tracks,
Kept his way without swerving,

I have not deviated from what his lips commanded;
I have treasured his words more than my daily bread (23.10-12).

He charges that the divine defendant did not have the necessary or sufficient justification to seize his property and therefore, the action constitutes *'šq*, unlawful appropriation.

A second important accusation against him that the Lord will address in the answer he files is an extension of the first: God is unjust in his role as Judge. Job and his friends share the assumption that God acts as Judge of human behavior. While his friends testify that the hero must have committed some offense that would justify the punishment he is receiving from God (8.4; 22.5-9), the plaintiff, holding firmly to his innocence, accuses the divine magistrate of injustice. He presents evidence from his own case (9.20c) as well as his observations on the widespread prosperity of the wicked (21.7-34; 24.1-25) to prove that the system of divine retribution is corrupt. His painful and shocking experience at the hands of the divine Judge leads the innocent man from Uz to complain before his peers:

'aḥḥat-hî'[16] *'al-kēn 'āmartî tām w^e rāšā' hû' m^e kalleh*

It is all one; therefore I say, 'He destroys the blameless and the guilty' (9.22).

Job hopes to resolve the issue of the miscarriage of divine justice through the human system of justice—litigation.

God appears before the tribunal to answer the charges Job brings against him. The author adroitly uses poetry about creation to provide the defendant with the opportunity to clear himself. He responds directly to the first charge, that of wrongful appropriation, by asserting his rightful title to the universe he created and rules. God testifies in 41.3: *taḥat kol-haššāmayim lî-hû'*, 'Everything under the heavens is mine'. In addition to this clear assertion of his own right of ownership, God dismisses through a series of cross-examining interrogatories any possible prior claim to title that Job might make:

'êpoh hāyîtā b^e yosdî-'āreṣ
haggēd 'im-yāda'tā bînâ.
mî-śām m^e maddêhā kî tēdā'
'ô mî-nāṭâ 'ālêhā qāw.

Where were you when I laid the earth's foundations?
Speak if you have understanding.

Do you know who fixed its dimensions,
Or who measured it with a line? (38.4-5).

The creator has original title. If Job cannot establish his participation in the work of creation, he would have no grounds for any claim to the property he has charged was unlawfully seized. God continues to present his defense when he closely questions the plaintiff about his knowledge of the creative process:

'al-mâ 'ădānêhā hoṭbā'û
'ô mî-yārâ 'eben pinnātāh.
b^{e}*ron-yaḥad kôk*^{e}*bê bōqer*
wayyārî'û kol-b^{e}*nê 'ĕlōhîm.*

Onto what were its bases sunk?
Who set its cornerstone
When the morning stars sang together
And all the divine beings shouted for joy? (38.6-7).

The creator would know the specifications for laying the foundation of the universe, as well as the nature of the celebration that accompanied it. If Job is claiming title to any property in this world, he would have to prove to the court that he has information about the construction details:

'ê-zeh hadderek yiškon-'ôr
w^{e}*ḥōšek 'ê-zeh m*^{e}*qômô.*
kî tiqqāḥennû 'el-gĕbûlô
w^{e}*kî tābîn n*^{e}*tîbôt bêtô.*

Which path leads to where light dwells,
And where is the place of darkness,
That you may take it to its domain
And know the way to its home? (38.19-20).

This cross-examination is intended to dramatize before the court that a human being cannot assume the original right as creator of ownership over any part of the universe. If Job is unable to respond effectively to these interrogatories, he would in effect confirm God's defense against the charge of unlawful appropriation—that everything under the heavens does indeed belong to the divine Creator.

Continued cross-examination by the divine litigant is directed at establishing the defense that he has never transferred the original title he holds to the universe he created. If Job, then, is claiming the right of ownership over any property he charges God has seized, he ought to be able to demonstrate that he has assumed or even is capable of assuming the responsibilities of ownership. The Almighty asks a series of questions intended to reveal the plaintiff's inability to exercise the most fundamental care for any land:

hăyādaʻtā ḥuqqôt šāmāyim
'im-tāśîm miṣṭārô bā'āreṣ.
hătārîm lāʻāb qôlekā
w^{e}*šipʻat-mayim t*^{e}*kassekkā.*

Do you know the laws of heaven
Or impose its authority on earth?
Can you send up an order to the clouds
For an abundance of water to cover you? (38.33-34).

Job is challenged to explain how he can charge God with appropriation of property clearly dependent upon the Lord for its continued survival.

Poetry about creation is appropriate for refuting Job's charge against God of wrongful deprivation. Traditionally, the concepts of creation and title are linked in Biblical Hebrew poetry. The founder of the universe automatically assumes title. A good example of the connection between these ideas is found in Psalm 24:

la-yhwh hā'āreṣ ûm^{e}*lô'āh*
  tēbēl w^{e}*yôš*^{e}*bê bāh*
kî-hû' ʻal-yammîm y^{e}*sā-dāh*
  w^{e}*ʻal-n*^{e}*hārôt y*^{e}*kōnĕnehā*

The earth is the Lord's and all that it holds,
  the world and its inhabitants.
For he founded it upon the ocean,
  set it on the nether-streams (Ps 24.1-2).[17]

Creation poetry makes clear that the Lord has never transferred title to any part of the universe he formed.

If creation poetry in Hebrew Scripture has traditionally affirmed that the Lord who established the world has title to it, how then was the biblical audience to understand the gifts that God promises to give in return for obedience? Moses, for example, assures the Israelites that, in return for obedience, they will be given the land promised to their forefathers (Deut 6.10-12) and prosperity (Deut 28.11). It would be easy to misconstrue the meaning of the verb *ntn* in these promises. Its intended meaning is not the transfer of title to property, but a grant for its use. Moses makes this clear to Israel in Deut 10.14:

hēn la-yhwh 'ĕlōhêkā hāššāmayim ûš^e^mê haššamāyim hā'āreṣ w^e^kol-'ăšer-bāh

Mark, the heavens to their utmost reaches belong to the Lord your God, the earth and all that is on it!

Lev 25.23-24 confirms this understanding:

w^e^hā'āreṣ lō' timmākēr liṣmitut kî-lî hā'āreṣ kî-gērîm w^e^tôšābîm 'attem 'immādî

But the land must not be sold beyond reclaim, for the land is mine; you are but strangers resident with me.

An additional example of God's clarification of the issue of title is found in Exod 19.5-6:

w^e^'attâ 'im-šāmôa' tišm^e^'û b^e^qōlî ûš^e^martem 'et-b^e^rîtî wihyîtem lî s^e^gullâ mikkol-hā'ammîm kî-lî kol-hā'āreṣ

Now, then, if you will obey me faithfully and keep my covenant, you shall be my treasured possession among all the peoples. Indeed, all the earth is mine, but you shall be to me a kingdom of priests and a holy nation.

The author of the book of Job firmly builds God's defense against the plaintiff's misconceived accusation on the foundation of accepted biblical tradition.[18] The Lord never authorized the hero's assumption of the right of ownership over any of his property, but has simply given a grant for its use. There can have been no wrongful deprivation committed by the Almighty against the man from Uz.

The second accusation which God answers simultaneously in his testimony is that of injustice in his role as Judge of the earth because of his indiscriminate punishment of the innocent Job. He does this first by describing his primary role in the universe as that of King rather than Judge, so that the hero can realize that the treatment he is receiving from God is not the result of a juridical decision but an administrative one. And second, God answers the complaint that he acted unjustly by defining for Job the true nature of divine justice as sovereignty. The redefinition frees the hero to see the divine action as the prerogative of the Ruler.

To establish that his primary role is that of King rather than Judge, God describes in intimate detail his dominion over the universe: His creation of the world (38.4-11); his knowledge of its structure (38.16-22); his command over natural forces (38.24-30) and animals (39.1-

30); and his ability as provider (38.39-41). God's administrative activity extends to all details of operating his realm. With a rapid series of interrogatories, he challenges the ability of his opponent as a human being to provide the necessary governance. Does the man from Uz need to concern himself as the Ruler does with the details of the life of the planet: the cycle of night and day (38.12, 19-20), the formation of the constellations (38.31-33), the wind and rain (38.24-28), and the welfare of the wild life (38.39-40)?

> *hămibbînātᵉkā ya'ăber-nēṣ*
> *yiprōś kᵉnāpāw lᵉtêmān.*
> *'im-'al-pîkā yagbîah nāšer*
> *wᵉkî yārîm qinnô.*
>
> Is it by your wisdom that the hawk grows pinions,
> Spreads his wings to the south?
> Does the eagle soar at your command,
> Building his nest high,
> Dwelling in the rock,
> Lodging upon the fastness of a jutting rock? (39.26-27; cf. 38:39-41).

Although the poet mentions briefly in 38.12-13 and 40.11-13 the Lord's responsibilities as divine judge of human beings, the emphasis of the speech is clearly on his duties as sovereign over a kingdom dependent on him for its continued existence:

> *mî yākîn lā'ōrēb ṣêdô*
> *kî-yᵉlādāw 'el-'ēl yᵉšawwē'û*
> *yitᵉ'û liblî-'ōkel.*
>
> Who provides food for the raven,
> When his young cry out to God
> And wander about without food? (38.41).

It is interesting to note that the poet uses the verb *šw'*, 'cry out', in this verse to show the dependency of the young ravens on God. This use of the verb echoes its earlier use in 19.7 where it signifies Job's legal action against the divine Judge for injustice in the punishment he is receiving:

> *hēn 'eṣ'aq ḥāmās wᵉlō' 'ē'āneh*
> *'ăšawwa' wᵉ'ēn mišpāṭ.*
>
> Behold, I cry out 'Offense!' but I am not answered;
> I call out, but there is no litigation (19.7).

There is irony in the poet's use of this verb in verses which contrast the wild birds' intuitive appeal to God as the very source of their continued life with Job's myopic appeal to the human court of law for justice with the divine Judge.

In the course of his testimony that he is primarily King not Judge in the world, God indirectly answers Job's charge of injustice by defining the nature of divine justice. When he uses the word *mišpāṭ* in 40.8 the context leaves no doubt that he is speaking not simply about his system of retribution but about his governance.

> *ha'ap tāpēr mišpāṭî*
> *taršî'ēnî lᵉma'an tiṣdāq.*
>
> Would you impugn my sovereignty,
> Would you condemn me that you may be right? (40.8).

As I discussed in an earlier article, 'The Meaning of *Mišpāṭ* in the Book of Job', the ancient Semitic root *špṭ / ṯpṭ* has two meanings—that of judging and that of ruling.[19] While Job and his friends have drawn their definitions from the sphere of the court, when God uses the term *mišpāṭ*, he draws his definition also from the alternate meaning of the root: ruling. This usage is verified in 1 Sam 8.9 where God describes to Samuel the authority (*mišpāṭ*) of the king. By using *mišpāṭ* in this context in 40.8 God teaches Job that he need not understand his profound loss as the result of the Lord's judgment for wrongdoing, but of his exercising his divine prerogative to administer a complex kingdom. This conforms with the characterization in the Prologue of God's action toward Job—testing of his subject's loyalty (1.8-11; 2.3-6).

Most commonly poetry with a creation motif is used in the Hebrew Bible to praise God as King or to petition his intervention.[20] But the author of the book of Job adapts the poetry for use in the arena of the courtroom, and therefore, several distinct characteristics emerge. First, it is spoken by God in chs. 38–41 in the first person, rather than in the usual second or third person, because he is a litigant testifying in the hero's lawsuit.[21] His opening challenge emphasizes this characteristic: *wᵉ'eš'ālᵉkā wᵉhôdî'ēnî*, 'I will ask and you inform me' (38.3b). Second, it is uniquely framed in an often rapid-fire series of interrogatories which God uses to cross-examine his co-litigant. For example:

> *hᵃtittēn lassûs gᵉbûrâ*
> *hᵃtalbîš ṣawwā'rô ra'mâ.*

h^e tar'îšennû kā'arbeh
hôd naḥrô'ēmâ.

Do you give the horse his strength?
Do you clothe his neck with a mane?
Do you make him quiver like locusts,
His majestic snorting (spreading) terror? (39.19-20).

The force of these queries is to discredit Job's accusation that his divine opponent unlawfully appropriated his property, and their effect is to establish God's power over the universe he created and his prerogative to administer it as he wills. How can the man from Uz accuse God of injustice when in fact he knows little about the very meaning of divine justice or the nature of God's responsibilties in the world?

The only possible equivalent biblical use in a juridical context of what might be considered a creation motif may be found in Psalm 50.[22] But here, rather than cross-examining the human plaintiff in a lawsuit brought against him, God is the initiator of litigation for breach of covenant. He testifies in the first person that his people are fulfilling only the ritual laws for sacrifice while neglecting the rest of the covenant (Ps 50.8, 16-21). What the Almighty requests is that Israel:

z^e baḥ lē'lōhîm tôdâ
w^e šallēm l^e 'elyôn n^e dārêkā

Offer to God praise as your sacrifice,
fulfill your vows to the Most High (Ps 50.14).

But the interesting element of this juridical psalm is God's explanation of why sacrifice is an insufficient fulfillment of the covenant.

lō'-'eqqaḥ mibbêt^e kā pār
mimmikl^e 'ōtêkā 'attûdîm.
kî-lî kol-ḥay^e tô-yā'ar
b^e hēmôt b^e har^e rê-'ālep.
yāda'tî kol-'ôp hārîm
w^e zîz śāday 'immādî.
'im-'er'ab lō'-'ōmar lāk
kî-lî tēbēl ûm^e lō'āh.

I claim no bull from your estate,
no he-goats from your pens.
For mine is every animal of the forest,
the beasts on a thousand mountains.[23]

I know every bird of the mountains
the creatures of the field are subject to me.
Were I hungry, I would not tell you,
for mine is the world and all it holds (50.9-12).

The Lord makes clear to his people that the sacrificial animal may not be considered their gift to him, since he already has title to it. The praise that motivates or accompanies the physical offering constitutes for God the gift. Although the legal issues are different in Psalm 50 and in the book of Job, the former being the legitimacy of a gift from man to God while the latter concerns the appropriation by God of what Job contends was a divine gift,[24] the answer filed by God in the two lawsuits is the same. Human beings simply cannot claim title to any part of the universe in which they reside. The meaning of the elaborate descriptions in Job 38–41 of the birds and animals living in God's realm is elucidated by Psalm 50. Curiously, in Ps 50.11, God supports his claim to title with the assertion (*yāda'tî*) that he has knowledge of the creatures living in his kingdom. This kind of knowledge evidently is considered necessary and sufficient evidence of title.

While creation poetry is used in Job 38–41 as testimony which allows God to enter the courtroom, accept accountability to man, and see the world from Job's perspective, it also works paradoxically to open divine vistas for the man from Uz beyond the limited confines of the human legal forum. God's opening challenge to Job in 38.2 (*mî zeh maḥšîk 'ēṣâ / b^{e}milîn b^{e}lî-dā'at*, 'Who is this that darkens my plan, / by words without knowledge?') criticizes the hero for his earlier speeches which obscured the divine design for the universe.

It is important to understand how Job may have darkened God's plan in order to appreciate the impact of his resulting enlightenment after hearing the Lord's speech. The hero's testimony obscured God's design, not simply because he wished for the blackness of extinction (ch. 3) after God had granted life, although that is, as Robert Alter suggests, an important purpose of the poet's imagery of darkness.[25] The hero darkens God's plan by having tunnel-vision in viewing divine justice in human juridical terms. The shadowed world that Job describes is a perverse one in which the wicked are free to operate in the dim night without punishment while he, an innocent man, is assumed by his peers to have the taint of sinfulness because of his loss at God's hands. The poet uses the imagery of darkness on this level to describe the world of the wicked who are 'rebels against the light (*b^{e}mōrĕdê-'ôr*)' (24.13a), using the cover of night to commit the crimes of adultery and theft. Job complains that his world, once lighted with God's lamp (29.3), has been destroyed by darkness (23.17):

w^{e}hiṣṣiganî limšōl 'ammîm
w^{e}tōpet l^{e}pānîm 'ehyeh.
watēkah mikka'aś 'ênî
wiṣuray kaṣṣēl kullām.

He made me a byword among the people;
I have become like Tophet of old.
My eyes fail from vexation;
All shapes seem to me like shadows (17.6-7).

The blackness Job is experiencing is interpreted by Eliphaz as proof of his wickedness. This friend charges:

'almānôt šillaḥtā rêqām
ûz^{e}rō'ôt y^{e}tōmîm y^{e}dukkā'.
'al-kēn s^{e}bîbôtêkā paḥîm
wibahel^{e}kā paḥad pit'ōm:
'ô-ḥōšek lō'-tir'eh
w^{e}šip'at-mayim t^{e}kassekkā.

You have sent away widows empty-handed;
The strength of the fatherless is broken.
Therefore snares are all around you,
And sudden terrors frighten you,
Or darkness, so you cannot see;
A flood of waters covers you (22.9-11).

Job sees that the only hope for light is litigation that will clarify his legal status. Because God does not answer immediately his accusations (30.20), the man from Uz says:

kî ṭôb qiwwîtî wayyābō' rā'
wa' ăyaḥălâ l^{e}'ôr wayyābō' 'ōpel.

I looked forward to good fortune, but evil came;
I hoped for light, but darkness came (30.26).

When God does testify before the court, the illumination that Job hoped for comes. The Lord's testimony does, as we have seen, enlighten Job about the reason for his action. But the clarification extends far beyond receiving specific answers to his juridical complaints. Creation poetry allows God to elucidate for Job his *'ēṣâ*, his design for the universe. He extends the hero's vision beyond the human realm, best exemplified in the legal forum where scrutiny and evaluation of man's behavior is of ultimate concern. Previously Job characterized God as a 'Watcher of man (*nōṣēr hā'ādām*)' (7.20) who is preoccupied with human judgment:

> *mâ-'ᵉnôs kî tᵉgaddᵉlennû*
> *wᵉkî tāšît 'ēlāyw libbekā*
>
> What is man, that you make much of him,
> That you fix your attention upon him? (7.17).

God is portrayed in the creation poetry of chs. 38–41 as Watcher over the cosmos, his attention fixed on the forces of nature, the land, and animals. By questioning Job, the Almighty wishes to teach him how little awareness he has had of the complexity of the world in which man lives and how myopic his previous vision of the Lord's relationship to the cosmos has been. For example, Job thought of darkness on one level as the extinction of human life which he wishes for and on another, as the black world of the sinner into which he was thrust by God's abusive action. But the Almighty shows him how little he really understands about darkness when he asks:

> *'ê-zeh hadderek yiškon-'ôr*
> *wᵉhōšek 'ê-zeh mᵉqômô.*
> *kî tiqqāḥennû 'el-gᵉbûlô*
> *wᵉkî tābîn nᵉtîbôt bêtô.*
>
> Which path leads to where light dwells,
> And where is the place of darkness,
> That you may take it to its domain
> And know the way to its home? (38.19-20).

The Lord is talking in these verses about events of creation beyond Job's previous understanding. Darkness has a reality of its own, not simply in relationship to human beings. Job's horizon is being extended.

God describes for Job in chs. 38–39 his broad, all-encompassing vista of the cosmos—earth (38.4-6), sea (38.8-11), the gates of death (38.17), snow (38.22), hail (38.22), wind (38.24), rain (38.25-28), grass (38.27), dew (38.28), ice (38.29-30), the constellations (38.31-32), clouds (38.34), lightning (38.35), the lion (38.39-40), ravens (38.41), mountain goats (39.1), the wild ass (39.5-8), the wild ox (39.9-12), the ostrich (39.13-18), the horse (39.19-25), and the hawk (39.26-30). Job is given a perspective once available only to the Creator.

While the poetic vision of the natural world in chs. 38–39 is broad and general, it is detailed and particular in chs. 40–41 in which God describes Behemoth and Leviathan.[26] The extensive cataloguing of the characteristics of these two creatures is the poet's way of demonstrating their deep significance to the Creator who says:

> *hinnēh-na'b^{e}hēmôt 'ăšer-'āśîtî 'immāk*
> *ḥāṣîr kabbāqār yō'kēl.*
> *hinnēh-nā'kōḥô b^{e}motnāyw*
> *w^{e}'ōnô biśrîrê biṭnô . . .*
> *hû' rē'šît dar^{e}kê-'ēl*
> *hā'ōśô yaggēš ḥarbô.*

> Take now behemoth, whom I made as I did you;
> He eats grass, like the cattle.
> His strength is in his loins,
> His might in the muscles of his belly . . .
> He is the first of God's works;
> Only his maker can draw a sword against him (40.15-16, 19).

The Lord provides information not readily accessible to human beings of Leviathan when he tells about his back (41.7), his scales (41.8-9), his sneezings (41.10), his eyes (41.10), his mouth (41.11), his nostrils (41.12), his breath (41.13), his neck (41.14), his flesh (41.15), his breast (41.16), and his underparts (41.22). The poetry communicates a divine caring that cannot be exceeded by the Lord's love for human beings:

> *hăyarbeh 'ēlêkā taḥănûnîm*
> *'im-y^{e}dabbēr 'ēlêkā rakkôt.*
> *hăyikrōt bĕrît 'immāk*
> *tiqqāḥennû l^{e}'ebed 'ôlām.*

> Will he plead with you at length?
> Will he speak in soft words to you?
> Will he make a covenant with you
> To be taken as your lifelong servant? (40.27-28).

God's relationship with Leviathan, as with man, is structured and defined by a *b^{e}rît*. The Almighty provides the hero with an opportunity to see his place in the universe in relationship to these enormous and fascinating beasts. He says about Leviathan in his closing words:

'ên-'al'āpār mošlô
he'āśû liblî-ḥāt.
'ēt-kol-gābōah yir'eh
hû' melek 'al-kol-bᵉnê-šaḥaṣ.

There is not on earth his like,
Made as he is without fear.
He sees all that is haughty;
He is king over all proud beasts (41.25-26).

The creation poetry in God's speeches, which works successfully as testimony in the courtroom, paradoxically opens for Job a transcendent perspective of the cosmos created and governed by God.

Job's initial response to the panoramic vision of God's *'ēṣâ* is silence. God's questions remain unanswered. When he does speak briefly in 40.4 before lapsing again into speechlessness, he expresses a new realization of his own insignificance in so vast a design for creation.

hēn qallōtî mâ 'ăšîbekkā
yādî śamtî lᵉmô-pî.

See, I am of small worth; what can I answer you?
I clap my hand to my mouth (40.4).

Job's final response in 42.6 shows his understanding that the creation poetry of God's speeches has worked on two levels: as testimony in his lawsuit, and as revelation of the divine plan for the universe:

'al-kēn 'em'as wᵉniḥamtî
'al-'apār wā'ēper.

Therefore, I withdraw and retract (my case),
being but dust and ashes (42.6).

As I discussed in 'The Meaning of *Mišpaṭ* in the Book of Job',[27] the final stich of this verse communicates the plaintiff's perception that until that moment the lawsuit has been in progress. Job ends the case with a formal retraction.

The hero's final concession works in a second way. He acknowledges with the phrase *'al-'āpār wā'ēper* that God's speech has helped him put his life in a cosmic perspective. The exact intent of this short phrase is difficult to determine precisely, the NJPS translating it adverbially as 'being but dust and ashes', while most translations prefer 'in/on/upon dust and ashes'.[28] A case may be made for each of these interpretations. It may be intended to communicate, as the

NJPS translators might argue, Job's new realization that he is simply one part of a complex cosmos, made of dust and ashes, the very stuff God used to create the universe. While he once complained against the Almighty for fashioning him of clay only to turn him back into dust (10.9), he now shows an acceptance of his humble composition, just as Abraham does when he acknowledges his being dust and ashes while boldly challenging the justice of God's destroying Sodom and Gomorrah (Gen 18.27). Some translators prefer the English '(sitting) in/on/upon dust and ashes' for the Hebrew *'al-'āpār wā'ēper*. If this is the intended meaning, Job, having just heard the description of Leviathan who cannot be dominated by any creature on earth (*'al-'āpār*. 41.25), would be symbolically expressing an acceptance of his modest place in the animal kingdom by sitting on earth and ashes.[29] The poet may have left this phrase intentionally ambiguous to evoke both meanings, a play on words that would be difficult to reflect in an English translation. In the very act of sitting upon dust and ashes, Job symbolically affirms that he is made of the same elements, dust and ashes, which God used in creating the earth.

Regardless of the precise English translation of *'al-'āpār wā'ēper*, the author's intent in 42.6 is clear. The verse communicates Job's awareness of the complexity of God's answer. To its juridical dimension, the plaintiff answers by retracting his case, recognizing the force of the divine litigant's defense. To its cosmic dimension, the man from Uz, by confirming the elemental nature of his being, acknowledges his humble place in the divine *'ēṣâ*.

The Almighty's speech from the whirlwind has had a profound impact on Job in his search for the meaning of divine justice. God, accepting accountability in man's court of law for the force of his action, has acknowledged the importance of the human system of jurisprudence within his universal order. But the creation poetry enlightens the man from Uz about a system of justice far more complex and awesome than the one he had known in the legal forum. Job accepts God's revelation that divine justice is the Lord's sovereignty over his universe.

NOTES

1. *'ēṣâ* is used in the creation poetry of Isa 40.13 to speak of God's design for the universe. It is used to refer to the divine plan for mankind in Isa 5.19; 46.10; Jer 32.19; 49.20; 50.45; Mic 4.12; Ps 33.11; 73.24; 106.13; 107.11; Prov 19.21.

2. Robert Alter, 'The Voice from the Whirlwind', *Commentary* (January, 1984), p. 34. Alter focuses on the beginning of what he calls 'the poetic argument' in the book of Job, Job's death-wish which he introduces in ch. 3. He contrasts the hero's self-involvement, his turning inward, with God's expansiveness, his 'panoramic vision' (p. 35), in chs. 38–41.

3. Alter p. 39.

4. While Alter does say that 'the poet works with an exquisite sense of the descriptive needs at hand and of the structural continuities of the poem and the book' (p. 41), his statements about the relationship between Job's speeches and those of God show his concern that there appears to be a degree of structural discontinuity. For example, he says: 'Obviously there can be no direct answer to Job's question as to why, having been a decent and God-fearing man, he should have lost all his sons and daughters, his wealth, and his health . . . Job surely does not have the sort of answer he expected, but he has a strong answer of another kind' (p. 41).

5. These scholars include B. Gemser, 'The *Rîb*- or Controversy-Pattern in Hebrew Mentality', *Wisdom in Israel and in the Ancient Near East* (ed. M. Noth and D. Winton Thomas; VTSup, 3; Leiden: Brill, 1955), p. 135; James Limburg, 'The Lawsuit of God in the Eighth Century Prophets', ThD thesis, Union Theological Seminary (Virginia), 1969; M.H. Pope, *Job, Introduction, Translation and Notes* (2nd edn; AB; Garden City: Doubleday, 1973), p. lxxi; Heinz Richter, *Studien zu Hiob, Der Aufbau des Hiobbuches, dargestellt an den Gattungen des Rechtsleben* (Theologische Arbeiten, 11; Berlin: Evangelische Verlagsanstalt, 1959); and Claus Westermann, *Der Aufbau des Buches Hiob* (Beiträge zur historischen Theologie, 23; Tübingen: J.C.B. Mohr [Paul Siebeck], 1956).

6. This subject is explored in my earlier article, 'The Meaning of *Mišpāṭ* in the Book of Job', *JBL* 104 (1982), pp. 521-29.

7. Dennis J. McCarthy, S.J., '"Creation" Motifs in Ancient Hebrew Poetry', *Creation in the Old Testament* (ed. Bernhard W. Anderson; Philadelphia: Fortress Press, 1984) p. 83.

8. Evidence for a juridical interpretation of the belt-wrestling metaphor is reviewed in my article, 'The Meaning of *Mišpāṭ* in the Book of Job', p. 527.

9. In Job 29.16 and 31.13, Job uses the root *rîb* to speak of former litigation in which he was involved. All other occurences of the root in the book refer to the lawsuit the hero initiates against God. The root in 13.8 refers to the friends' participation in the suit on behalf of God. James Limburg (p. 67) argues that *rîbot* in 13.6 refers to the hero's arguments in a second suit against his friends. But his request for their silence in 13.13 argues against this interpretation because, were the companions litigants in a suit, they would be required to testify, as Job says about this responsibility of a defendant in 13.22. As the hero makes clear with the idiom *rîb lĕ*, 'to testify in behalf of', in 13.8, a meaning known from its use in Judg 6.31, he considers the friends as witnesses for God.

10. N.H. Tur-Sinai, *The Book of Job: A New Commentary* (rev. edn, Jerusalem: Kiryath Sepher, 1967) p. 554.

11. *ḥāmās* is a technical term for 'wrongdoing' or 'offense', as verified by its use in the Hebrew law in Exod 23.1 and Deut 19.16 where, in construct with *'ēd*, meaning 'offending witness', it refers to one who testifies falsely in a case-at-law. Giving false testimony is a justiciable offense, according to Deut 19.

12. In this verse *ṭôb* may have the force of 'defensible', as its meaning in 2 Sam 15.3, 'defensible cases (*d^ebārekā ṭôbîm*)', would indicate.

13. *Black's Law Dictionary*, (5th edn, 1979), p. 300.

14. Although most translators of the term into English choose the non-technical 'oppress', the NJPS correctly recognizes its juridical force with 'defraud'. But 'defraud' in English civil law refers to deprivation of a right, usually property, through false representation, and therefore does not accurately convey the meaning of the Hebrew. The technical forensic intent of the root *'šq* in Hebrew and Aramaic law is documented in 'A Case of Wrongful Deprivation: Job's Lawsuit Against God', a paper I delivered at the 1983 AAR/SBL/CTS Southeastern Region Annual Meeting.

15. Moshe Greenberg, 'Reflections on Job's Theology', *The Book of Job: A New Translation According to the Traditional Hebrew Text* (Philadelphia: The Jewish Publication Society of America, 1980), pp. xvii-xviii. There has been disagreement among scholars as to whether the Prologue and Epilogue may have been written by an earlier or later author than the one who wrote the poetic Dialogue. Regardless of the process of writing and editing that may have occurred, the book must finally be treated as a whole in the form in which it appears in the Hebrew Bible. In that sense, it is possible to speak of the author of Job.

16. The words *'aḥḥat-hî'*, which may be translated 'It is all one', could be interpreted to mean that it doesn't matter whether one lives or dies, as S.R. Driver and G.B. Gray (*A Critical and Exegetical Commentary on The Book of Job Together With A New Translation*, [Edinburgh: T.& T. Clark, 1921], p. 92) suggest, or that God treats guilty and innocent alike, a more common interpretation preferred, for example, by E. Dhorme (*A Commentary on the Book of Job* [transl. Harold Knight; New York: Thomas Nelson 1967], p. 139); Robert Gordis (*The Book of Job. Commentary, New Translation and Special Studies* [New York: The Jewish Theological Society of America, 1978], p. 108); Pope (p. 71); and Tur-Sinai (p. 167).

17. Other psalms in which there is a link between the ideas of creation and title include Pss 89.12 and 95.3-5.

18. Job in the Prologue responds to his loss with the pious statement: 'The Lord has given (*nātan*), and the Lord has taken away (*lāqāḥ*); blessed be the name of the Lord' (1.21). The poetic Dialogue explores the hero's process of coming to terms with the meaning of divine giving and taking.

19. Scholnick, p. 522.

20. Poetry with a creation motif is used to praise God, as in Isa 40.12; 51.9-10; Am 4.13; Pss 8; 24.1-2; 33.6-7, 9; 89.10-13; 95.4-5; 96.5; 100; 119.73, 90; 147.4, 8-9, 16-18; and to petition his intervention, as in Pss 65.6-8; 74.13-17; and 90.1-2.

21. Praise about God in the third person is found in Isa 40.12; 51.9-10; Pss 24; 33; 95.1-5; 96; 100; 147 and in the second person in Pss 8; 65; 74; 89; 90; 119. It is a general characteristic that poetry with a creation motif is in the second or third person. In these verses, God speaks in the first person, as he does in Job, about his creation.

22. Although Ps 50 does not mention God's founding of the universe, it might broadly be classified as creation poetry because of its description of his kingship, if we accept Loren Fisher's definition of the genre in 'Creation at Ugarit and in the Old Testament' (*VT* 15 [1965], pp. 313-24). He writes: 'Those who say "no creation at Ugarit" must have a very narrow definition of creation. Certainly they do not consider "re-creation" or the ordering of chaos as creation . . . I hope to show . . . that conflict, kingship, ordering of chaos, and temple building are all related to an overarching theme that I would call "creation"' (pp. 315-16).

23. As the NJPS points out, the Hebrew of this verse is uncertain.

24. In the book of Job, the hero is presented in the Prologue as considering his property and family as gifts of God (1.21) which he takes back and, in the poetic dialogue, he speaks of his life as a divine gift (10.12).

25. Alter, pp. 35-36.

26. In the context of God's speeches in chs. 38–41, Behemoth and Leviathan are treated as natural creatures described in a landscape which includes other real animals: the ibis and cock (38.36), the lion (38.39-40), the raven (38.41), the mountain goat (39.1-4), the wild ass (39.5-8), the wild ox (39.9-12), the ostrich (39.13-18), the horse (39.19-25), the hawk (39.26-30). Robert Gordis in Special Note 37 (pp. 569-72), after reviewing the two interpretations that these animals have historically been given—as mythical and as real creatures—presents a strong case for viewing these two beasts as real animals described by God as part of the natural world in which Job lives. After giving five reasons why it makes sense contextually to understand Behemoth and Leviathan as real rather than mythical beasts, Gordis concludes by saying: 'We are, therefore, convinced that only a description of actual flesh-and-blood monsters, unbeautiful in man's eyes, but a source of delight to God, is relevant to the poet's purpose. Hence, *Behemoth* is to be identified as the hippopotamus and *Leviathan* as the crocodile' (p. 571).

27. Scholnick, pp. 528-29.

28. *'al-'āpār wā'ēper* is rendered 'in/on/upon dust and ashes' in the majority of modern translations of the book of Job into English, most recently in Gordis, p. 491.

29. Edouard Dhorme, translating *'al-'āpār wā'ēper* as 'on dust and ashes', suggests that 'This self-humiliation springs from an act of repentance' (p. 647).

12

FOLKTALE STRUCTURE IN THE BOOK OF JOB
A Formalist Reading

Carole Fontaine

The question of genre in Job and the relationship between the prose framework and the poetic speeches of the book's core have posed numerous problems for critics of the work. Various theories of genre have characterized the book as a dramatized lament,[1] a series of legal proceedings,[2] an 'answered lament paradigm' (*Klageerhörungs-paradigma*),[3] and a comedy,[4] each with appropriate intentions and life settings attributed to the author(s) based on the favored genre designation. While current trends in exegesis show considerable interest in dealing with the whole text as a literary unit,[5] no one interpretive scheme seems to account adequately for the symbiotic relationship existing between the prose and poetry in Job. Marvin Pope concludes in his commentary, 'there is no single classification appropriate to the literary form of the Book of Job. It shares something of the characteristics of all the literary forms that have been ascribed to it, but it is impossible to classify it exclusively as didactic, dramatic, epic or anything else. The book viewed as a unit is *sui generis* and no single term or combination of terms is adequate to describe it.'[6]

The historical relationship of the narrative sections in Job 1.1–2.13 and 42.7-17 to the central portion of the book has posed a set of vexing questions for interpreters. Clearly, the Prologue and Epilogue belong together, for style, content and structure exhibit too many similarities for this to be seriously questioned, and the folkloric quality of the narrative is widely recognized.[7] However, did the prose story exist in oral or written form available for the poet's use, or was it composed *ad hoc* to frame the dialogues, or perhaps even composed and added at a later time?[8] The 'poeticity' of the Prologue and Epilogue have led some to posit an 'epic substratum' for this portion of the text, assuming that the story as we have it is derived from this earlier poetic source.[9] The patriarchal setting of the narrative and the mention in Ezek 14.14, 20 of Job in the company of two other renowned men, Noah and Daniel, do not necessarily vouch for the antiquity of the prose, but discovery of a Dan'l in the Ugaritic corpus adds weight to the contention that both poet and audience knew the story of a righteous individual named Job. The numerous parallels to Job found among the 'problem literature' of Egypt and Mesopotamia similarly support the notion that the tale of a good and upright person who suffered at the hands of a god and was restored existed in the ancient 'public domain', both in literary and folk (oral) forms.[10]

While precise determinations of the textual prehistory of the prose lie beyond the scope of this study,[11] it is proposed here that the Prologue and Epilogue in their entirety display, as one might expect, the structural features of a folktale manifested at the syntagmatic level of plot composition and characterization,[12] and hence, this must be taken seriously in any literary interpretation. Further, it will be shown that the poetic speeches also follow and continue that folktale in structure, thus providing a key to the interpretation of several intriguing features.

A FORMALIST APPROACH

In 1928, Vladimir Propp published his analysis of a corpus of Russian fairy tales, *Morfológija skázki* (*The Morphology of the Folktale*),[13] in which he attempted to provide a careful synchronic analysis of the structure, or in his words, the 'morphology' of the tale at the syntagmatic level. This work formed the beginning of his attempt to account for the structural similarities to be found in this tale type, but his chapter on diachronic analysis was omitted from the original publication, and was published in 1946 as *Istoriceskiye korni volshebnoy skázki (The Historical Roots of the Fairy Tale)*.[14] In fact, the patterns Propp identified in the Russian *Zaubermärchen* had been noted and characterized as the '*Arische Aussetzungs- und Rückkehr-Formel*' by J.G. von Hahn, a collector of Albanian and Greek tales, in the nineteenth century.[15]

With the publication of the first English version of Propp's work in 1958, interest in such a 'structural' approach to traditional texts blossomed, and moved out beyond application to folklore into the realm of literature where Propp's work has been a key point of departure for the investigations of some French semioticians and literary critics.[16] Though not himself an orthodox and active proponent of Formalism, that politically suspect literary school which flourished at the beginning of this century in Russia in opposition to literary atomism and symbolism, Propp is usually cited as one of Formalism's major contributing members,[17] and in fact, his work shares much with the approaches of the Prague linguistic school, another offshoot of Formalism.[18] Propp's method, with and without modifications, has been successfully applied to the study of North American Indian folktales, African and Swedish folktales, and recently, to the biblical book of Ruth.[19]

Propp's approach to the folktale starts with the consideration of those features of the tale which are invariant, rather than focusing on individual motifs or themes. Tales display a vast number of actors or *dramatis personae*, the 'subjects' of the tale; but the actions of these characters, the 'predicates' of the tale, are actually fairly limited. These predicates, which Propp termed 'functions', are 'understood as an act of a character, defined from the point of view of its significance for the course of the action.'[20] They constitute the recurring, stable elements which make a given folk narrative into a folktale, regardless of the variation of characters who might possibly perform the function. Propp catalogued 31 functions (exclusive of connective elements and the initial situation) which together accounted for all the action in his corpus of tales. While not every function occurred in every tale, the sequences of the functions which did appear were identical. Often, functions might become assimilated to one another, or a tale might show a reduplication or incorporation of another series of functions (such as a new act of villainy or another series of tests of the hero), thus creating a mini-tale within the tale; and these series Propp referred to as 'moves'.[21] The 31 functions isolated by Propp are:

	(Initial situation: α)
I	Absentation (β)
II	Interdiction (γ)
III	Violation (δ)
IV	Reconnaissance (ε)

V	Delivery (ζ)
VI	Trickery (η)
VII	Complicity (θ)
VIII	Villainy (A)
VIIIa.	Lack (a)
IX	Mediation: the connective incident (B)
X	Beginning counteraction (C)
XI	Departure (↑)
XII	The first function of the donor (D)
XIII	The hero's reaction (E)
XIV	Provision or receipt of a magical agent (F)
XV	Spatial transference; guidance (G)
XVI	Struggle (H)
XVII	Branding: marking (J)[22]
XVIII	Victory (I)
XIX	The initial misfortune or lack is liquidated (K)
XX	Return (↓)
XXI	Pursuit (Pr)
XXII	Rescue (Rs)
XXIII	Unrecognized arrival (O)[23]
XXIV	Unfounded claims (L)
XXV	Difficult task (M)
XXVI	Solution (N)
XXVII	Recognition (Q)
XXVIII	Exposure (Ex)
XXIX	Transfiguration (T)
XXX	Punishment (U)
XXXI	Wedding (W)[24]

Though Propp chose to concentrate on the actions of the personages of the tale rather than on the individuals performing them, he was able to categorize the various actors one might find in a tale according to the spheres of functions associated with given *dramatis personae*. The characters in a tale, based on the functions which they fulfill are:

Villain
Donor (provider)
Helper
Princess (the sought-for person) and her Father
Dispatcher
Hero
False Hero[25]

There are three ways in which functions are distributed among the tale personages. The character may be identified exactly with the sphere of action (functions), as in the case of Donors who provide the Hero with a magical agent, or Helpers who assist the Hero in escape or rescue of the sought-for person, and so on. Second, a single *dramatis persona* may fulfill functions from several spheres of action: thus there are Donors who are also Helpers, Villains who make the claims of False Heroes, Heroes who act as their own Helpers, and other variations. Third, one sphere of action may be fulfilled by several characters. A number of personages may act as Donors, 'testing' the Hero prior to another character's actually providing the magical helper or agent.[26]

Criticisms and refinements of Propp's work have pointed up the need for greater attention to the aspects of characterization in folk narrative, and the desirability of linking syntagmatic to paradigmatic analyses, since Propp's linear axis for plot progression gives only one, albeit a critical, dimension of the story.[27] B. Nathḥorst's monograph raises important questions about some of Propp's methodological formulations,[28] and C. Lévi-Strauss and A.J. Greimas, among others, have suggested the possibility of viewing some functions as transformations of even more basic underlying forms.[29] However, as a starting place for the analysis of the principles of plot composition, Propp's work continues to hold promise, expecially for comparison across tales, and for other sorts of narratives, both folk and literary, where the same rules of narrative 'syntax' may be in operation.[30] Bearing in mind these criticisms, let us now focus our attention on the folktale of Job which has received little or no form critical attention of this kind.

THE MORPHOLOGY OF JOB

The Initial Situation (α^2) Job 1.1-3

Although Propp, perhaps wrongly,[31] does not consider the initial situation a function per se, it is an important morphological element in the tale. Beginning with a spatial-temporal determination ('A man there was in the land of Uz'), the Hero is named, and indicated by status designations important to the tale, including important qualities such as spiritual ones ('and that man was blameless and upright, one who feared God and turned away from evil').[32] Family members are enumerated ('There were born to him seven sons and three daughters'). There is repeated emphasis placed on the Hero's well-being in domestic, agrarian and fabulous terms, no doubt because these will soon be placed in jeopardy ('He had seven thousand sheep, three thousand camels, five hundred yoke of oxen, and five hundred she-asses, and very many servants; so that this man was the greatest of all the people of the east').[33]

The opening formula of the Hebrew departs from the normal means of beginning a historical narrative (*’îš hāyâ* here instead of *way^{e}hî ’îš*), and marks the work as a story with its own clearcut beginning (cf. 2 Sam 12.1 and Est 2.5). As such, it may be considered an example of a formulaic 'framework' which opens and concludes a tale, leading into an initial situation (see below).[34]

The Preparatory Section

Propp considers the first seven functions as preparation for 'The Complication', Villainy/Lack, and the functions which lead to the Hero's departure.[35]

Absentation (β^3) Job 1.4

A member or members of the family is absent from home, thus opening up the possibility for further developments, such as violation of commands in the absence of those who enforce them, opportunities for villainy, and so on. The form of absentation here is (β^3), 'sometimes members of the younger generation absent themselves', with a motivation given ('His sons used to go and hold a feast in the house of each on his day; and they would send and invite their three sisters to eat and drink with them').[36]

Interdiction (γ°) *and Violation* (δ°) Job 1.5a

The negative command and its violation (or, in inverted form, the fulfillment of a request) are paired functions, the second of which may occur without the first (since a violation presumes an interdiction). The Interdiction may occur in strengthened or weakened forms, and its Violation signals the entrance of the Villain onto the scene. In Job 1.5, we see only a weakened form of the Violation in the motivation for Job's attempt to ward off evil consequences, since it is based on the probability of a violation of an implicit interdiction ('You shall not curse God in your heart') having occurred.[37]

Connective Element (§) Job 1.5b
Propp uses the notation (§) to indicate elements which link one group of functions to the next.[38]

Reconnaissance ($\varepsilon^3 2$) Job 1.6-7 *and Delivery* (ξ^2) Job 1.8
Here the Villain first appears in tales which contain the function Villainy, as opposed to Lack. An indication is given as to how the character has been included in the action (entering from the outside, flying in through the ceiling, etc.), as in Job 1.7 ('The Lord said to the Satan, "Whence have you come?" The Satan answered the Lord, "From going to and fro on the earth, and from walking up and down on it"'). This element also includes the motivation for the Villain's interrogation, since it emphasizes the 'job description' of the Satan. This character alludes to his actions of Reconnaissance, in the word-play on the root of *haśśāṭān* as he answers about his habitual activities of surveillance of humankind (*miššûṭ bā'āreṣ ûmēhithallēk bāh*).

The Villain's desire is to obtain information about the victim/Hero, which may be done by directly questioning that character, or another personage as we see here. In inverted forms, the Villain may be questioned rather than perfoming the interrogation, and so receives information through that process, as in Job 1.8. Typically, the auxiliary elements describing Job's fabled righteousness are trebled (Propp's notation:).[39]

> And the Lord said to the Satan, 'Have you considered my servant Job, that there is none like him on the earth, a blameless and upright man who fears God and turns away from evil?'

Trickery (η^1) Job 1.9-11 *and Complicity* (θ^1) Job 1.12a
In this set of paired functions, the Villain uses deceitful persuasion or other forms of (magical) coercion to take possession of the victim and/or his belongings (Job 1.9-11, with trebling(:) at the textural level of the preposition *b'd*). The Hero/victim agrees or responds automatically and involuntarily (Job 1.12a), for as Propp points out, 'one notes that interdictions are always broken and conversely, deceitful proposals are always accepted and fulfilled'.[40] Given the seriousness of the self-curse/wager form in the ancient Near East, one might be tempted to view this as a form of magical coercion to which Yahweh must naturally respond (η^2, θ^2). Often the complicity

in this 'deceitful agreement' takes place because the Villain has created some difficult situation to which the deceitful suggestion seems to supply an answer, as we see in the dialogue between Yahweh and the Satan.[41]

Connective Element (§) Job 1.12b
This connective contains the motif of 'spatial transference', which allows the action to move from one location to another, here from the divine court to the earth.

The First Complication

Connective Element (§β^3) Job 1.13
As the tale moves into the first complication of Villainy, function (β^3) is reprised to set up the report of the misfortunes which have befallen Job. The restatement of the element of Absentation confirms Propp's observation that it is the separation of family members which creates the opportunity for the complication.[42]

Villainy (A^5, A^{14}, assim.) *and Mediation, The Connective Incident* (B^4) Job 1.14-19
The preparatory functions all lead irrevocably to Villainy, an instance of misfortune or perception of Lack, which causes the Hero to be dispatched from home to seek a solution. In the case of victim-heroes, Villainy simply causes the Hero to leave home, so that adventures which will lead to the restoration of the family's fortunes may take place. In this tale syntagma, the function of Villainy, in which a number of villainous acts may take place together, appears in forms A^5, 'plunder' and A^{14}, 'murder', both of which may be considered variations of 'seizure'.[43] However, as sometimes happens,[44] this function itself has been assimilated to function B, Mediation, which makes the misfortune known. In our text, this occurs by means of report (B^4), and features of repetition are prominent, both in the words of the servants who report, and in the structural variation between disasters caused by human agency (Job 1.14-15, 17) and disasters caused by 'divine' agency (Job 1.16, 18-19).

Beginning Counteraction (C neg.) Job 1.20-21 *and Connective Element* (§) Job 1.22
Although Propp notes that the function of Counteraction, where the

Hero agrees to or decides upon a response to the misfortune caused by the villainous acts, generally occurs in tales of seeker-heroes,[45] Job does respond to his situation, refusing to curse God (hence, making this a negative outcome for the function, C neg.). This leads to the connective element of Job 1.22, which gives the motivation for the onset of another complication through its evaluation of Job's conduct.

The Second Complication

Reconnaissance ($\varepsilon^3 2$) Job 2.1-2
Delivery (ζ^2) Job 2.3
Trickery (η^1) Job 2.4-5
Complicity (θ^1) Job 2.6
Connective Element (§) Job 2.7a
Villainy (A^6) Job 2.7b
Beginning Counteraction (C^1) Job 2.8a
Departure (↑) Job 2.8b

Job's counteraction to Villainy in the first complication, though the 'proper' response for the thematic development of Job as the 'righteous believer', demands that a new complication of Villainy ensue, since it produced no movement on Job's part. The logic of the tale requires that its Heroes set out, whatever the reason for those departures might be. Hence, the functions which lead up to a new act of Villainy (A^6, bodily injury) are reduplicated, with Yahweh once again setting the limits of the function (Job 1.12a; 2.6). The involuntary nature of Yahweh's response to the Satan's Trickery (η^2, θ^2, employment of magical or other means) is evident in the statement in 2.3b, 'He still holds fast his integrity, *although you moved me against him, to destroy him without cause*'. The second complication shows an intensification of action, in form and content. Not only does the Villainy now touch Job personally (although Propp considers bodily injury to be a morphological equivalent to other forms of seizure, since the injured party is deprived of health),[46] but the Satan also dispenses with the use of intermediaries for performance of the Villainy, which is narrated directly and not through the medium of report. If it is indeed the case that the Satan's wager with Yahweh is also an implicit self-curse, then our Villain has reason to 'up the ante', so to speak, since he is by no means disinterested in the outcome.

The second attack on Job is successful, from the perspective of the tale's syntagmatic demands of plot action. Job's Counteraction to bodily injury is a simple response to his physical condition as he scrapes himself with a potsherd. The key point to which the functions have pressed relentlessly occurs when Job leaves home to sit among the ashes. It is here that his future tests and struggles will take place before he may return home in triumph.

Entry of Donors and Helpers

Now that Job has 'set out' as the tale demanded,[47] the inclusion of more *dramatis personae* begins. These new characters appear in the form of Donors and Helpers, those providing much-needed information, guidance, magical objects, and objects or beings provided by the Donors which directly affect the hero's ability to liquidate Lack and reverse misfortune. Hence, their contributions to the solution of the Hero's problems is critical to plot development, for without their appearance at this point the Hero could not proceed.

Some of the most interesting post-Proppian research into the morphology of the tale has concerned itself with the character and function of these secondary *dramatis personae*. The Donor normally administers a 'test' of some sort, often in the form of a simple greeting or interrogation, a request for help or mercy, or even hostile challenge and competition. These 'preliminary tests', as they have been termed by E. Meletinsky,[48] lead to the acquisition of further help, and often seem to be designed to test the Hero's knowledge of the 'rules of the game', as well as his courtesy, wisdom, willingness to oblige and take initiative. Heroes who answer politely and respond positively to their potential Donors receive the help they need; surly Heroes who respond negatively receive nothing (other than an occasional harsh reprisal), and must be tested again until they finally make the appropriate reply, so that the action may continue.

The tale shows a tendency to construct its action upon a triadic hierarchy of tests, preliminary (Donor) tests, basic tests (struggle with the Villain), and supplementary tests (which expose the False Heroes). Successful completion of the first test yields an ever-increasing 'tale value', which leads to the ability to complete the next test, and so on. This intensive expenditure of energy is necessary in order to overcome the 'entropy' introduced by the villainous act.[49] Trebling of the function of the test itself (the Hero fails twice and succeeds on the third trial; the Hero passes three tests, each more difficult than the last; the Hero succeeds after two companions have failed, etc.) as well as trebling of auxiliary elements, is habitual (but not obligatory) for these sets of functions. It is common to find whole test syntagma repeated in triads with very little alteration, as a Donor first tells the Hero about the upcoming (basic) test. This may then be repeated as the Hero actually completes the basic test. Finally, in the supplementary test to determine the identities of the Hero who performed the deed and the False Hero who only claims to have performed the deed, the test episode may be recounted yet again, serving as 'proof'. In all these instances, trebling (⁝) seems to operate as one of the formulaic components by which a storyteller fleshes out the skeleton of plot functions.[50]

First Function of the Donor (D^2) Job 2.9
The Hero's Reaction (E^2 neg) Job 2.10a
Connective Element (§) Job 2.10b

Job's first preliminary test is administered by a potential Donor in the character of his wife, who may be designated as a 'Princess-Tester', since she will be associated with the ultimate tale value, W, 'wedding' in the form of resumed marriage.[51] Ancient commentators did not overlook the 'test' quality in this interchange between Job and his unnamed but equally distraught wife. Incipient misogyny interpreted this in the light of Woman as 'temptress', and found her here as the 'helper' of the Satan who through her inflicts yet another test upon Job.[52] However, as P. Trible has noted,[53] the question raised by Job's wife is by no means devoid of critical theological reflection on the matter at hand, and though paired with the injunction to 'curse God and die', intimates that holding fast to integrity is at the heart of Job's search for an understanding of God's actions and redress of wrongs done. Job's answer, though it shows that he does indeed know the rules of the game as formulated by the piety of antiquity ('Shall we receive good at the hand of God, and shall we not receive evil?') is hostile, and hence, the crucial information which the potential Donor attempted to transfer is unavailable to him. The connective element approves Job's response both to the Villainy of the second complication and, implicitly, his response to the Donor. From the perspective of the tale, however, this signals the need for further preliminary Donor tests. Job will respond no less negatively to his encounters with further Donors, in the triad of his friends, and hence, additional trebling in the function of the preliminary tests occurs.

Mediation, The Connective Incident (B^4) Job 2.11-13
In order to advance the action, the tale retraces its steps in another connective incident which will provide mediation of the problem. This is done by allowing the misfortune of the Hero to be made known, here to Job's three friends, potential Donors, each of whom will test Job three times. C. Bremond's observation that Propp's classification of functions tells the plot's story only from the privileged point of view of the Hero is applicable here.[54] A small cluster of 'heroic' functions which apply to the actions of the Donors may be noted within this connective: misfortune is made known (B^4 2.11a); Departure (↑ 2.11a); beginning Counteraction (C^1, 2.11b) and Unrecognized Arrival (O, 2.12a). This feature, along with the shift to third-person narrative, suggests some support for the contention that this syntagma has been reworked or added by the author of the poetic speeches.[55]

Mediation, The Connective Incident (B^7) Job 3.1-26
The specific form of Mediation which occurs here is the Lament (B^7), which is the typical function associated with acts of Villainy which include murder.[56] While lament is appropriate here, since Job's friends have not yet heard of Job's distress directly from the Hero, it is also common to see tale Heroes deliver long monologues prior to the performance of arduous tasks.[57] Whether the lament is viewed as a reprise of the preceding functions or a preliminary to the cycles of Donor tests, it clearly stands as a bridge between the tale proper and the poetic speeches.

First Function of the Donor (D^2) Job 4.1–5.27; 8.1-21; 11.1-20; 15.1-35; 18.1-21; 20.1-29
The Hero's Reaction (E^2 neg) Job 6.1-7.21; 9.1–10.22; 12.1–14.22; 16.1–17.16; 19.1-29; 21.1-34
While it is not necessary to posit exact correspondences between folktale action sequences and the poetic speeches, it is clear that both in content and syntagmatic structure, the core of the book of Job does not diverge greatly from what would be expected had the central functions of the tale been continued in prose form. The poet found in the form of the folktale itself a ready-made format for the expansion

of certain segments of the action of the narrative. The dialogues of Job with his friends rely heavily on the triadic pattern associated with tests of the hero. While the friends of Job may leave much to be desired as comforters due to their insensitivity to their friend's position, they make admirable Donors. In numerous places, they suggest actions (i.e. basic tests) which Job might perform, and attempt to impart information which might help Job resolve his dilemma. Their growing hostility at Job's intransigence and the increasing irony of Job's responses may easily be interpreted in the framework of the accelerating difficulties encountered in a series of tests. Job's replies, lacking in civility and attentiveness to the proposed mediating behaviors suggested by the potential Donors, insure that the testing must and will continue.

However, Job's responses should not be interpreted merely as failure of preliminary testing, since his speeches, generally longer than those of his Donors,[58] do refute—at least to Job's satisfaction—his friends' positions, hence acting as a stimuli for more intensive testing. Job also acts as his own Donor-Helper by describing the upcoming basic test, including its outcome: struggle with God (Job 9.1–10.22; etc.). It is noteworthy that Heroes often take part in lengthy dialogues before performance of the basic test, so that whatever specific interpretation of the outcome of the dialogues may be chosen, the general activity can be accounted for within the complex of functions which go to make up a tale. The genres most frequently found in the poetic speeches—disputation speeches, juridical forms, rhetorical questions and appeals to ancient tradition[59]—are all ones which call to mind the notion of 'testing' or conflict over transmission of needed information.

First Function of the Donor (D^9) Job 22.1-30; 25.1-6
Hero's Reaction (E^9, *trial of the magical agent*) Job 23.1–24.25; 26.1–27.23; 31
Receipt of a Magical Agent (F^3) *and Guidance* (G^4) Job 28.1-30.31
The difficulties in extending any interpretive theory to the third cycle of Job are notorious, since the third speech of Zophar is missing, the speech of Bildad is much too short, and Job's replies include the infamous Hymn to Wisdom (Job 28), which seems incongruous to some when placed in Job's mouth. Critics conclude that the text as it stands cannot have been transmitted properly, and that perhaps the best interpretation may be to conclude that the dialogue breaks down at this point.[60]

Despite the problems inherent in any reconstruction of these chapters, it is possible to extend our observations of folktale structure to these portions of the work. First, given our comments on the occurrence of trebling (:) in the test syntagmata, we would naturally expect to find the most significant action located in the last third of the third cycle of tests—precisely where the dialogue breaks down! We can only speculate about the original form of the text, but there are hints remaining, when viewed through the matrix of folktale functions, of how the movement from preliminary test with the friends to the basic test of competition with God might have been achieved.

In the third cycle, such as it is, we see the intertwining of two function sequences, as Job's donor tests mutate to include three trials of the operation of a 'magical' agent. Three instances are found here where Job makes 'avowals of innocence': in his reply to Eliphaz (Job 23.10-12); following his response to Bildad (Job 27.2-6); and in the position which would be occupied by the reply to Zophar (Job 31), had the cycle followed the pattern of the preceding two. It is possible to see Job's first two oaths as special forms of the preliminary test to 'try out' the magical aid one has received from the Donor (Propp does not assign these tests a label, since he views them as developments from the essential donor test[61]). Again, we must regard the last element of those trebled as the most important for thematic development, as ch. 31 clearly is, since it ends the discourses of Job. The power of the word in the negative confession of the oath operates like the more traditional sort of magical agent recommended to the Hero to bring about the *dénouement*.

Much simplified, the action in 28.1–30.31 may be described as follows: Job, acting as his own Helper, receives information from God about the 'true' nature of wisdom (28.28); and his reflections on his own exercise of that wisdom in his former life (chs. 29–30) guide him to pronounce his third and final oath of innocence (ch. 31). Recalling here Propp's general principle that in assessing the presence of assimilated functions, it is necessary to consider the outcome of a given segment for its impact on plot development,[62] 28.1–30.31 should be considered the general fulfillment of functions F, 'provision or receipt of a magical agent', and G, 'the hero is transferred, delivered, or led to the whereabouts of an object of search', where 'the object of search is located in "another" or "different kingdom". This kingdom may lie far away horizontally, or else very high up or deep down vertically' (p. 50).[63] Following the first two preliminary tests for the use of the magically powerful oath of innocence, Job's successful response to the donor tests of the third cycle leads him to search out wisdom (F), a magical Helper with access to cosmic information and proven ability to guide her followers. Searching, a task integral to the tale, is never a simple matter:

> But where shall wisdom be found?
> And where is the place of understanding?
> Man does not know the way to it,
> and it is not found in the land of the living.
> The deep says, 'It is not in me',
> and the sea says, 'It is not with me'.
>
> 'Whence then comes wisdom?
> And where is the place of understanding?
> It is hid from the eyes of all living
> and concealed from the birds of the air.
> Abaddon and Death say, 'We have heard a rumor of it with our ears' (Job 28.12-14, 20-22).

Job's quest for the wisdom which could not be found in the outermost boundaries of the tale universe (up/down, far/near, natural/supernatural, hidden/obvious, true/false)[64] leads him to a God who proclaims, 'Behold, the fear of the Lord, that is wisdom; and to depart from evil is understanding' (28.28, function G). In 28.23-28. Yahweh, displacing the expected Zophar, acts as a successful Donor to Job, thus providing the vehicle for further development and movement toward the basic test, precipitated through the oath of ch. 31. Far from viewing v. 28 as an appendage to the hymn, and the hymn as extraneous to the Donor disputation cycles, the presence of wisdom here is critical. It reaffirms Job's basic righteousness (cf. 1.1, 8; 2.3) even while emphasizing the impossibility of human wisdom totally to comprehend the divine (by means of the motif of hiddenness). The evidence of the effect of wisdom's Guidance on Job is found in the reaffirmation of his own position as truly blameless and upright. The functional meaning of this moral stance before the Lord is fully exegeted in Job's monologue following the wisdom hymn (29.1–30.31). Using wisdom themes, this speech forms a thematic bridge to Job's third and successful use of an oath whose seriousness is heightened by the inclusion of the frequently omitted apodosis. Driven to conclude the final triad of tests by his now hostile Donors, having searched for and been given a definition of wisdom which allows him to trust in his own righteousness, Job is able finally to take the action (ch. 31) which will move him toward fulfillment of the basic test.

Reduplication of Receipt of a Magical Agent (F^9) Job 32.1–36.33 *and Guidance* (G^4) Job 37.1-24

If the interpretation here is accepted thus far and the desire to read the text synchronically is honored, what then is to be done with the sudden appearance of Elihu on the scene? Indeed, Propp's model lists the next function expected as H, 'struggle: the hero and the villain join in direct combat'.[65] As we have seen, it is common to find a new 'move' (sequence of functions) beginning in a tale before the previous move has been entirely resolved, or 'episodic moves' interwoven or reduplicated,[66] and such may be the case here. Since Helpers often appear out of nowhere to describe the upcoming test, lead the hero to the site of the competition, and generally make themselves useful in other ways (sometimes to the exclusion of action of the part of the Hero), it is possible to view the inclusion of Elihu as a repetition and fulfillment of functions F, receipt of a magical agent (here in the form of Elihu the Helper; 32.1–36.33), and G, guidance (37.1-24). That Job's use of the oath in ch. 31 is followed by the appearance of Elihu, a Helper who directly foreshadows Yahweh's arguments and the upcoming thunderous theophany, then, is not beyond the bounds of what one might expect of structural repetition seen in the tale. The unexpectedness of Elihu's appearance is resolved by the recognition that, unlike the friends who are potential Donors (and subsequently False Heroes), he is a Helper, and as such, is apt to appear suddenly, and exit in the same manner. Since Elihu claims, however indirectly, that it is the spirit of God which prompts him to speak (32.8ff.), Yahweh is again the Donor and source of a Helper to Job.

It is interesting to consider the possible reasons for the occurrence of this second move of functions FG at the conclusion of the triad of preliminary tests. Given that the placement and content of the Elihu speeches reduplicate functions F and G, these chapters may have been added as an attempt to clarify the structure of action in the Third Cycle after it had become disarranged. However, another explanation based on the structure of the tale presents itself: the repetition of the functions of the Helper in 28.1–37.24 formally balances the two complicating moves of Villainy of the Prologue, the two conflicts with Yahweh and double restoration to come (42.10, 12).

Struggle (H^2) Job 38.1–40.2; 40.6–41.34
Victory (I^2 neg.) Job 40.3-5; (I^2) Job 42.1-6
The 'basic test', as one might expect, is differentiated from the tests which precede and follow by analysis of its outcome: the major misfortune or lack is overcome by means of this test, whereas the other test syntagmata operate to provide the Hero with means to succeed in the basic test (preliminary donor tests), and act as validation of the authorship of the deed (supplementary tests to expose the False Hero). The form of struggle here is that of H, 'competition', which seems to be a development from more violent forms of combat.[67] This is appropriate, for Job's complaint all along has been the impossibility of meeting God on equal grounds for normal combat, thus providing the needs for a shift from the physical to the legal sphere. The overtones of aggression in the encounter are evident in Yahweh's opening words, 'Gird up your loins like a man, I will question you, and you shall declare to me' (38.3). The outcome of the first struggle must be considered negative (40.3-5), since it leads to a reduplication of the struggle and response.

Tale motifs are evident in the Yahweh-speeches. The cosmological descriptions of 38.4-38 emphasize the overwhelming strangeness of the world into which the Hero has been catapulted, thus playing out the tale's basic opposition of own/foreign and its fascination with boundaries.[68] The diverse animals of 38.29–39.30 recall the animal Helpers so familiar to the tale. Such creatures often form a more supportive and informative 'kinship' unit for the Hero than do his real family and friends,[69] a fact upon which Job comments when he claims to be 'a brother of jackals and a companion of ostriches' (30.29). The appearances of Behemoth and Leviathan recall the 'wondrous' animal, an intensification of the normal animal Helper, and their occurrence in the second incidence of H^2, Struggle, is apt, since they obviously play some part in bringing about the final victory.[70]

It should be noted that while Yahweh fulfills the role of Villain here, as the *dramatis persona* who engages Job in combat, the role of 'False Villain' or pseudo-villain, who inflicts evil but makes multiple restitution, is not unknown to the tale.[71] We suggest that, given the equivocal nature of the character of Yahweh in the book of Job, a

False Villain is present here, for two reasons. First, Job's second response to Yahweh makes clear that he is not going to use his audience to curse to God's face (1.11; 2.5), so it is really the Satan, rather than Job or Yahweh, who has been defeated in this final interchange of the basic test (I pos.). Second, it is Yahweh who doubly restores the fortunes of Job and punishes the False Heroes (see below), acts which are clearly not found in the sphere of the Villain.

Connective Element (§) Job 42.7a
Unfounded Claims (L); *Difficult Task* (M); *Solution* (N); *Recognition* (Q) *and Exposure (Ex assim.)* Job 42.7b-9
Immediately following the Yahweh speeches, the tale resumes with a cluster of functions which act to form the episode of the supplementary test. This deals with Job's friends, who now play the role of the 'False Hero' (i.e. '... you have not spoken of me what is right, as my servent Job has', 42.7b). Included in the Difficult Task proposed to Job (intercession on behalf of the False Heroes, but one might note that this function could also apply to the friends) is the recognition of Job as the Hero who has spoken properly, and hence, this is an allusion to the full liquidation of lack yet to come (42.8-9). With the acceptance of Job's prayer, the Hero is recognized as irrevocably marked off from those making heroic claims who are finally exposed for what they are, although the functions Q and Ex have assimilated to one another. As is generally the case with complex tales of many moves, only the most recent antagonists of the Hero (i.e. the False Heroes instead of the Villain of the complications) are punished.[72] These supplementary functions which vindicate Job and dispose of his friends are linked paradigmatically to those in Job 2.11-13, which introduce the friends.

The Initial Misfortune or Lack is Liquidated (K^4) Job 42.10
Return (↓) Job 42.11a
Transfiguration (T) 42.11b-12
Wedding (W^2) Job 42.13-16
The tale concludes with functions which center upon the reinstatement of the Hero. The action of a tale does not simply return the Hero to his initial situation, but, as a result of the values gained by successful completion of all the tale tests, leaves the Hero at a higher level than that at which he began (42.10b, 12, 15).[73] The scene is a familiar one

from classical *Zaubermärchen*: surrounded by relatives and friends the Hero is transfigured in some way. Functions T^2 'the hero builds a marvelous palace', and T^3, 'the hero puts on new garments' are represented here, as Job accrues more wealth (42.12) for his house, and receives ornaments of gold and money from his kin. Given the repetition of the statement of restoration by Yahweh, one might also understand another occurrence of function K^4, liquidation of the initial misfortune, at this point. This second statement has the effect of allowing Job's lacks, caused by Villainy, to recede much as a case of the measles does: the first area stricken (lack of children and goods) is the last to be restored.

The final tale value is found in function W^2, 'resumed marriage', implicit in the account of Job's children (42.13-17). Although the number of children born to Job is not subject to double restoration, (though the form of the numeral 'seven' is unusual and may refer to doubling) the emphasis on the exceptional beauty of Job's three daughters, along with the statement that Job has given them an inheritance among their brothers, shows that there *are* more children than before, since the daughters have become more fully human in their father's sight.

Concluding Frame Job 42.17
Paralleling the opening frame of the tale, a concluding formula appears here. For similar examples, see Gen 15.6; 35.29; 1 Chron 29.28.

CONCLUSION

Structural analysis of Job confirms that, taken as a whole, the work may be considered a 'poeticized folktale'. At the syntagmatic level, the narrative and the poetic speeches together form a tale of the 'victim-hero' type of considerable complexity, with at least two moves (using this term in Propp's narrow sense of functions which repeat functions A-K)[74] and several episodic moves (see Figure 1). Two beginning complications (functions A-↑) are balanced by two liquidations of lack (K^4, understood either in content of the double restoration, or by means of the possible repetition of K^4 in Job 42.12); two differentiated sets of Donors (female and male) test Job, with a triad of tests administered by the males who, because of their failure, become False Heroes. Two episodes of help and guidance (functions

Figure 1: *Folktale Functions in Job*

Prologue

Move I. $(\alpha^2)\beta^3[\gamma]\delta^1\S\varepsilon^3{}_2\zeta^2\eta^1\theta^1\S\S^{\beta^3}[A^5{}_{14}]B^4\ C^{neg}\S$

Move II. $\varepsilon^3{}_2\zeta^2\eta^1\theta^1\S$ A^6 $C^1\uparrow D^2E^2neg$

$B^4(C^1\uparrow O)$

Poetic Speeches

$B^7D^2E^2neg$ ⁝

D^2E^2neg ⁝

$D^9E^9D^9E^9$ E^9

F^3G^4

$F^9G^4H^2I^2neg$

H^2I^2

Epilogue

$\S LMNQ[Ex]K^4$ Move II Resolved

$\downarrow T^2{}_3(K^4)W^2$ Move I Resolved

——— = Move

— — — = Episodic Move

[ ] = Assimilated Function

( ) = Proposed Function

⁝ = trebling

Figure 2: *Paradigmatic Relationships Among Functional Sequences*

Initial Situation/ Final Situation	Preparatory/ Concluding Functions	Complication/ Resolution	Preliminary/ Supplementary Tests	Basic Test
$(\alpha^2)\beta^3[\gamma]d^1$§	$\varepsilon^3 2\zeta^2\eta^1\theta^1$§	§$\beta^3[A^5 14]B^4$ Cneg§		
	$\varepsilon^3 2\zeta^2\eta^1\theta^1$§	A^6 C^1 ↑	D^2E^2neg	
			B^4 (C^1↑O) B^7	
			D^2E^2neg ⋮	
			D^2E^2neg ⋮	
			$\underline{D^9E^9D^9E^9 \quad E^9}$	
			F^3G^4	
			F^9G^4	
				H^2I^2neg
				H^2I^2
			§LMNQ[Ex]	
		K^4↓		
	$T^2 3(K^4?)$			
W^2 Frame				

( ) = Proposed Function
[ ] = Assimilated Function
—— = Interwoven Move
⋮ = Trebling

FG) precede two struggles (HI). Paradigmatic relationships between the larger groupings of functions are shown in Figure 2.

Almost all of the *dramatis personae* expected in the tale are present in Job. The role of Hero is, of course, Job's, but he is also his own Helper. Donors are represented by the friends, the Bride-Tester, and Yahweh. Elihu and Wisdom, whether understood as personified (and hence, a magical helper) or as a cognitive process of wondrous capabilities (a magical agent) appear as Helpers. The Satan is clearly the Villain of the first two moves, with Yahweh appearing as False Villain in the remainder of the tale. Eliphaz, Bildad and Zophar fulfill a second collective role of False Hero. Since it is Yahweh who restores Job's wealth, the usual role of the Father who bestows the Sought-for marriage partner (Princess), it is tempting to view Yahweh as the realization of this role in a modified form. If our interpretaion of the operation of Wisdom as a *dramatis persona* is valid, then this may also provide us with an insight into the relationship which exists between Yahweh and Wisdom.

Assessment of how well Propp's method of analysis holds for tales of the ancient Near East cannot be fully judged without more comparative data. (Sasson's *Ruth* is less helpful for our purposes here, since it is of the seeker-hero tale type.) Divergence from the model used should call not only for ongoing refinements of the classifications made, but also for greater scrutiny and revision of the model itself, especially along the lines suggested by Bremond and Meletinsky. For example, it may be desirable to redraw the structure outlined above using the categories of Lack-Search-Difficult Task instead of Villainy-Struggle. Disagreements in analysis may simply reflect the difference between modern European tale types and ancient tales, or the intrusion of literary features, since the ancient texts have almost certainly been subject to literary embellishment.[75]

Preliminary surveys of three Middle Egyptian texts (Tale of the Eloquent Peasant, The Shipwrecked Sailor, and the Westcar Papyrus) and two Late Egyptian tales (Tale of Two Brothers, and Tale of the Doomed Prince) show supporting evidence for both the validity of Propp's scheme and the need to apply it to these literary texts with greater flexibility (as has been the case with North American Indian tales and African folktales). The importance of Absentation in the complication is found in the several tales, and the necessity of the Hero's departure from home is likewise attested.[76] Tests appear in triads, with success in the final trial, brides appear as

Helpers and testers, and animal Helpers and Donors abound.[77] Propp's discussion of the preparatory section of tales, however, where certain functions are considered mutually exclusive, does not hold for the works under consideration, nor does the observation concerning the complementary distribution of Lack and Villainy as the complications in tales. Tales may proceed from Lack (as in the Westcar Papyrus),[78] Villainy (Two Brothers),[79] or both (Doomed Prince).[80] Episodes of semantically linked functions, such as DEF, MN, and others, need not occur in the order suggested by Propp. A transfer of an animal Donor test (DE) in the Tale of the Two Brothers occurs in the preparatory section, in order to pave the way for animal Helpers in the complication who warn the Hero of intended Villainy,[81] and other sequences may also deviate from Propp's suggested order. Given these analogies, the occurrence of the supplementary test in Job before (rather than after) function K^4, liquidation of lack, need not be viewed as a serious challenge to the general applicability of the model.

Diachronic studies of the differentiation of the tale from myth and its subsequent developments give further parameters for the evaluation of Job as a tale.[82] A high-status Hero whose misfortune 'disguises' him as low-status, Job is an example of a 'heroic' tale, where the interest in deeds tends to be for their own sake and the renown they bring their doer, although strong mythological tones and other features suggestive of more archaic tales are also present. '*Märchen* biology', the realm of folktale study concerned with the life of the form and its narrator in the community, has rightly emphasized the impact of not only the narrator but the audience as well on the shape of the tale.[83] Though the author of Job has not violated the structural constraints of the tale in its literary telling, only this frozen version remains for study, and direct study of the communal dimension of creation of the text is impossible. We must conclude that, given the work's preservation, tradition must have considered the 'poeticized folktale' to be an example of *Zurechterzählen*, the constitutive way to narrate a tale, rather than *Zerzählen*. It is hoped that the reading presented here may be evaluated similarly as a constructive, rather than destructive, retelling of Job's tale.[84]

NOTES

1. Claus Westermann, *The Structure of the Book of Job: A Form-Critical Analysis*, tr. C.A. Muenchow (Philadelphia: Fortress, 1977), pp. 1-13,

following a suggestion of Aage Bentzen, *Introduction to the Old Testament* (2nd edn; Copenhagen: G.E. Gad, 1952), II, p. 182.

2. H. Richter, *Studien zu Hiob* (Theologische Arbeiten, 11; Berlin, 1959); Michael B. Dick, 'The Legal Metaphor in Job 31', *CBQ* 41 (1979), pp. 37-50, and 'Job 31, The Oath of Innocence, and the Sage', *ZAW* 95 (1983), pp. 31-53.

3. H. Gese, *Lehre und Wirklichkeit in der alten Weisheit* (Tübingen, 1958).

4. J.A. Holland, 'On the Form of the Book of Job', *Australian Journal of Biblical Archaeology* 2 (1972), pp. 160-77; David Robertson, 'The Book of Job: A Literary Study', *Soundings* 56 (1973), pp. 446-69; J.W. Whedbee, 'The Comedy of Job', *Semeia* 7 (1977), pp. 1-39; William Urbrock, 'Job as Drama: Tragedy or Comedy?', *Cur TM* 8 (1981), pp. 35-40.

5. David Robertson, *The Old Testament and the Literary Critic* (Philadelphia: Fortress, 1977); John F.A. Sawyer, 'The Authorship and Structure of the Book of Job', *Studia Biblica 1978* (JSOT Supp Series 11), I, pp. 253-56; John A. Baker, 'The Book of Job: Unity and Meaning', *Studia Biblica 1978*, I, pp. 17-19; Alan Cooper, 'Narrative Theory and the Book of Job', *Studies in Religion* 11 (1982), pp. 35-44.

6. Marvin Pope, *Job* (Anchor Bible, 15; 3rd edn; New York: Doubleday, 1973), p. xxxi.

7. Pope, *op. cit.*, pp. xxii-xxiv; Robert Gordis, *The Book of God and Man: A Study of Job* (Chicago: Univ. of Chicago, 1965), pp. 66ff.

8. Sawyer, pp. 253-57; Baker, pp. 17-26; Yair Hoffman, 'The Relation Between the Prologue and the Speech-Cycles in Job: A Reconsideration', *VT* 31 (1981), pp. 160-70.

9. S. Spiegel, 'Noah, Danel, and Job', in *Louis Ginzberg Jubilee Volume* (New York, 1945), pp. 305-55; N. Sarna, 'Epic Substratum in the Prose of Job', *JBL* 76 (1957), pp. 13-25. See also W.J. Urbock, 'Oral Antecedents to Job: A Survey of Formulas and Formulaic Systems', *Semeia* 5 (1976), pp. 111-37.

10. M. Noth, 'Noah, Daniel und Hiob in Ezekiel XIV', *VT* 1 (1951), pp. 251-60; Pope, pp. xxiv-xxvi.

11. Alt believed that the tale could be divided into an earlier (ch. 1 and 42.11-17) and later tale (ch. 2 and 42.7-10), based on his analysis of repetitions ('Zur Vorgeschichte des Buches Hiob', *ZAW* 14 (1937), pp. 265-68. Gordis contends, rightly, that there is only one tale, viewing 2.11-13 and 42.7-10 as 'jointures' composed by the poet (*op. cit.*, pp. 72-73).

12. S. Bar-Efrat refers to this type of structural analysis as that at 'the level of the narrative world', where one may deal with characters and/or events ('Some Observations on the Analysis of Structure in Biblical Narrative', *VT* 30 [1980], pp. 161-66). For a different analysis dealing with paradigmatic structures in Job, see R. Polzin, 'The Framework of the Book of Job', *Interp* 28 (1974), pp. 182-200; *Biblical Structuralism* (Semeia Supp.; Philadelphia: Fortress, 1977).

13. Vladimir Ia. Propp, *Morphology of the Folktale* (2nd edn with a Preface by Louis A. Wagner and New Introduction by Alan Dundes; Austin: Univ. of Texas, 1968).

14. E. Meletinsky, 'Structural-Typological Study of Folktales', in *Soviet Structural Folkloristics: Texts by Meletinsky, Nekludov, Novik, and Segal with Tests of the Approach by Jilek and Jilek-Aall, Reid, and Layton*, introduced and ed. by P. Maranda (Approaches to Semiotics, 43; The Hague: Mouton, 1974), I, pp. 19-25. Cited hereafter as *SSF*.

15. Archer Taylor, 'The Biographical Pattern in Traditional Narrative', *Journal of the Folklore Institute* 1 (1964), pp. 114-17.

16. C. Bremond, 'Le message narratif', *Communications* 4 (1964), pp. 4-32; 'The Logic of Narrative Possibilities', *NLH* 11 (1980), pp. 387-411; R. Barthes, 'Introduction à l'analyse structurale des récits', *Communications* 8 (1966), pp. 1-27; A.-J. Greimas, *Structural Semantics; An Attempt at a Method*, tr. by D. McDowell, R. Schleifer, and A. Velie, with an introduction by Ronald Schleifer (Lincoln: Univ. of Nebraska, 1983). For a general review, see Michael Riffaterre, 'French Formalism', in *The Frontiers of Literary Criticism*, ed. with an introduction by David H. Malone (Los Angeles: Hennessey & Ingalls, 1974), pp. 93-119.

17. I. Levin, 'Vladimir Propp: An Evaluation on his Seventieth Birthday', *JFI* 4 (1967), pp. 32-49; V. Erlich, 'Russian Formalism', *Journal of the History of Ideas* 34 (1973), pp. 627-38.

18. D.S. Avalle, 'Systems and Structures in the Folktale', *Twentieth Century Studies* 3 (1970), pp. 70-73.

19. Alan Dundes, *The Morphology of North American Indian Folktales* (FF Communications, 195; Helsinki: Academia Scientiarium Fennica, 1964); R.A. Georges, 'Structure in Folktales: A Generative-Transformational Approach', *Conch* 2 (1970), pp. 4-17; P.V. Vehvilainen, 'The Swedish Folktale; A Structural Analysis' (Diss., 1964; Ann Arbor: University Microfilms No. 65-5472, 1965); D. Paulme, *La Mère dévorante: Essai sur la morphologie des contes africains* (Paris: Gallimard, 1976); J.M. Sasson, *Ruth: A New Translation with a Philological Commentary and a Formalist-Folklorist Interpretation* (Baltimore: Johns Hopkins Univ. Press, 1979).

20. Propp, p. 21.

21. *Ibid.*, p. 59. V. Voigt has suggested that a new function emerges whenever there is a change in (1) the scene of the action, (2) the time, (3) the performer of the action, or (4) the action performed ('Some Problems of Narrative Structure Universals in Folklore', *Acta Ethnographica* 21 [1972], p. 67).

22. Propp, pp. 51-53. The alphabetic order deviates here.

23. Although an uppercase 'O' sometimes marks this function, it is also represented by a smallcase 'o' and a degree circle.

24. Propp, pp. 25-65.

25. *Ibid.*, pp. 79-83. For further refinement in this scheme, see E.

Meletinsky, S. Nekludov, E. Novik, and D. Segal, 'Problems of the Structural Analysis of Fairytales', in *SSF*, I, pp. 111-17.

26. Propp, pp. 84-86. 'Magical Helpers' are animate; 'magical agents' are qualities or objects which operate in the same way as living Helpers.

27. J. Culler, *Structuralist Poetics* (Ithaca: Cornell Univ., 1975), pp. 209ff.

28. B. Nathḥorst, *Formal or Structural Studies of Traditional Tales* (Stockholm Studies in Comparative Religion, 9; Stockholm: Kungl. Boktryckeriet P.A. Norstedt & Soner, 1969), pp. 16-29. For example, if clusters of functions are subject to embedding within the main sequence of the tale, can one actually conclude that the sequences of such complex tales are indeed identical? For an approach to dealing with this question, see R.A. Georges, pp. 5-13.

29. C. Lévi-Strauss, 'L'analyse morphologique des contes russes', *International Journal of Slavic Linguistics and Poetics* 3 (1960), p. 142; A.-J. Greimas, 'Le conte populaire russe: analyse fonctionelle', *IJSLP* 9 (1965), pp. 152-75; *Du Sens* (Paris: Seuil, 1970), p. 187.

30. W.O. Hendricks, 'Folklore and the Structural Analysis of Literary Texts', *Language and Style* 3 (1979), pp. 83-108.

31. Lévi-Strauss, p. 134; Nathḥorst, pp. 23-24.

32. The specifics of these features will vary, depending on the culture from which the tale comes. Elli K. Maranda and Pierre Maranda, *Structural Models in Folklore and Transformational Essays* (The Hague: Mouton, 1971), p. 27.

33. Propp. pp. 25-27, 120-21.

34. Linda Dégh, 'Folk Narrative', in *Folklore and Folklife: An Introduction*, ed. Richard Dorson (Chicago: Univ. of Chicago, 1972), pp. 60-61.

35. Propp, pp. 30-31.

36. *Ibid*., pp. 26-27, 120-21.

37. *Ibid*., p. 27.

38. *Ibid*., pp. 71-74.

39. *Ibid*., pp. 28-29, 74-75, 121.

40. *Ibid*., p. 30.

41. *Ibid*.

42. *Ibid*., p. 27.

43. *Ibid*., pp. 31-35.

44. *Ibid*., pp. 66-70.

45. *Ibid*., p. 38.

46. *Ibid*., p. 32.

47. Spatial transference may be absent or extremely limited in some tales (Propp, p. 39). It might be argued that Job does not actually travel very far from home, but since both scene and action have changed, the function ↑ may be said to be represented here.

48. Meletinsky *et al.*, 'Problems', p. 78.

49. *Ibid*., pp. 134-39; Pierre Maranda, 'Introduction', in *SSF*, pp. 11-12.

50. Meletinsky *et al.*, 'Problems', pp. 76-80; Dégh, pp. 60-62.
51. Meletinsky *et al.*, 'Problems', pp. 111, 117-19.
52. Pope, pp. 21-23.
53. P. Trible, 'Biblical Theology as Women's Work', *Religion in Life* 44 (1975), pp. 7-13.
54. 'Each agent is his own hero' (C. Bremond, 'Logic', p. 392).
55. A. Alt, p. 268.
56. Propp, p. 38.
57. Dégh lists 'monologue' by the hero, and dialogues between heroes and secondary dramatis personae as 'formulatic verbal sequences' which are part of the stable, building blocks of the tale (pp. 60-62).
58. P.W. Skehan, *Studies in Israelite Poetry and Wisdom* (CBQMS, 1); Washington: CBA, 1971), pp. 96-126.
59. R.E. Murphy, *Wisdom Literature: Job, Proverbs, Ruth, Canticles, Ecclesiastes, Esther* (FOTL, 13; Grand Rapids: Eerdmans, 1981), pp. 15-45.
60. Westermann, pp. 131-32; B.S. Childs, *Introduction to the Old Testament as Scripture* (Philadelphia: Fortress, 1979), pp. 530, 535-36.
61. Propp, p. 74. Westermann (pp. 97-98) feels that asseverations of innocence outside the third cycle (6.28-30; 9.21) fill essentially different roles than do those found here.
62. *Ibid.*, p. 67.
63. *Ibid.*, p. 50.
64. Meletinsky *et al.*, 'Problems', pp. 93-97.
65. Propp, p. 51.
66. *Ibid.*, pp. 92ff. 'Episodic moves' are sequences of semantically linked functions which are embedded within individual moves.
67. *Ibid.*, p. 52.
68. Meletinsky *et al.*, 'Problems', pp. 93-95.
69. M. Lüthi, 'Aspects of the Märchen and Legend', *Genre* 11 (1969), p. 165.
70. J.G. Gammie, 'Behemoth and Leviathan: On the Didactic and Theological Significance of Job 40.15–41.26', in *Israelite Wisdom: Theological and Literary Essays in Honor of Samuel Terrien*, ed. J.G. Gammie, W.A. Brueggemann, W.L. Humphreys, and J.M. Ward (Missoula: Scholars Press, 1978), pp. 217-31.
71. Meletinsky *et al.*, 'Problems', p. 97.
72. Propp, p. 63.
73. Meletinsky *et al.*, 'Problems', p. 129; Dégh, p. 63.
74. Propp, p. 92.
75. Richard Dorson, 'Foreword' in Hasan M. El-Shamy, *Folktales of Egypt*, with a Foreword by Richard Dorson (Chicago: Univ. of Chicago, 1980), pp. ix-xii.
76. Tale of the Eloquent Peasant (in *The Literature of Ancient Egypt: An*

Anthology of Stories, Instructions, and Poetry (new edn; ed. with an introduction by William Kelly Simpson; (New Haven: Yale Univ., 1973), pp. 31-32); Shipwrecked Sailor, pp. 51, 54; Tale of the Doomed Prince, p. 86; Tale of the Two Brothers, pp. 94-95.

77. Marriage (preliminary) test triads occur in the Tale of the Doomed Prince (Simpson, pp. 87-88), as does a triad of basic tests with a bride-helper/tester (p. 91). Animal helpers and donors are found in the Tale of Two Brothers (p. 94), the Shipwrecked Sailor (p. 54), and elsewhere.

78. Simpson, pp. 19-22.

79. *Ibid.*, pp. 95-96.

80. *Ibid.*, pp. 85-86.

81. *Ibid.*, p. 94.

82. E. Meletinsky, 'Problem of the Historical Morphology of the Folktale', in *SSF*, pp. 53-56; E. Meletinsky *et al.*, 'Problems', pp. 74-78.

83. Lüthi, pp. 162-63.

84. The research presented here was made possible by a sabbatical leave granted by Andover Newton Theological School. Special thanks are in order to my colleagues Charles E. Carlston and Elsie A. McKee, and to Billie Poon and Judith Carpenter for their technical assistance in the preparation of this manuscript.

13

SAMSON: A PLAY FOR VOICES

William J. Urbrock

Foreword by the Author

My ideas for *Samson: A Play for Voices* began to develop in 1968, when I wrote an original version for entry in a public radio competition.

A full decade later, in 1978-79, at the same time as I was chairing the Biblical Hebrew Poetry Section of the Society of Biblical Literature, an opportunity arose for revising the play for presentation before a live audience. I had taken on the task of Program Chairperson for the Annual Meeting of the Conference on Christianity and Literature, Region XI, that convened at St Mary's College in Notre Dame, Indiana, in April, 1979. While casting about for ideas for a final plenary session, I discovered that CCL member Sr Maria Assunta Werner of St Mary's was teaching a rather ambitious course on The Bible and the Arts. She was happy to assent to my suggestion that together we prepare a program that would feature a representative portion of her course augmented by an original artistic contribution of sorts from me. That year her course was divided into four sections, three of which centered on Moses, Samson and John the Baptist. Each character was studied on the basis of the Biblical traditions, later Jewish and Christian traditions, and interpretations in the arts, (specifically painting, literature and music). We opted, of course, to feature her segment on Samson and an updated version of my play.

Samson attempts to recreate some of the Biblical lore about the illustrious ancestors (see Ben Sira 46.11-12; Hebrews 11.32-34), a kind of lore common to most societies, both ancient and modern. It has been placed into the mouth of an ancient singer of tales,[1] that creative custodian of a community's oral traditions whose songs developed many of the themes that were to characterize early literature and drama.

Like much of that ancient lore, *Samson* carries a moral. The theme of wisdom and folly is introduced before the song-cycle proper gets under way, and the lesson is carefully reviewed at the cycle's end. Throughout, the Voices of Wisdom bring constant reminders that a moral struggle is in progress. Moreover, in fashion not unknown in ancient tales, ethical concern often recedes before some aesthetic embellishments. These include the sensuous imagery of the Love duets, the repetitive subsections of the Downfall, the contrast of crude taunting and exalted hymn in the Mocking and Celebration sections, and the ritual nature of the Lament. At various points musical accompaniment has been suggested as an additional ornament.

The verse in this play consists largely, although not entirely, of direct translations and paraphrases (all my own) from the Hebrew Scriptures. Specifically, the admonitions of Wisdom are from Proverbs 1–9, augmented by a few lines from Ben Sira, and the Love duets are from the Song of Songs. Samson's Lament borrows motifs from Psalm 22, with an eye to Job as well. The Hymn of Praise to Dagon is, of course, a translation of Psalm 29. That psalm, itself perhaps a Hebrew-Yahwistic adaptation of an earlier Canaanite song honoring Baal Haddu,[2] is here ascribed to yet another deity once worshipped on Palestinian soil.

One might argue that the juxtaposition of these disparate verse portions of the Scriptures, notably Proverbs and the Song of Songs, now relocated within the context of the Samson legends, results in a horse of altogether a different color from any of the originals. On the contrary, however, I would argue that precisely the juxtaposition of legend, love song, and wisdom verse may help convey the richly textured, more inclusive vision of life commended to readers and hearers of the ancient Biblical tradition.[3]

I have not attempted to impose a meter, in the strict sense of the term. On the other hand, I have adhered rather consistently to the Biblical mode of parallelism, and I have inclined to pairing cola of equal or nearly equal syllable counts in English. I have noticed, too, in directing the reading aloud that a certain sense of balancing needs to be reflected in long and short vowel tones or in slowing or speeding the delivery of paired lines. I have tried to add color through alliteration and assonance, two phenomena well attested in Biblical Hebrew verse, wherever possible. On occasion, especially at climactic points, I have taken the liberty of composing very simple rhyming couplets.

The choice of female voices to portray the Voices of Wisdom obviously was dictated by the fact that in the Bible, as in the Ancient Near East, Greece, and elsewhere, wisdom was often personified as a Lady. She appears as such in the excerpt I chose from Proverbs.

The episodes of the play develop roughly in chiastic order[4] as follows:

I. The Prologue
II. The Love Affair
III. The Downfall
IV. The Mocking
V. The Celebration
VI. The Lament and Vindication
VII. The Epilogue.

The Love Affair and Lament are paired antithetically, both accompanied by the same music. Behind Samson's single and relatively shorter Lament soliloquy, the music serves to evoke his several, altogether longer songs of Love in the earlier dialogue with Delilah. The Downfall and Celebration are also paired antithetically around the motif of Samson's strength. He avoids downfall so long as his secret is not told, since behind the secret stands the God of Israel. Once the secret is out, however, he is at the mercy of the devotees of Dagon. There is also a synonymous pairing in the motif of binding and loosing. Thus, in the Downfall scene Samson is able to break free, except at the last, while in the Celebration he must step to the tune of his tormentors. The Mocking scene also pairs with the Downfall in this same manner.[5]

There are other connections between scenes as well. The Downfall continues with echoes of the earlier Love poetry. The Lament is sharply juxtaposed to the Hymn to Dagon in the scene just preceding. The Mocking is climactic in portraying the awful results warned of by the Voices of Wisdom in the two scenes preceding. Similarly, in it all the Philistines bring into the open an undercurrent of mockery that had been present already in Delilah's words in the Downfall scene. As a more continuous thread, of course, the voice of the Storyteller recurs from time to time along with admonitions and remarks of the Voices of Wisdom.

As noted, the play has been scored for ten voices: the Storyteller, Delilah, Samson, a quartet of Female Voices, and three Male Voices. Alternatively, the female and male Voices could be limited to only two each. When the play was first presented in April, 1979, Samson and Delilah stood center, flanked by the Female Voices on Samson's side and the Male Voices on Delilah's. Off to the side of the Female Voices was the Storyteller, next to whom was set an easel for displaying large scene titles. Musical accompaniment was provided by timpani (kettle drums), guitar, flute, and tambourines. We also used whip-sticks and slap-sticks during the Mocking and Celebration scenes. Actors and musicians for the performance were University of Wisconsin Oshkosh students and faculty.

The version of Samson printed here is essentially what was performed in 1979, with some minor revisions.[6]

NOTES

1. Discerning readers will recognize a nod here to a pathfinding study to which I am greatly indebted: Albert B. Lord, *The Singer of Tales* (Cambridge, Mass.: Harvard University Press, 1960).

2. The hypothesis was developed by H.L. Ginsberg, 'A Phoenician Hymn in the Psalter', in *Atti del XIX Congresso Internazionale degli Orientalisti* (Rome, 1935), pp. 472-76. It was taken up by F.M. Cross, Jr ('Notes on a Canaanite Psalm in the Old Testament', *BASOR* 117 [1950], pp. 19-21), M. Dahood (*Psalms I 1–50* [Garden City, NY: Doubleday, 1966], *ad loc.)*, and others, but recently has been questioned by P. Craigie ('Parallel Word Pairs in Ugaritic Poetry: A Critical Evaluation of Their Relevance for Psalm 29', *UF* 11 [1979], pp. 135-40).

3. Recently, Phyllis Trible has juxtaposed analyses of the Song of Songs and the 'Love Story Gone Awry' in Gen 2–3 so as to show how the texts may be mutually illuminating: *God and the Rhetoric of Sexuality* (Philadelphia: Fortress Press, 1978).

4. The phenomenon of chiasm for both smaller and larger sections of Biblical verse and narrative is by now so well attested as to require no additional comment. It may be of interest to note, however, that I was not aware of the chiastic structure (more or less) that was developing for *Samson* until I had completed a first draft.

5. About the time I was revising *Samson* in 1979, I was reading Othmar Keel's *Jahwes Entgegnung an Ijob* (Göttingen: Vandenhoeck & Ruprecht, 1978). His provocative discussion of the Divine Speeches in Job alerted me

to the phenomenon of the pairing of verse segments larger than adjacent cola or lines (see, e.g., pp. 32-44, 82-85, 159).

6. During my tenure as chairperson of the SBL's Biblical Hebrew Poetry Section, I also wrote a voice drama for presentation at the Upper-Midwest Regional Meeting of the SBL in St Paul, Minn. in April, 1978. Although much shorter than *Samson*, the play was constructed in a similar manner, viz. by using quotations from Lamentations, Second Isaiah, Job, Psalm 8, the Priestly creation account and even the Enuma Elish. At the performance all the voices were heard from offstage, while one actor mimed before the audience. The play has since been published: W.J. Urbrock, 'Creation 1: A Play for Voices', *Cur TM* 6 (1979), pp. 68-76.

SAMSON: A Play for Voices

William J. Urbrock

Dramatis Personae
Story Teller
Delilah
Samson
Quartet of Female Voices
Trio of Male Voices

The Female Voices (Women 1 and 2, sopranos; Women 3 and 4, altos) serve as the Voices of Wisdom. They also speak as the Philistine Women.

The Male Voices introduce the song cycle. They also speak as the Philistine Men.

Scene Long ago and far away, yet very close to home

Episodes
Prologue
The Love Affair
The Downfall
The Mocking
The Celebration
The Lament and Vindication
Epilogue

PROLOGUE

[*Music up and out*]
[*A howling of wind and crackling of fire*]
[*Gradually fade in the voice of*:]

THE STORY TELLER: . . . and so it is said to this very day, 'Fools step in where angels fear to tread!' What? Shhh! Listen! Do I hear someone?

You there! Who are you? Who comes to eavesdrop, peeping-tom-looking over the shoulder of our tale? Step out of the dark. Let's have a look at you. Oh, so it's you, is it?

Well, come in, come in. Join our circle. Here where it's cozy and warm around the embers. Here where old and young, friend and enemy, Easterner, Westerner, ancient, modern, rub hands and wiggle toes together before the ever-burning flames. Here where myth and legend flicker in the imagination. Here where the flint of the soul's hope and the draft of the heart's yearning kindle epic and folktale into a blaze of truth.

That's it. Find your own comfortable spot, up close to the fire. Blanket yourself among the dwarves and dragons, near the elves and ents, next to the wizards and witches, beside the gods and goblins.

Now, then, what will it be? We have an inexhaustible repertoire. Will you have a saint or a sinner, a prince or a princess, demon or devil? Fairy godmother, flying horse, phantom king? The lore of the ages is at your disposal. Choose what you will hear.

What? Wisdom, you say? And folly? Wise wisdom and foolish folly. So be it. A tale of wisdom and folly.

Closer to the fire, please. Look deep into the flickering coals, into the pile of burning logs. Now: eyes purged, vision cleared, ears attuned, soul awake!

[*Fire and wind*]

Sages of long ago, tell us your story. Teach us about wisdom and folly. From the fire of the past, from the flames of the ages, conjure up for our imagination a hero foolish and wise: Tell us of Samson, chosen by God, deceived by man, chastened by life, vindicated by death. Voices of long ago, tell us the story of Samson.

[*Fire and Wind*]

MALE VOICES:

VOICE 1: In his days Israel was at the mercy of the Philistines. But the God of Israel grew jealous for his people. His angel appeared to the wife of Manoah of Zorah, of the tribe of the Danites, and said to her, 'You are barren and childless, but you shall become pregnant and bear a son. He shall belong to the God of Israel. Never shall a razor touch his head. He shall be dedicated to God from birth, and he shall begin to free Israel from the power of the Philistines. To God he shall be dedicated from the day of his birth until the hour of his death. Then the Spirit of the LORD will stir in him, and he shall have strength to deliver Israel.'

VOICE 2: As the angel had promised, so it came about. Manoah's wife became pregnant and gave birth to a son. They called him Samson and dedicated him to the God of Israel. They let his hair grow as a sign fo his consecration. Never did a razor touch his head.

VOICE 3: When he became of age he found occasion to begin harassing the Philistines. Once he slew thirty in the city of Ashkelon, plundering their garments to pay a debt. Once he tied torches to the tails of 300 foxes and turned them loose to burn the Philistine orchards and wheat fields. Once he slew a thousand of them with the jawbone of an ass. As his fame spread among the Philistines, he grew ever bolder, entering their very strongholds and cities to consort with their women. Once, while he was being entertained by a prostitute in Gaza, they barred and surrounded the town to lie in wait for him until morning. But at midnight he arose and left her house, single-handedly tore out the city gate—posts, bars, hinges, and all—and ran away unscathed.

VOICE 1: After this he became infatuated with a woman in the valley of Sorek. Her name was Delilah. Now the Philistine leaders had struck a bargain with her, saying, 'Entice him and find out the secret of his great strength. Tell us how we may overpower him, tie him, and subdue him. Find out for us, and we will pay you eleven hundred pieces of silver.'

THE LOVE AFFAIR

VOICES OF WISDOM (FEMALE QUARTET):

ALL:	Beware, Samson, beware! Beware of folly!
Vv. 1-2:	Wisdom cries out in the streets, In the squares she lifts up her voice.

From the top of the walls she shouts,
At the gates of the town she speaks:

V. 3: 'Hear, prudent one, gain instruction!
'Hear, wise one, learning and counsel!
'Attention to my proverb!
'My thoughts I pour out for you!
'My mind I speak out for you!

V. 4: 'My son, if you take admonition,
'If you treasure my prudent advice,
'If your ear is attentive to wisdom
'And your reason attuned to insight,
Vv. 3-4: 'You'll be saved from adulterous women,
'Whose delight is loose morals and speech,
'Who forsake their lawful companions,
'Who abandon their marriage and vows,
Vv. 2, 3: 'Such women whose houses are pitfalls,
Vv. 2, 4: 'Whose bedrooms are outposts of hell.
ALL: 'Who enter their deadly apartments
'Bid life, love, and fortune "Farewell!"'

DELILAH: Samson, my love. Come, come to me. Share your bull-strength with me, your lion-strength with Delilah.

Kiss me with kisses from your lips!
Your caresses are sweeter than wine!
How fragrant your anointing oils!
Your name is perfume outpoured!
Take me! Hurry! Draw me to you!
Hold me! Clasp me in your embrace!
I'll exult, I'll rejoice in your love.
I'll extol your love more than wine.

Refresh my heart with kisses!
Restore my soul with love!
I am sick, I am sick with love!

A bag of myrrh is my sweetheart
That lies between my breasts.
A cluster of orange blossoms
That circle round my head.

Oh! You are handsome, beloved!
You are lovely! Your eyes are doves!
Oh! You are comely, beloved!
You are mine, you are mine to love!

Our couch, all uncovered, is ready;
Our roof-beams all cedar and pine.
Come! Enter my chamber! Be mine!

SAMSON: Delilah, my love. I come, I come to you. I will share my bull-strength with you, my lion-strength with Delilah.

Like a mare of Pharaoh's chariots
You are bejeweled, my love.
Your cheeks are adorned with spangles,
Your neck with strings of bead.
I will make you bracelets of gold,
Studded with points of silver.

You are a saffron of Sharon,
A lily of the valleys.
A rose among the brambles
Are you among maidens.
A flow'ring tree in the thicket
Are you among young women.

Oh! You are charming, beloved!
You are lovely! Your eyes are doves!
Oh! You are comely, beloved!
You are mine, you are mine to love!

I long for your couch all uncovered,
For your bedroom of cedar and pine.
Come! Enter your chamber! Be mine!

VOICES OF WISDOM:

ALL: Beware, Samson, beware! Beware of folly!

Vv. 1-2: My son, pay attention to Wisdom!
Listen! Take my advice.
Don't play the fool like a madman,
Don't fondle a strange woman's breast!
Let knowledge and insight preserve you,
Save your lips from a harlot's kiss.

Vv. 3-4: Yes! A loose woman's mouth drips honey;
Her palate is smoother than oil.
But her wine-kiss sours to vin'gar;
Her tongue is a poisoned foil.
By devious paths and passage
She leads you on towards ruin.

V. 1: Turn back! Resist her advances!
Her footsteps speed towards doom!

V. 3: Do you think God's eyes are not open?
V. 4: Think he winks at human fault?
Vv. 1-2: No! The fool must pay for folly,
Must stumble and trip in his sin.
ALL: A person is lost without training;
And will die without discipline!

DELILAH: Samson, my love. Come, come to me. Share your bull-strength with me, your lion-strength with Delilah.

I'll lead you to my mother's room,
To the chamber of her who bore me:
'Strip naked, my love, strip naked.
'Bare your strength to Delilah's eyes!'

[*Music up and in*]

My love, tanned and ruddy,
My love, like burnished bronze,
Your head is finest gold,
Your neck is polished brass.
Your locks are wavy-dark,
All raven-black your curls.

Your eyes are like doves
By springs of water,
All swimming in milk,
All bathed in cream.
Your cheeks are beds of spices,
Sweet herbs and fragrant mint.

Your lips distill ambrosia,
Sweet nectar, spiced tea.
Your muscles are metal,
Your arms tempered steel,
Your torso white ivory,
Set with lapis lazuli;

Your thighs alabaster,
Your knees granite-stone;
Your legs marble columns
On bases of gold.

Fragrant like cedar,
Like redolent pine,
Your lips exude syrup,
Your mouth berry-wine.

Your hands smell of resin,
Your palms reek of sap;
Aglisten like amber
The sweat on your back.

Awake, O North Wind!
Blow, Wind of the South!
Sweep over my garden,
Lift its odors aloft!
Let Samson breathe in my aroma,
Let him sniff my tempestuous desire!
Bring him here! Let him taste of my passion!
Let my lust set his heart on fire!

SAMSON: Delilah, my love. I come, I come to you. I will share my bull-strength with you, my lion-strength with Delilah.

I come to your garden, my sister.
I enter your orchard, my love.
Until the morning dawns,
Until the darkness flees,
I will visit your garden of myrrh;
I will lie in your balsam bed.

Oh! You are charming, beloved!
You are lovely! Your eyes are doves!
Your eyes are in a gilded cage
Like turtle-doves behind your veil.
Your hair is black like flocks of goats
Grazing on the slopes of Gilead.
Your teeth are smooth like shorn ewe-lambs.
Like sheared sheep fresh from the washing.
Your lips are threads of scarlet,
Your mouth is crimson stuff.
Your cheeks are pomegranates,
Ripe fruit behind your veil.

Your breasts are like two fawns,
Like offspring of stag and doe,
Who feed among the lilies,
Who produce only twins,
Who are never bereaved.

Oh, you are charming, beloved!
Perfected in beauty, all fair!
Your sculptured thighs are like jewels,
The work of a master hand.

Your navel is a rounded bowl,
Brim-full, overflowing with wine.
Your belly is a heap of wheat,
Wreathed, encircled with lilies.

How fair you are! How pleasant!
Dainty! Delectable! Sweet!
You are stately like a royal palm;
Your breasts are like bunches of dates.
I will climb among your branches;
I will taste your delicious fruit.
Your bosom is ripe like grape-clusters,
Full-mellowed like grapes on the vine.
I will drink the must of your nipples,
Take my fill of heady new wine.

Enflame me, beloved, with kisses!
Make me drunk with your love divine!

[*Music up and out*]

VOICES OF WISDOM:

ALL: Beware, Samson, beware! Beware of folly!

V. 1: I have looked out of my window;
I have peered through lattice and shutter.
I have seen a simple fellow,
I have noticed among the lads
A young man without any sense.

Vv. 1-2: A prostitute grabs him, hugs him,
Kisses him, laughs in his face:
V. 3: 'I have decked my couch with covers,
'With pillows, fine linens, and quilts.
'I have sprinkled my bed with perfume,
'Scent of cinnamon, almond, and cloves.
'Make love to me! Love me till morning!
'Take your fill! Drench your soul with delight!'

V. 4: Her seductive advances lure him,
Her smooth talk persuades him to come.
He follows; he goes along with her
To the slaughter like a stupid ox;
V. 2: To the pitfall like a witless beast;
V. 4: To the ambush like a senseless buck,

Vv. 2-4: When an arrow pierces his entrails,
Brings him low and robs him of life.

V. 1: My son, pay heed! Don't ignore me!
Pay close heed to the words of my mouth!
She has wounded a hundred, a thousand;
Ten thousand, a million her slain.
Her house is a gate to destruction.
Vv. 1-2: Don't go in! You won't come out again!
Vv. 3-4: Stand back! Keep your feet from her path!
ALL Stay away! She will lead you to death!

DELILAH: Samson, my love. Come, come to me. Share your bull-strength with me, your lion-strength with Delilah.

[*Music up and in*]

I am my beloved's
His longing is for me.
Come, my beloved,
Come out to the field!
To the peasant huts!
In the morning dew
We'll look for blossoms:
For budding grape vines,
For flow'ring pomegranates.
There I will give
My love to you.

The mandrakes give off fragrance.
Fancy fruit adorns our doors:
Apples fresh-picked and apricots dried
I have reserved for you, my love.

Oh, that you were like my brother,
Like a twin at my mother's breast!
Should I meet you in public, I'd kiss you
Without shame, like next of kin.
I would lead you to my mother's room,
to the chamber of her who bore me.
I would serve you mulled wine to drink,
Sweet wine squeezed from pomegranates.

Hurry, beloved!
Make haste like a stag!
Speed like an antelope
Over mountain and crag!

SAMSON: Delilah, my love. I come, I come to you. I will share my bull-strength with you, my lion-strength with Delilah.

You have ravished, my sister, my love,
Ravished my heart with a single glance,
With a single turn of your jewelled neck.

How sweet your charms, my sister, my love,
How much sweeter than spicy new wine!
Sweeter than balsam
Your oils and perfume!

Your lips drip nectar, my sister, my love,
Your tongue tastes of honey and cream.
Sweeter than incense
The scent of your clothes!
A garden locked is my sister, my love,
A sealed fountain, a private domain;
A watered garden of pomegranates,
An orchard of choice spices and fruit;
All rosemary, basil, and mint;
All cinnamon, henna, and nard.
All lemon trees, oranges, and limes;
All olive trees grow in her yard.

I come to your garden, my sister.
I enter your orchard, my love.
Until the morning dawns,
Until the darkness flees,
I will visit your garden of myrrh;
I will lie in your balsam bed.

DELILAH AND SAMSON:

My love is a fountain,
A fresh-flowing stream,
A well of contentment,
A river of dreams!

[*Music up and out*]

VOICES OF WISDOM:

Vv. 1-2: A fool self-destroyed
Who can restore?
Vv. 3-4: Who will honor
A fool self-disgraced?

ALL: The wise perceives hidden dangers;
The prudent flees and is saved.
But a fool rushes in without forethought;
And folly leads straight to the grave!

THE DOWNFALL

DELILAH: Samson, my love, tell me. Tell me the secret of your strength. How could you be bound that one might overcome you?

VOICES OF WISDOM: No, Samson, no! Folly!

DELILAH: Tell me, Samson. Tell me your secret.

SAMSON: Delilah, my love, I will tell you. If I were bound with seven fresh bowstrings which have not yet been dried, I would become as helpless as any other man.

DELILAH: See, Samson, my love. I have seven fresh bowstrings not yet dried. Do you love me? Let me tie you; let me tie you in my love.

The seven strings are bonds of love:
First: the bond of loyalty;
Second: the bond of faith;
Third: the bond of steadfastness;
Fourth: the bond of trust,
Fifth: the bond of constancy;
Sixth: the bond of troth;
Seventh: the bond of helplessness—helpless in my love.

See, Samson, my love. I have tied you, tied you in the sinews of my love.

SAMSON: Delilah, my love.

Let me see your face.
Let me hear your voice.
For your face is sweet,
And your voice is comely.
Sustain me with kisses,
Refresh me with smiles,
For I am sick with love!

DELILAH: Samson, my love! The Philstines! The Philistines are upon you!

VOICES OF WISDOM:

ALL:	No, Delilah, no! Not yet does folly reign.
V. 1:	Rise, Samson, rise!
Vv. 1-2:	Snap your fetters!
Vv. 3-4:	Break your shackles!
ALL:	Burst your bonds!

[*Sound of fire*]

THE STORY TELLER: Just as dry wood cracks upon the fire, the seven bowstrings were exploded by the flaming strength of Samson. So his secret was not known.

DELILAH: Why do you scorn me, Samson? Do not mock me. Do not lie. Tell me, Samson, my love. Tell me the secret of your strength. How could you be bound that one might overcome you?

VOICES OF WISDOM: No, Samson, no! Folly!

DELILAH: Tell, me, Samson. Tell me your secret.

SAMSON: Delilah, my love, I will tell you. If I were bound with seven new cords which have not yet been used, I would become as helpless as any other man.

DELILAH: See, Samson, my love. I have seven new cords not yet used. Do you love me? Let me tie you; let me tie you in my love.

The seven cords are bonds of love:
First: the bond of loyalty;
Second: the bond of faith;
Third: the bond of steadfastness;
Fourth: the bond of trust;
Fifth: the bond of constancy;
Sixth: the bond of troth;
Seventh: the bond of helplessness—helpless in my love.

See, Samson, my love. I have tied you, tied you in the sinews of my love.

SAMSON: Delilah, my love.

Let me see your face.
Let me hear your voice.
For your voice is sweet,
And your face is comely,

Sustains me with kisses,
Refresh me with smiles,
For I am sick with love!

DELILAH: Samson, my love! The Philistines! The Philistines are upon you!

VOICES OF WISDOM:

ALL: No, Delilah, no! Not yet does folly reign.

V. 1: Rise, Samson, rise!
Vv. 1-2: Snap your fetters!
Vv. 3-4: Break your shackles!
ALL: Burst your bonds!

[*Sound of wind*]

THE STORY TELLER: Just as wisps of straw are driven before the wind, the seven cords were dispersed by the tempestuous strength of Samson. So his secret was not known.

DELILAH: Why do you scorn me, Samson? Do not mock me. Do not lie. Tell me, Samson, my love. Tell me the secret of your strength. How could you be bound that one might overcome you?

VOICES OF WISDOM: No, Samson, no! Folly!

DELILAH: Tell me, Samson. Tell me your secret.

SAMSON: Delilah, my love, I will tell you. If the seven locks of my head were to be woven into the web on the loom, I would become as helpless as any other man.

DELILAH: See, Samson, my love. I will weave your locks into the web on the loom. Do you love me? Let me tie you; let me tie you in my love. The seven locks are bonds of love:

First: the bond of loyalty;
Second: the bond of faith;
Third: the bond of steadfastness;
Fourth: the bond of trust;
Fifth: the bond of constancy;
Sixth: the bond of troth;
Seventh: the bond of helplessness—helpless in my love.

See, Samson, my love. I have tied you, tied you in the sinews of my love.

SAMSON: Delilah, my love.

Let me see your face.
Let me hear your voice.
  For your voice is sweet,
  And your face is comely.
Sustain me with kisses,
Refresh me with smiles,
For I am sick with love!

DELILAH: Samson, my love! The Philistines! The Philistines are upon you!

VOICES OF WISDOM:

ALL:	No, Delilah, no! No yet does folly reign!
V. 1:	Rise, Samson, rise!
Vv. 1-2:	Snap your fetters!
Vv. 3-4:	Break your shackles!
ALL:	Burst your bonds!

[*Sound of tempest*]

THE STORY TELLER: Just as trees are uprooted before the hurricane, the seven locks were torn from web and loom by the whirlwind strength of Samson. So his secret was not known.

DELILAH: Three times you have scorned me, Samson. Three times mocked me. Three times lied.

How is it you say, 'I love you;
'Delilah, you I love'?
  You mock me with your face,
  Deceive me with your voice.
But your words are bitter,
And your thoughts are false.
  Taste no more my kisses,
  Drink no more my smiles,
  For I have done with love!

VOICES OF WISDOM:

ALL:	Have done, Samson! Have done with Delilah!
Vv. 1-2:	Wisdom has constructed her house, Set it up on seven pillars. She has dressed her game,

She has mixed her wine,
She has trimmed her banquet table.

V. 3: She has sent out her maids to call
From the highest places in town,
V. 4: 'Whoever is simple, come here!'

V. 3: To the unlearned man she speaks,
V. 4: 'Come in! Partake of my bread!
'Come in! Drink a draught of my wine!
'Leave ignorance behind, and live!
'Set your feet on wisdom's way!
'I'll reward you with happy years!
'You'll find joy and length of days!'

ALL: Have done, Samson! Have done with Delilah!

SAMSON: Delilah, my love, tell me. What shall I do for you? How shall I regain your love?

Let me see your face.
Let me hear your voice.
For your voice is sweet,
And your face is comely.
Sustain me with kisses,
Refresh me with smiles,
For I am sick with love!

VOICES OF WISDOM: No, Samson, no! Folly!

DELILAH: Samson, my love, tell me. Tell me the secret of your strength.

VOICES OF WISDOM: No, Samson, no!

SAMSON: Yes, Delilah, yes! I will tell you the secret, the secret of my strength.

Never has a razor touched my head,
Never have my hairs been shaved.
I am the servant of God,
Slave of the God of Israel,
Consecrated from the womb.
Dedicated from my birth.
Now, then, if my locks were cut,
my hair were clipped,
my head were shaved,
surely my strength would leave me and I would become as helpless
as any other man.

VOICES OF WISDOM:

Vv. 1-2: No, Samson, no!
ALL: Woe, Samson, woe!

DELILAH: Now, Samson, now! Now I know you love me. Now I have tied you, tied you in my love!

VOICES OF WISDOM:

V. 1: Folly has caught her game,
V. 2: snared his soul,
Vv. 1-2: trapped his heart,
Vv. 1, 2, 3: bagged his strength!
ALL: Woe, Samson, woe!

DELILAH: So, Samson, so!

Sleep like a babe in Delilah's bosom,
Like a helpless infant at my breast.
Until the morning dawns,
Until the darkness flees,
Lie in my fragrant garden,
Rest among my budding vines,
Lodge in my shaded orchard,
Sleep among my choices fruits.

SAMSON: So, Delilah, so!
I will sleep like a babe in your bosom,
Like a helpless infant at your breast.
Until the morning dawns,
Until the darkness flees,
I will lie in your fragrant garden,
I will rest among your budding vines,
I will lodge in your shaded orchard,
I will sleep among your choicest fruits.

THE STORY TELLER: At last, like a stag brought down by the hunter's arrow, Samson fell to the shafts of folly. And his secret was known.

DELILAH: Sleep, Samson, sleep!

VOICES OF WISDOM: Wake, Samson, wake!

DELILAH: Sleep like a babe in Delilah's bosom,
Like a helpless infant at my breast.

Now you have told the secret,
Told the secret of your strength.
Sleep, while my shears clip you hair;
Sleep, while my razor shaves your head;
Sleep, while I trim your seven locks.
Loose the braid of power!
Loose the braid of brawn!
Untie the web of valor!
Untie the web of might!
Cut off the strand of mettle!
Cut off the strand of strength!
Cut off the strand of courage!
Now! You are mine at length!

VOICES OF WISDOM: Woe, Samson, woe!

DELILAH: So, Samson, so!
Samson, servant of God,
Slave of Israel's God,
Consecrated from the womb,
Dedicated since your birth!
I have cut your locks,
I have clipped your hair,
I have shaved your head!

Surely, your strength has left you, and you have become as helpless as any other man.

Samson, my love! The Philistines! The Philistines are upon you!

VOICES OF WISDOM: Yes, Delilah, yes!
Now does folly reign!

SAMSON: No, Delilah, no!
I'll be free again!
Let me run!
Let me flee!

VOICES OF WISDOM: Doom, Samson, doom!

DELILAH: Your fate was sealed by me!

PHILISTINES:

MAN 1: Catch him!
MAN 2: Seize him!

MAN 3: Hold him fast!
MEN 1-2: Beat him!
MEN 2-3: Blind him!
ALL MEN: Ours at last!

[*Cries of Samson*]
[*Shouts of Philistines*]

THE STORY TELLER: Thus was Samson brought low by folly! The Philistines captured him and gouged out his eyes. Handcuffed and fettered, he was dragged to prison. There he was hitched to the millstone, harnessed to grind grain like a broken beast.

THE MOCKING

[*Whip lashes; jeers*]

PHILISTINES:

MAN 1: Samson, bull of Zorah!
Samson, ox of Gath!
In dust and grime
You spend your time.
Would you like a bath?

ALL MEN: Not a beast,
Not a man,
Gaze on Gaza
If you can!

VOICES OF WISDOM:

V. 1: Because I called, but you ignored;
V. 2: Because you laughed when I implored;
V. 3: Because you rejected my counsel,
V. 4: My advice you refused to take;
Vv. 1-2: So, I, too, laugh at your downfall!
Vv. 3-4: I jeer at your terrible fate!

ALL When distress and despair break upon you,
When terror swoops down like a storm,
A tornado of ruin rips your inwards,
You'll be left devastated, forlorn!

[*Whip lashes; jeers*]

PHILISTINES:

MAN 2: Samson, bend your back!
Samson, bow your head!
We'll pay you well—
Enjoy your swill!
Here, have a crust of bread!

ALL MEN: Not a beast,
Not a man,
Gaze on Gaza
If you can!

VOICES OF WISDOM:

V. 1: When you cry to me, I will keep silent;
V. 2: When you seek me, I will run and hide.
Vv. 3-4: For you refused to learn
Fear of God or the ways of men.
V. 1: You rejected my counsel,
V. 2: You despised my reproof;
Vv. 3-4: I will never advise you again!

ALL: Now taste the result of your folly,
Eat the rotten fruit of your ways.
Fill your stomach with refuse and garbage!
Gorge your belly with filth and decay!

[*Whip lashes; jeers*]

PHILISTINES:

MAN 3: Samson, crush our grain!
Samson, grind our wheat!
You loved a whore
Who knew the score!
She taught you how to sweat!

ALL MEN: Not a beast,
Not a man,
Gaze on Gaza
If you can!

VOICES OF WISDOM:

Vv. 3-4: Can a man carry coals in his bosom
Without setting his garments ablaze?

Vv. 1-2: Can a man walk barefoot through a bonfire
Without burning the soles of his feet?

V. 1: So the simpleton courts disaster,
His complacency dooms him to ruin.

V. 2: The fool must pay for his folly,
Must stumble and trip in his sin.

ALL: A man is lost without training,
He dies without discipline.

[*Whip lashes; jeers*]

PHILISTINES:

MAN 1: Samson, taste the whip!
MAN 2: Samson, feel the rod!
MAN 3: Step lively now,
You clumsy cow!
MEN 1-2: Don't stumble in the mud!

ALL MEN: Not a beast,
Not a man,
Gaze on Gaza
If you can!

[*Whip lashes; jeers*]

THE CELEBRATION

THE STORY TELLER: Now the rulers of the Philistines assembled for a carnival, a great feast before thir god, a victory celebration before Dagon.

[*Flourish of timbrels; fade in chanting of priests in background*]

PHILISTINES: [*Hymn of Praise to Dagon*]

WOMEN: Nathan Dagon beyadēnu
Shimshon, Shimshon 'oyevēnu!

Dagon, our god, is grand!
Samson subdued by his hand!
[*Flourish of timbrels*]

ALL: Ascribe to Dagon, O heav'nly gods,
Ascribe to Dagon glory and strength.
Ascribe to Dagon glorious fame.

Bow down to Dagon, O heav'nly gods,
Bow down to Dagon when he appears,
When he appears in holy vision.

WOMEN: Nathan Dagon beyadēnu
Shimshon, Shimshon 'oyevēnu!
[*Flourish of timbrels*]

ALL: The voice of Dagon over the storm,
The voice of Dagon upon the floods,
The voice of Dagon crashes and roars!

The thunder of god shatters and breaks,
The thunder of god batters and shakes,
Battters and shakes mountains and hills!

WOMEN: Nathan Dagon beyadēnu
Shimshon, Shimshon 'oyevēnu!
[*Flourish of timbrels*]

ALL: Enthroned is Dagon over the storm!
Enthroned is Dagon over the floods!
Enthroned is Dagon as sov'reign and lord!

The blessing of Dagon let us implore!
The blessing of Dagon let us enjoy!
Let us enjoy his vict'ry and peace!

WOMEN: Dagon, our god, is grand!
Samson subdued by his hand!

Nathan Dagon beyadēnu
Shimshon, Shimshon 'oyevēnu!
[*Flourish of timbrels and timpani*]

WOMEN: Bring on Samson!

MEN: Bring on Samson!

WOMEN: Samson, who ravaged our land!
MEN: Samson, who ravished our women!
WOMEN: Samson, who slew our men!
ALL: Bring on Samson to entertain us!

[*Applause and roar of crowd*]

THE STORY TELLER: So they summoned Samson from prison, from grinding the grain, to cavort before the crowd.

[*Whine of whips; applause and roar of crowd*]

PHILISTINES:

MAN 1: Make way! Make way for Samson!
ALL: Make way! Make way for Samson!

MAN 1: Whom will you slay today?
MAN 2: Whom will you plunder?
MAN 3: Ho, ho, Samson, Hey hey!
ALL: Who stole your thunder?

MEN: Look at the blood!
WOMEN: Look at the gore!
MEN: Look at the clod!
ALL: We want more!

[*Whips*]

MAN 1: Give us a dance, Samson!

[*Whips*]

ALL: [*Chanting to rhythmical clapping, timbrels*]
Dance - - - - - dance - - - - - dance - - - - - dance!
Clown - - - - - clown - - - - - clown - - - - - clown!
Twist - - - - - turn- - - - - twist - - - - -turn!
All - - - - - fall - - - - - down!

[*Cheers; flourishes*]

WOMEN: Look at the blood!
MEN: Look at the gore!
WOMEN: Look at the clod!
ALL: We want more!

[*Whips*]

MAN 2: Give us a song, Samson!

[*Whips*]

ALL: [*Chanting to rhythmical clapping; moans from SAMSON*]
Moan - - - - - moan - - - - - moan - - - - - moan!
Clown - - - - - clown - - - - - clown - - - - - clown!
Sing - - - - - song - - - - - sing - - - - - song!
All - - - - - fall - - - - - down!

[*Cheers; flourishes*]

MEN: Look at the blood!
WOMEN: Look at the gore!

MEN: Look at the clod!
ALL: We want more!

[*Whips*]

ALL: Give us a show, Samson!

MAN 1: Bark like a fox!

[*Whips*]

SAMSON: Yip, yip, yip!

MAN 2: Roar like a bear!

[*Whips*]

SAMSON: Grror—grrowr!

MAN 3: Squeek like a mouse!

[*Whips*]

SAMSON: Meep, meep, meep.

[*Cheers, flourishes*]

ALL: Reward! Reward!
MAN 1: Scraps for the pig!
MAN 2: Slop for the hog!
WOMEN: Crumbs for the cur!
MEN: Bones for the dog!

[*Jeers, laughter*]

ALL: Whom will you slay today?
Whom will you plunder?
Ho, ho, Samson! Hey, hey!
Who stole your thunder?

[*Cheers, timpani*]

THE STORY TELLER: Now the temple was filled with men and women and with all the Philistines lords and ladies. So great was the crush that another three thousand were jammed on the roof to look in while Samson made sport. Then Samson called to the God of Israel.

THE LAMENT AND VINDICATION

SAMSON: O God, with you is wisdom,
Who knows your works,

Who was present when you formed the world,
Who perceives your plans.
She understands what is pleasing in your sight;
She knows what is right.

[*Music up and in*]

Send her forth, send her forth from your heaven,
From your throne of glory.
Let her come to me and assist me
Let her turn me to the fear of God;
Let her clear my mind.

Let me fall into the hands of the LORD,
But save me from mankind!
For God's mercy limits his anger,
But human hatred knows no bounds.

How long will you look on, O LORD?
How long keep silent?
Make haste! Save my life from man-eaters,
My soul from the jackals.
Gaunt wolves bare their teeth, stalk me
Snapping and snarling.
Hungry beasts of the forest attack me;
Roaring lions,
Growling bears, grunting boars, screeching wildcats,
Laughing hyenas.

They snicker, they jeer at my stumbling;
They circle around me.
They gather to mock, to insult me;
They taunt without ceasing.
They have sharpened their teeth like arrows,
Their tongue like a sword.

So I am a worm and no man,
An object for hissing,
A target for sneers and derision,
A sight for gaping.

Will you forsake me, O LORD, forever?
Abandon your servant?
How long will you hide your face from me?
Leave me defenseless?
How long must I bear with your anger?

How long endure sorrow?
How long will my enemies triumph?
Victorious forever?

Your arrows, O LORD, have pierced me;
Your blows have crushed me.
I am utterly battered and beaten,
Mortally wounded.
I acknowledge my guilt and rebellion,
My sin and my folly.

[*Music out*]

You put me in my place.
My strength was not my own;
My power came from you.
Now save me from disgrace.

PHILISTINES: Ascribe to Dagon, O heav'nly gods,
Ascribe to Dagon glory and strength.
Ascribe to Dagon glorious fame.

SAMSON: Will you permit your foes to deride you?
Let your enemies scorn your great Name?
Help me, O God of salvation!
Act to defend your great Name!
Cover up my sins; re-instate me!
Consecrate me by your great Name!
Do not let the scoffers insult you!
Don't allow them to put you to shame!

PHILISTINES: Bow down to Dagon, O heav'nly gods,
Bow down to Dagon when he appears,
When Dagon appears in holy vision!

SAMSON: O LORD God, remember me! Remember poor Samson! Restore my strength this one last time, that I may be avenged upon these Philistines for but one of my two eyes!

Repay them for their cruelty!
Repay their wickedness!
Deal back to them their hatred!
Bring their sins upon their heads.

They, too, are fools, O God!
Preferring wrong to right!
They disregard sound wisdom,
Cast mercy out for spite!

[*Laughter, jeers*]

PHILISTINES: The thunder of god shatters and breaks,
The thunder of god batters and shakes,
Batters and shakes mountains and hills!

[*Timpani*]

SAMSON: Vengeance, O God! Vindication!
Lightning and thunder! Damnation!

[*Timpani*]

THE STORY TELLER: Then Samson grasped the two central pillars, the main supports of the building; and he leaned his weight upon them, his right hand on the one and his left hand upon the other.

PHILISTINES: The blessing of Dagon let us implore!
The blessing of Dagon let us enjoy!
Let us enjoy his vict'ry and peace!

[*Timpani*]

[*The following speeches are spoken simultaneously*]

PHILISTINES: (*first WOMEN, then ALL*)
Dagon, our god, is grand!
Samson subdued by his hand!
Dagon, our [etc., *ad lib*]

SAMSON: Vengeance, O God! Vindication!
Lightning and thunder! Damnation!
Now let me die with the Philistines!

THE STORY TELLER: He strained with all his might! The pillars gave way, and the temple came crashing in ruins upon everyone in it.

[*Timpani; crash of the building; the Philistine chant ends in screams and moans.*]

[*Silence*]

THE STORY TELLER: So those whom Samson destroyed at his death were more than those he had slain during his lifetime. Then his family and all his relatives came and bore him away. They carried him in funeral procession and buried him between Zorah and Eshtaol in the tomb of Manoah, his father.

[*Silence*]

EPILOGUE

VOICES OF WISDOM:

Vv. 1-2: Wisdom cries out in the streets,
In the squares she lifts up her voice.
From the top of the walls she shouts,
At the gates of the town she speaks:

V. 3: 'Listen! I speak noble thoughts!
'My lips announce what is right.
'I will utter only the truth;
'My mouth abhors gossip and lies.

V. 4: 'Every word on my tongue is straight,
'Nothing slanted or twisted or warped.
'I talk sense for the open-minded,
'Good sense for the seeker of wisdom.

Vv. 3-4: 'Happy are those who follow my ways!
'Happy whoever takes my advice.
'Who daily watches at my door,
'Who daily waits at my gate.

ALL: 'Whoever finds me, finds life;
'Obtains God's favor and light!
'But whoever strays from my path
'Will be lost in darkness and night!'

THE STORY TELLER: Well, that is our story. And this is the sum of the matter: Samson rejected the admonitions of wisdom. Because he could not harness his ego nor rein in his passions, his God forsook him, his common sense faltered, and his strength failed him. He was tamed and muzzled and shackled, set to work like brute beasts, those irrational creatures who know neither wisdom nor folly. A yoke of hard labor and a whip of public ridicule were his reward for unthinking behavior.

[*Music up and in*]

Now listen, my child, hear my opinion.
Reject not my considered advice:
Put your feet into Widom's fetters,
And place your neck into her collar.
Bend your shoulders and carry her;
Do not balk under her saddle.
In the end she will give you rest;
Her discipline bring you contentment.

Her bonds will become your security;
Her cords become beautiful clothes.
  Her yoke be a necklace of rubies,
  And her harness a choker of gold.

My child, if you really want insight,
Then ponder the end of this tale:
  What Wisdom reveals to her children
  Brings happiness! All else will fail!

[*Music up and out*]

[*Fire and wind*]

FINIS

14

TWO SONGS OF VICTORY:
A COMPARISON OF EXODUS 15 AND JUDGES 5

Alan J. Hauser

Exodus 15 and Judges 5 are two of the oldest[1] pieces of poetry in the Tanak. They are also the only two extensive victory songs we possess, each celebrating Israel's conquest in a particular battle.[2] There are numerous differences between these two songs. One is the extensive and highly metaphorical treatment of the battle in Exod 15, which contrasts with the very brief battle scene in Judg 5. Another is the specific focusing on the leader of the enemy, Sisera, in Judg 5 (along with his mother and her maidservants), which contrasts with the relative ambiguity of the foe in Exod 15, where he is simply 'Pharaoh', as in the preceding narratives in Exodus. Another difference is the lengthy delineation of specific tribes in Judg 5, where some are praised for sending troops while others are chastised for their reluctance, which contrasts with Exod 15, where Israelite warriors are never discussed and the people Israel are not specifically mentioned until vv. 13-18. Furthermore, the structure of each poem is different. For example: Exod 15 contains only two basic scenes (the battle at the sea and the entrance into Palestine), while Judg 5 continually modulates from one brief vignette to another; Exod 15 addresses much of the poem to Yahweh in the second person (vv. 6-8, 10-13, 16-17), while Judg 5 addresses Yahweh this way only in vv. 4 and 31.

Despite these and other differences between the two poems, there is a great deal they have in common, much of which clearly derives from their function as songs of victory. This paper will explore in detail the similarities and differences between these two songs, looking both at the elements they hold in common and at the unique way each poem develops these elements. After the study is completed, there will be an assessment of the possibility that both poems are modeled after a victory song 'form' known in early Israel.[3]

1. *The Use of the Divine Name*

As one would expect, there is repeated emphasis in both songs on Yahweh as the hero who comes to Israel's deliverance. This may be seen first of all in the heavy usage of the divine name in both poems. In Exod 15 the tetragrammaton (יהוה) is used extensively in vv. 1, 2,[4] 3, and 6, where the reader's attention is focused on God's vital role in defeating Israel's enemy. 'My God' (אלי) and 'God of my father' (אלהי אבי) are also used in v. 2.[5] While references to God do occur later in the poem (יהוה in vv. 11, 16, 17,[6] 18), the clustering of so many references at the beginning focuses the reader's attention from the outset on the God who has brought Israel the victory. The references to God are especially frequent in vv. 1 and 2, where the singer joyfully celebrates in first person rhetoric the strength and victory of his God.

Judg 5 also opens with a heavy emphasis on Israel's victorious God.[7] In vv. 2-5 the tetragrammaton is used six times, at least once in each verse. The opening section also uses 'God of Israel' (אלהי ישראל) in vv. 3 and 5, and 'the One of Sinai' (זה סיני)[8] in v. 5. As in Exod 15, there are references to God later in the poem (יהוה is used in vv. 9, 11, 13, 23, and 31), but the clustering of so many references at the beginning rivets the audience's attention on Israel's victorious God. Several references to Israel's God by name come at the point (v. 3) where the singer celebrates in the first person the victory of his God, just as in Exod 15.1-2.

The numerous references to God at the beginning of each of the two poems, coupled with the repeated use of the divine name in those verses where the singer speaks in the first person and breaks forth in ejaculatory praise[9] of his/her victorious God, are precisely what one would expect in a song of praise to God after a battle. While it certainly is not unusual for the name of Israel's God to be used several times in a song or psalm, what is remarkable in Exod 15 and Judg 5 is the *frequency* and *intensity* with which God is mentioned at the beginning of each song of victory. Thus, whether one claims that the songs are by Moses or Miriam (Exod 15) and Deborah and Barak (Judg 5), or by subsequent poets writing on behalf of these famous figures, it is clear that the introductory sections of both songs exude a spontaneous, irrepressible enthusiasm for Israel's God.

2. *Other Means of Stressing Yahweh's Role in Winning the Victory*

Exod 15 also emphasizes Yahweh by means of the numerous descriptions applied to him in the poem. In Exod 15.2 the singer calls him 'my refuge' (עזי) 'my strength' (זמרת) and 'my salvation' (ישועה), and emphasizes his closeness to God by calling him 'my God' (אלי) and 'God of my father' (אלהי אבי). In v. 11 the singer asks, 'Who is like you among the Gods, O Yahweh?' (מי כמכה באלם יהוה), and God is said to be 'splendid in holiness' (נאדר בקדש), 'awesome in glorious deeds' (נורא תהלת), and a 'doer of wonders' (עשה פלא). In a more specifically military description, Yahweh is called a 'man of war' (v. 3, איש מלחמה), and his right hand (ימין) is said in v. 6 to be 'awesome in power' (נאדרי בכח).[10] In v. 16 the greatness of God's arm (זרוע) causes the terrified rulers in Palestine to be as still as a stone.

Exod 15 also describes God's victory by means of numerous action-packed scenes. In v. 1 God is said to be 'exalted in triumph' (גאה גאה),[11] having thrown the horse and his chariot[12] into the sea. Verse 4 continues this picture, with Yahweh casting Pharaoh's chariots and his army into the sea. Verses 6 and 12 contain two pictures of God's right hand fighting the enemy. In v. 6 his hand shatters (רעץ) the enemy, much as a king would use his mace to bash in his enemy's forehead.[13] In v. 12 there is the rather unusual picture of God extending (נטה) his hand, causing the earth to open and swallow the enemy. Verse 7 contains two pictures: God, in the greatness of his majesty (גאון), throws down (הרס) his enemy; and God sends forth his burning anger (חרון), which devours the enemy like stubble (קש).[14] Verses 8-10 contain a three-part, balanced image. With the breath (רוח) of his nostrils God causes the waters to be piled up (ערם, niphal), an image repeated in different words in the last two lines of the verse. The Egyptians view this as their opportunity, and greedily pursue Israel into the waters (v. 9). God then blows once again with his wind (רוח), and the waters cover the Egyptians (v. 10).[15] Finally, in vv. 13-16, which shift the focus from the conflict with the Egyptians to the entry into Palestine, we do not have a description of Yahweh's wondrous deeds in battle (except for the brief reference in v. 13a), but rather of the consternation caused among the leaders of Palestine by Yahweh's great victory. Hearing of Yahweh's acts, and fearing the worst for themselves, the people tremble (v. 14, רגז). Those who dwell in Philistia are seized by pangs (חיל). The chiefs of Edom are terrified (v. 15, בהל), and the chiefs of Moab are seized by trembling (רעד). The inhabitants of Canaan totter back and forth (מוג), weak-kneed. Fright (v. 16, אימה) and trembling (פחד) fall on all of them.

Unlike Exod 15, Judg 5 does not apply numerous descriptive words and phrases to Yahweh, nor does it present a number of scenes which vividly and explicitly describe God taking on the enemy. It does, however, use other means to emphasize Yahweh's crucial role in the victory over the Canaanites. While the song in Exod 15 never once mentions Israelite warriors, Judg 5 deals with the Israelite warriors in considerable detail in vv. 2, 8-9, and 11-18. The phrase 'Bless the Lord' (ברכו יהוה) is used twice in the poem (vv. 2, 9), and both times it appears immediately after the leaders and people in Israel are praised for coming out to fight. The clear implication is that it is Yahweh who caused the people to come out to form an army for Israel. Verse 11 speaks of the triumphs of the Lord's peasantry (פרזן) in Israel, and in vv. 11 and 13 there is the picture of the people of the Lord (עם יהוה) marching against the enemy. Verse 23 curses Meroz because its inhabitants did not come to the help of Yahweh against the mighty (גבורים), thereby again underlining the fact that the tribes and clans came out in response to Yahweh's initiative. Verse 31 concludes the poem by again attributing the victory to Yahweh, who causes his enemies to perish (אבד), while those whom Yahweh loves, presumably Israel and her warriors, are to be like the sun rising in his might.

Surprisingly, while the poet spends a great deal of time listing the Israelites who came to fight and those who did not (vv. 14-18, 23), the actual description of the battle is very brief (vv. 19-22), and the Israelite warriors are not mentioned once as taking part in the battle. In fact, God is not even mentioned by name in these verses. The poet in Judg 5, unlike the poet of Exodus 15, has chosen to celebrate Israel's victory by means other than vividly describing Yahweh in action on the battlefield, as will be discussed below when the water motif and the final two scenes of Judg 5 are analyzed. The allusion to Yahweh's role by means of the stars fighting from heaven against Sisera (v. 20) is indirect, as is the allusion by means of the water imagery in v. 21.

The scenes in vv. 3-5 are crucial in developing the role of Yahweh in the victory. As noted previously, God is in the forefront in these verses, where various forms of the divine name are used quite frequently. In v. 3 there is a scene from after the battle.[16] The poet, speaking in the first person, calls on the kings and princes to listen while praises are sung to Yahweh, God of Israel. Since the only kings around at this point in Israel's history would have been the kings of the Canaanites, whom Israel had just defeated, these Canaanite rulers are being sarcastically told to listen while praises are sung to the God who has just defeated them.[17] This has the effect not only of putting down the Canaanite kings, but also of praising Yahweh and thanking him for the victory. Unlike Exod 15.1-2, all this is done without any specific references to the battle and without any descriptive nouns or adjectives applied to God. We are told only that 'I will sing' and 'will make melody' to Yahweh.

In this verse the three major forces that will clash on the battlefield—the victorious Israelites, the vanquished foe, represented by the kings, and the victorious deity—are all encapsulated in one brief unit, where the focus of praise is on Israel's God. The same is true in Exod 15.1-2, where the victorious 'I' sings on behalf of Israel, the vanquished horse and chariot are pictured being thrown into the sea, and the victorious Yahweh is the center of all the praise. Thus, both poems open with an ebullient first-person praise of Israel's God for having delivered his people by crushing the enemy.

Judg 5.4-5 continues the stress begun in v. 3 on Yahweh's vital role. The specific picture is of Yahweh marching (צעד) to the scene of the battle from southern Palestine. Accompanying him are powerful natural phenomena, including the quaking (רעש) of the earth and a heavy rainstorm. The power of God through the forces of nature is thus heavily stressed at the beginning of the song, and the reader is led to conclude that in the face of this power the Canaanite kings, their armies and their chariots (vv. 19-22), are puny and easily swept away. Since vv. 4-5 set the tone with Yahweh in power as the God of creation who controls the forces of nature, there is no need to mention him specifically in vv. 19-22 as a warrior; his might has already determined the outcome of the battle. One should not say that, by comparison, the poet of Exod 15 downplays God's power over the forces of nature. He does, in fact, frequently emphasize that power (vv. 1, 4-8, 10-12). But he also chooses to depict Yahweh vividly as a man of war, fighting on the battlefield with a strong right arm. These are images the writer of Judg 5 has chosen to avoid, perhaps because he felt they would detract from the picture of God's cosmic power and majesty which he meant to convey. The differences in the way the two poets have described God's role in the two battles are a matter of style, and perhaps also a matter of theology. Both poets, however, clearly lay heavy stress on Yahweh as victor.

3. *The Water Motif*

Another similarity between the two poems is their use of water imagery. One might say that the reason for such use lies in the events surrounding each victory: the Egyptians drowning according to Exod 15, and the Canaanites being swept away by the onrushing flood in Judg 5. Nevertheless, it is clear that both poems do more than just allude to historical events. They use the water motif as a means of intensifying the struggle on the battlefield and emphasizing the significance and power of Yahweh's victory over the enemy. In the process, the water imagery goes beyond mere literal description and becomes poetic metaphor. This does not necessarily mean, however, that the poets intended to introduce a strong mytho-poetic theme, with Yahweh struggling against primordial chaos. As Cross and Freedman note regarding Exod 15, the sea is never personified as the enemy, and in fact is used by Yahweh as one of his weapons against the enemy.[18] Even though, as will be noted below, the water in each poem briefly constitutes a potential threat to Israel, this threat is a ploy used by the poets to intensify the drama of their poem, and does not imply any attempt to introduce the theme of a cosmic struggle between Yahweh and primordial chaos.

Exod 15 uses several clusters of images to develop the water motif. The picture in v. 1 of Yahweh throwing the horse and his chariot into the sea is repeated in slightly varied form in v. 4 where Yahweh, just described as a man of war (v. 3), casts Pharaoh's chariots and his army into the sea. Here both the sea and the Egyptians are passive, with the mighty warrior Yahweh casting the Egyptians into the sea like toys. Verse 7 also mentions Yahweh overthrowing (הרס) his adversaries. The second picture is of the submerged Egyptians. In v. 4b Pharaoh's choice warriors are sunk[19] in the sea. The abyss (תהמת) covers them (v. 5), and they go down into the depths like a stone. This image is also present in v. 10, where the sea covers the Egyptians, and they sink like lead in the mighty waters. The third picture is of Yahweh causing the waters to pile up, creating a passageway (v. 8). By the wind (רוח) of God's nostrils the waters are dammed up (ערם); they stand upright (נצב) like dams of water; the abyss thickens (קפא)[20] in the midst of the sea.

Verses 8-10 form a tightly compacted, three-part unit. After the wind of God's nostrils causes the waters to stand up, the Egyptians, seeing a passageway, decide to take advantage of it to pursue and destroy the Israelites. God's action in holding back the waters is thus seen briefly as a potential threat to Israel, allowing the Egyptian army access to Israel. This potential threat is used by the poet to misdirect the audience, leading them briefly to fear for Israel's safety. This makes v. 10 more powerful and effective, for God then quickly and easily turns the congealed waters into a trap for the Egyptians. He again blows with his wind, and the sea engulfs the greedy warriors.[21]

Verse 16 carries the water motif beyond the confrontation with the Egyptians to the entry of Israel into Canaan. The reference to the enemy being filled with dread and as still as a stone while Israel passes over (עבר) should be understood, in this particular context, as a reference to the crossing of the Jordan.[22] Thus, Yahweh's defense of Israel at the sea against the Egyptians, who wanted to destroy Israel as it passed through the waters, has implications for later confrontations. The new enemies now stand in dread when Israel once again passes through the waters.

In Exod 15 the water motif thus plays a very significant role. It is the body into which God throws the Egyptians; it is the body which covers the Egyptians as they sink to their death; it is the body used by Yahweh to entrap the Egyptians as they pursue Israel; and it is the body which Israel crosses, having gained respect from her new enemies due to Yahweh's destruction of the Egyptians.

Even though Judg 5 does not explicitly depict Yahweh using water to fight against the Canaanites on the battlefield, the water motif also plays a major role in Judg 5, and one can even argue that the paratactic style of the poet leads the audience to envision Yahweh's presence on the battlefield more effectively than if he had been specifically mentioned.[23] The water motif begins in vv. 4-5, where Yahweh marches from Edom to the battlefield. There is a threefold reference to water accompanying this theophany: the heavens dropped (water); the clouds dropped water;[24] and the mountains flowed (with the water).[25] Thus, when Yahweh comes to the battlefield, he comes as the powerful God of the storm.

However, in the paratactic style of the poet, we do not move directly to the role of water in the battle scene, but instead to a post-battle scene at the משאבים ('watering places' or 'watering troughs'), where Yahweh and his people Israel celebrate the victory (v. 11). Due to our lack of knowledge regarding the meaning of מחצצים,[26] the precise function of the water motif at this point in the song cannot be determined. Nevertheless, we can say that the poet depicts the water as being domesticated and tranquil, rather than the potent tool of Yahweh in the storm. Before the battle scene is described, wherein the full fury of the storm overwhelms the enemy, the poet hints at the peaceful domestic conditions which will follow the Israelite victory. No longer will travelers keep to the byways (v. 6) due to the unsettled conditions, and no longer will the Israelite peasants 'cease' (v. 7).

This post-battle scene ends in v. 11, and the writer moves on in vv. 12-18 to a description of the Israelite army. Just as in Exod 15 the waters Yahweh controls pose a potential threat to Israel (when the Egyptians decide to pursue Israel through the dammed up waters, v. 9), so in Judg 5 the waters threaten to deny Israel an army. In vv. 15-17 four tribes are listed among those who did *not* come to aid in the battle, and three of them failed to come for reasons associated with water: Gilead elected to stay beyond the Jordan River; Dan stayed with his ships; and Asher stayed by the sea coast at his piers. It is hardly an accident that three of the tribes that fail to come are described by the poet as holding back due to the influence of water. The poet is teasing the reader, suggesting that, despite vv. 4-5, water may not be under Yahweh's control, may not be available to help with the Israelite victory. This teasing serves to set up the reader, so that the overpowering use of water in v. 21 will be even more effective as a literary image.

Even though Yahweh is not specifically mentioned in the battle scene (vv. 19-22), the very failure to mention his name intensifies his presence, given the background prepared by the poet in preceding verses. Since the writer has already associated storm imagery and vast quantities of water with the appearance of Yahweh in vv. 4-5, the image of the torrent Kishon in v. 21 will automatically bring to the mind of the audience the theophany of Yahweh. But by forcing the reader to make that association, rather than directly using Yahweh's name, the poet places even greater emphasis on Yahweh's presence. The association is helped by the poet's use of 'waters of' (מי) and 'heaven' (שמים)[27] in the two preceding verses, both being important words in the development of the water imagery in vv. 4-5. The power of Yahweh over the storm in vv. 4-5 is also echoed by means of the three-fold repetition[28] of נחל (torrent): 'Torrent Kishon (נחל קישון) swept them away'; 'torrent onrushing' (נחל קדומים); 'torrent Kishon' (נחל קישון). The onrushing verbiage onomatopoetically depicts the irresistible power of the onrushing waters, and paratactically brings to mind Yahweh, who unleashed the awesome storm already before the battle began.

The water motif is continued in one final, brief way. When Sisera flees the battlefield, he comes in desperation to Jael, his throat parched (v. 25). The two words מים שאל (he asked for water) succinctly present a juicy irony. Sisera, whose forces had been defeated because he had too much water (v. 21), now must beg a bit of water from a woman, an act which will shortly lead to his death at the hands of the cunning Jael.

Both Exod 15 and Judg 5 make thorough use of water imagery. Exod 15 associates it more directly with the battle, picturing Yahweh throwing the Egyptians into the water, in which they are repeatedly said to sink, and picturing Yahweh holding back the waters to entrap the Egyptians. In Judg 5 the poet carefully develops his water imagery before the battle begins (vv. 4-5), describing Yahweh as the powerful storm God. While the onrushing waters are one image[29] used to emphasize God's victory over the Canaanites, his presence on the battlefield is never described, and the poet relies on paratactic association to impress on the audience the vital role of Yahweh in the victory through the forces of the storm.

4. *The Mocking of the Enemy*

In both Exod 15 and Judg 5 there are a number of ways in which the enemy is mocked. Examples of those alluded to previously are: God's tossing the Egyptians into the sea like toys (Exod 15.1, 4); God's right hand shattering the enemy (Exod 15.6); or the scene in which the torrent Kishon sweeps away the enemy (Judg 5.21). There are, however, a number of additional techniques and scenes used in the two poems to mock the enemy.

We begin by looking at Exod 15.9. It was noted previously that this verse comes at the middle of a three verse sequence in which God parts the waters (v. 8), the Egyptians eagerly pursue Israel (v. 9), and God blows with his wind and covers the Egyptians (v. 10). One of the reasons this verse is so effective is because of its close association with vv. 1-2. These three verses alone of all those in the poem contain a heavy first-person emphasis. Verses 1 and 2 contain three first-person verbs expressing the singer's praise of God (see note 9). The singer also refers to Yahweh as: עזי, 'my refuge'; זמרת, 'my strength'; ויהי לי לישועה, 'my salvation'; אלי, 'my God'; and אלהי אבי, 'God of my father'. Verse 9 also uses many first-person forms: ארדף, 'I will pursue'; אשיג, 'I will overtake'; אחלק שלל, 'I will divide the spoil'; תמלאמו נפשי, 'my desire will be satisfied'; אריק חרבי, 'I will draw my sword'; and תורישמו ידי, 'my hand will seize them'. The repeated use of first-person forms in vv. 1-2 and v. 9 leads the audience to compare the two 'I's; and the contrast could hardly be sharper. In vv. 1-2 the stress is clearly on the joyous outburst of the grateful singer who praises his God for the victory he has wrought. Verse 9, by contrast, presents an 'I' greedy for destruction and plunder. This latter picture of a cocky, bloody despoiler of Israel sets the Egyptians up for their fall in v. 10. The God of the first 'I' simply blows with his wind and engulfs the Egyptians in the waters. Thus, in Exod 15 we have two 'I's, each asserting itself strongly. The first 'I', who enthusiastically praises God and looks to him for salvation, is victorious. The second, haughty 'I' cannot envision anything but victory and plunder, but is humbled and sunk in the depths of the sea.

As noted previously, Judg 5 also contains a scene in which the 'I' or singer praises God for the victory. In v. 3, which refers to a time after the battle, the 'I' sings boldly and enthusiastically in the presence of the Canaanite kings of the victory Yahweh has wrought. אנכי ליהוה אנכי אשירה[30], 'I, to Yahweh, I, I will sing!'; אזמר ליהוה אלהי ישראל, 'I will sing to Yahweh, the God of Israel'. While we are not specifically told that the Canaanite kings have been defeated, the poet provides a strong hint through the singer's command[31] that the kings listen while praises are sung to the God of Israel, who the audience knows has defeated the Canaanites. This indirect allusion to the defeat of the Canaanites contrasts with the blunt statement in Exod 15.1 that God had thrown the horse and his chariot into the sea. Even though Judg 5, unlike Exod 15, does not contain a corresponding first-person speech by the enemy warriors, it does develop the idea of the haughtiness of the enemy (as in Exod 15.9), it does depict the proud enemy being overpowered (as in Exod 15.10), and it does provide brief speeches by Sisera's mother and her female attendants (Judg

5.28-30) as a means of mocking the enemy's confidence and thirst for spoils.

We turn first to v. 19, which opens with the repetitive באו מלכים נלחמו, 'The kings came, they fought', and אז נלחמו מלכי כנען, 'then fought the kings of Canaan'. The writer has used standard poetic repetition[32] to lengthen and thereby emphasize the picture of the kings coming and fighting.[33] The repetition causes the audience to dwell on the picture, as does also the next line, בתענך על מי מגדו, 'at Taanach by the waters of Megiddo'. All this emphasis on the fighting of the Canaanite kings makes more effective the last line of the verse בצע כסף לא לקחו, 'Spoils of silver they did not take', for there the fighting of the kings and their pre-battle confidence is contrasted with reality: they failed to take the spoils that go to the victor.

However, the defeat of the Canaanite kings is not explicitly mentioned here, since the audience is forced to infer it from the failure of the Canaanites to take spoils, just as the defeat of the Canaanites was not explicitly mentioned in v. 3. In both instances the poet's indirect, paratactic style leads the audience to the conclusion the poet wants them to reach regarding the defeat of the Canaanites. This contrasts sharply with the style of Exod 15, where the defeat of the Egyptians is on center stage already in the first verse.

Having thus far held back from providing an explicit description of the defeat of the Canaanites, the poet presents, beginning in v. 21, a dramatic sequence of scenes vividly depicting their downfall. The threefold image in v. 21 of the torrent Kishon sweeping away the enemy was previously discussed under the water motif. This is followed in v. 22 by the frantic retreat of the Canaanites from the battlefield. The poet pictures the pounding (הלם) of the horses' hoofs, and twice uses the word 'galloping' (דהרות) to reinforce the image of the panic-stricken enemy warriors desperately fleeing for their lives. This provides a striking contrast to the confident approach of the kings in v. 19, just as the picture of the enemy being engulfed by the waters in Exod 15.10 provides a striking contrast to the confident enemy who wanted to pursue Israel through the walled-up waters and destroy her (v. 9).

Verses 24-27, which describe the fall of Sisera at the hands of a woman, form both the climax of the poem and the key description of the defeat of the Canaanites. However, since I will deal in detail with this scene in the next section of my paper, 'The Fall Motif', let me simply say here that Sisera's humiliating death at the hands of a woman and the drawn-out description of his fall to the ground provide the cathartic moment of release for the audience, who can vent in their savoring of the downfall of the Canaanite leader the intense hatred of the Canaanites that had built up for so many years.

The reason for that intense hatred comes to focus in the sarcastic final scene (vv. 28-30), in which Sisera's mother and her attendants are mocked. As the scene opens, Sisera's mother gazes out the window and asks, מדוע בשש רכבו לבוא, 'Why does his chariot tarry so long?'; מדוע אחרו פעמי[34] מרכבותיו, 'Why do they delay, the hoofbeats of his chariots?' Sisera's mother is genuinely worried about her son, and the audience might be tempted to feel a bit of sympathy for her, especially since they know that Sisera is dead and will not be returning. However, any potential feelings of sympathy are quickly removed in vv. 29-30, where the scene reaches its climax.

As noted earlier, the poet had used the statement in v. 19 that the Canaanite kings got no spoil to allude to the Canaanite defeat, but the spoils motif was not developed further at that point. In vv. 29-30, however, Sisera's mother and her 'wise' ladies go into elaborate detail itemizing all the spoil they think Sisera is collecting for them. With heavy sarcasm, the poet expresses the defeat of the Canaanites by having the Canaanite women gloat over the spoils while the audience still has fresh in its mind the picture of the dead Canaanite leader lying on the floor of the tent with his brains scattered around him. Rather than taking spoils, the Canaanites themselves have become the spoils of Israel. The Canaanites had no doubt seized considerable spoils from Israel after previous battles, intensifying the Israelite hatred of them. The knowledge that this time the greedy women would get no spoil would have been very gratifying to the Israelite audience. This would have been especially true since Sisera's mother, despite the growing evidence that her son will not return, simply cannot bring herself to entertain the idea that the Canaanites have lost.

The words of Sisera's mother and her ladies itemizing the spoil parallel the words in Exod 15.9, אחלק שלל תמלאמו נפשי, 'I will divide the spoil; my desire will be satisfied'. In both instances there is a scene in which the enemy (or the enemy's mother) is on center stage confidently speaking of the spoils that will be taken. In Exod 15 the words come immediately before the enemy is engulfed by the waters, while in Judg 5 they come after the outcome of the battle has already been determined and serve as a means of deriding the defeated enemy. Thus, even though Judg 5 does not contain a scene with numerous first person singular verbs spoken by the enemy, as does Exod 15, the words spoken by Sisera's mother and her ladies have the same effect as Exod 15.9—the enemies of Israel are mocked for their confidence of victory and spoils.

Thus, Exod 15 and Judg 5—each in its own way—mock the enemy. Exod 15 dwells more explicitly on the battle itself, showing Yahweh tossing around the humiliated Egyptians and consuming them like stubble. Judg 5, which devotes little time to the battle, initially uses a more indirect style, only alluding to the Canaanite defeat until v. 20, but then using vivid scenes to picture the Canaanites being swept away (v. 21), retreating from the battlefield in panic (v. 22), and having their leader pounded into oblivion by the woman Jael. Both poems employ the spoil motif, the enemy in Exod 15 desiring to despoil Israel but being engulfed by the returning waters, the enemy in Judg 5 being mocked through the picture of the confident Canaanite women 'counting' the spoil even as their leader lies dead.

5. *The Fall Motif*

It is quite natural to think of an enemy falling when one thinks of his defeat. This was certainly as true for the ancients as it is for us today. The victory palette of King Nar-mer shows him striking with a mace a prisoner kneeling at his feet, while the panel below his feet depicts two nude enemies lying prostrate on the ground.[35] A relief from the palace of Tiglath-Pileser III at Nimrud depicting the siege of an unknown city shows various enemies scattered on the ground below the city wall, and two figures who are falling from the top of the wall toward the ground.[36] Perhaps the most striking example of this fall motif is the victory stela of Naram-Sin of Agade celebrating his victory over the Lullubians.[37] He is pictured ascending a mountain, with various enemies lying scattered at his feet or standing below him begging mercy, while one figure plummets from the mountain-side.

Both Exod 15 and Judg 5 employ this fall motif. In Exod 15 the motif is developed, not in terms of a battle scene in which the enemy is seen falling to the ground, but rather in terms of the enemy sinking in the waters or falling into the abyss. Since this sinking was discussed earlier under the water motif, let me at this point simply summarize by saying that the descent or fall motif is present in vv. 1, 4, 5, 7, and 10. The final iteration of the fall motif (v. 12) does not refer to water, but rather to the earth, which swallows or engulfs (בלע) the Egyptians, no doubt symbolizing not only the defeat of the Egyptians but also their descent into the underworld.

In Judg 5, the fall motif centers on vv. 24-27, which form the climax of the poem. Here we have the poem's cathartic moment, in which all the pent up hatred of the Canaanites and the way they have previously defeated Israel and lorded over them finds release.[38] Sisera clearly embodies in himself the Canaanites, and his fall is their fall. In v. 24 the threefold emphasis on the fact that Jael is a woman heightens the joy of Israel over the fall of Sisera. Not only does he die: he dies in a humiliating way at the hands of a woman. After Jael lulls Sisera into trusting her (v. 25) and then seizes her lethal weapons (v. 26a), there follows a rapid-fire and highly repetitive sequence of clauses describing Sisera's fall:

והלמה סיסרא	And she hammered Sisera
מחקה ראשו	She crushed his head
ומחצה וחלפה רקתו	And she shattered and she pierced his temple
בין רגליה כרע נפל שכב	Between her feet he sank, he fell, he lay still
בין רגליה כרע נפל	Between her feet he sank, he fell
באשר כרע	Where he sank
שם נפל	There he fell
שדוד	Dead!

Such repetition far exceeds what is normal in Hebrew poetry. This does not, however, mean that the text is corrupt: rather, the poet, who elsewhere speeds up or slows down the action to suit his purposes, has here chosen to slow the action almost to a standstill in order to allow the audience to vent their hatred of the Canaanites as they savor Sisera's fall. It takes Sisera a very long time to fall to the ground as one verb is piled upon another. First there are the four verbs describing the bashing of Sisera: הלמה, 'She hammered'; מחקה, 'She crushed'; מחצה, 'She shattered'; חלפה, 'She pierced'. Then follows in v. 27 a sequence of seven verbs describing Sisera's fall to the ground: כרע, 'He sank' is used three times; נפל, 'He fell' is used three times; and שכב, 'He lay still' is used once. The configuration of the words also slows the action as we move through the verse. The first line has five words, בין רגליה, 'Between her feet' and one usage of each of the three verbs. The second line is the same, except that the last verb (שכב) is omitted. Then there are two two-word lines, each with a verb: באשר כרע, 'Where he sank' and שם נפל, 'There he fell'. This all then comes to focus, like an inverted pyramid, on the one final word, שדוד,[39] 'Dead!' The vivid effect is to portray Sisera slowly slumping to the ground in a heap, where he, like the Canaanites he represents, lies crushed and fallen before Israel. The poet has skillfully used his words to achieve an image almost as frozen and certainly as permanent as that presented in the graphic art discussed earlier.

Thus, both Exod 15 and Judg 5 make major use of the motif of falling, with the enemy weakly and passively sinking in defeat before Israel. Exod 15 uses the motif at several points in the first twelve verses of the poem, picturing God throwing the Egyptians into the sea, causing the sea to cover them, or opening the earth to swallow them. This use of the sea and earth provides a somewhat modified form of the fall motif, but it is a very effective one. Judg 5 focuses its fall motif in one intense section, vv. 24-27. Unlike Exod 15, it is not all the enemy who are pictured going down, but their leader, Sisera, who represents all the Canaanites. The enemy does not fall before Yahweh, as in Exod 15, but rather falls before a woman. But in both Exod 15 and Judg 5 the end result is the same: the enemy has fallen before Israel, and is no more.

Conclusion

Even though there are numerous similarities between Exod 15 and Judg 5, the differences between them in both form and content are also considerable, as this study has shown. It therefore would not seem appropriate to suggest that there is an established 'form' for victory songs that was followed by both Exod 15 and Judg 5. Claus Westermann, in discussing songs of victory, claims that 'The original form of the song of victory, looking back to the time of need, the report of the victory, and the praise of God, can no longer be recognized . . .'[40] However, Westermann provides no evidence beyond his own intuition for the existence of such a form as the model followed in early Israel. While it may be appropriate to talk of isolating a form such as an individual lament in the book of Psalms, there is not enough patterned regularity held in common by Exod 15 and Judg 5 to make it reasonable to propose something so set as a victory song form lying behind these poems.

It would also be a mistake simply to include Exod 15 and Judg 5 in a larger genre. Westermann's pointing to the similarity between the structure of Judg 5 and the structure of a psalm of praise of the people is in some ways helpful.[41] But to leave matters there would tend to obscure the unique connection of each poem with a particular Israelite victory. Both poems are clearly more than just psalms of praise.

It would seem best to suggest that what the two poems have in common are several features or modes of description that would automatically come to mind as someone was creating a song of victory to celebrate an Israelite success on the battlefield. These elements, which evidence much more the spontaneity and exuberance of victory than they do an attempt to follow a set form, include:

1. a focusing on the specific name of Israel's God (Yahweh, God of Israel, my father's God, etc.) as a way of emphasizing his all-important role in the victory;
2. the application of specific terms or phrases to God (my strength, my salvation, etc.) and/or a description of God's role in the victory (God's coming to the battlefield, his fighting against the enemy, etc.);
3. a description of God's use of the forces of nature to give Israel the victory;
4. the mocking of the enemy;
5. a description of the enemy's fall.

While these elements came naturally to mind for the writers of Exod 15 and Judg 5 as they celebrated their people's victories, each poet developed the various elements in a unique way. One example would be the way each writer dealt with God and his role in the battle. Exod 15 applies a number of descriptive phrases to God, and has him active as a powerful warrior combating the enemy, while Judg 5 uses a number of different names for God but no descriptive phrases, and never directly pictures God taking part in the battle. As noted earlier, the style of Exod 15 is blunt and direct, while the style of Judg 5 is indirect and paratactic.

Another example would be the way each poem presents the forces of nature. Although both do so by means of the water motif, Exod 15 uses that motif throughout most of the battle scene (vv. 1-12, which constitute more than half the poem), and links water directly to

God's action on the battlefield. Judg 5 develops the water motif extensively before (vv. 4-5, 11, 17) and after (v. 25) the battle scene, which is rather brief (vv. 19-22), and devotes a larger share of its battle description than does Exod 15 to motifs that do not directly focus on water (vv. 19-20, 22). When water is mentioned (v. 21), the battle scene does not specifically link God with the water, but relies on the audience's associating the water with the theophany of vv. 4-5, where God demonstrates his awesome power over the storm, a power so great he need not appear personally on the battlefield.

Thus, in Exod 15 and Judg 5 we find diversity within commonality. While both poems employ several common themes, and exhibit a strong reverence for Israel's God, this commonality does not derive from a concerted effort by each poet to imitate a well-known formal structure for victory songs, but rather from the writer's basic instincts regarding what was necessary and important in a song praising Israel's God for the victory. Using these basic elements, each poet has composed, in his own creative way, an impressive and powerful tribute to Israel's triumphant God.

NOTES

1. While there is relatively little debate about the antiquity of Judg 5, there has been considerable debate about the dating of Exod 15. W.O.E. Oesterley claims that its vocabulary and style indicate a relatively late date, *Ancient Hebrew Poems* (London: SPCK, 1938), p. 18. Claus Westermann, in *The Praise of God in the Psalms* (Richmond: John Knox, 1965), p. 91, calls the Song of Deborah 'the only extensive song of victory from pre-exilic times that has been transmitted fully', thereby implying that Exod 15 is post-exilic. See also Martin Noth, *Exodus: A Commentary* (London: SCM, 1962), p. 123. I am inclined to agree with Frank M. Cross and David Noel Freedman, who call Exod 15 a 'song of triumph' and give it an early date on the basis of comparative analysis with Ugaritic literature, 'The Song of Miriam', *JNES* 14 (1955), pp. 237-40.

2. Some of the Psalms, such as Ps 21, are designed for celebration after a victory, but give no appearance of being tailored to a *particular* victory. There are other victory songs clearly celebrating specific events, but they are quite brief (e.g. Judg 15.16; 16.24; 1 Sam 18.7).

3. The question of the unity of Exod 15 is an appropriate discussion for another paper. While noting that I do consider Exod 15.1-18 a single poem (see Cross and Freedman, 'Song', pp. 237-38), let me also indicate that almost all the points of comparison with Judg 5 lie in vv. 1-11, whose essential unity few would dispute. The unity of Judg 5 is not often

questioned.

4. יה, with the subsequent ו appended, may be taken as an early form of יהוה (Yahweh) (*ibid*., p. 243).

5. I disagree with the claim of Cross and Freedman (*ibid*.), that v. 2 is out of place where it stands and does not fit with the 'prevailing' metrical pattern in the rest of the ode. Scholars have for too long incorrectly assumed that metrical regularity was very necessary in ancient Israelite poetry, with all kinds of accompanying suggestions for textual emendations. But variation in metrical pattern is itself an important poetic device, as may be seen, for example, in Judg 5. Also, I fail to see any contextual incompatibility between vv. 1 and 2, for both sing praises in the first person to Israel's victorious God. See George W. Coats, 'The Song of the Sea', *CBQ* 31 (1969), p. 1, and James Muilenburg, 'A Liturgy on the Triumphs of Yahweh', *Studia Biblica et Semitica* (Wageningen: H. Veenman, 1966), pp. 237, 239-40.

6. Read יהוה (Yahweh) for ארני (Lord), following the Samaritan text and many other manuscripts.

7. For much of what I say regarding Judg 5, my earlier article 'Judges 5: Parataxis in Hebrew Poetry', *JBL* 99 (1980), pp. 23-41, may serve as a detailed resource should the reader seek more extensive discussion. Scholarship regarding Judg 5 is also discussed in the paper.

8. Regarding the translation of זה סיני as 'The One of Sinai', see W.F. Albright, 'The Song of Deborah in the Light of Archaeology', *BASOR* 62 (1936), p. 30.

9. Exod 15.1-2 employs three intensive verbs: the qal cohortative אשירה, 'I will indeed sing!'; the hiphil imperfect אנוהו, 'I will praise him!'; and the polel imperfect ארממנהו, 'I will exalt him!' Judg 5.3 twice uses אנכי, 'I', suggesting that the singer is bubbling with enthusiasm and eager to be heard, uses the qal cohortative אשירה, 'I will indeed sing!' and uses the piel imperfect אזמר, 'I will sing!'

10. Regarding the translation of נאדרי as 'awesome', see Cross and Freedman, 'Song', pp. 245-46, where they argue for the archaic translation of the verb as 'to fear'.

11. Note the emphasis added by the infinitive absolute.

12. ורכבו (and his rider) is no doubt to be understood here to refer to a chariot. See Cross and Freedman, 'Song', p. 243.

13. This image is seen commonly in Egyptian art as, for example, in the relief showing King Snefru smiting an Asiatic, or the relief of Thut-mose III smiting his captives; cf. James B. Pritchard, *ANEP* (2nd edn; Princeton: Princeton University Press, 1969), pls. 295 and 312.

14. Is this not a sarcastic allusion to the stubble the Israelites had to gather (Exod 5.7, 12) in order to make bricks for the Egyptians?

15. This scene will be discussed in detail when the water imagery and the mocking of the enemy are analyzed.

16. The poet's paratactic style allows him to shift from scene to scene

without following any strict rules of chronological order. See Hauser, 'Parataxis', pp. 26-29.

17. This would be akin to asking Napoleon to listen while the events at Waterloo are recited. Note, however, that at this point in the poem the defeat of the Canaanites is not specifically mentioned. The poet only hints at it.

18. 'Song', p. 239.

19. Note the passive verb טבעו, in pual.

20. I disagree with Cross and Freedman, 'Song', p. 246, who argue it is better to translate קפא as 'churn' rather than 'congeal', because 'In the present context the former idea, involving action, is preferable'. But it is precisely the *inactivity*, the standing still of the waters, that is stressed in this verse. See Coats, 'Song', pp. 14-15, who gives solid reasons for dismissing the idea of Cross and Freedman that the basic image in vv. 8-10 is that of a storm at sea, rather than a path through which the Egyptians pursue Israel.

21. The use of verbs in vv. 8-10 greatly enhances the effect of these verses. In v. 8 the wind of God's nostrils (note the lack of a verb) causes the waters to pile up. Two of the three verbs describing the reaction of the waters to God's wind are passive niphals (נערמו, 'they are dammed up', and נצבו, 'they stood upright') and the third suggests passive action (קפאו, 'they thickened'). Before Yahweh, whose activity does not even need to be expressed by a verb, the waters meekly obey. In v. 9 the desire of the Egyptians for the slaughter and despoiling of Israel is expressed through six verbs which vividly describe the Egyptians' greed and confidence. But the fact that all six verbs are in the imperfect also implies that the Egyptians still need to do a lot of striving: everything they want is in the future. In contrast, God's response to the Egyptians (v. 10) is given in one qal perfect verb, נשפת, 'You blew'. The sixfold striving of the Egyptians is overcome by one action of God, which causes the sea to engulf them (note the intensive piel כסמו ים, 'The sea covered them'). The Egyptians passively go down (צללו, 'They sank') like lead in the mighty waters. See the briefer but similar discussion by John D.W. Watts, 'The Song of the Sea—Exod XV', *VT* 7 (1957), p. 373.

22. עבר is used in Josh 5.1, which describes Israel's crossing of the Jordan as she enters Palestine. See Coats, 'Song', p. 11.

23. See Hauser, 'Parataxis', p. 33.

24. Note how the structure of the poetry makes the audience focus on מים (water). After the words 'The heavens also dropped' (גם שמים נטפו), the poet does not tell immediately what the heavens dropped, but adds the line 'Indeed the clouds dropped' (גם עבים נטפו), and only then adds the word 'water' as a completion to both lines. The temporary delay in the completion of the first line piques the audience's curiosity, making the listeners pay more attention to the word when it is finally given.

25. נזל (flowed) makes perfectly good sense in this context, fitting in with the water imagery preceding it by pointing to the rainfall rushing through

the mountains. One need not emend the text, as Robert Boling has attempted, *Judges: Introduction, Translation, and Commentary* (AB; Garden City: Doubleday, 1975), p. 108. See George Foot Moore, *A Critical and Exegetical Commentary on Judges* (ICC; Edinburgh: T. & T. Clark, 1895), pp. 141-42.

26. See Moore, *Judges*, p. 148 and Boling, *Judges*, pp. 102, 110, whose interesting proposal for v. 11a fails to take account of the ambiguity of מחצצים.

27. Note that שמים (heaven) contains within it the sound of the word מים (water).

28. Recall the three-fold reference to water in the theophany (vv. 4-5).

29. The other images are the description of the advancing Canaanite kings (v. 19), the kings' failure to obtain spoil (v. 19), the stars fighting from heaven (v. 20), and the hooves of the Canaanites' horses galloping in retreat (v. 22).

30. This is exactly the same cohortative form used in Exod 15.1.

31. The verse opens with two imperatives: שמעו, 'Hear!'; and האזינו, 'Listen!'

32. The poet of Judg 5 on occasion chooses to amplify, condense, or even omit repetition when it suits his purpose. For an example of elaborate amplification, see Judg 5.26-27, which will be discussed below. When the poet omits repetition altogether, as in בצע כסף לא לקחו, 'Spoils of silver they did not take' (v. 19), or מים שאל, 'He asked water' (v. 25), he thereby provides emphasis by means of the abruptness, which contrasts with the usual repetition. See Hauser, 'Parataxis', pp. 32-38.

33. אז (then) strengthens the effect of the repetition, since one expects something new after it, but instead most words from the first line are repeated.

34. Even as Sisera's mother asks her question, the reader is reminded of the defeat of the Canaanites by the reference to hoofbeats, which calls to mind the hoofbeats of v. 22, where the Canaanites fled the battlefield in defeat.

35. Pritchard, *ANEP*, pl. 296.

36. Yigael Yadin, *The Art of Warfare in Biblical Lands* (New York: McGraw-Hill, 1963), pp. 406-407.

37. Pritchard, *ANEP*, pl. 309.

38. See Hauser, 'Parataxis', pp. 34-38.

39. Note the passive participle.

40. *Psalms*, p. 92.

41. *Ibid.*, p. 91. For a brief discussion of some forms proposed for Exod 15, see Coats, 'Song', pp. 7-8.

15

THE SONG OF MIRIAM POETICALLY AND THEOLOGICALLY CONSIDERED

Bernhard W. Anderson

The Song of Miriam (Exod 15.21), one of the shortest pieces of ancient Israelite poetry, has almost been crowded out by the much longer Song of the Sea (Exod 15.1b-18) which precedes it in the present scriptural arrangement.[1] Miriam's song is set in the narrative framework by a prose introduction (15.20) which portrays her going at the head of 'all the women', who accompanied her with timbrels and dancing, and singing the song 'to them' (*lāhem*)—apparently to the women in this context. The Song of the Sea, on the other hand, is placed in the narrative context by a prose introduction (15.1a) which announces that Moses led 'the Israelites' in the singing of 'this song' to Yahweh in hymnic praise. After the singing of the hymn, which is redolent of Canaanite language and imagery and which is endorsed with the prestigious authority of Moses, the song of Miriam strikes the reader as anticlimactic, even though her song marks the conclusion of the whole Exodus story. (The ensuing verses, beginning with 15.22, open a new movement in the narrative, dealing with 'crises in the wilderness'.) Understandably, commentators—as in the case of Brevard Childs's excellent commentary on Exodus—concentrate on the Song of the Sea and leave the Song of Miriam on the periphery of attention.[2]

It is interesting that the redactors of the Torah have associated the Song of the Sea with Moses, who dominates the Exodus tradition in its present form, although there is no allusion to Moses' leadership in the song itself. On the other hand, Moses is completely ignored in the Song of Miriam and its own narrative context. There Miriam is introduced only as 'the prophetess' (*hann*^{e}*bî'â*) and 'the sister of Aaron'—the man who elsewhere is regarded as the brother (Exod 4.14) and spokesman of Moses. All of this leads Martin Noth to say that the Song of Miriam and its narrative introduction belong to a tradition older than the present Pentateuchal narrative in which Moses is the dominant figure[3] and therefore, as one might say, finally 'upstages' Miriam in the singing of a song that celebrates the divine victory at the sea. In the summary of Israel's sacred history given in Mic 6.3-5, however, Miriam retains her place along with Moses and Aaron as a leader of early Israel.

Let us take a critical look at the place of the Song of Miriam in its present scriptural context. After this is done, we shall examine the piece of poetry itself and consider its relation to the Song of the Sea. Finally, we shall consider in outline some of the theological implications of Miriam's song, which stands at the fountainhead of a poetic and singing tradition that leads, at least in Christian imagination, through the Song of Hannah (1 Sam 2.1-10) to Mary's Song of Thanksgiving, the Magnificat (Luke 1.46-55).

1. *Miriam's Song in its Context*

Consider, first, the narrative context in which the Song of Miriam is placed. The Exodus Story reaches a climax in Exod 14 with the dramatic portrayal of the passage of the fugitive Hebrews through the Sea of Reeds and the discomfiture of the pursuing Egyptians. The conclusion of the narrative itself is reached in Exod 14.30-31:

> So at that time Yahweh liberated Israel from the power of Egypt. Seeing the Egyptians dead upon the seashore, Israel perceived the great power that Yahweh demonstrated against Egypt. The people feared Yahweh and put their trust in Yahweh and in Moses, his servant.

After that we find not one hymn, but two, celebrating Yahweh's liberating power. The first, the Song of the Sea, picks up the theme—almost verbatim—that is stated in the second, the Song of Miriam (compare 15.1b with 15.21). Is there a redactional explanation for this literary overlap?

It is evident that the horizon of the Song of the Sea is much wider than that of the immediate narrative context where the subject is the victory at the Sea of Reeds. The passage through the sea is, to be sure, a crucial event which demonstrates the incomparable majesty and power of Yahweh, the Divine Warrior. This event, however, is the prelude to a further divine triumph. Immediately after recapitulating the victory over the Egyptians (v. 12), the poet proceeds to announce Yahweh's further demonstration of power:[4]

> You faithfully led
> the people whom you redeemed:
> You guided in your might
> to your holy encampment (Exod 15.13).

Then the poet goes on to describe how panic overwhelmed the leaders of Edom and Moab, as well as other rulers of Canaan:

> While your people passed over, Yahweh,
> while your people passed over whom you have created
> (Exod 15.16b).

This 'passing over' (the verb is *'ābār*) is not the crossing through the sea but the movement toward the goal ahead. The poet says (15.17a), addressing Yahweh, that 'you caused them to go in' (*t^ebi'ēmô*) and 'you planted them' in the sacred mountain, the sanctuary where Yahweh is praised. Admittedly, the poem seems to reflect the Canaanite mythic pattern: the conflict of the Divine Warrior with adversaries, the building of a sanctuary on the sacred mountain for the triumphant deity, and the celebration of the god's everlasting kingship.[5] The poetry, however, reflects the twofold confession that Yahweh 'brought the people out of Egypt' and 'brought them in to the promised land'. The entry into the land of Canaan is in view.

The broader horizon of the Song of the Sea raises the question as to whether it belongs to another literary phase than that represented by the Song of Miriam. In the past, traditio-historical investigation, initiated by George Coats[6] and followed up by Brevard Childs,[7] has proposed that the event at the sea belongs to the wilderness wanderings tradition, not to the Exodus tradition in the larger sense of Yahweh bringing the people out of Egypt and into a new land. Childs's study in particular argues that 'Ex. xv reflects a poetic tradition of the event of the sea, which although equally old as that in the J account, has been transmitted within the larger framework of the exodus and conquest traditions'.[8] He suggests that in the early stage of the Old Epic tradition, the sea event was an episode in the people's plunge into the wilderness where they continually murmured (see Exod 14.10-14). By the time of the final redaction of the traditions in the post-exilic period, however, this event 'had become central in the tradition and identified with the exodus from Egypt itself'.[9]

However one reconstructs the traditio-historical development from Old Epic tradition to the final text, there is strong reason to believe that the Song of the Sea is an intrusive element, as various scholars recognize.[10] This judgment, of course, says nothing about the relative ages of the traditions that have been combined. Literarily, the poetic tradition reflected in the Song of the Sea may be older than—or just as old as—the Old Epic tradition (JE). Certainly this essay does not challenge the judgment of scholars of the Albright school regarding the antiquity of Exod 15.1b-18. From a purely literary point of view, however, the Song of the Sea, with its larger horizon, appears to be an expansion of the epic tradition which once moved from the narrator's conclusion in Exod 14.30-31 to the singing of Miriam's song in Exod 15.20-21. The intrusion of the passage now found in Exod 15.1-18 into this narrative context necessitated the somewhat awkward, and certainly prosaic, recapitulation in Exod 15.19:

> For when the horses of Pharaoh with his chariots and charioteers went into the sea, Yahweh caused the waters of the sea to overwhelm them, but the Israelites walked on dry ground in the middle of the sea.

2. *The Song of Miriam Itself*

Assuming, then, that originally the story of Israel's liberation concluded with the Song of Miriam (perhaps harking back to the beginning when the baby Moses' unnamed sister watched over him; 2.2, 7-8), let us turn to the song itself.

The song is composed of two distichs (bicola), each element of which is articulated in a 2/2 rhythm:

šîrû le YHWH	Sing to Yahweh!
kî gā'ô gā'â	For he is powerfully ascendant.
sûs werōk^{e}bô	Horse and charioteer
rāmâ bayyām	he has hurled into the sea.

While the song has a superficial affinity with songs of victory, like the Song of Deborah (Judg 5), mainly it displays the formal features of the hymn, the genre delineated by Hermann Gunkel. It opens with an imperative plural verb (cf. Pss 113.1; 117.1; etc.) which summons a community to praise Yahweh: 'Sing to Yahweh!' This invitation is followed by the motive for praise, a characteristic element of a hymn, introduced by the particle *kî* ('for'): 'For Yahweh is powerfully ascendant!' This translation attempts to render the force of the finite verb *gā'â* which is strengthened and made emphatic by the preceding infinitive absolute *gā'ô*. The verbal meaning is that Yahweh rose up in power, became 'ascendant' (meaning 'in control', 'dominant', 'superior'). The motive for praise is followed by a further hymnic ascription which portrays Yahweh's rising to the height of divine power in a wonderful moment of liberation of fugitives from pursuing enemies: 'Horse and charioteer Yahweh has hurled into the sea'. 'The image for the victory', writes George Coats, 'is mythopoetic', and 'in all probability is the oldest recounting of the event of the Sea in the Old Testament'.[11]

In both form and brevity the Song of Miriam corresponds closely to Psalm 117, the shortest psalm in the Psalter. The psalm also begins with plural imperatives which summon people to praise Yahweh:

hall^{e}lû 'et-YHWH kol-gôyîm	Praise Yahweh all nations,
šabb^{e}ḥûhû kol-ha'ummîm	Glorify him all peoples!

This *Aufgesang* is followed by the motive for praise, also introduced by the particle *kî*:

kî gābar 'ālēnû ḥasdô	For his loyalty prevails over us,
we'ĕmet-YHWH l^{e}'ôlām	and Yahweh's faithfulness is endless.

Unlike the Song of Miriam, Psalm 117 concludes with an *Abgesang*, as hymns often do, although there is some uncertainty as to whether this concluding refrain, *hall^{e}lû-yāh*, belongs intrinsically to the psalm. (In the LXX it is the opening of Psalm 118; it is lacking in the Syriac version.)

The comparison of Miriam's song with Psalm 117 discloses two matters. First, brevity does not provide a sure clue to the relative antiquity of a literary unit. The notion that priority belongs to short literary units formulated in concise style in contrast to extended pieces composed in discursive style is a weak premise of past form criticism.[12] It is hazardous to argue on the basis of brevity alone that Miriam's song is earlier than the Song of the Sea. On the other hand, and this is the second point, the brevity of the Song of Miriam does not necessarily indicate that we have here a poetic fragment or a torso of a once longer poem. It is interesting to recall that Frank M.

Cross and David Noel Freedman in their initial study designated the longer poem in Exod 15.1b-18 'The Song of Miriam', despite the fact that in the present text this poem is introduced by a statement that identifies Moses as the leading singer. The argument given was that 'the opening verse also served as the title of the song in antiquity, in accordance with standard practice in titling poems'. This is said to account for the similarity of the opening of (what they now title) 'The Song of the Sea' and the poetic piece usually called 'the Song of Miriam'. 'Hence verse 21 [the Song of Miriam proper]', they wrote, 'is not a different or shorter or the original version of the song, but simply the title of the poem taken from a different cycle of tradition.'[13] If this be so, it is hard to understand why the poem in Exod 15.21 survives only in title and why it is now placed after the Song of the Sea which elaborates on the title. Martin Noth plausibly suggests that 'the older hymn' has provided the inspiration for the Song of the Sea. The poet has re-sounded the keynote of Miriam's song, although shifting from the plural imperative invitation to a cohortative introduction, *'ašîrā* ('I will sing' or 'Let me sing'), and has given the hymn a new poetic elaboration.[14]

Another explanation for the brevity of Miriam's song may be found in the narrative context. In the Old Epic tradition we are given a picture of Miriam taking the lead, while the women went out after her dancing and playing their tambourines (cf. 1 Sam 18.6; Judg 11.34; Jer 31.13). Miriam 'answered them' (*watta'an lāhem*, v. 21a), we are told, by singing her song. The verb *'ānâ* ('answer, respond') suggests that Miriam sang responsively. This has been noted by older commentators, e.g. W.H. Bennett: 'Miriam and her choir sang antiphonally'.[15] Umberto Casssuto has gone a step further. The song, he suggested, was intended as a 'refrain at the end of each strophe'—that is, each strophe of the preceding Song of the Sea.[16] Here Cassuto seems to be bent upon harmonizing traditions that were once independent. However, even when we bracket out the Song of the Sea and concentrate on the Old Epic tradition, the brevity of Miriam's song is appropriate to its function. It served to punctuate the rhythms of 'the dance of the merrymakers' (cf. Jer 31.4) or perhaps to give a musical interlude to the narrative of 'the Singer of Tales', to recall the important book by Albert Lord.

To summarize: The Song of Miriam, which now stands under the shadow of the superb Song of the Sea, deserves to be considered in its own right. This is an independent song which was an immediate poetic response to the event of Yahweh's liberation that it celebrates.[17] In song and dance Miriam and her companions celebrated with the people the wonder of the event at the sea. In so doing, they inaugurated a liturgical tradition in which other poets and singers stood, including those who have given us the laments, thanksgivings and hymns of the Psalter.

3. *Some Theological Reverberations of Miriam's Song*

It is not enough, however, to consider only the poetic dimensions of Miriam's song and to try to assess its place in the history of Israel's literary traditions. This song resounds with hymnic praise to Yahweh, the liberating God, and therefore it makes a claim upon faith. Here we can only consider in brief outline some of the theological reverberations of the early song which were picked up and elaborated by other Israelite poets and storytellers in later situations and in various circles of tradition.

First of all, Miriam and her companions took the lead in celebrating and in vocalizing the event of liberation at the sea. If we may take the song as a theological clue, the event has two sides, which are the obverse and reverse of the same coin. On the one hand, the event was experienced as wonder—one could even say 'miracle'—in the sense that God was experienced as being present as liberator in a crucial moment. On the other hand, the event was expressed in poetic language that communicated its saving power and hence made it a social experience to be shared and celebrated. These two dimensions—historical event and word-event—belong together inseparably. Here we are not dealing with pure poetry, for the poet witnesses to a historical reality. Even the radical historian Martin Noth concluded that the event at the Sea belongs to the primary stratum of tradition which rests on 'the bedrock of an historical occurrence'.[18] Nor are we dealing with a miraculous act of God which resulted in speechless ecstasy, for 'the sensuous power of an event', as Martin Buber puts it, 'has streamed into [the historical situation] and lives on', precisely because it was given poetic expression. The prophetess Miriam, Buber comments, in this instance 'fulfilled the second of the two basic prophetic functions, of bearing God's words to the community and bearing the words of the community to God'.[19]

Martin Buber's essay on 'The Wonder on the Sea', to which I have just alluded, could well be the starting point for a theological exposition that would far exceed the given limitations of this essay. In an illuminating monograph on *God's Presence in History*, Emil Fackenheim has resumed the discussion initiated by Buber. He begins with a Jewish Midrash which asserts that what the humblest woman saw at the Reed Sea was not seen by Isaiah, Ezekiel, and other prophets of Israel. For instance, Ezekiel, according to the first chapter of his prophecy, speaks of how the heavens were opened and he beheld visions of God which cannot be fathomed—visions that pertain to the holiness of God who is beyond the human world. Miriam and her companions, on the other hand, saw something which constitutes a 'root experience' of the whole Jewish tradition: that the God, who is completely beyond the phenomenal realm and who transcends all human categories, 'was unmistakably present to a whole people at least once'.[20]

Here I shall not pursue further Fackenheim's thesis that the modern historian has expelled God from history just as the modern scientist has banished God from nature. Nor would it be fruitful to launch into a discussion of what really happened at the Reed Sea. My theological interest is rather in the relation between deed and word—historical event and speech event. If indeed the Holy God was present to a people 'at least once'—and that seems to be the witness of the Song of Miriam—then that presence became a 'saving experience' (Fackenheim's expression) as it was articulated in poetic speech. The word-event expressed—even evoked—the wonder that was shared and celebrated in community. Buber remarks: 'the miracle is revelation through the deed, which precedes revelation through the word'.[21] That may be so, though here we may face the proverbial problem of the priority of the hen or the egg. In any case, inspired poetry—and, I may add, engaging story-telling—has an indispensable place in the sharing, communication, and transmission of the 'root experiences' that give Israel its identity and vocation as a people.

Second, the poetic celebration of the presence of the Holy God in the liberating event at the Sea indicates that the problem of evil, as a theological issue, is incipient at the beginning of Israelite tradition. God's liberating action 'leads to the saving of the one and the downfall of the other', as Buber remarks in passing, without pondering the theological implication of the statement.[22]

Theologies of liberation must take this problem seriously, especially those that appeal to the Exodus as a paradigm of God's liberating work today. Martin Luther King once presented a sermon on the subject, 'The Death of Evil upon the Seashore', based on the text which in Old Epic tradition just precedes the Song of Miriam (according to the above analysis): 'And Israel saw the Egyptians dead upon the sea shore' (Exod 14.30).[23] In this powerful sermon he vividly portrays the flight of Hebrew slaves from Egypt: 'Egypt symbolized evil in the form of humiliating oppression, ungodly exploitation, and crushing domination'. The wonderful event occurred, and 'when the Israelites looked back, all they could see was here and there a poor drowned body beaten upon the seashore'. 'For the Israelites', he goes on to say, 'this was a great moment... It was a joyous daybreak that had come to end the long night of their captivity.' Yet King adds a major qualification. 'The meaning of this story is not found in the drowning of Egyptian soldiers, for no one should rejoice at the death or defeat of a human being. Rather, this story *symbolizes* [italics mine] the death of evil and of inhuman oppression and unjust exploitation.'[24]

This symbolic interpretation belongs within the trajectory of the Exodus tradition. To be sure, in the Song of Miriam the enemies are Pharaoh's hosts, and that is true also in the Song of the Sea, even though the poet was influenced by the *Chaoskampf* myth. Other poets, however, portrayed the mythical sea as Yahweh's adversary, as in Ps 114, 'When Israel came out of Egypt...' or Ps 77, 'The waters saw you, God... and writhed' (vv. 16-20); or they depicted Yahweh as the divine Warrior who conquered Rahab and made the depths of the sea a way for the redeemed to pass over (as in Isa 51.9-10).[25] This poetic tendency can also be seen in the Psalms, where the enemies are faceless and are associated with the powers of chaos at work in human history.[26] Furthermore, in Isa 59.15b-20, a passage that stands on the frontier of apocalyptic eschatology, Yahweh is portrayed as the Divine Warrior who comes to achieve justice, clad in the full armor of God including the 'breastplate of righteousness' and the 'helmet of salvation'.

The theological point is that the problem of evil (or even the issue of theodicy) did not arise only late in the history of Israel's traditions, owing to a crisis in covenant theologies occasioned by the fall of Jerusalem and the exile of the people. The problem was present, at least incipiently, from the beginning. It was not linked exclusively with monotheism but with God's action as liberator who, to use the language of Mary's psalm in the New Testament, brings about the downfall of the high and mighty and exalts those of low degree (Luke 1.46-55).

Third, and finally, the event at the sea as poetically expressed is open toward the future and is fraught with universal implications. In part the future horizon is based on the disclosure of the God—the sole Power, the Holy One—who was present in the event. As Emil Fackenheim remarks, 'If God is ever present *in* history, this is not a presence-in-general, but rather a presence *to* particular [people] in particular situations'. Of course, if this is the disclosure of the God who is truly God and not just a tribal deity or cultural idol, 'such a presence must have universal implications'. He goes on to say: 'These implications, however, are manifest only in the particular; and they make of the [people] *to whom* they are manifest, not universalistic philosophers who rise above their situations, but rather witnesses *in*, *through*, and *because* of their particularity to the nations'.[27]

It should be added, I believe, that the event of liberation was pregnant with universal implications not only by virtue of the presence of the Holy God in a concrete, particular historical situation but also by virtue of the poetic expression of the event. The dominant metaphor in the Song of Miriam is a military one: Yahweh is the warrior—not Yahweh is *like* a warrior (simile) but Yahweh *is* the warrior (metaphor)—who comes to the rescue of the weak and the helpless. This language is not just a nominalistic convention, although admittedly it was derived from the social experience of the time; in this poetic context it is a metaphor that participates symbolically in the reality that is apprehended.

Thus the Song of Miriam as metaphor is open toward the future. There may be a poetic reference to Miriam and her companions in an exquisite poem found in Jer 31.2-6, where the Virgin Israel is to take the lead in the new time of Yahweh's salvation.

> Again I will build you, and you shall be built,
> O virgin Israel!
> Again you shall adorn yourself with timbrels,
> and go forth in the dance of the merrymakers
> (Jer 31.4 RSV)

Here the poet speaks of Israel—'the people who survived the sword' and who 'found grace in the wilderness' (31.1)—in an inclusive sense that transcends the brokenness of north and south Israel. And in the poetry of Second Isaiah, the revelation of Yahweh, made known through deed and word at the Reed Sea, is the paradigm of a new exodus of salvation in which Israel will mediate Yahweh's blessing to all nations and peoples.[28]

NOTES

1. For a rhetorical study of the Song of the Sea and references to other studies, see James Muilenburg, 'A Liturgy on the Triumphs of Yahweh', *Studia Biblica et Semitica*, Festschrift for Th. C. Vriezen (Wageningen: H. Veenman, 1966), pp. 233-51.

2. Brevard S. Childs, *The Book of Exodus* (OTL; Philadelphia: Fortress Press, 1974), pp. 240-53.

3. Martin Noth, *Exodus*, trans. by J.S. Bowden (OTL; Philadelphia: Westminster, 1962), pp. 122f.

4. Translation by Frank M. Cross, Jr, 'The Song of the Sea and Canaanite Myth', *Canaanite Myth and Hebrew Epic* (Cambridge, Mass.: Harvard University Press, 1973), p. 130.

5. Cross, *ibid.*, p. 142.

6. George W. Coats, 'The Traditio-Historical Character of the Reed Sea Motif', *VT* 17 (1967), pp. 253-65.

7. Brevard S. Childs, 'A Traditio-Historical Study of the Reed Sea Tradition', *VT* 20 (1970), pp. 406-18.

8. *Ibid.*, p. 412.

9. *Ibid.*, p. 418.

10. See Noth, *Exodus*, p. 123, who regards the poem as a secondary insertion; also Coats, 'The Song of the Sea', *CBQ* 31 (1969), pp. 4f.

11. Coats, 'The Song of the Sea', pp. 13f.

12. See my comments in the introduction to the translation of Martin Noth's work, *A History of Pentateuchal Traditions* (Chico, Calif.: Scholars Press, 1980), p. xxv.

13. 'The Song of Miriam', *JNES* 14 (1955), p. 237.

14. Noth, *Exodus*, p. 123. See also Coats, 'Song of the Sea', pp. 3-4.

15. W.H. Bennett, *Exodus* (Century Bible; Edinburgh: T.C. & E. Jack, 1908 [?]), p. 137.

16. Umberto Cassuto, *A Commentary on the Book of Exodus*, trans. by Israel Abrahams (Jerusalem: Magnes, 1967), p. 182. In private correspondence Baruch A. Levine advances another proposal: the referent of *lāhem* in 15.21 is the Israelites of 15.1 who, with Moses as soloist, responded to Miriam's song. This view requires construing *'anâ* in 15.21 as 'recite, sing' (cf. Exod 32.18; Num. 21.17) and saying that the sequence has been altered in the history of transmission.

17. See Claus Westermann, *The Praise of God in the Psalms*, trans. by Keith R. Crim (Richmond, Va.: John Knox, 1965), pp. 87-88.

18. Noth, *History of Pentateuchal Traditions*, p. 50.

19. Martin Buber, *Moses* (London: East & West Library, 1946), p. 74.
20. Emil L. Fackenheim, *God's Presence in History: Jewish Affirmations and Philosophical Reflections* (New York: Harper & Row, 1970), p. 4.
21. Buber, *Moses*, p. 79.
22. *Ibid.*, p. 75.
23. Martin Luther King, Jr, *The Strength to Love* (New York: Harper & Row, 1963; Pocketbook Edition, 1964), pp. 71-81.
24. *Ibid.*, p. 73.
25. In his book, *Exodus* (Maryknoll, N.Y.: Orbis Books, 1978), Severina J. Croatto writes: 'The more Israel becomes engaged in forming itself as a people the more it focuses on that decisive event, which therefore is represented in creational language (cf. Isa 44.21-24; 51.9-11), the allusion to creation as a struggle against the forces of chaos (Isa 54.5; Deut 32.6; etc.) . . . As important as origins are, the Hebrew world shifts them to another epicenter, the salvific event of the Exodus . . .' (p. 13).
26. See my discussion of this motif in *Out of the Depths: The Psalms Speak For Us Today* (revised edition; Philadelphia: Westminster, 1983), pp. 88-90.
27. Fackenheim, *God's Presence*, p. 8.
28. See further my essay, 'Exodus Typology in Second Isaiah', *Israel's Prophetic Heritage*, Festschrift for James Muilenburg, ed. by B.W. Anderson and Walter Harrelson (New York: Harper, 1962), pp. 177-95: Walther Zimmerli, 'Der "neue Exodus" in der Verkündigung der beiden grossen Exilspropheten', *Gottes Offenbarung* (Munich: C. Kaiser, 1963), pp. 192-204.

16

A RESPONSE TO 'THE SONG OF MIRIAM' BY BERNHARD ANDERSON

Walter Brueggemann

In recent years Professor Anderson has offered to the Society a series of papers (including his presidential address[1]) that amount now to something of a corpus with a distinctive character. Three elements mark these papers, including the present paper:

a. They are models of clarity and restrained argument.
b. They are methodologically self-conscious, making some most significant moves.
c. They are primarily concerned with the theological function of the text.

I am particularly grateful for the way in which Anderson has relentlessly insisted on the priority of the theological agenda. That insistence is at times a lonely one in the guild.

I

Anderson's paper, it appears to me, divides into two parts. The turn between the two parts is marked by the sentence that Miriam and her contemporaries 'inaugurated a liturgical tradition in which other poets and singers stood'.

Until that point, the paper is concerned with rather conventional questions and judgments concerning the tradition-critical formation of the text. Those questions (carefully dealt with) concern the relation between prose and poetic traditions, between the long poem of vv. 1-18 and the short poem under discussion, between mythic patterns and epic tradition. My impression is that on most of these points, Anderson does not greatly advance things, nor does he seem to me to be primarily interested in such questions. He tends to follow the Albrightian consensus on the formation of the text. He does, however, argue one important gain in this regard. The song of Miriam is understood independently and seriously as a major poetic referent point, whereas it is often taken only as an echo of, anticipation of, or title for the larger poem. And if its independent character may be acknowledged, then we are free to consider its influence. And that is the question of the remainder of the paper.

II

It is the latter part of his paper that I find more interesting, and I suggest it is the area about which Anderson himself is most concerned. I wish to comment on four elements found in it.

1. The structure of the hymn and the relation of the word and deed are at the heart of Anderson's concern. He observes that the song of Miriam is closely paralleled to Ps 117 and has the two hymnic parts of *summons to praise* and *reason for praise*, introduced by *kî*. Concerning such hymns, my suggestion is that while the Psalm must be 'recited down' (as that is the order of the words) it must be 'understood up' from reason to summons. I take the summons, 'sing to Yahweh', as an act of world construction in which Yahweh is celebrated as ruler of the new poetic world now constructed by the poet. But the warrant for such a world is given in the reason, the actual concrete experience of liberation which evokes both the poem and the new world. So there is a *move up* from *experience* to *world*, from *event* to *structure*, from *story* to *system*. Israel in its most poignant faith does its praise precisely by reiterating the *experience* which is both concrete and transformative.

I am interested in articulating a typology that argues that where the *reason* prevails, Israel stays close to concrete, raw experience. But where the Psalm loses its reason, and has only *summons* (most clearly in Ps 150), then the Psalm is largely cut off from the experiential factors which give it life, and it becomes an ideology which asks for assent without giving any reasons related to experience. The song here is a symmetrical hymnic statement of summons and reason, indicating that the world constructed by the poet is held tightly informed by the actual experience of liberation. (I have not done so, but it would be interesting to investigate to see if there is a correlation between the balance of summons and reason and the use of the divine names that are more 'militant' or 'syncretistic', as Freedman has proposed as a grid.[2])

2. The 'chicken-egg' problem bothers Anderson and needs to bother us all. We must take care not to have *the historical event* precede *the speech event*, or to separate them. Rather, we must insist (in my judgment, as I think Anderson suggests) that the poetic characterization of the event belongs to, decides, and shapes the nature of the event which is remembered. It is this poetic reading of reality that causes Israel to experience *this* experience and not some other experience. The language evokes the experience. And so the poetic articulation is at the heart of the liberation offered here. That is, presumably it was not visibly evident to anyone that Yahweh had pushed the horse and the rider into the sea. One might have thought, for example, that the horses panicked and were drowned. Or, that the slaves were lucky and the Egyptians lost interest and faded away. One might conjecture many different readings of the event, none of which is fully available to us. But this particular reading, which is now normative, depends on the poet to create an event which did not happen so until she uttered it so. Thus, the *liberation of politics* depends on the *liberation of imagination*. And until there is a poetic release of imaginative language, the political liberation from Egypt cannot be experienced, and certainly cannot have continuing power for coming generations. The hymn wrought by the poet makes the world. Had there been no poet, the world offered would not have been this particular world. The 'root experience' is not only a happening in public purview, but the 'root experience' is a poem which shapes, decides, and nuances what happens. And one may well wonder why these world-creating poems that run from Miriam to Mary are preserved in the tradition as the speech of women, who then are the 'world-makers' in Israel. Perhaps in that society they are the only ones free enough from the 'known world' to have the capacity to speak an alternative world.

3. Anderson's comments on the problem of evil are important, but we are offered only an adumbration yet to be filled out. And perhaps his statement is not without problem. While I do not finally disagree with Anderson's point, I think it must not be reached too soon. If the hymn is a liberation song sung by a community until just now oppressed (which I take it to be), it must be understood in terms of

social release of much pain and rage that are pent up. Specifically the hymn is a partisan statement by a community at a new moment of unexpected well-being. The power, vitality, and credibility of the hymn depend on this partisan quality. If the hymn be taken as a first reading of the new reality after release, and only the first reading, then the partisan expression of reality need be given full play. No recently oppressed community can afford to care too much or too soon about the oppressor. Israel does not regard the destruction of the Egyptians as a moral problem. We must not miss the raw decisiveness that makes sense as a first reading.

It is only later, in a season of equilibrium and well-being, that one can move past the partisan rage to care genuinely about equity and even-handedness. This move to a concern for the Egyptians is a legitimate move for Martin Luther King, and one can argue that King represents a considerable moral advance beyond Miriam. And it is a legitimate move for Anderson and for us in our season of equilibrium. But we must take care that we do not impose such a view on the hymn, and of course, Anderson knows this well. After all, the hymn is not systematic theology, nor is it a full-blown moral code. It is simply a glad statement about a transformation. It could be that this powerful and passionate partisan speech comes from the myth of the battle with chaos. It could be. But it is not necessary. It could be a raw voice growing out of an actual human experience: the voice of those unexpectedly freed from long-term pain and despair. And that requires dancing and singing!

Anderson is surely correct in noting shrewdly that the problem of theodicy is already present here at the outset of Israel's hymnic tradition. But it is important to notice the character of this injustice and evil. Evil here is not a theoretical question, as it has become for so many philosophically inclined, but it is an immediate threat concerning survival. I would not want to pose the problem of evil in Israel's tradition as centered around the matter of the destruction of the Egyptians. In other contexts, and later on, that is a problem. But the problem of evil as Israel teaches it to its young is this: '*The Egyptians treated us harshly and we cried out to the Lord*'. That is, Israel in its first moment of speech speaks about the problem of evil which is the problem of the strong over the weak. But in the same phrasing, this problem of evil (which is not to be reduced to symbol) is coupled with an act of complaint that Gerstenberger has shown to be an act of hope.[3] The problem of evil, in Israel's poetic reading of it, is a problem of *oppression and hope*. That is the main fix for Israel. Israel's poets, storytellers, and credo-shapers stay close to that perception. Problems of responsive violence and vengeance certainly loomed subsequently. But not now. Now, the evil is the rapacious inhumane power of the strong one. Israel's reading of evil in history is offered, nonetheless, in the horizon of Yahweh's sovereignty which over-matches Egyptian power. That is Miriam's rendering of the matter of evil. Already here the parameters of theodicy are present, as Anderson says. But the problem admits of no moral, romantic or liberal reading. It is simply that, from the outset, Israel taught its young that the experiential process we call history is conflicted. Theodicy tends to become an intellectual problem only when the reality of conflict wants to be overcome in some comprehensive harmony. Dance is possible in Israel because Yahweh is the stronger party. If that raw claim were watered down, there never would have been energy or imaginative freedom to depart the empire. And that is to say, there would have been no poem, no text, no Israel. That is, the drowning of the Egyptians is definitional to the raw, abrasive hope of early poetic Israel.

4. Finally, I like very much Anderson's comment that the text inaugurates a liturgical tradition which has futures for other peoples. I believe this to be Anderson's most important methodological move in which he is not so interested in the process 'behind the text', as the 'possibilities in front of the text' which are generated by the text. Because revelation is a word-event, the text keeps generating new disclosures of an odd dimension in the historical process.[4] That odd dimension of disclosure, again available in the poetry of Hannah and Mary, is made to those who are treated harshly and who cry out in grief and hope. The odd disclosure, evoked in the poem again and again, is that the rapacious social process is not closed. It is the poem, and only the poet, who keep that process open, not closed, disclosed, not undisclosed. The rapacious social process is real, but it is under judgment and is open to the abrasive rule of Yahweh.

As we all recognize, the problem of the particular and universal is an acute one. But in this movement from cry to dance, from grief to hymn, it is always concrete and particular. Jacob Neusner has recently written: 'Religion exists in the mind and imagination of the scholar of religion. Only religions flourish in the "real" world of nations and churches'.[5] And I should say, poems of hymnic liberation exist only in the concrete, out of particular oppressions into concrete liberations. Any who universalize are out of touch with concrete pain and concrete joy, which are the only kind of pain and joy that matter at all.

One must take care not to generalize or universalize from a mythic perspective on the poem. Rather the transference and repeated utilization is not from concrete to universal, but from this one concrete to another concrete setting. It is sometimes noticed that the poetic experience of oppression and dance in Israel speaks faithfully about another experience of oppression and dance which now takes on poetic power. The poem has generative power because it discloses what is present in other experiences beyond this one of Miriam. Israel insists that what is present for those who can notice is oppression and transformation. Where the disclosing poem is not sung, the experience may not be disclosed. Then there will be only hopeless subservience and knuckling under. Where there is no poem, there will be no new social possibility, no new act of God, no text, and no community. This poem in its concreteness generates other poems also concrete, which function in disclosing ways about other odd situations of oppression and hope.

NOTES

1. Bernhard W. Anderson, 'Tradition and Scripture in the Community of Faith', *JBL* 100 (1981), pp. 5-21.

2. David Noel Freedman, 'Divine Names and Titles in Early Hebrew Poetry', *Magnalia Dei; The Mighty Acts of God*, ed. by Frank Moore Cross, Werner E. Lemke and Patrick D. Miller, Jr (Garden City, N.Y.: Doubleday, 1976), pp. 55-107.

3. Erhard Gerstenberger, 'Der klagende Mensch', *Probleme biblischer Theologie*, ed. by Hans Walter Wolff (München: Chr. Kaiser Verlag, 1971), pp. 64-72.

4. On the 'oddness' of this speech to match the oddness of historical experience, see Paul Ricoeur, 'Biblical Hermeneutics', *Semeia* 4 (1975), pp. 123-28.

5. Jacob Neusner, 'Judaism within the Disciplines of Religious Studies: Perspectives on Graduate Education', *Bulletin, The Council on the Study of Religion* 14 (Dec. 1983), p. 143.

INDEX

INDEX OF BIBLICAL REFERENCES

INDEX OF AUTHORS

JOURNAL FOR THE STUDY OF THE OLD TESTAMENT

Supplement Series

1 I, HE, WE AND THEY:
A LITERARY APPROACH TO ISAIAH 53
D.J.A. Clines

*2 JEWISH EXEGESIS OF THE BOOK OF RUTH
D.R.G. Beattie

*3 THE LITERARY STRUCTURE OF PSALM 2
P. Auffret

4 THANKSGIVING FOR A LIBERATED PROPHET:
AN INTERPRETATION OF ISAIAH CHAPTER 53
R.N. Whybray

5 REDATING THE EXODUS AND CONQUEST
J.J. Bimson

6 THE STORY OF KING DAVID:
GENRE AND INTERPRETATION
D.M. Gunn

7 THE SENSE OF BIBLICAL NARRATIVE I:
STRUCTURAL ANALYSES IN THE HEBREW BIBLE (2nd edition)
D. Jobling

*8 GENESIS 1-11: STUDIES IN STRUCTURE AND THEME
P.D. Miller

*9 YAHWEH AS PROSECUTOR AND JUDGE:
AN INVESTIGATION OF THE PROPHETIC LAWSUIT (RIB PATTERN)
K. Nielsen

10 THE THEME OF THE PENTATEUCH
D.J.A. Clines

*11 STUDIA BIBLICA 1978 I:
PAPERS ON OLD TESTAMENT AND RELATED THEMES
Edited by E.A. Livingstone

12 THE JUST KING:
MONARCHICAL JUDICIAL AUTHORITY IN ANCIENT ISRAEL
K.W. Whitelam

13 ISAIAH AND THE DELIVERANCE OF JERUSALEM:
A STUDY OF THE INTERPRETATION OF PROPHECY
IN THE OLD TESTAMENT
R.E. Clements

14 THE FATE OF KING SAUL:
AN INTERPRETATION OF A BIBLICAL STORY
D.M. Gunn

15 THE DEUTERONOMISTIC HISTORY
M. Noth

16 PROPHECY AND ETHICS:
ISAIAH AND THE ETHICAL TRADITIONS OF ISRAEL
E.W. Davies

17 THE ROLES OF ISRAEL'S PROPHETS
D.L. Petersen

18 THE DOUBLE REDACTION OF THE DEUTERONOMISTIC HISTORY
R.D.Nelson

19 ART AND MEANING: RHETORIC IN BIBLICAL LITERATURE
Edited by D.J.A. Clines, D.M. Gunn, & A.J. Hauser

20 THE PSALMS OF THE SONS OF KORAH
M.D. Goulder

21 COLOUR TERMS IN THE OLD TESTAMENT
A. Brenner

22 AT THE MOUNTAIN OF GOD:
STORY AND THEOLOGY IN EXODUS 32-34
R.W.L. Moberly

23 THE GLORY OF ISRAEL:
THE THEOLOGY AND PROVENIENCE OF THE ISAIAH TARGUM
B.D. Chilton

24 MIDIAN, MOAB AND EDOM:
THE HISTORY AND ARCHAEOLOGY OF LATE BRONZE AND IRON AGE JORDAN AND NORTH-WEST ARABIA
Edited by J.F.A. Sawyer & D.J.A Clines

25 THE DAMASCUS COVENANT:
AN INTERPRETATION OF THE 'DAMASCUS DOCUMENT'
P.R. Davies

26 CLASSICAL HEBREW POETRY:
A GUIDE TO ITS TECHNIQUES
W.G.E. Watson

27 PSALMODY AND PROPHECY
W.H. Bellinger

28 HOSEA: AN ISRAELITE PROPHET IN JUDEAN PERSPECTIVE
G.I. Emmerson

29 EXEGESIS AT QUMRAN:
4QFLORILEGIUM IN ITS JEWISH CONTEXT
G.J. Brooke

30 THE ESTHER SCROLL: THE STORY OF THE STORY
D.J.A. Clines

31 IN THE SHELTER OF ELYON:
ESSAYS IN HONOR OF G.W. AHLSTRÖM
Edited by W.B. Barrick & J.R. Spencer

32 THE PROPHETIC PERSONA:
JEREMIAH AND THE LANGUAGE OF THE SELF
T. Polk

33 LAW AND THEOLOGY IN DEUTERONOMY
J.G. McConville

34 THE TEMPLE SCROLL:
AN INTRODUCTION, TRANSLATION AND COMMENTARY
J. Maier

35 SAGA, LEGEND, TALE, NOVELLA, FABLE:
NARRATIVE FORMS IN OLD TESTAMENT LITERATURE
Edited by G.W. Coats

36 THE SONG OF FOURTEEN SONGS
M.D. Goulder

37 UNDERSTANDING THE WORD:
ESSAYS IN HONOR OF BERNHARD W. ANDERSON
Edited by J.T. Butler, E.W. Conrad & B.C. Ollenburger

38 SLEEP, DIVINE AND HUMAN, IN THE OLD TESTAMENT
T.H. McAlpine

39 THE SENSE OF BIBLICAL NARRATIVE II:
STRUCTURAL ANALYSES IN THE HEBREW BIBLE
D. Jobling

40 DIRECTIONS IN BIBLICAL HEBREW POETRY
Edited by E.R. Follis

41 ZION, THE CITY OF THE GREAT KING:
A THEOLOGICAL SYMBOL OF THE JERUSALEM CULT
B.C. Ollenburger

42 A WORD IN SEASON: ESSAYS IN HONOUR OF WILLIAM McKANE
Edited by J.D. Martin & P.R. Davies

43 THE CULT OF MOLEK:
A REASSESSMENT
G.C. Heider

44 THE IDENTITY OF THE INDIVIDUAL IN THE PSALMS
S.J.L. Croft

45 THE CONFESSIONS OF JEREMIAH IN CONTEXT:
SCENES OF PROPHETIC DRAMA
A.R. Diamond

46 THE BOOK OF THE JUDGES: AN INTEGRATED READING
B.G. Webb

47 THE GREEK TEXT OF JEREMIAH:
A REVISED HYPOTHESIS
S. Soderlund

48 TEXT AND CONTEXT:
OLD TESTAMENT AND SEMITIC STUDIES FOR F.C. FENSHAM
Edited by W. Claassen

49 THEOPHORIC PERSONAL NAMES IN ANCIENT HEBREW
J.D. Fowler

50 THE CHRONICLER'S HISTORY
M. Noth

51 DIVINE INITIATIVE AND HUMAN RESPONSE IN EZEKIEL
P. Joyce

52 THE CONFLICT OF FAITH AND EXPERIENCE IN THE PSALMS:
A FORM-CRITICAL AND THEOLOGICAL STUDY
C.C. Broyles

53 THE MAKING OF THE PENTATEUCH:
A METHODOLOGICAL STUDY
R.N. Whybray

54 FROM REPENTANCE TO REDEMPTION:
JEREMIAH'S THOUGHT IN TRANSITION
J. Unterman

55 THE ORIGIN TRADITION OF ANCIENT ISRAEL:
THE LITERARY FORMATION OF GENESIS AND EXODUS 1-23
T.L. Thompson

56 THE PURIFICATION OFFERING IN THE PRIESTLY LITERATURE:
ITS MEANING AND FUNCTION
N. Kiuchi

57 MOSES: HEROIC MAN, MAN OF GOD
G.W. Coats

58 THE LISTENING HEART: ESSAYS IN WISDOM AND THE PSALMS
IN HONOR OF ROLAND E. MURPHY, O. CARM.
Edited by K.G. Hoglund

59 CREATIVE BIBLICAL EXEGESIS:
CHRISTIAN AND JEWISH HERMENEUTICS THROUGH THE CENTURIES
B. Uffenheimer & H.G. Reventlow

60 HER PRICE IS BEYOND RUBIES:
THE JEWISH WOMAN IN GRAECO-ROMAN PALESTINE
L.J. Archer

* Out of print